ESSAYS IN THE CONCILIAR EPOCH

ESSAYS IN THE CONCILIAR EPOCH

BY

E. F. JACOB

UNIVERSITY OF NOTRE DAME PRESS

1963

© E. F. JACOB

U.S.A.

UNIVERSITY OF NOTRE DAME PRESS
Notre Dame, Indiana

First published by
the University of Manchester at
THE UNIVERSITY PRESS
316-324 Oxford Road, Manchester 13, U.K.

revised edition 1963

Library of Congress Catalog Card
Number 63-15295

Printed in Great Britain by Butler & Tanner Ltd, Frome and London

PREFACE

THE Conciliar Epoch is the period of the Great Schism and the General Councils of the Western Church (1378–1448). The Councils were the last collective act of medieval Christendom. To the re-making of religious unity in Europe and the reform of the Church the best minds of the age gave of their best. Unity they achieved at length, but not reform : the Conciliar system, as the decree *Frequens* planned it, was comparatively short-lived.

I have not attempted to do more here than to hint the answer or answers to the question why this was so. Elsewhere, in a work specially devoted to the Council of Constance, it will be suggested that a solution is to be found as much in the diplomatic as in the ecclesiastical history of the time. It is enough now to point to the zeal of the Conciliars, to their hopes—and to some of their shortcomings and the limitations of those they represented ; to show how urgent their work seemed at a time when the foundations of authority in the Church were being challenged by the loyal as well as the disloyal. The challenge went back to Ockham and Marsilius, and indeed further still.

For the historian of religion it is an age abounding in deep currents : piety had reawakened and was seeking new forms of expression both for the life of the community and for the conduct of the individual. The human spirit was conscious that it was on the brink of new things, but could not everywhere take the plunge. Part of the fascination of the age lies in the coexistence, the overlapping, of old and new : in all the self-frustrated efforts to get free. One luminous mind, the mind of Cusanus, could transcend the antagonisms, but few had either the power, or (like Thomas of Agnetenberg) the humility. They turned back, as Dietrich of Niem, to the ancient ways : their radicalism, where it existed, was based on courses no longer applicable or relevant.

I am indebted to the Governors of the John Rylands Library and to the Librarian, Dr. Henry Guppy, for permission to reprint here certain articles that have already appeared in the *Bulletin* of the Library (chs. II and IV to IX), and to the Council of the Historical Association for similar permission to reproduce two articles in *History* (chs. III and X). Revision has made several of them barely recognizable : the publication of the new edition of Ockham's political works involved drastic changes in the article now printed as ch. V, while chs. VI (" Sir John Fortescue "), VIII (the *De Imitatione Christi*), and X (" Middle Ages " and " Renaissance ") have undergone much transformation.

v

My grateful thanks are due to the Rev. John Flitcroft, who read the proofs and made a number of helpful suggestions ; to Dr. Dorothy Sarmiento, for the Index ; to Mr. H. M. McKechnie, Secretary of the Manchester University Press, for his kindly assistance ; and to the Committee of the Tout Memorial Publication Fund, for a generous subsidy.

E. F. J.

1943.

PREFACE TO THE SECOND EDITION

AT the end of these reprinted essays, originally published in 1943, I have added two chapters : one on the florid style in the Latinity of later medieval England, the other upon the economic position of English University clerks during the period and their efforts to secure promotion from the court of Rome.   The former may help to illustrate p. 181–182 of ch. XII " ' Middle Ages ' and ' Renaissance ' " ; the latter may serve to acquaint the reader with what was, to a good many people, an important aspect of the more general problem of Papal provisions.   These chapters are followed by some brief reconsiderations of, and supplementary notes upon, certain of the original essays, necessitated by the rapid advance of study and research in many departments of later medieval history.

My thanks are due to the Royal Historical Society and to the Governors of the John Rylands Library for permission to reprint, from the *Transactions* (4th Ser., Vol. XXVII), and the *Bulletin* of the Library (Vols. 17, No. 2, and 29, No. 2), material now included as chs. XI and XII.

E. F. J.

1952.

PREFACE TO THE THIRD EDITION

IN this edition I have substituted for ch. VIII of the 1953 edition (" The *De Imitatione Christi* ") an Essay on Gerard Groote, which originally appeared in *The Journal of Ecclesiastical History* Vol. III, No. 1, by kind permission of the Editor and Consultative Committee. The Notes and Comments are brought more nearly up to date.

E. F. J.

1962.

CONTENTS

CHAP.   PAGE

I   CONCILIAR THOUGHT 1

II   DIETRICH OF NIEM 24

III   ENGLISHMEN AND THE GENERAL COUNCILS OF THE FIFTEENTH CENTURY . 44

IV   ENGLISH CONCILIAR ACTIVITY, 1395–1418 57

V   OCKHAM AS A POLITICAL THINKER 85

VI   SIR JOHN FORTESCUE AND THE LAW OF NATURE 106

VII   THE BRETHREN OF THE COMMON LIFE 121

VIII   GERARD GROOTE AND THE BEGINNINGS OF THE " NEW DEVOTION " IN THE LOW COUNTRIES 139

IX   CUSANUS THE THEOLOGIAN 154

X   " MIDDLE AGES " AND " RENAISSANCE " 170

XI   VERBORUM FLORIDA VENUSTAS 185

XII   ENGLISH UNIVERSITY CLERKS IN THE LATER MIDDLE AGES :

       1. THE PROBLEM OF MAINTENANCE 207

       2. PETITIONS FOR BENEFICES DURING THE GREAT SCHISM . . 223

       NOTES AND COMMENTS ON CHAPTERS I TO X 240

       INDEX 253

Et quia manifestissimum est omne esse et vivere per concordantiam constitui : tunc in illa divina essentia, ubi vita et esse unum sunt summa aequalitate, est summa et infinita concordantia ; quoniam ibi nulla contrarietas locum habere potest, ubi aeternitas vita est.

CUSANUS, *De Concordantia Catholica*, I. i.

CHAPTER I

CONCILIAR THOUGHT

MANY people are influenced in their view of the Conciliar Movement by the assertion of Dr. Figgis that it was the work of academics. "It"—he was referring to the "Conciliar party"—"had the weakness of an academic movement except in so far as it expressed the general desire to close the Schism." [1] There can be no doubt that prominent university figures took a notable part in advocating a Conciliar solution for the Great Schism, and in justifying the acts of the Councils on the basis of law, historical precedent, and theology. But how far was the initiative in summoning the Councils, in holding them on their course when once they had been assembled, or in conducting the debates and arranging the agenda, due to such men and to the universities they represent?

This is a difficult question, barely answerable in general terms. At the start it is well to be clear what the word "academic" means. The modern distinction between the "academic" and "non-academic" way of regarding a question is inapplicable to the Middle Ages. There was no serious constructive thought that was not "academic." Any competent civilian or canonist argued along lines determined by the practice of the great law schools. Any solid philosopher divided his material, distinguished, and syllogized as he had learned at Paris or Oxford or some other studium; and on any question when the past history or present policy of the Church was in question, it was the first instinct of its leaders to turn to the *viri magne litèrature* (to quote the summons to the Canterbury Convocation in November 1433) for an opinion. The fact that the opinion was given in a flowery or an allegorical way (or both) may make it seem to us remote and strained, but this was not how contemporaries regarded it. Henry of Langenstein, writing his *Epistola pacis* at a critical moment in May 1379, when Clement VII's envoys were in Paris begging for their master's recognition as Pope, uses a purely allegorical setting for an argument of the most practical sort in favour of the University's suspending judgment until a General Council should decide between the rival Popes. At such a time contemporaries would find nothing odd in his introduction of Jupiter, Satan and the Genius of Peace.[2] Correctness, learning, and

[1] *From Gerson to Grotius* (2nd ed., 1931), pp. 37–38.
[2] For a full account of this letter, cf. Franz Bliemetzrieder, *Das Generalkonzil im Grossen abendländischen Schisma* (Paderborn, 1904), pp. 44 f.

subtlety in observing these conventions greatly affected the listener or reader ; *eleganti* (the name for them) captured his good will ; but the historian today is concerned with the interpretation and purpose of the treatise or memorandum, not with its contemporary adornments, and it is absurd to suppose that because much Conciliar thought is wrapped in these conventions, it is therefore nebulous and lacking in practical sense.

So much is obvious, and is another way of saying that medieval controversy demands much patience. But "academic" has another shade of meaning. It may be the attribute of the would-be university reformer, whose theories break down before the hard facts of royal administration and papal finance ; and that, I think, is the sense which Figgis had in mind. He considered that the academics, borrowing from the current doctrine and practice of representation, were advocating for the Church a constitutional system which that deeply-rooted monarchy found alien to its structure and repugnant to its dominant theory of the Petrine supremacy ; and that in so doing they left out of account forces which less intelligent and more worldly men might easily have appreciated : some degree of nationalist sympathy for one or other of the contending Popes (as in the case of Aragon with Benedict XIII) ; the vested interest of the *curiales* ; the conservatism of ecclesiastical corporations like cathedral chapters, and so forth. Perhaps this was the main cause why the movement, "so reasonable and so respectable," is considered to have broken down : yet for Figgis and other more recent writers, the academics did at any rate leave to posterity statements of theory that became part of the liberal tradition of Western Europe. These men thought that the Church was a polity, a mixed government, not a unitary absolutism ; that the Popes were subject to natural and divine law, and that the papal power could be both curtailed and regulated by periodical assemblies of Western Christendom. They struck a blow for constitutional freedom by treating the Church as a society amenable to the enlightened remedies of the time ; they had a view of history which enabled them to justify their theories by precedents drawn from earlier periods in the life of the Church.

This may, perhaps, stand as a statement of present-day opinion about Conciliar thought. The tendency of critics has been to regard it, so far as method is concerned, as a body of speculation applying to the Church the terms and concepts used by contemporary liberals and constitutionalists in discussing the scope and limits of secular authority.[1] Without denying the usefulness of this approach, one may suggest that

[1] This is the tendency—though it is not more than that—in R. W. and A. J. Carlyle, *A History of Medieval Political Theory in the West*, vi, ch. 3.

the passages where the constitutional analogy is pressed are not always the most essential part of Conciliar doctrine, save, perhaps, in the writings of Peter d'Ailly : and that the concept of the Church advanced by the great Conciliars has a theological, rather than a political or constitutional, basis. Further, it should be pointed out that there is a body of administrative and reforming thought which may equally be regarded as Conciliar : the thought represented by men like Dietrich of Niem, with which I shall deal in a later chapter.

A few preliminary reservations about the academics are suggested by modern Conciliar study both here and abroad. In the first place, the original suggestion for a General Council was advanced while the Great Schism was, so to speak, incubating ; it did not come from the Universities, but from three Italian cardinals, James Orsini, Peter Corsini and Simon de Borsano, and was made before the election of Robert of Geneva as Clement VII took place.[1] The three cardinals very quickly and (we now know) with some justification [2] developed doubts about Urban VI's election, but were not prepared to join their thirteen ultramontane colleagues at Anagni, who had met to discuss the proposal for a new conclave. In asking for a Council to clear up the circumstances of the election, they took up a midway position between their own pontiff and their Spanish and Gallican colleagues. The group at Anagni naturally thought their advocacy of a General Council both harmful and dangerous. It was rejected because, as Peter Flandrin said, nobody had the power or jurisdiction to summon such a council except the Pope or his legate, and because " every general council receives its authority from the Pope, and the things that are decided and declared there receive their efficacy from the Pope." [3] There was no precedent, according to Anagni, for such a council, although on other occasions there had been schisms in the Holy See, as now. The matter was entirely one for the College of Cardinals, since, when they elected, they represented the whole Church,[4] " and the duty of making a valid election is imposed on them by the whole Church." Yet these rebuffed Italian cardinals held to their point after Clement had been elected, and lost no opportunity of making propaganda. They did not live long enough to see results : but their grain of mustard seed was to grow into a great tree.

In the second place, it was the Sacred College, not the Universities or even the secular princes, that eventually brought the Councils of Pisa

---

[1] Their efforts are described by Bliemetzrieder, *op. cit.*, p. 6.

[2] " Tractatus domini cardinalis sancti Eustachii," in *Literarische Polemik zu Beginn des Grossen abendländischen Schismas* (ed. F. Bliemetzrieder, Vienna, 1909), pp. 6–12.

[3] *Ibid.*, p. 63.   [4] *Ibid.*, p. 69.

and Constance together, and kept Constance at least true to its original aims of unity, peace in the Church, and reform. Whatever may have been Cardinal Baldassare Cossa's motives in helping his colleagues to clear the ground for the Council of Pisa—an anonymous writer at Constance called him " father of the Council of Pisa "—the fact remains that the initiative of the two obediences brought that Council into being. When Cardinal Uguccione, archbishop of Bordeaux, was sent to address Henry IV in the presence of the three estates of his kingdom at Westminster Palace on 28 and 29 October 1408, he delivered from the Cardinals an official message worth consideration. To do anything less than summon the General Council and seek the help of the kings and princes of Christendom in so doing, would, he said, be contrary to the vow and oath of every cardinal then in the conclave " to pursue the business of union by way of resignation (*cessio*) or any other reasonable way." They had solemnly sworn to do this : to that task they were bound by divine natural law (*jure naturali divino*) ; neither party could pursue union in the presence of its own Pope, when he offered the opposition already described (in the earlier part of the address). The cardinals were therefore right in forsaking the Pope and in going to a safe place where they could concert their plans. The envoy pointed out that Gregory XII had sworn to resign the papacy, so that his continued holding of it constituted an act of perjury and schism, and any supporting him would be similarly involved. The unanimity of the cardinals was proof that the Holy Spirit was with them. They had sworn to stay where they were, and not to retire without the consent of the majority : in the interests of the Church as a whole they were prepared to face the consequences of their action, and to maintain that the General Council " has to judge the Pope " (*habet judicare papam*) : they could cite their authorities for this assertion, and were prepared to refute the opposing position.[1]

It is easy to point out that by the eve of the Council of Pisa thirty miserable years had elapsed since the double election of 1378, and that the cardinals might have acted before. But nobody who seriously studies the internal history or the external diplomacy of France during these years, as Noel Valois and, of late, M. de Boüard and M. Perroy have revealed it, can maintain that there was any substantial hope— even on Clement VII's death in 1394—of such action, in view of the rival, and sometimes internally inconsistent programmes, of French political factions. Until the French withdrawals of obedience from the Avignonese pontiff in 1398 and 1406, perhaps even during those experiments, the possibility of union in the Church ultimately rested, as all

[1] *St. Albans Chronicle* (ed. V. H. Galbraith), pp. 136–152.

policy during the incapacity of Charles VI rested, on the attitude of the royal dukes, Orleans, Berry and Burgundy. Both in its nations and in its faculties the University of Paris was divided upon the right course to follow, and for years the court discouraged discussion or resolutions in that quarter.

Finer intelligences, like Gerson, while deeply deploring the obstinacy of Avignon, called for charity and patience towards supporters of the rival Pope, and advocated persuasion rather than forcible methods with the pontiffs. Only slowly did the conviction mature that if Avignon was obdurate and the " way of resignation" (on the part of the *contendentes*) proved impracticable, the Gallican Church had better go its own way ; but when that decision was taken, it was discovered that the king (or rather his officials) was getting many a foothold where he had never been before, and that it was not the Church that was profiting, but the Crown. It needed the bitter discovery of administrative difficulties in working a headless Gallicanism [1] to convince France as a whole that withdrawal of obedience was not enough, and that a more constructive move towards union was necessary. Throughout this long and painful process our opinion of the effectiveness of the university partisans of the Council must depend upon the strength we attribute to French political factors and to ducal ambitions. Projects for an Italian state under French rule, the alliance with the Visconti and the move against Genoa, Orleanist ambitions in the Mediterranean—all the devices and stratagems of a partisan religious policy stood in the way of union. It would surely be difficult to maintain that after the meetings of 1379 and the pamphleteering of the German masters Henry of Langenstein and Conrad of Gelnhausen, the University of Paris could do more than keep alive the ultimate hope. It did much in this direction, but very many grievances had to accumulate and much experience be gained before the "royal way of the Council" (*via regalis Concilii*) could be opened.

It was the cardinals who by their collaboration with Sigismund made the Council of Constance a reality, and held it on its course, even to their own detriment, when it was threatened with dissolution by the flight of John XXIII. The critical moment in the preliminaries was the death of Ladislas of Naples (7 August 1414). It was the Pope's intention, as soon as he heard the news, to reoccupy Rome, and to restore the papal state, instead of meeting the Council at Constance, as he had promised the College to do. The cardinals one and all resisted

---

[1] G. Barraclough, " Une document sur la soustraction d'obédience en 1398," *Revue d'histoire ecclésiastique*, t. XXX, no. 1, Jan. 1934, 101–115, gives an excellent summary of the difficulties experienced in the first withdrawal.

and held him firm to his original proposal.[1] It was a notable achievement. But more notable is the fact that in the early stages of Constance two of them, first D'Ailly and later Fillastre (Cardinal of St. Mark), told the Italian supporters of John XXIII bluntly that they were not prepared to have the Council of Pisa confirmed and then return home after a few pious resolutions which would have left John XXIII in power without settling the problem of his rivals. The questions of unity and reform, they urged, were still unsolved.[2] When this brave attitude won support from the English delegation, and later from the French, the two cardinals were able to recruit in the Council a solid and critical opposition to the Pope and to maintain it in spite of the gravest provocation. That provocation no reader of Fillastre's diary will' fail to understand. The Sacred College had no vote as such : individual members might speak and vote within the four nations into which the Council of Constance was organized. Though represented on the Standing Committee (*deputati nacionum*), the cardinals could not determine the agenda, and often, as Fillastre complains, they did not know in advance what was being debated. Slighted at times, not always unintentionally, by the Emperor, they had to steer a course between the radicalism of the Patriarch of Antioch and the Avignonese view of papal administration that was so natural to many of them and so comfortable to their pockets. They held to their course even when they saw the sacred chair lowered in the general estimation by crude and inexperienced administrators, and discipline in the Church endangered. They did not follow the Pope to Schaffhausen or into Baden ; some visited him in his retreat, protested, and returned. Had they gone with him, either the Council would have come to an end, or the cardinalate have suffered an irrecoverable blow. They understood this and held on, but they had to endure the sequestration of their cameral revenues, had to put up with receiving paltry allowances from a Conciliar bursar. They were prepared for humiliation in order to keep the Council in being both for the election of a new pontiff—two long years ahead— and for the reform of the Church, which most of them never burked.

The generalization of Figgis is much more applicable to the Council of Basel, though it by no means fits all the facts. Undoubtedly he had in mind the great work of Nicholas of Cues, written especially for the Council, the *De Concordantia Catholica* with its ideal of an organic and harmonious Christian society, and its proposals for a system of electing

---

[1] " Sed cardinales sentientes, quod, si illuc irent, non reverterentur ad concilium et idem concilium non fieret neque procuraretur unio et reformatio ecclesie . . . fortiter restiterunt " : Fillastre, in H. Finke, *Acta Concilii Constanciensis*, ii. 15.

[2] *Ibid.*, ii. 17-18 ; iii. 42, and von der Hardt, *Magnum Oecumenicum Constantiense Concilium*, ii. 193.

all prelates and ministers of the Church ; he also noted that in the system of voting by deputations at Basel the senior ranks of the hierarchy played a less important part than in that of voting by nations, and this consequently implied that university doctors and masters had a voice. It is, however, far from certain that the deputation system played into the hands of academics *per se* ; it was not so much the universities that took the lead against Eugenius IV, after he had been obliged to recognize the Council which he had declared dissolved, as the adherents of Cardinal Aleman in the Deputations of the Faith and Reform, and they were the lower clergy in general rather than university doctors and masters in particular.

An important effect of the Great Schism had been to make men think more seriously about the institution which they had accepted as part of their daily lives. Not that in the normal course of events the government of the Church went undiscussed. As Dr. Owst has pointed out, medieval congregations must have listened to plenty of sermons satirizing the clergy and complaining about the venality of the Roman Curia.[1] People heard this sort of thing, believed it in a dull way, and did nothing. Then came the religious division of Europe, and in course of time scandals like Bishop Despenser's Crusade in the Low Countries or the siege of Benedict XIII in his own palace at Avignon. Slowly there formed in more thoughtful minds the conviction that unity must be fought for, whatever the existing law of the Church might say about the means of achieving it ; and that it was impossible to dissociate the Schism from the prevailing *difformitas* in the Church. To secure an uncontested Pope, but to do no more than this, was to perpetuate a system which on another occasion might prove unequal to the shock of division and then heresy would have its day. Both lines of reasoning led back to first principles. Before reform could be embarked upon, what was the Church and what ought its constitution to be ?

Inevitably such questions had been asked before, indeed from the days of Cyprian onwards. They had come particularly to the front in the struggle between Philip IV of France and Boniface VIII, when James of Viterbo had defined the Church as a *regnum ecclesiasticum*, a divinely-commissioned monarchical government. A little later the views of the " spiritual " Franciscans emphasizing the poverty of Christ and His apostles had necessitated a defence of the Church as a holder of property, and led to an analysis of its lordship or *dominium*. Around this raged a battle which must have interested most young clerks at Oxford when they searched for the subject of their weekly disputa-

[1] *Literature and Pulpit in Medieval England*, ch. **v**.

tions, especially when Wyclif was re-stating the doctrine in terms of
feudal law and moral philosophy. We might follow the contest back
—as Father Gwynn has done—to the *De potestate ecclesiastica* of Giles
of Rome : it is enough here to note that any discussion of this hardy
topic might quickly lead to a consideration of authority and channels
of authority in the visible Church. Yet the schism was a challenge of
a different sort. It was not with the propaganda of militant temporal
power, nor (at this moment) with a perverted Augustinianism that the
Church had to reckon, but with an administrative situation that drew
its strength and its inveteracy from the divisions of secular Europe.
Occasio schismatis et fomentum erat discordia inter regna, Richard Ullerston
truly remarked. In his *consilium pacis* of 1381 Henry of Langenstein
states—to refute them—some of the arguments of those opposing the
projected General Council. Councils, he makes them say, were suitable to the primitive Church, when there was no canon law and no
hierarchy ; but now the world has changed, customs are different : [1]
" princes and prelates have long been divided among themselves and
have become, as it were, fixed and immovable in their opinions, practically refusing to receive any further information." [2]   Langenstein is,
in his own way, expressing not merely the cleavage in religious allegiance
but the sort of conditions that made it inevitable that when England at
the Gloucester parliament of 1378 accepted Urban VI's election without
properly investigating the facts,[3] Scotland, with similar lack of information, should side with Clement VII.[4]   The schism, in fact, underlines
the diplomatic grouping of the powers brought about by the Hundred
Years War. English subjects abroad were not permitted to obey
Clementine prelates, and that was how the March of Calais came to be
detached from the Clementine see of Thérouanne and given by Urban
to the Archbishop of Canterbury as a kind of Continental peculiar.[5]
Catholic concord, and the success of the Council, were therefore in no
small degree to depend on international peace, and the point is one
that can never be sufficiently stressed when considering the supposed

[1] In Gerson, *Opera* (ed. E. du Pin), ii. 821 : " alter mundus est quam tempore
ecclesiae primitivae, alii fidelium mores, alia praesidentium studia et affectiones."

[2] *Loc. cit.* : " eo quod tam principes et praelati diu fuerint contra se divisi, et
sint quasi in suis opinionibus immobilitati, nolentes quasi ampliorem informationem
accipere."

[3] E. Perroy, *L'Angleterre et le grand Schisme d'Occident*, p. 50 f.

[4] See the authorities cited by J. H. Baxter in *Copiale Prioratus Sancti Andree*,
Introd., pp. xxxvi–xxxvii.

[5] Similarly, for support and protection given to an Urbanist bishop of Tournai,
cf. E. Perroy, " Un évêque urbaniste protégé de l'Angleterre, Guillaume de Coudenberghe, évêque de Tournai et de Bâle," *Revue d'histoire ecclésiastique*, t. XXVI,
no. 1, Jan. 1930, p. 103 f.

shortcomings of the leading academic Conciliars. When Sigismund, who at first showed signs of understanding the real significance for the Church of the Anglo-French struggle, joined the anti-French block by making the Treaty of Canterbury, the step must have dismayed all minds that could appreciate the relationship between politics and religion.

The main obstacle as it presented itself to the advocates of the Council was the legal *impasse*. This may be expressed in the words of the Provost of Worms, Conrad of Gelnhausen :

> It is impossible for the general Council to be held or celebrated without the authority of the Pope. But to convene such a council in the present case the authority of the Pope cannot step in, because no single person is universally recognized as Pope, nor is any individual generally obeyed as Pope, and if the council were to be convoked by the authority of the one or the other person now in question, he would in virtue of this be recognized as Pope ; and from this it is to be inferred that they cannot *both* authorize it, because there cannot be more than one supreme Pontiff.[1]

In other words, papal authority is necessary for the summoning of the Council and no such undisputed authority exists. It was in reply to this that both Langenstein and Gelnhausen urged the necessity of interpreting the canon law or, as they said, of using *epikeia*. At first this took the form of discussing the passages of the canon law that seemed particularly intractable so as to find out " the intention of the legislator " ; and Gelnhausen takes certain texts where the " sollers et acutus epikeias," the clever and shrewd interpreter, displays his method, and brings out the fact that " necessity and reasonable and urgent cause " demands the Council. It was this argument that deeply impressed Gerson, who is never tired of dwelling on the virtues of *epikeia*.

> The unity of the Church does not demand in those that practise such equity or interpret positive law that they should have mathematical or demonstrative warrant for their action : it is enough if they can count upon moral or civil or political authority : the good exponent of equity considers all the particular circumstances which the legislator has not been able to foresee or express. Beholding them, he looks to the end which might follow, were he to observe the express letter of the law rigorously. If from his observation he finds that the end is liable to be noxious according to Divine or eternal law and against the right intention of the legislators, he lays down that the law is to be interpreted in such and such a way, or else that for the present it must not be applied.[2]

In the *De potestate ecclesiastica* (April 1415) he reached by this method

---

[1] " Epistola Concordiae," c. 2, in Bliemetzrieder, *Literarische Polemik*, p. 127.

[2] " De unitate ecclesiastica," Consideratio 3, in Gerson, *Opera*, ii. 120 ; " Sermo facta coram Anglicis," *Opera*, ii. 127. Dr. Bernhard Bess (*Johannes Gerson und die Kirchenpolitischen Parteien Frankreichs vor dem Konzil zu Pisa*, Marburg, 1890, p. 6) called *epikeia* " das Zauberwort, welches alle Schwierigkeiten losen sollte, der Schlüssel für die Schlösser des kanonischen Rechts."

a statement of three exceptions to the canonical rule that the Pope must summon the General Council : one of these, it may be noted, is when, on being required to summon the Council, the Pope declines to do so, to the detriment of the Church ; or if he does not observe the date fixed by the Council for its subsequent meetings, whether at five- or ten-yearly intervals.[1] The latter point shows that the germ of the decree *Frequens* (1417) was already in Gerson's mind.

But the deeper question was whether the Church had the power to proceed at all in the matter. If there were two contending parties for the papacy, it was in fact a double-headed monster (*monstrum biceps*), or as good as headless, and then arose the question where true authority was to be found ; did it lie in the executive, the Pope and cardinals ? This takes us back to the old problem of the definition of the Church, and here the Provost of Worms had much of importance to say.

The holy Catholic Church, whose unfailing Head is Christ . . . is not the College of the Pope and Cardinals, nor any particular College in the world, because any such body can culpably fail. [It is] the congregation of the faithful in the unity of the Sacraments. . . . Of this kindly Mother to the universal Church there are, or should be, two subordinate spiritual heads, one of them the principal head, always sound and never failing, which is Christ our God, governor of the true faith, Who preserves the Church as His unblemished bride ; whence it cannot be headless, since He promised to be with us for ever till the end of the world, a promise that gives us the greatest consolation in this trial of the Schism ; for we shall ever have a Bishop and Pastor of our souls (1 Peter ii.). The other is the secondary head of the Church, to wit the Pope, but that head can sometimes cease to exist through death or for some other reason, such as falling from grace, although the papacy does not die.[2]

---

[1] *Opera*, ii. 249 : " Excipiuntur tamen tres casus ubi congregatio Concilii generalis sit legitime sine Papa. Unus dum desi[n]it esse per mortem naturalem, vel civilem, sen canonicam, quae est depositio, vel si cadat in perpetuam maniam ; aut si ad eum captivatum non pateat accessus.

Alius, dum sufficienter requisitus de convocando Concilio, renuit contumaciter in perniciem ecclesiae, praesertim si tangat ipsum. Tertio, si Concilium, postquam est a Papa legitime congregatum, statuat certum tempus et locum pro celebrando generali Concilio ; sicut infra triennium, vel de decennio in decennium, etiam ubi Papa renueret, nec refert in primo et secundo casu per quos evocetur Concilium, dummodo congregetur, quemadmodum fuit Pisis. Nihilominus expedit decernere pro futuro modum convocationis, sicut in reformatione salubriter est avisatum, utinam et synodaliter jam esset definitum. "

[2] Epistola Concordiae, c. 3, in *Literarische Polemik*, p. 129. Cf. a very similar statement in Langenstein's *Concilium pacis*, in Gerson, *Opera*, ii. 824. The universal Church, of which the General Council is the representative, is superior to the College of Cardinals and any other particular grouping (*congregatio*) of the faithful, and to every single person of whatever dignity or precedence (*praesidentiae*) he may be. This is undoubtedly the source of the decree *Sacrosancta* (1415) of the Council of Constance, called (with exaggeration) by Figgis " probably the most revolutionary official document in the history of the world " (*op. cit.*, p. 31).

Then follows a passage which Gerson must have read and taken to heart : [1]

> For Christ is called Head of the Church, inasmuch as the grace of a unique person, overflowing in Him according to the plenitude of that fount of all grace dwelling in Him, pours sense and motion, both of spirit and of grace into that Church, to wit, into all that adhere to Him by faith and the sacrament of faith, and in so far as He is God, causes the grace of the Head to flow in authoritatively, but in so far as He is Man, to flow in by means of His merit, and this merit . . . He has from His union with the Word. And because of this unfailing influence from its Head the Church has the privilege of indeviability.

This was the contemporary way of stating the doctrine of the unity of the Church in Christ which owes its foundations to St. Paul, the Apostle of unity. In the first epistle to the Corinthians, St. Paul makes it his aim to check the excess of individualism and the diminishing sense of corporate responsibilities in the church of Corinth and in Greek life generally by setting forth the relation of the Holy Spirit to the *Ecclesia*. The local congregation of believers was a sanctuary, a ναος, in which God dwells by His Spirit—a body of Christ in which all the members have been admitted by being baptized in one Spirit ; *etenim in uno spiritu omnes nos in unum corpus baptizati sumus*. In the epistle to the Ephesians, the field is wider ; here the danger of strife between Jew and Gentile is met by upholding the work of the Spirit in *ecclesia* ; but now the local congregations are thought of as parts of the universal Church, the Church of all believers, the university of Christian brothers. All its members are bound together by the Holy Spirit in a corporate unity. In his book on *The Holy Spirit in the New Testament*, Dr. Swete expressed the point cogently :

> The individuals who composed the Church are members of a living body ; it is the common life of the body that makes them one, and this life is inspired by the Spirit of Christ. The Church is the body of Christ : Christ is incomplete without His Church, as the Church is incomplete without Christ : from the exalted Head, the life of the Spirit flows down into all members : there is vitality and there is growth in every part which is in real union with the Lord and with the body as a whole. [2]

On the 23rd March 1415, just after the escape of John XXIII to Schaffhausen, Gerson preached on behalf of the University of Paris a sermon on the text, " Walk while ye have the Light," in the course of which he uses these identical arguments and cites the famous texts of St. Paul comparing the spirit-guided Christian society to the human body. At such a moment of profound crisis, the Council, representing the Church, must be of one mind, must continue, and guide the body

---

[1] Cf. *De auferibilitate Papae ab ecclesia*, Gerson, *Opera*, ii. 211.
[2] P. 311 ; cf. *ibid.*, pp. 309–11.

whose secondary head, or vicar of Christ, has failed to do so. Some
of his conclusions [1] will give the essence of his ecclesiology in its more
mystical form :

(1) The Church is united by its attachment to one Head and
is fastened to Him through the loving bond of the Holy Spirit by
the mediation of divine gifts (carismata), the qualitative dispositions
(he calls them) that in the mystical body make its complexion harmonious, vital, and pleasing to behold, adequate to fulfil all the
spiritual works of life.

(2) The Church, when united to one secondary Head, who is
called the supreme pontiff, Vicar of Christ, is more multiform,
richer and greater than was the congregation of the synagogue or
than is a civil community, whether under rector, king or emperor.

(3) The Church has the power or faculty in virtue of the life-
giving seed planted within her by the Holy Spirit, to prolong her
existence by maintaining the integrity and unity of her limbs, essential
or formal, as much as material or in a state of transition (fluentium).[2]

(4) The Church, or the General Council representing her, is the
rule laid down by the Holy Spirit given to us by Christ, so that
everyone of whatever estate, even papal (here the decree Sacrosancta
is anticipated), is bound to obey her, otherwise he is to be called a
Gentile and a publican.

(5) When the Church or the General Council lays down any
rules concerning the Government of the Church, the Pope is not
so much above even positive law that he can at his own will dissolve
such rules dictated by the Church for the purposes for which they
have been so laid down.

(6) The Church or the General Council, though it cannot take
away the plenitude of papal power supernaturally and mercifully
granted by Christ, can yet limit its use under certain rules and laws,
to the edification of the Church, for which the papal authority and
the authority within it of one man over another has been granted,
and this is the stable foundation of all ecclesiastical reform.

It will be seen that Gerson thinks of the Church as a society bound
by law, the law made by the whole body through its representatives,
the General Council. He accepts the plenitudo potestatis ; he thinks that
the papacy guarantees a richer life to the Church as a whole ; yet he
distinguishes between the senses in which papal power should be understood, for it is not a simple or unitary phenomenon. These distinctions

---

[1] Opera, ii. 205.
[2] "Morally and in present fact," is a rough way of expressing it.

he had already made in an earlier treatise, *Liber de vita spirituali animae*, written at Bruges (probably during the second half of 1399),[1] where he defined the papal power under four categories. Dr. A. J. Carlyle has pointed out Gerson's admiration of a mixed government and his advocacy, in a secular community, of what he quaintly called "timocracy" (by which term democracy is obviously meant) ;[2] but Gerson's analysis of the papal power both here and in the *De auferibilitate Papae ab ecclesia* suggests he did not regard the Church altogether in the same way as constitutional writers regarded the State ;[3] it was more than a *politia*, it was a mystical body ; the papacy could not be treated by the same methods as a civil monarchy.

> The Pope has first of all from Christ spiritual lordship over the whole Church with the plenitude of power in the things that belong to the spiritual government of the Church properly called. He has, secondly, canonical power over the goods of the Church which are called, by an improper use of the term, spiritual, like the collations and benefices and jurisdiction over quasi-temporal things and revenues. Thirdly, he has the power by the consent of princes, particularly the emperor . . . to appropriate certain temporalities, which obviously cannot belong to him by divine law, and if he is called lord of all things in temporalities, he yet does not possess every kind of civil dominion. . . . He has, fourthly, the kind of power which by natural law a superior has over his subjects.[4]

I cannot find that Gerson ever departed from his notion of the plenitude of power in matters strictly spiritual ;[5] but he emphasised most strongly the corresponding responsibilities of the Pope and the fact that he has a *proportionalis obligatio servitutis*. Further, though the papal power " has been so immediately conferred by God that the whole Church could not destroy it nor build it again if it were destroyed," it can fail through human and personal weakness, and if it fails it is the duty of the Church to restore it by means of the common action of the whole body represented by the General Council. He put the matter symbolically in saying :

> The Church has an unfailing Bridegroom, Christ ; so that as law stands, Christ cannot give a bill of renouncement to his spouse the Church ; nor,

---

[1] E. Vansteenberghe, " Gerson à Bruges," *Revue d'histoire ecclésiastique*, Jan. 1935, p. 27.
[2] *Medieval Political Theory in the West*, vi. 161–162.
[3] Cf. " De auferibilitate Papae ab Ecclesia," Gerson, *Opera*, ii. 213 : "Auferibilis est, lege stante, quaelibet Politia civilis monarchica seu regalis, ut fiat aristocratica, et non sic de Ecclesia quae in uno Monarcha supremo per universum fundata est a Christo." [4] *Opera*, iii. 34–35.
[5] Cf. " De Potestate ecclesiastica," Consideratio 10, in *Opera*, ii. 239–240, where this is made perfectly clear, yet is combined with the doctrine " quod et sine Papa generale Concilium convocari, et a concilio Papa judicari certis casibus potest."

conversely, is the Church so bound by the tie of marriage to the unfailing Vicar of her spouse, that they cannot by consent part and a bill of renouncement (*libellus repudii*) be given.

This is the language of his treatise (1409), the *De Auferibilitate Papae ab Ecclesia*. Here Gerson argues that Christ cannot be parted from His Church. Christ's presence gives it an influx of vital power that sustains the hierarchy and all orders within the Church, creates in it the ability to continue and perpetuate its life, and implants there the *vivificum semen* to raise up new generations. From this, he says, " One may infer that the Church or the Council representing it has power to institute, elect or nominate the supreme pontiff in the sacred See of Peter and to determine the manner in which he acquires his office." [1] But if the Bridegroom cannot be taken away from the Church, His vicar can, in certain instances, whether he consents to resign or not. If, as Pope Celestine did, the vicar of the Bridegroom could renounce his office, so too can the Bride renounce that vicar, as long as adequate reasons can be alleged for such a step ; for God granted no estate, no form of administrative power, except for the edifying of the Church.

It is very important not to regard Gerson as a radical attacking the See of St. Peter ; he is first and foremost a devoted French scholar and patriot, a loyal member of the Faculty of Theology in the greatest centre of theological studies, and a churchman with a high regard for the papacy and for the purity of that exalted office. These ideas he had imbibed, as he tells us, from his master, his predecessor in the rectorship of the College of Navarre. It is Peter d'Ailly's particular distinction to have applied to the Church constitutional doctrines which political philosophers used in connexion with the State, and to have done so in a way which both supported the General Council in its claim to superiority over the Pope, and at the same time upheld the dignity of the papacy. In his *De ecclesiae et Cardinalium auctoritate*, read in one of the churches in Constance on 1 October 1416, he steered a course between extreme Franciscan and extreme papalist views. The truth about the power of the Church, he says, lies between two errors, that of the Waldensians who would withhold from the Church every sort of temporal property and authority, and those who, like Herod, suppose Christ to have been an earthly king, and attribute to the Pope supreme power over temporalities and spiritualities alike.[2] The position of the Pope and Cardinals and lesser dignitaries resembles that of St. Peter and the Apostles.[2] All spiritual powers, save the *potestas dispositionis ministrorum* were common to the Apostles : so they are common to the ministers of the Church, who hold their power from Christ. The Pope is head only in so far

[1] Gerson, *Opera*, ii. 212.   [2] *Ibid*, p. 926.   [2] *Ibid*., p. 930.

as he is *principalis inter magistros* ; none the less from him, as from the high priest and architect, the whole ecclesiastical order of ministers in some sort depends. Yet he is elected by the community, the Roman people acting through their leaders or representatives, the Cardinals.[1] The government of the Church should not be regarded as an unmixed monarchy : it has elements of aristocracy, a form of government or principality " according to virtue," and of democracy, and such a mixture or " polity " is best, because in a mixed government all have some part in ruling.[2]

D'Ailly makes it clear that all office derives from the community, which has the right to elect its rulers. Even the aristocratic part or element, the Pope's *fratres* or Cardinals, should be elected—he would have seventy-two elected, like the elders of Israel, from the provinces of the Church. Any official member of the hierarchy in the Church should be regarded as a representative of the community, holding his office on trust, though his spiritual powers are from God. It follows that if the Pope, himself a *minister*,[3] errs in faith or in the government of others, he retains nothing but the ordinary right of an accused man to a fair trial. For practical purposes the judge to try him is the General Council, which represents the community of Christendom : more than any other body it is likely to be inspired and infallible.

This constitutional doctrine is combined with a notable respect for, even a defence of, the Roman Church. Although this Church is a *particularis ecclesia*, and as such subject in head and members to the judgment of the General Council, yet so high is its authority and pre-eminence that it must not be lowered or depreciated. Its advice must be " reverently heard " when it comes to a consideration of reform.

> Wherefore it is clear that we ought not to listen to a number of voices in this council saying repeatedly : " We will call the cardinals when we see fit, but not when it is a question of their reform " ; whereas it belongs no less to the Cardinals to cite *them* and reform *them*, than *vice versa* ; and in reforming each estate, individuals of those estates should be heard and not repelled by the Council's verdict ; each element should be induced to mutual caritative correction .[4]

This attitude is the opposite of the anti-curialist tendencies I shall later describe.

By the time of the Council of Basel, seven years after Martin V had succeeded in reducing the Council of Siena to a meaningless conventicle, people had forgotten the arguments of Gerson and d'Ailly and, as Nicho-

---

[1] From this he concludes that though in the Council of Constance the cardinals should not be the sole electors, they should not be " totally excluded " from the election of the Pope : Gerson, *Opera*, ii. 937.

[2] *Ibid.*, p. 946.   [3] *Ibid.*, pp. 942–943.   [4] *Ibid.*, p. 939.

las of Cues observed, were thoroughly divided and confused in their ideas about papal authority. This, Nicholas tells us, is why he wrote the *De Concordantia Catholica*. Some have been surprised that in all Conciliar writing, the work of highest perfection should come from the man who, in 1437, passed, along with his friend Cardinal Giuliano Cesarini, to the papal side. That such a staunch upholder of the Council as Nicholas of Cues should have become " the Hercules of the Eugenians " has been thought to detract from the value of the book as well as to cast doubt upon the sincerity of its author. But those who read this great work as well as the second and third letters to the Bohemians (1432) with the care they deserve, are not likely to rest content with such a view. In spite of his firm and reasoned support of the decree *Sacrosancta* (1415) and his almost exaggerated faith in the merits of election both in Church and Empire, Nicholas's fundamental conviction was of the need to preserve the unity of the Church and to close the ranks, with the Bohemians and the Greeks—this is very important—inside. The *De Concordantia Catholica* is not aimed simply at demonstrating the superior authority of the Council, at recruiting support for its continued existence, but at showing the Church to be a united, comprehensive, *and welcoming* body, ready to receive, not with sharp definitions to repel. For without sacrificing the discipline and the doctrine of the Western Church, Nicholas of Cues believed in a tolerance and latitude sufficient to allow for differences of outlook on theological matters provided that they were not pressed to extremity. *Omnis enim concordantia differentiarum est.*

This is the secret of his admiration for, and frequent citations from, St. Cyprian, and of the use he makes of St. Augustine's treatises against the Donatists. He saw the parallelism between the problems of the early African Church and the plight at the moment of writing of the churches on the periphery of Rome. Of the *ecclesia militans* he writes :

> We should consider that since the Church is so called from its unity and its harmonious congregation, it is composed of a fraternity, which nothing so essentially contradicts as division or schism. For though the one faith is the cable (*funiculus*) of its collectivity, yet sometimes variety of opinion without doctrinaire obstinacy (*pertinacia*) is compatible with unity. For Cyprian and the whole council of seventy bishops held different views within the faith of the Church ; yet they were not cut off, since they did not prefer their own opinion to fraternal unity, because they were without obstinacy, as Augustine agrees, in his second book against the Donatists. . . . Wherefore that Church militant, which is subject to human judgment, has within its body many armies that by external sign do not appear unfaithful, though secretly they are cut off from the agreement of the faith ; and they are not expelled or condemned, unless these hidden things are known.[1]

---

[1] " De Concordantia Catholica," ch. V ; ed. G. Kallen (Heidelberg, 1939), p. 49.

The passage in the *De Baptismo* [1] is one where Augustine is turning against the Donatists their own argument that as Cyprian was not prepared to take a rigorist view on the re-baptism of heretics, so neither must the African Church with themselves. Cusanus cites this passage in the sense that Augustine approves, i.e. as showing the *humilitas Cypriani*, [2] his desire to leave to his colleagues, the African bishops, the fullest freedom of action in the matter of re-baptism. This was exactly the attitude which the papal legate, Cardinal Cesarini, took when he decided to keep the Council of Basel in being, after the bull of dissolution issued by Eugenius IV: the bitter and suspicious Bohemians must be treated with a mixture of charity and firmness, and brought into the Council, if they were prepared to admit that they alone were not the true Church, and did not prefer their own utraquist ritual to the sacramental rite of Western Christendom. But, as Cusanus added in the second of his letters (*Ad Bohemos*), "In that Church, so long as unity remains, nobody doubts that without danger there can be a variety of rite." [3] It was the first duty of the Council to secure, by reasoning and appeal, the willing acceptance of that unity by communities without. The opposition of the Curia must be countered by demonstrating the unanimity of Christendom assembled there in its representatives; and if the Council has to proceed without the Pope, it should still remember the patriarchal subjection which it owes to him, and must treat him with the utmost kindness (*mansuetudine*), the only conduct possible to a fraternity.

I am not quite sure why Dr. Figgis said that the Catholic Concord "sheds a sunset glory over the medieval world." It contains, however medieval the form in which it is couched, a discussion of representation that is of considerable interest even to-day. It is on its representative function that the supremacy of the Council over the Pope is made to turn. In his précis of contents he summarized the crucially important Chapter XVIII of the second book thus:

> The foundation of this consideration that the Council is superior to the Pope lies in Augustine, since the representation of the Church (to which verity and Christ's presence are assured) in the universal Council is surer and more infallible than in the Pope alone. And here is revealed the basis of the whole matter of representations and administration, and why prelates should be elected, and what order shall be kept, and how the Cardinals should be elected by the provinces as their legates, so to speak. [4]

---

[1] II. 3 (*Corpus Script. Eccl. Lat.*, li. 177 f.).

[2] "Non me terret auctoritas Cypriani, quia me reficit humilitas Cypriani."

[3] *Opera* (1565), p. 832: "in eadem quidem ecclesia remanente unitate varium posse ritum esse sine periculo nemo dubitat."

[4] Ed. Kallen, p. 13.

" Surer and more infallible." In Ch. XVIII Cusanus cites a statement of Augustine that St. Peter, because of the primacy of his apostle-
ship, represented the Church *figurata generalitate*, and argues accordingly
that the Roman pontiff has a *figuratam et repraesentiuam personam* : that
is, he represents the universal Church, but only *in figura*, only as a symbol
or a figure represents the truth. (Cusanus was a mathematician as well
as a philosopher, and the *figura* may in his mind be the mathematical
symbol or the geometrician's illustration.) Between the rock on which
the Church is built and Peter himself there are " several stages of representations and significations before the real rock is reached ": the progress
is, he says, " from a most confused representation and figure up to the
truth by increasingly sure and true intermediaries." The surest and
truest approximation to verity, the rock of the Church, is the General
Council, which represents the universal Church " less confusedly and
more by holding in the truth " (*plus tenendo in veritate*). What then
are the grades by which surer representation is reached ? A very revealing passage explains :

> the Pope "figures" the Church in a very confused fashion : in nearer
> manner he represents his patriarchate, nearer still his metropolis : still more
> surely his diocese, more surely still his clergy, and lastly, as if in one body,
> his daily council. Whence it happens that the Cardinals or legates of pro-
> vinces who are the Roman pontiff's assistants are called principal limbs and
> part of the Pope's body. Thence moreover it is clear that the more specific
> (*particularior*) the presidency, the surer is the representation in the person
> of the president, and the less confused.

In other words, the more concentrated and narrow the unit, the more
faithfully is it personified by its head.[1] The foundation of the claim that
the General Council is a clearer and more definitive representation of
the Church than the Pope will be plain : in the General Council the
small units are fully represented : the *particulars* are present. Cusanus'
theory of representation is the Roman Lawyers' theory of impersona-
tion : and though it is this, it is as far as possible removed from the
universalism of Hobbes who makes the Leviathan " alone to bear the
person " of the commonwealth.

◂ An important type of Conciliar thought concerns the problem of
administrative reform. In the treatises that have come down to us
one feature is very prominent : the concentration of the would-be
reformers upon the head (the Pope) and the Roman Curia, rather than
upon the members (the provinces and dioceses). In blaming the papacy
for the ruin of the Church, the publicists and pamphleteers were giving

[1] *Opera* (1565), p. 741.

attention to the governing opinion of the time. The authors of the *Speculum aureum de titulis beneficiorum* and of the *Squalores curiae Romanae* are very characteristic of their epoch : later, in 1410, Dietrich of Niem in his *De modis uniendi et reformandi ecclesiam in concilio universali* puts the point with all the earnestness of a reformer : to heal the Schism will not necessarily lead to reform ; nor is there much hope of the Church being reformed until the real cause of all the trouble is removed. If the General Council works both to heal the Schism and to cleanse the Church, in fact to make an end of those things out of which schisms arise, it must either limit or do away with the powers which the Popes have usurped. And by this phrase Dietrich, like all those of his generation—and indeed the generation before him—was stigmatizing the centralized administration of the Church, the beneficiary and financial policy of the papacy.[1] That was the root cause of the evil. This is not the place to trace the steps by which the administrative centralization of the Church was accomplished. Let it suffice to say that by 1300 the development was well on its way and the theory enunciated by Innocent III—*omnes ecclesie et res ecclesiarum sunt in potestate Pape*—had already been given a practical turn by the famous decretal *Licet ecclesiarum* of Clement IV (1265) which added the principle of general reservation to that of provision : a principle which the successors of Clement IV found to be capable of considerable expansion ; for from this time onwards new categories of reserved benefices were added by the constitutions of Boniface VIII, Clement V, and John XXII ; and these, after being codified and still further extended by Benedict XII, received confirmation and what appeared to be permanent validity in the Rules of the Papal Chancery during the Schism. Opposition was not directed merely against the extended scope of papal patronage : it was the ability of the Curia to turn its administration of patronage—through provisions and reservations— into a money-making concern that evoked the most violent criticism. The development of taxes upon consistorial and non-consistorial benefices, *servitia* and annates respectively, and the need to satisfy the papal merchants before the bulls of provision were released by them to the impetrants, formed a cause of much dissatisfaction, though the money was paid right enough. It was against these closely linked systems of patronage and finance, together with the attendant evils of pluralism and non-residence, the conferment of prebends upon foreigners, the unsuitability of many provisors and the evils of the system of expectatives that, as Dr. Haller has shown,[2] the attacks of the reformers were concentrated throughout the fourteenth century. The demands of the reformers at Constance and earlier were the same—the restoration, as

[1] Ch. II, *infra*, p. 39.   [2] *Papsttum und Kirchenreform* (1903), p. 169 f.

Dietrich had demanded, of the *antiqua via*, the good laws instead of the bad new ones. The bad new laws are those which the Popes have instigated during the last hundred years in their constitutions for the *Camera Apostolica*, and particularly in their Chancery regulations. It is the business of the reformers therefore to get rid of the abuses by restoring the old rights of collation to the ordinaries. The cameral constitutions must disappear when the next general council meets : so also the reservations—no matter whether they have been created through the canon law or through the Chancery regulations. They are thievish, execrable and rapacious. We have only to look back a century to the Council of Vienne (1311-1312) to see how old these questions really are, and how old the plans of reform. But it would be wrong to suppose that reform at the Council of Vienne had quite the same meaning as it had for the reformers of the great fifteenth-century councils ; reform at Vienne meant the removal of certain abuses which had arisen within the framework of the existing constitution—not the abolition of that constitution. For the latter view would have been utterly unthinkable in a generation for which the *plenitudo potestatis* of the Popes was not merely an acknowledged fact but a positive creed. The conception of reform as a *constitutional* question was more particularly the fifteenth-century contribution to the subject. And here we can classify our reformers. The moderates would not deny the plenitude of the papal power : they would limit its use. The radicals like Dietrich were charging the Popes not with having abused their power, but with having usurped powers to which they had no right.[1]

Was the centralized system so bad as to warrant this uncompromising attitude ? With Dr. Haller, we may well ask : " Was the effect on the Church as a whole of the corrupt state of the Curia actually so great that we are justified, indeed compelled, to accept the attitude of the fifteenth-century reformers at its face value and declare that the papacy must be considered the principal cause of the decline of Church institutions ? " No conclusive answer can be forthcoming before we have thoroughly tested the evidence of contemporaries by other contemporary evidence. Now the question of the reliability of contemporary evidence is absolutely vital. How far can we trust what Dr. Haller has termed " the acrid phrases of preachers " or the boundless accusations of the *gravamina* literature ? Haller suggested that an answer to some of our questions might be discovered through statistical use of the papal registers, by means of which the historian might be able to check the assertions of the chroniclers, pamphleteers and reformers.[2] This view Professor

[1] On the radicals, cf. Haller, *op. cit.*, pp. 186–187.
[2] Haller, *op. cit.*, pp. vi–vii.

Barraclough has submitted to a searching criticism. He maintains that, quite apart from the difficulty of trying to estimate the effect of the provision system upon the life and character of the fourteenth-century Church from the papal documents, the evidence of the archive material itself is still not definitive. Basing himself mainly on the studies of the Belgian school of research (Berlière, Tihon and Baix) and the work done by Rieder for the history of the Cathedral of Constance, he points out that, if the statistics so far drawn up are correct, it would seem that, in the cases investigated, only half the number of supplications granted led to the issue of papal letters, and that only half the number of letters resulted in the actual conferment of a benefice; and therefore that, before a conclusive answer may be given, not only does the record of the petitions require to be checked by reference to the papal letters, but they in turn need checking by reference to the accounts of the papal collectors, " whose detailed statements of annates paid or owed offer final proof whether a providee eventually obtained real possession of his benefice or not." [1] What is required is evidence to determine whether a man got the benefice or not. And where such checking has been done, the results have been interesting. The papacy has been shown to have had a strict regard for the rights of lay patrons and to have given the question of nationality much deeper consideration than is usually supposed. Although from time to time there might have been real objection to provisors on account of their nationality, in actual fact questions of class were more likely to have been at issue.

> Thus [says Professor Barraclough] even if provisions were often used to further family interests and connexions, it is generally admitted that papal intervention, in counteracting the growing spirit of nepotism and introducing new elements into the chapters, exercised a salutary influence in cathedral and collegiate churches.[2]

(We recollect the remark of Erasmus in regard to a certain cathedral that " Christ Himself could not have been admitted into this college without dispensation."). The same writer suggests that if we were to look at the whole development of Church History from the tenth to the fifteenth century instead of considering the fourteenth and fifteenth in isolation, we should probably discover that

> the abuses which have ordinarily been ascribed to the centralized administrative practices, and above all to the centralized administration of church benefices through the papacy, appear as the result of developments which were already inveterate long before the day of Babylonish exile at Avignon.[3]

He is therefore inclined to ask whether the depressing picture drawn

[1] *Papal Provisions*, p. 34.   [2] Barraclough, *op. cit.*, p. 57.   [3] *Ibid.*, p. 59.

by the reformers is not due to long-standing abuses in provincial churches, e.g., the lack of an adequate system of episcopal visitation, rather than to the maladministration of the centre. The real trouble, he thinks, was not so much what the Popes did as what they did not do. They did not offer sufficient resistance to the aristocratic tenants, and did little or nothing to correct the recognition of privileged classes within the Church ; to use a banker's metaphor, they let themselves be " acted upon by the public " and allowed the tide of petitions for benefices to flow in upon them, so that only when the waters were upon them did they consider how to canalize that flood. At bottom this may have been because they accepted a conception of the ecclesiastical benefice which, broadly speaking, identified it with other non-ecclesiastical types of property—as an object of private rights, not of public interests.[1] That they dealt most systematically and efficiently with petitions when they were received, there can be no doubt ; in Professor Barraclough's paper on the executors of papal privileges (1934) the carefulness of the judicial inquiry that followed the act of provisions was specially emphasized.[2] As the result of much recent research, therefore, papal administration has been shown to be not as capricious as Dr. Haller has asserted, but on the contrary a carefully weighed and well-balanced legal system which gave the ordinary collators ample opportunity in which to defend themselves.

Professor Barraclough's study brings us face to face with a very real problem. If, as the evidence which has been collected suggests, only a comparatively small number of those who sought provision eventually obtained them : if, in actual fact, the Popes were careful to provide people acceptable to the localities, and if their intervention was devised and used so often with willing co-operation, what are we to make of the various reform projects put forward by the separate nations at the General Councils during the first half of the fifteenth century ? What indeed of the *Avisamenta* at Constance ? How did all the trouble arise ? Why did the members of the Council challenge the legitimacy of the papal system, and why did they decide that the spiritual needs and welfare of the Church could only be met by a return to the more ancient methods of appointments to benefices by the ordinaries ? It is important not to be premature or hasty in generalizing on these topics. Many years will have to pass before the statistical method can give really secure results. All that we have gained at present is enough to

[1] Barraclough, *op. cit.*, p. 77, pointing out that this had become the accepted view of the canon lawyers.

[2] " The Executors of Papal Provisions in the Canonical theory of the thirteenth and fourteenth centuries," *Acta Congressus Iuridici Internationalis Romae* 12–17 Novembris 1934, iii. 109–153.

put us on our guard against accepting the judgment of fifteenth-century churchmen too readily. It is certain now that much of the contemporary criticism which historians in the nineteenth century were accustomed to take at its face value, was unjustified and exaggerated. And it is equally clear that, in Professor Barraclough's words, the " disorders in the fourteenth- and fifteenth-century church cannot be ascribed to any single group of causes, and any attempt to-day to settle the whole responsibility on the papacy and its administration of benefices and finances is doomed to failure."

With these words of caution in mind, we may now turn to one of the most radical opponents of the papal centralization, Dietrich of Niem.

CHAPTER II

DIETRICH OF NIEM

THE average civil servant does not write memoirs or reminiscences. After retirement, he may translate the classics, or fulminate against departmental extravagance from some riverside retreat. Reluctance to write out of office hours was equally true of the medieval clerk, who laid down his *stylus* with pleasure. Even outstanding figures like the jurist who wrote the *Tractatus de Legibus et Consuetudinibus Regni Angliae* on the secular side, or the exalted compiler of the *Liber Censuum* on the ecclesiastical, left no histories of their own times. But every now and then there are exceptions to this rule : men like Godfrey of Viterbo, Acerbus Morena the Podesta of Lodi, and the great Otto of Freising in the service of Frederick Barbarossa ; Petrus de Ebulo, the court poet of Henry VI ; Joinville, devoted biographer of his sacred master ; or Nicholas of Butrinto, attached to the court of the Emperor Henry VII in Italy. In England the outstanding example must have been Richard fitz Neal, the author of the *Dialogue of the Exchequer*, whose large *Tricolumnis*, or three-columned history of Henry II's period, seems irrevocably lost. Among the *curiales* proper there is Cardinal Bozo, who revised and continued the biographies in the *Liber Pontificalis*, and his exact contemporary in the Curia, that splendour of English scholarship, John of Salisbury, who was in the Pope's household from 1148 to 1153 and was later clerk to Archbishop Theobald of Canterbury. John's *Historia Pontificalis* comes nearest to personal reminiscences, for, as Dr. Poole shows, much of it was written amid the events it describes. Then in Boniface VIII's time, nearly 150 years later, we have Cardinal James Stefaneschi, who took verse for his medium. Most of these— and there are others—are not persons who spent the greater part of their lives at the royal or the papal court. They came to the service of their masters when they were mature men, sometimes, like John of Salisbury or Otto, Barbarossa's uncle, after a prolonged period of academic study or cloistral government. More significant are those who, having made the court and its administrative services their life's work, narrated from the inside, whether in verse or prose, the history of their masters' doings and times, or the circumstances of their own existence. The period of the Schism and the Councils provides particularly good instances of this type : in England there is in fact Hoccleve, secondary in the privy seal office, and Adam of Usk, the ecclesiastical lawyer, who passed from the court of Canterbury to the Roman Curia ; and in Rome itself there are Gobelin Person, Dietrich of Niem and Leonardo Bruni of Arezzo, the papal secretary.

Bruni, so useful historically, has about him something of the detachment of the humanist, and perhaps loved Florence better than Rome ; but the Germans Gobelin and Dietrich, both originally clerks of the diocese of Paderborn, were the true professionals, men of an older and more genuinely medieval stamp than Bruni, and their careers are alike in several ways. Each lived in the midst of the exciting events of the Schism and the Councils of Pisa and Constance. Each wrote the history of his own times, Gobelin in his *Cosmodromion* (printed by Meibomius), the book of the " Course of the World," in which he is not an original authority till chapter lxix of the Sixth Age ; Dietrich in his book *On the Schism*, and his *History of the life and deeds of Pope John XXIII till his flight and imprisonment*. Each was so impressed with the abuses of the Schism under which he lived and worked that he turned reformer, Gobelin (to quote Creighton) " as an asserter of the episcopal jurisdiction as a practical means of reforming the Church " : [1] Dietrich as a convinced Conciliar, returning in spirit and in letter to the primitive days of the Church, when the Emperor might summon General Councils to secure unity and the eradication of evils. Both show remarkable perception of the significant events in the period they describe ; but Dietrich, in many ways more passionate and partisan than Gobelin, has a more speculative mind, and analyses with greater depth the theory and practice of ecclesiastical sovereignty. In his later days he wrote what Gobelin was perhaps too disillusioned to attempt. On a basis of principle and history alike, he pinned all his faith to the Council, and became one of its most active propagandists : a true radical, passionate and without mental reservations. The conversion of such an experienced administrator is too striking an event to be passed over.

There is something pathetic in the spectacle of a faithful man watching the disintegration of the machinery which he has helped to work successfully and efficiently. The curial system evolved by the Avignonese Popes certainly worked. If a largely increased revenue for the papacy, through reservations and expectatives, was one of its achievements, justice was not forgotten ; the Curia illustrated the old tag about the intimate connexion of that commodity with finance. The censorious view of this system prevalent among English historians is mainly due to acceptance of literary rather than administrative evidence, without any attempt at statistical exploration ; but it also comes from the habit of looking at a papal bull of provision, or a grace conferring a benefice

[1] *History of the Papacy during the Reformation*, i. 428–29.

when it fell vacant, as a document complete in itself, a papal bolt from the blue; whereas in practice it was usually only one of a series of transactions begun at the request of an individual or community on behalf of its members, and ending with a thorough examination of the local situation by independent persons, so as to determine the right of the impetrant to the benefice.[1] In fact it marks one stage in a judicial process. The method of making the request, the exact words by which it was granted, and their implication, were determined by custom, embodied in the rules of the Papal chancery : subtle and delicate regulations added to, here a little and there a little, by each successive Pope with the co-operation of the vice-chancellor and other leading members of the chancery. When it is recollected that for a majority of churchmen throughout Western Europe the obtaining or augmentation of a livelihood was dependent, in the initial stages of the process, upon the observance of these rules by petitioning party and by Curia alike, the responsibility of senior office in the chancery becomes abundantly clear.

Such office Dietrich [2] held. He was born sometime in the 1340's (the exact year is uncertain) in the little Westphalian town of Brakel, close to Nieheim, and he owned property there and in Hameln. Like Gobelin he joined the Curia at Avignon. We first hear of him during Urban VI's pontificate in 1370 as a notary of one of the auditors of the Rota, Franciscus Lando, later Cardinal of Venice. He was, in fact, a judge's clerk, employed in writing and attesting documents in the processes referred by the pontiff to his master. The first great change in his life must have been his migration with the Curia of Gregory XI to Rome on the stormy journey of the early days of January 1377. Here in the city he witnessed some of the scenes at Urban VI's election, wrote his two treatises on curial administration, the *Liber Cancellariae* and the *Stilus Palatii abbreviatus*, the fruits of the position to which Urban VI almost immediately appointed him. For on the 11th of May 1378 he appears as *scriptor*, and in his *Liber Cancellariae* (1380) he is called *abbreviator et scriptor*. Although the division of the abbreviators into the "greater" and the "lesser parks" appears in documents of a somewhat later date, the former class is distinguished at this time by the titles "assistant to

---

[1] Cf. G. Barraclough, *Papal Provisions*, ch. vii.

[2] The most recent biography is that of Hermann Heimpel, *Dietrich von Niem* (*c. 1340–1418*), Münster (Westf.), 1932. His chapter "Dietrich von Niem (Nieheim)" in *Westfälische Lebensbilder* (Münster, 1937) gives Dietrich's local connexions. Georg Erler, *Dietrich von Niem* (Leipzig, 1887) is still valuable for the details of Dietrich's life, as is also the monograph of H. V. Sauerland (*Das Leben des Dietrich von Nieheim*, Göttingen, 1875). For Dietrich, at Constance, cf. the chapter of Dr. Heinrich Finke, "Dietrich von Niem in Konstanz," *Forschungen und Quellen zur Gesch. d. Konstanzer Konzils*, 1889.

the vice-chancellor " and " those in the greater presidency." Now a notice of Dietrich at the time of the Council of Basel speaks of him as " *inter praesidentes in cancellaria domini nostri unus de maioribus et toti curiae tempore suo notus.*" [1] We may take it, I think, from various references in the *De Schismate* and from the knowledge shown by him in the technical treatises on administration, that from the time of Urban VI onwards Dietrich belonged to the more important category. The drafting of the minute for papal letters might be entrusted to an individual abbreviator ; but the examination of the document was the task of a committee or " rota," i.e. the presidents. It was responsible business, and required legal knowledge and experience greater than was exacted by the mere business of drafting, which could be done by anyone who had learned the *stylus curiae.* That Dietrich was trusted and respected in the Curia appears from a letter from the abbreviator Johannes Stalberg (another fellow-countryman), saying that without him nothing could go forward at the Curia ; and a younger contemporary historian, Dietrich Engelhus of Brunswick, calls him *cortisanus maximus in modernis.* Such was his position throughout Urban VI's pontificate, as well as under Boniface IX, until he was provided with the bishopric of Verden in 1395. From June in that year, throughout 1397 and during part of 1398, he was in Germany, but without ever residing in his cathedral city. Some of his letters are dated from Lüneberg, and he appears never to have obtained effective possession of the see. The explanation is probably to be found in Archbishop Otto of Bremen, his predecessor in the diocese of Verden, who had secured possession of Rothenburg and allied himself with the Duke of Brunswick and the city of Verden to keep Dietrich out. Dietrich was back in Rome at the beginning of July 1398 ; but Boniface IX, to his great annoyance, gave the Bishopric of Verden next year to Conrad of Soltau. Yet Dietrich still called himself " Elect of Verden " ; in 1401 he matriculated under that title in the University of Erfurt. This is the only certain reference we have of his connexion with any university, though he professes to have studied deeply in both laws. He did not stay long in the university town. At the beginning of 1403 he was again in Rome, present at the consistory wherein Boniface IX recognized Rupert of the Palatinate as king of Germany. He remained there under Innocent VII and Gregory XII, until the Curia moved northwards, ostensibly to meet, and negotiate with, Benedict XIII. He accompanied the Pope on the unhappy journey through Viterbo and Siena to Lucca (January to July 1408). At Lucca in May 1408 one can see him beginning to waver in his loyalty to Gregory, as it became abundantly clear that the Roman pontiff, under the pressure of his

[1] Quoted in Heimpel, *op. cit.*, p. 27.

relatives,[1] was not taking the negotiations with his opponent seriously. The complete break came when Gregory left Lucca on the 14th of July 1408. We do not know exactly when Dietrich passed over to the Conciliar interest; nor was he at Pisa when the Council opened in March 1409. But he had been working in Germany for the cardinals. At Cologne towards the end of 1408 he presented Archbishop Frederick with his *Nemus Unionis*, a document book of the futile negotiations between the pontiffs, and he is found corresponding with Cardinal Landulf Maramaldi, who was actively working for the Council in Germany. After November 1409 we find him back in his old place at Alexander V's Curia, and later on serving John XXIII, whose career he later depicted in a remarkable polemical memoir. From 1411 to 1413 he was still in Rome, but plying his pen in the Conciliar interest. In August 1410 he issued the first draft of his most important Conciliar work, the *De modis uniendi et reformandi ecclesiam in concilio universali*, and in the days between the summoning and the opening of the Council of Constance he completed the treatise, *Avisamenta edita in concilio Constanciensi*, which was for a long time attributed to Gerson. In the Council of Constance he concerned himself mainly with the process against John XXIII; a number of the tracts on this topic written by him for the Council are published in Dr. Finke's *Acta*. We have other glimpses of him in the German nation at the Council, but with John's deposition his main task had been accomplished. It is possible indeed to criticize him for working during the years 1411–1413 in the service of the man who, he was convinced, must be discarded by the Church. But he evidently regarded it as his duty to carry on the administration of the Curia as he had known and practised it before the crooked days of Boniface IX, while awaiting the decisions which he hoped that the Church would later take, and an attentive reading of his Conciliar treatises shows that he is not open to the charge of serious inconsistency. He lived to see Martin V's election, but not the Concordats, and he died in occupation of a canonry in St. Salvatius at Maastricht towards the end of March 1418.

These bare dates show that his working career extended over a most formidable crisis in the history of the Church. His written works reflect nearly every phase of events, and are the record of disappointment and later of recovered hope. They give us in the first place an intimate picture both of the *curialis* himself and of his surroundings in the early days of the Schism. Rome, despite the Romans, was evidently not an

---

[1] " Spes vero sua requiescit in Paulo et aliis nepotibus suis quos satis exaltat " : William Swan, notary and proctor at the Papal Curia, to John Launce, Canon of Chichester, 12 Dec. 1407, in MS. Bodl., Arch. Seld. B 23, fo. 48.

uncongenial place for the Teuton. In the early fifteenth century, a letter of Joan Swan, the wife of William Swan, a resident English proctor, mentions the fact that her husband had asked her to come out to him in Rome and to learn German (which he regarded as essential). She would come out, she said, but the vernacular she could not manage.[1] Now the phrase Joan uses is *eruditio vulgaris lingue*, which implies that it was regularly spoken among certain of the *curiales* ; and so many were the German pilgrims that came to Rome that in his later days, when he was well off from prebends, canonries and fees, Dietrich founded, to the west of the Piazza Navona, the Church and hospice of Santa Maria dell' Anima. Not far away, but nearer the river, was the English hospice of St. Thomas the Martyr and the Holy Trinity, and in its vicinity the various dwellings which the English house leased to our countrymen attached to the Curia or staying on business in Rome.

The *curiales* were a peculiar international community, a class of more cultured and sensitive fibre than the turbulent Romans or the sly and superstitious Neapolitans. They were fair game for plunder, for, like the modern bank messenger, they seemed to be marked down by the ill-disposed. When the Romans heard that Robert of Geneva had been elected by the cardinals at Anagni, they set upon the innocent members of the Papal Curia in Rome, particularly upon the northerners (*ultramontani*), and maltreated them badly. Dietrich saw Roman matrons stirring up the inhabitants of the city against these unfortunate men, and even spitting in their faces.[2] One of Dietrich's complaints about Urban is that when he took his cardinals and curials about with him, he did not see to it that they had good quarters. At Nocera (in 1383) where he occupied the castle (which, he grumbled, was hardly big enough for him), he left his cardinals and officials to find what lodgings they could in the seventy-odd houses of the Borgo ; the result was that as many as could made off to the sea coast and elsewhere. The reason for their flight, Dietrich told Urban, was that " they lacked protection." Dietrich calls them " *delicati et imbelles* "—not used to roughing it.[3] He tells how, when escaping from the intolerable conditions at Nocera, large numbers reached Castellamare, the governor of the place deprived them of such weapons as they had, and turned them all out, only to fall into the clutches of the local sailors, who were in league with some Catalan pirates on the Island of Capri. The sailors, who pretended not to understand Italian, took them out to sea, where they were at once overhauled by the pirates, robbed of their possessions, and landed penniless

---

[1] MS. Bodl., Arch. Seld. B 23, fo. 137v.
[2] *De Schismate* (ed. Erler), I. xiv. 29.
[3] *Ibid.*, I. xxxvii. 70.

at Naples ; while those who escaped to Naples by land were relieved of their goods by highwaymen *en route*.[1]

Dietrich himself (who did not escape from the attentions of these raiders) was of rather tougher quality. Perhaps the Germans as a whole had greater determination than the other *curiales*. When, upon Clement VII's election, many officials of the Curia deserted Urban, so that he was left alone " like a sparrow on the house-top," only the Germans stayed behind together with a few English, Bohemians and Hungarians.[2] But even the robust Dietrich admits that he could not control his emotions when at Nocera he saw Cardinal Leonardo de Sangro (suspected of complicity in the cardinals' plot of 1384) stripped, bound with ropes, and swung three times to the ceiling by the papal torturers, while the pontiff's miserable nephew, Francesco, looked on and laughed (*immoderate ridebat*).[3] It was not a gentle age, and none so hard-hearted as the first Roman pontiff of the Schism, the Neapolitan " born in the Piazza Nido, in a place which is commonly called Hell ".[4] *Fuit enim duri cordis*. But as Gregory XI's regent in the chancery, Bartholomew Prignano knew a trustworthy official when he saw one, and Dietrich was in his good books. " For many years," says Dietrich, " I was with him every night ; after he had gone up to his chamber to repose, he made me read to him in the Bible until he fell asleep." [5] In later years there were numerous occasions when Dietrich boldly faced Urban and remonstrated with him for his conduct towards the cardinals and *curiales*. It was natural, for, as a high permanent chancery official, Dietrich had access to the Pope and acted as referendary for petitions. In 1385 he represents himself as being handed by Urban a *rotulus* of petitions submitted to the Pope for signature. The *rotulus* came from unscrupulous people in Naples who wanted the red hat either for themselves or their friends. " As I read these petitions," says Dietrich, " I was astonished; and before each of them I made a sign, to show the scandalous behaviour of the petitioners, putting the Pope on his guard against their temerity and ignorance of curial procedure." As a practised administrator Dietrich was shocked to see the Neapolitans petitioning to be made cardinals, " just as poor clerks were wont to supplicate for expectatives "; [6] but Urban " trusted too much in the sowers of tares " and promoted, as Gobelin tells us,[7] a number of Neapolitans to the cardinalate, thus causing much amusement and gossip in Naples : for, says Dietrich, rather scandalously, " I heard a number of Neapolitan ladies, who knew the circumstances of the new cardinals, say to their friends : ' I

---

[1] *De Schismate* (ed. Erler), I. xlvii. 87–88.   [2] *Ibid.*, I. xi. 27.
[3] *Ibid.*, I. li. 92.   [4] *Ibid.*, I. i. 8.   [5] *Ibid.*, p. 9.
[6] *Ibid.*, I. xliii. 80.   [7] *Cosmodromion*, vi. 84.

hope I may see your husband a cardinal.'" The new Neapolitan cardinals, he says, " were jolly fellows " (*boni socii*), and each one of them was said " to have somebody with him and other hangers-on." [1]

Like Dietrich, we are digressing. His usefulness as an administrator is clearly seen in the *Liber Cancellariae Apostolicae*, a short but comprehensive handbook compiled by him for Chancery officials, giving the formulae of the oaths taken by newcomers, the names of dioceses throughout the Church, a large group of privileges granted to the religious, especially the Hospitallers, the constitutions on the subject of administration made in the Council of Lyons, John XXII's reforming ordinances for the Chancery, and other regulations for each class of officials, together with a table of salaries and a list of fees payable for apostolic letters. In his rubrics Dietrich shows himself an admirer of the Chancery in its earlier days. *Sequuntur mirabilia pennata*, he writes, *regimen et jura Cancellariae Apostolicae more antiquo*.[2] The *mirabilia* mainly consist of allowances for food and transport, the old and liberal regime before Urban took to moving about into uncomfortable places as well as to curtailing expenses. Later in the book he comes to certain thirteenth-century constitutions on the office of *scriptor*, again in " the old style." [3] The first of these, enjoining celibacy, instructs all writers that openly keep mistresses to put them away within eight days. In his *De Schismate* Dietrich praises Innocent VII because he made all writers of Apostolic letters dismiss their housekeepers (*focarias*).[4] We may well imagine that even the legitimately wedded Joan Swan would have had a difficult time, if she had joined her husband in Rome. The last of the clauses in this group is headed : " Even this constitution is kept to-day and deservedly." It gives warning that papal writers will be suspended from their office for seven days if they write " other " letters before those of the Curia. In cases where no payment for curial letters or for exemplifications (*rescribendae*) was offered, " the business of the Curia is to be preferred." [5] Dietrich tells us that he made his handbook from extracts faithfully copied " out of the book of the aforesaid chancery, dilapidated with age, with which I compared this present book, diligently hearkening to it in all things. And I arranged its chapters in a better manner, as far as I could, adding certain rubrics lacking in the original." After the date is a sigh : " Heu bona fortuna, cur non es omnibus una ? " [6]

The *Stilus Palatii*, or " Method of the Papal Court, conceived from the common practice of the said palace by T. de Nyem, least of all abbreviators," is an auditor's handbook, devised for the judges of the

[1] *De Schism.*, I. xliv. 81.
[2] *Liber Cancellarie Apostolicae* (ed. Erler), pp. 168–170.
[3] *Ibid.*, p. 171.   [4] *De Schism.*, II. xli. 202.
[5] *Liber Cancellariae Apostolicae*, p. 171.   [6] *Ibid.*, p. 203.

Rota. It answers all sorts of practical questions which a papal judge might want to know. What commissions can the vice-chancellor issue, what belong to the Pope alone? [1] What action is the auditor to take when he receives a commission; when is he to cite the parties and how much notice ought he to give them? [2] What articles ought he to admit? [3] How are witnesses to be treated? [4] And much besides. A most practical work, which many may find more interesting than the longer textbook on the chancery, though in this case the author obtrudes himself hardly at all. These two books are, in the words of fitz Neal, " non subtilia, sed utilia." They have no graces of style nor the pungency that marks his other writings.

Indeed nobody would call Dietrich a stylist, though naturally he had the *cursus* at his fingers' ends. But, as an historian of his times, he has advantages. He calls the *De Schismate*, the work for which he is best known, a labyrinth, in which the reader will find here and there displeasing things that must not disturb him, " since they who write histories in their search for truth often recite what they would prefer to suppress." He has made, he says, many digressions : for these have a way of enticing the reader, just as a tasty and unusual dish delights those at a banquet. Prolixity, where it is noticed, must be attributed by his readers to his inexperience in this sort of work. Of the utility of reading history there can be no question. It has a moral function. Memorable deeds deserve commemoration. To rehearse them leads to emulation on the part of the listeners, who learn to choose the good and to avoid the evil [5]— *declinando vitia, virtutes sectando*, as Gobelin said.

Dietrich has a shrewd eye for the significant, and, though he is never elegant, an enviable power of vivid and sometimes amusing description. Frequently he is carried away by his prejudices, and repeats scandal. Urban's nephew Butillo comes off very badly, but there seems no evidence for the gross immorality which Dietrich attributes to him at Naples.[6] The three Italian cardinals who met and deliberated at Fondi are treated with great scorn, although their negotiations with the disgruntled ultramontanes were originally undertaken at Urban's express bidding, and despite the fact that they early arrived at the Conciliar solution which Dietrich was later to adopt. He persists in calling them Peter, James and John, whereas the name of the third was Simon de Borsano. Robert of Geneva he cordially dislikes, and attributes his election partly to his noble relatives and kinsmen.[7] He is large, rather corpulent, fond of his food.[8] Conversely, Dietrich is too lenient to the

---

[1] *Stylus Palatii*, in *Liber Canc. Apost.*, p. 217.   [2] *Ibid.*, pp. 218–220.
[3] *Ibid.*, pp. 221–222.   [4] *Ibid.*, pp. 224–225.
[5] *De Schism.*, " Praefatio Auctoris," pp. 4–5.
[6] *De Schism.*, I. xxxiii. 63.   [7] *Ibid.*, I. x. 25.   [8] *Ibid.*, II. i. 124.

group that plotted against Urban in January 1380. But as an eye-witness he is admirable. There are unforgettable pictures. Urban taking no notice of the cup proffered him by Otto of Brunswick, husband of Johanna of Naples, to the dismay of all present : [1] Urban with his face " blazing like a lamp," and his voice raucous with passion against the disloyal cardinals : [2] Urban, as he paced the garden of the Castello di Parco, reading aloud from his breviary to drown the expected cries of the aged Cardinal of Venice who was being tortured in the cellar below : but the cardinal, as often as the ropes pulled him up to the ceiling, only repeated the words : " Christus pro nobis passus est." [3] There are the crowds of Romans gathering excitedly on the steps of St. Peter's at Urban's election, the relations and supporters of possible candidates for the papacy riding in expectation of success through the streets of Rome, the flight of the cardinals after they had done the deed and elected Urban ; numerous intimate touches written from the street rather than from the study. And the digressions are morsels both rich and tasty. The first of these comes in the form of a description of the delectable country round Nocera, a welcome relief after the story of Urban's cruelty to his officials and his strained relations with Charles of Durazzo. Dietrich speaks of the great chestnut trees that grow larger fruit than he has ever seen, and of the nut-groves on the road to Salerno, that might provide food for the whole district : " but now pigs are fed thereon, whose flesh makes the finest bacon, firm and delicious, and I have never seen larger and fatter capons and so cheap as are found there on that plain. And therefore the *curiales*, as long as they were safe, preferred to remain there than in any other part of the kingdom of Sicily." He then describes the wonderful wine that comes from the slopes of Monte Chiunzo and is shipped to various foreign countries : a good vintage, if kept for five or six years, grows stronger and better : in fact, the longer it is kept, the better it is.

Whence it once happened that I was admitted to the cellar of the Arch-bishop of Naples at the Castle of Torre by a certain German, then keeper of the castle, along with a proctor, a responsible man (*satis discreto*) in the Roman Curia, and some others, the captain wished us to taste the wine stored for many years in the cellar, and after we had tried the wine from several vessels, taking a little from each, the proctor suddenly became so inebriated that he could neither speak nor stand upright, but we carried him speechless and incapable to his lodging, where placed he slept continu-ously till the next day. But on waking up, when we asked him what had happened, he had no notion at all. At which I marvelled greatly. But whether this arose from weakness of brain or because he had drunk too greedily, I know not. The captain, seeing the said proctor so drunk in the

---

[1] *De Schism.*, I. vii. 19.   [2] *Ibid.*, I. xlv. 85.   [3] *Ibid.*, I. lii. 94.

cellar, told me with a smile that I should not be surprised that it had so chanced with my friend. He had seen the same thing happen to many that drank in the cellar.[1]

Following the narrative of the civil discord in Perugia, where, in 1393, Dietrich witnessed a horrible massacre of one faction by the other, there is an account of a visit paid by Boniface IX to the baths at Pozzuoli, when he was ill with stone. With some friends Dietrich made an expedition to the warm springs in the volcanic rocks of Monte Solferata, and entered the caves of pumice which the bathers frequented, stripped naked because of the heat and gaseous steam. It was a famous cure for gouty maladies. The place was dangerous when the south wind blew and forced the vapours back into the holes whence they arose. " After I had entered the said mountain," says Dietrich, " while I crept about the place exploring, for I was still fit and active (*dum iuvenis essem*), I broke out into a powerful and excessive perspiration, promising God that if he would permit me this time to return safe from this mountain, I never would go back again." He took with him to the bath " called St. Margaret's " a friend with a swollen and painful hand, which, when the vapours came up, was immediately cured, though the redness left by the inflammation remained. He describes Monte Gauro, four miles from Baiae,

> which many deluded Germans call in their tongue *Der Gral*, saying, as the natives affirm, that in it are many men alive and living till the day of judg-ment, who are given up to revelling and sensuous delights, and perpetually ensnared in devilish pastimes. Near which, in a certain house, is a bath without water : people merely sit upon a large round stone, and in a short while begin to sweat, and receive much pleasure and relief therefrom, as I myself proved. Near which is a pool in which harmless snakes appear in great quantities. And in this region crops ripen and are gathered in May, and about the middle of April fresh fruits are found in great abundance, to wit beans and cherries : and small and sweet pears, luscious to taste, about the middle of April each year. . . . You will always see grapes on the vines trained upon the fruit trees and elms in the winter right up to Christmas, great bunches of them, and many gardens green with trees and grass all the year long.[2]

The Neapolitan country he associates particularly with Virgil's tomb, and he mentions the wonders wrought there by that seer. He had been studying Gervase of Tilbury.[3]

---

[1] *De Schism.*, I. xxxviii. 71–73. It was, of course, the exhalations in the cellar rather than the wine itself which laid the proctor low.

[2] *Ibid.*, II. xix., xx. 153–157.

[3] Cf. *Gervasii Otia Imperialia* (ed. Liebrecht), pp. 14 *et sqq.* Dietrich cites him again both in the same work and in the *De Modis*, to demonstrate the duty of the Emperor to summon the General Council.

To read the *De Schismate* is to understand why, as the long duel of the Schism worked itself out and impatience grew generally, Dietrich made reform as well as union his aim. One might think that the chancery official would desire unity rather than internal change ; or that at least he would not believe in change coming through the medium of so untried a body as the council. But with Dietrich it was not so. Yet the new conviction must have grown very gradually, for he was a loyal spirit. He is fully alive indeed to Urban's faults : he does not spare the Pope for his tactlessness and doctrinaire obstinacy ; he shows how utterly mistaken was Urban's visit to the Regnum in 1383–1385, how unfortunate his dealings with the unscrupulous Charles of Durazzo, how grievous and expensive his wars ; yet, as he says,

> Urban never committed simony, nor in any way burdened those whom he promoted to cathedral churches and monasteries that were vacant ; and the benefices that fell vacant within or without his court he conferred liberally, and tenaciously remembered upon whom he had conferred a vacant benefice in his reservation, since he was unwilling to collate any competitor to it. He consented to no sharp financial practices, but duly contented himself with the ancient rights of the apostolic camera, however moderate, and he was of such high heart that he never lamented his poverty, and on his death he left more money in the camera than he found there on his election, so that his obsequies were more decently carried out than those of Boniface IX and Innocent VII.[1]

But with Boniface IX everything was different, and money the sole aim. No more devastating picture of financial corruption in the Middle Ages has been painted than in the early chapters of Dietrich's second book. It is more convincing than the *Squalores Curiae Romanae* of Matthew of Cracow. Boniface IX, a large, fine-looking man, was a curious mixture of mental confusion and crafty unscrupulousness. He did not really understand the petitions and graces that he signed ;[2] he would give a benefice to the highest bidder, and when a still higher one came along, he found means of revoking the earlier grant, while the same benefice was often sold to a number of competitors. He said that those who offered little intended to deceive him. New expectatives with an antedating clause were devised, then another and much more expensive kind, with a special clause antedating even those. He made new ordinances suppressing the traffic, and immediately got round them by exemptions sold at a high price. " These things were done commonly

---

[1] *De Schism.*, I. lxix. 122–123.

[2] For examples of this, cf. his signatures to the *rotulus* put forward on behalf of William of Wykeham by the proctor John Fraunceys, printed by H. Chitty and E. F. Jacob, " Some Winchester College Muniments," *Eng. Hist. Rev.*, Jan. 1934, together with the authorities cited there.

and openly," says Dietrich with bitterness. " All fear of God and shame of men set aside ; and so frequently, that the *curiales* for the most part affirmed that such things were legitimate, since in such matters the Pope, as he said, could not sin." [1]   His last iniquity was to refuse to sign any petition, until he had received from intermediaries a gold florin for each signature ; and he made everyone, however poor he was, pay him as much as was paid to the abbreviator for the minute.[2]   In December 1402 he revoked all his expectatives and other graces " as if he had erred in all of them," and yet issued (upon payment) others for a term of years.[3]   We are back once more with the evil which Gregory VII fought, for which Dante consigned Boniface VIII to the lowest hell, the evil in comparison with which the sins of the flesh are but slight ; and as the book proceeds, its temperature subtly rises ; yet there is no invective, only simple statements, many of which modern writers on papal administration like von Hofmann have shown to be reliable. We should, however, abstain from taking Dietrich, who wrote at an exceptional time and under exceptional circumstances, as an invariably reliable witness to the abuses in the curial system as a whole.

Throughout the later part of the book Dietrich shows how powerless in effect were Boniface and his successor Innocent VII against the external dangers like Ladislas of Naples.   The Roman See, threatened by enemies and internal feuds, was breaking up.   Yet it is not till Gregory XII is reached that the note of despair is sounded ; it is clearly heard in the last chapters of the second book,[4] which tell us that Dietrich in his mortification had collected the damaging materials for the meeting of those last days in the *Nemus Unionis* or *Forest of Union*, the volume which was finished on 30th July 1408.   In the third book of the *De Schismate* he outlines the futile negotiations of the Commissioner for union who ran away from his commission.   He no longer calls him by his papal name.   Errorius it has become, since he has deceived the world,[5] and the biting satire never spares him.   As far as the end of Innocent VII's pontificate the *De Schismate* is a serious historical work : but in the third book it changes its character and grows curiously stylized. It is no longer steady writing, with entertaining digressions ; a sort of macabre *Totentanz*, the grim posturing of skeletons, is now depicted, with quotations from the documents and appropriate moralizing.   Very characteristic is Dietrich's view of the Emperor as the right resort in such a struggle.[6]   We have returned to Dante with his appeal to the prince whose power depends immediately upon God.   Dietrich cites

[1] *De Schism.*, II. viii., ix. 132–133.   [2] *Ibid.*, II. xi. 136.
[3] *Ibid.*   [4] *Ibid.*, II. xlii. 202–204.   [5] *Ibid.*, III. vi. 216.
[6] *Ibid.*, III. vi. 216.

the well-known passage from the *Decretum* in which Theodoric is repre-
sented as convoking a council to deal with the charges brought against
Pope Symmachus [1]—the very same passage that was cited in the council
at Paris which determined on the withdrawal of obedience in 1398.
It is very natural that Dietrich, conveniently forgetting the Emperor's
Arianism, should go back to his great namesake, the legendary lord of
Bern. This leads to a historical demonstration of the right of the
Emperor in such cases, and Dietrich makes much play with the treatment
of John XII by the Emperor Otto I. This, as can be seen elsewhere,
was a favourite argument. We also hear a more specifically Conciliar
note in his application to the Pope of what the earlier political thinkers
wrote about the *rex iniustus*. If the Pope is *tyrannus potius quam dei
minister*, and despised by all because of his demerits, he is removable
from his sacred government, " since a bad priest is not [rightly] called a
priest and a bad bishop is not a bishop." The first of these propositions
is generally admitted by the early Conciliars, and forms a common
argument in their treatises.[2] The second comes dangerously near the
opinion of Wyclif, that *papa praescitus et malus homo* has no power over
Christ's faithful.[3]

Some years ago Dietrich's *Life and deeds of John XXIII* was the only
further work of a major kind that could by general consent be attributed
to him. But the studies of Dr. Finke and of his pupil Dr. Heimpel have
revealed a Conciliar sequel to the political and historical tracts, and
given a new unity and logic to Dietrich's life. After much learned
discussion lasting for many years, the *curialis* has now been conclusively
proved to be the author of the important dialogue *De Modis uniendi et
reformandi ecclesiam in Concilio Universali* first published in August 1410.[4]
Furthermore, this is now revealed as the basis of the *Capitula agendorum
in Concilio Generali Constanciensi* discovered some years back by Dr. Finke
in a Vienna Manuscript and attributed by him to Dietrich. The *Capitula
agendorum* is in fact an amended version of the *De Modis*, written during
the Council of Constance, with necessary alterations and corrections.
The first of these treatises, the *De Modis*, printed by von der Hardt,
was ascribed by him, on the strength of a faulty attribution in the Munich
manuscript, to Gerson. Schwab in his *Johannes Gerson* effectively disposed of this, but assigned the treatise to the Spaniard Andres of Escobar ;

---

[1] *De Schism.*, l. xvii., vi. (ed. Friedberg, i. 51).

[2] See the references in Erler's n. 2 to *De Schism.*, III. xi. 224–225.

[3] Walsingham, *Historia Anglicana*, I. 343 ; this was admitted to be heresy by
Hereford and Repingdon at the Blackfriars, London, on 20 June 1382 : *Fasciculi
Zizaniorum*, p. 319.

[4] This was suggested by Dr. Max Lenz in his *Drei Tractate aus dem Schriftencyclus
des Constanzer Conzils*, 1876.

and it has been left to Dr. Heimpel, after a careful weighing of the internal evidence and on the strength of a Stuttgart Manuscript discovered by Professor Bartos of Prague, to show that Dietrich is its author.[1] As the result of modern criticism, Dietrich stands out as the author of the *De Modis* in its two versions ; of the treatise on the summoning of General Council, written 1413–1414 (also printed by Dr. Heimpel) ; of the *Avisamenta edita in Concilio Generali* (after August 1414), formerly also attributed to Gerson, but suspected by Lenz to be Dietrich's work ; and of a quantity of other shorter Conciliar works printed by Dr. Finke in his great edition of the *Acta* of Constance.[2] It is no exaggeration therefore to call Dietrich one of the leading publicists of his age.

At Constance, during the early months of the Council (November 1414—March 1415) Dietrich acted consistently with the *Avisamenta*. He protested energetically against the *Curia* continuing to function along its old lines : petitioning for benefices must cease, curial officials should be relieved from all duties in connexion with this impetration until Easter, for at present they are so occupied with it that they cannot give themselves up to the pursuit of union ; the thirty or more titular bishops who have arrived in Constance (to swell the number of John's supporters) must be excluded from the Council ; and the mendicant religious must likewise be forbidden the assembly, since they are suspect on various grounds, principally for coming there to maintain their position against the charges that are likely to be pressed against them by the secular clergy.[3] At the beginning of February 1415, he warned the Council that the work of union would make no progress *nisi suspendatur curia Romana, cessentque iste impetraciones*.[4] It was outrageous that at Constance, the city of reform, flocks of clergy seeking benefices should be found, as if no change was imminent in the Church's way of living. Such polemics powerfully reinforced the more constitutional campaign against the three *contendentes* that was being conducted through memoranda and debate in the nations, and even broached in the sacred college, by Cardinals d'Ailly and Fillastre. It cannot have escaped comment that a man, who had been engaged in the apostolic administration since Avignonese days, should now turn his back on the system he had helped to work and see in it the main obstacle to Conciliar progress. Towards the end of February, Dietrich, in exhorting the Council to deal immediately with the question of union, urged that if Benedict and

---

[1] *Dietrich von Niem*, pp. 79–124, pages of fundamental importance for the authorship of the various treatises written 1410–1415.

[2] Conveniently listed by Heimpel, *op. cit.*, pp. 298–300.

[3] Finke, *Acta Concilii Constanciensis*, iii. 76–79.   [4] *Ibid.*, iii. 108–109.

Gregory were willing to cede, and John unwilling, the Council could legitimately invoke the secular arm and proceed forcibly against him.[1] On the 18th March, at a time of great tension, when John, meditating escape, was encouraging members of the Council to complain that their freedom of movement was being curtailed and that they were being forcibly constrained to remain in Constance, Dietrich tried to steady opinion and to allay suspicion of the counter-measures that were being taken by Sigismund.[2] He must, therefore, have acted as a mouthpiece of the more eager German reforming opinion.

The *Avisamenta* are remarkable for their evidence of Dietrich's conviction that union—to be obtained, if possible, by the cession of all three *contendentes*—shall be accompanied by the drastic reform of the Curia. Dietrich relates that he had been present some five years earlier when the projected Council of Pisa was being discussed by some high personages, and had heard Alexander V, then Cardinal of Bologna, say that it was no use restoring unity unless the " abusive power" of the papacy was limited and the old practices and ceremonies of the Curia revived and maintained by its officials : " but when afterwards he came to the papacy, he forgot what he had then said, nor was that power limited in any way in that said Council or thereafter—nay rather, it was increased even more vehemently when he was dead."[3] A scorching attack is then delivered upon the general reservations, " whether enrolled in the Corpus Iuris or written in the books of the Apostolic Chancery."[4] If they cannot be abolished, they should at least be suspended for five years, i.e. till the next General Council. The authority of the Archbishops and diocesans ought to be restored, and the ordinaries be allowed to function freely and unimpeded by the restrictive final clauses (*clausule*) in papal letters. Nor should the lands of the Roman Church be entrusted to papal kinsmen or nephews, but " to wise and prudent cardinals appointed by the Sacred College."[5] One of Dietrich's more interesting charges is against Boniface IX for exacting immoderate fees for the collation of benefices, first in England, afterwards in Hungary and elsewhere, and then dissipating the money so gained ; with the result that clerks from these kingdoms no longer resort to the Roman Curia, but are " headless and disobedient to the Vicar of Christ."[6] Whatever may be the reference here, there were good reasons on the English

---

[1] *Ibid.*, iii. 128–129. He cites the arguments in the *Epistola de Cathedra Petri* and the *Consilium Pacis* of Henry of Langenstein.

[2] *Ibid.*, iii. 133–134.   [3] *Ibid.*, iv. 595.

[4] This distinction between the beneficiary legislation of the Corpus and post-Corpus periods is maintained in the German Concordat with the papacy (1418), which admits the legislation of the former, but rejects the latter.

[5] Finke, *Acta*, iv. 596.   [6] *Ibid.*, iv. 598.

Statute Roll why clerks from England should not go to Rome for the purpose of seeking benefices—at least without a royal licence.

Dietrich is not a theologian, like Gerson or d'Ailly, but a lawyer and practical administrator, with a plan of unity and reform argued upon a basis of history and experience. In reading him, one feels oneself in contact with a passionate nature and a realistic mind rather than with the intellectualism and subtler abstractions of Conciliar theory. In the *De Modis* Dietrich's first desire is the health and effective working of the spiritual community, which, like the State, has a common good : for the *conservacio et salvacio boni communis*. It is for this that law exists. When in an emergency the care for the common interest and the preservation and retention of " any private person " are brought into comparison, the public welfare must be put first.[1] Now the point to be emphasized is that this statement is made in the first part of the dialogue, where the *unio capitis* is treated. *Iam primo de unione capitis volo presupponere, et potestatem usurpatam diu ab eodem capite limitare.* The conjunction is striking. You cannot unite without going back to the original law of the Church and curtailing papal accretions to that sound old body of enactment. The implication is that it is no use deposing the *contendentes de papatu*, unless you restore or re-create the constitution. But this solicitude for the common good, to preserve which law exists, is itself implied in the liberal and discriminating analysis of sovereignty in the Church that Dietrich had already propounded a little earlier in the treatise. Here he draws a notable distinction between the Catholic, universal Church, including " Greeks, Latins, and barbarians that believe in Christ, men and women, bond and free," [2] and the particular and private Church, composed of the Pope, the cardinals and the prelates. These two, he says, " differ as genus and species, since every apostolic Church is catholic, and not the other way round, and therefore the Apostle said in his letters : ' The Church that is in Babylon saluteth you.' ", " *Which* Church therefore," the older speaker in the Dialogue asks, " must one labour to unify and restore ? " " We must work," comes the reply, " above all else for the salvation and restoration of that *Universal* Church and of the faithful that err and the limbs that go astray because of the *second* Church, since apart from the Universal Church there is no salvation." [3] Here indeed are echoes of the arguments which, as Dr. Haller has shown, were used at the French national synods of 1398 and 1406, when the withdrawal of obedience was under discussion. That the Church was the *coniunctio omnium existentium in caritate* was the

[1] Dietrich von Niem, *Dialog über Union und Reform der Kirche* 1410 (*De Modis*) (ed. Heimpel), p. 15.

[2] *De Modis*, p. 7.   [3] *Ibid.*, p. 9.

thesis of Pierre Plaoul, while his contemporary Pierre Leroy had maintained that the Pope is simply the functionary of the Church.[1] Dietrich's
distinction, sharper than theirs, between the *congregatio fidelium* and the
Roman species of it, is a development of views that owe their inception
to William of Ockham.[2] It may, however, have been borrowed from
a nearer source than the English thinker : a short while ago Dr. Richard
Scholz drew attention to an anonymous treatise completed on the
16th November 1406, the work, he argues, of an ecclesiastic of French
sympathies, possibly the Dominican Bishop of Siena, Michael Pauli de
Pelagallo.[3] This treatise, now preserved in a Vatican codex, is a plea
for the Council, based upon the practice of the primitive Church. The
writer shows a striking sympathy with the Greeks, *qui christianitatis
nomen et omen radicarunt in nobis*. After the Hebrews, they were helped
to found the Latin Church, a subordinate member (*Latinam inferiorem*),
and are an essential part of the Universal Church from which the author
distinguishes the hierarchy. To him the Catholic Church begins with
Christ's Passion in Jerusalem, and Jerusalem was originally the most
honoured of the patriarchates. Dietrich elaborates this theme of the
comprehensive Church in which " the Greeks and barbarians believing
in Christ " are included. There seems little chance of knowing whether
he was acquainted with the anonymous treatise, though he must have
met and known its author ; it is in the same dialogue form, but with
the teacher rather than the pupil (as in the *De Modis*) giving the information. Dietrich has the same egalitarian view of the power of the
Apostles ; but the concentration on the Greek Church and its problems
finds no echo in the German writer.

I have referred to Dietrich's debt to Ockham, which he shares with
the early Conciliar theorists ; but there is more than Ockham in Dietrich's
view of sovereignty ; there is Marsilius of Padua as well, whom in one
place he calls *magnus theologus* ;[4] and, as Dr. Haller has pointed out, the
central point in Marsilius' thought, the notion that the Church received
from Christ no dominion over worldly things but a spiritual power only,
is represented in the *De Modis* partly in the very words of Marsilius.[5]
Dietrich had paid special attention to the beginning of Dictio II of the

---

[1] J. Haller, *Papsttum und Kirchenreform*, pp. 347–348.

[2] Ockham, *Dialogus*, V. xxiv., in Goldast, *Monarchia* ii. 494. The crucial words
are : " et ideo quamuis Romana ecclesia post Papam fit membrum principale
ecclesiae, sine ipsa tamen potest ecclesia esse." Cf. Haller, *op. cit.*, p. 507, and
Andreas Posch, *De Concordantia Catholica des Nicolaus von Cusa*, p. 89.

[3] " Eine Geschichte und Kritik der Kirchenverfassung vom Jahre 1406," *Papsttum
und Kaisertum im Mittelalter* (Kehrfestschrift), p. 597, *et sqq.*

[4] *De Modis*, p. 61.

[5] *Papsttum und Kirchenreform*, p. 508. Dr. Haller does not, however, admit that
Dietrich is the author of the *De Modis*.

D

Defensor Pacis, especially the passages in which Marsilius defines *ecclesia*, *spiritualis*, and other such terms. He quotes from Marsilius the statement that Christ " gave no principate or office of secular judge to Peter or any other Apostle." [1] Like Marsilius, too, he strongly emphasizes the human limitations of the ecclesiastic. Office does not sanctify the holder or render him immune from responsibility. If the Pope is called *sanctus* it is not because of his dignity or authority, but because of the grace and charity of God. " We see with our own eyes that the actions of many prelates and priests to-day, at least a majority of them, are not spiritual, but temporal and carnal." [2] The division in the Church is proof of this. Like Marsilius he would restrain clerical usurpations, and would go back upon the Sext and the Clementines, and much indeed in the Decretals of Gregory IX that usurped the power of the ordinaries and made for the suppression of the imperial, that is, the secular power. [3] This should not be taken to imply that Dietrich would go all the way with the Paduan and limit the priesthood to the performance of divine office and the hearing of confessions ; but he was as conscious as Marsilius of the danger of extending the spiritual power beyond the constitutional limits observed before the papal jurists got to work and advanced their master's pretensions. It is the new decretalism, the *novellae constitutiones*, that he regards with suspicion : perhaps with the kind of suspicion that led the older and more conservative *curiales* to dislike the new papal secretaries of the fifteenth century. In this attitude he is no innovator. Bishop Stephen of Tournai said the same thing about the new civilian spirit in legislation at the end of the twelfth century : *antiquiores sacri canones abiciuntur, respuuntur, expuuntur*. The complaint is found in several of his contemporaries. [4]

It is the spectacle of private interest, which he had seen operating since the time of Boniface IX, that shocked Dietrich. The fear of this led him to find in the universal Church, lay as well as clerical, the censor and organ of correction and reform. All the possible objections to such

---

[1] *De Modis*, p. 61.   [2] *Ibid.*, pp. 20, 21.

[3] *Ibid.*, p. 19 : " Revertor ergo ad propositum et dico, quod tantam fraudem in administracione huius papatus fecerunt aliqui antiqui, qui cum multis viris peritis, imo maliciis imbutis, Deum non habentes pre oculis, multa iura sibi usurparunt, et meliorem partem sibi attribuerunt, et de re publica non curarunt. Et quis fecit illos libros, Sextum et Clementinas, arroganciam, superbiam, iuris ordinariorum locorum usurpacionem, imperatorum Romanorum iniuriosam detractionem et eorum aliorumque potestatis periculosissimam suppressionem et alia ~~multa in~~ spiritualis et secularis rei publice lesionem maliciose et pertinaci ambicione fabricata, in omnibus et per omnia concludentes ? "

[4] Thus, at the end of the twelfth century, the same complaints were made of decretal law that two or three generations earlier had been made of the Novels, Code and Digest : G. Barraclough, *Papal Provisions*, p. 135.

control, exercised through the General Council, he meets ; [1] and to history he appeals for support in the characteristic thesis which we encounter at the end of the *De Schismate* : the historic duty and privilege of the Emperor to summon and preside over the representative body that is to carry out the task of unity and reform.   In the present passage he invokes the examples of Henry II and Henry III,[2] while towards the end of his book he emphasizes the part taken by German Emperors in heading the Crusade to the Holy Places.[3]   In treating of the Emperor, he shows himself in strong agreement with the imperialist argument in favour of the independence of the Empire from the papacy, even in Italy, where the imperium had been invaded and broken up, so that petty tyrannies had become established in the cities.[4]   It is impossible to read the *De Modis* without seeing in it the practical application of the morals drawn and lessons learned in the *De Schismate*.   The two works hang together, explain one another.

It should not be necessary here to examine the question of Dietrich's originality.   The arguments in the *De Modis* are certainly expressed with a rare force of personal conviction ; but he who predicates originality of any single passage of Conciliar theory is a bold man.   Often indeed in medieval thought what constitutes originality is not the nature of the thesis sustained so much as the quality and character of the person who sustains it and the occasion upon which he does so.   Of Dietrich two things may be affirmed.   Nobody before him had stated the case for the Council so completely from the legal and administrative point of view ; and no man of his period burned with a fiercer desire for that justice, apart from which every kingdom is nothing but robbery on a large scale.

[1] *Ibid.*, pp. 51–57.   [2] *De Modis*, pp. 71–72.   Cf. p. 90.
[3] *Ibid.*, p. 89.   [4] *Ibid.*, p. 111.

CHAPTER III

ENGLISHMEN AND THE GENERAL COUNCILS OF THE FIFTEENTH CENTURY

MANY that have taken part in international conferences, political or academic, will have experienced feelings common at all periods to our fellow-countrymen in such assemblies : a desire to return home as soon as they reasonably can ; irritation at the inaudibility of speakers and lecturers as well as at the length of their contributions ; and, probably, a sense of frustration if promising measures have been shelved or defeated, or if interesting people have not been encountered.   Supposing these experiences to be true of to-day, when the aerodrome at Basel is now less than two and a half hours from London and letters come quickly from home, it is likely that they affected people even more strongly in 1409, when the Conciliar experiment had really begun at Pisa, or in the winter of 1414-1415, when an even greater assembly was packing itself into Constance.   A General Council was not a picnic.   If an Englishman's journey to Rome took from six to eight weeks, it would take him fully five, and probably more, to reach the· mouth of the Arno ; and quite that to arrive in Constance, in approaching which he was liable to be relieved of his valise and any cash that he had about him.   Once at the Council, he could not be sure of good lodgings, and might very likely be prevented from leaving without special licence.   Money for his expenses came slowly and fitfully : by the end of 1415 the levy for the delegation sent six years previously to Pisa had not yet been completed and the accounts of the collectors were still unaudited [1]—a telling comment on the clergy's attitude towards the Council.

An account of a journey to one of the Councils—Siena, originally convened at Pavia—has been left by John Whethamstede, abbot of St. Albans.[2]   It was evidently written up after his return, but the style and mythological allusions make up for the loss of detail, and the whole is in the abbot's best manner.   In reply to the Archbishop's letter conveying to him the royal (i.e. the Council's) wish that he should attend, the abbot professed himself ready, though his flesh quaked " at the prospect of drinking the cup of that journey overseas," to take up the

---

[1] *Reg. Chichele* (ed. Jacob), iii. 7-8.

[2] For Whethamstede, see R. Weiss, *Humanism in England* (1941), pp. 30-38, and bibliography there cited. The most complete account of him is the dissertation (Manchester Univ. Library) of Dr. Esther Hodge, *The Abbey of St. Albans under John Whethamstede*.

cross with Christ and to work for the redemption of the tottering Church. Before he left St. Albans he put the government of the house in the hands of the prior and two senior monks, told the obedientiaries not to quarrel, and warned the townsmen to submit to the lawful orders of their abbey. Then, after adoring the shrine of St. Alban and osculating the relics, he took a tearful leave of the convent in chapter, where he was so overcome that, strangely enough, he was unable to finish his sermon. In London he got his passport (or letters of credence), and had an interview with Archbishop Chichele, whom he strongly disliked. The crossing to Calais was most unpleasant, and he depicts it with a wealth of classical mythology. From Calais his way was through Picardy and Brabant to Cologne, when he had a touch of fever ; but a doctor found the right plaster (*emplastrum curationis*), and in a fortnight he recovered. Thence to Mainz, and on to Worms, Speyer, Ulm, Kempten, and over the Alps, not by the Brenner, but by the upper Inn Thal and the Vintschgau ; thence to Meran, Bozen, Trento, Cremona, and so to Pavia. At Pavia he found that the Council had been moved to Siena because of an epidemic. So he decided to go by Piacenza, Parma and Bologna over the Apennines to Florence, for he wanted to consult a physician there, to whom he had been given an introduction. The days were warm and he was subject to gout.

After stopping a while in Florence he reached Siena, his goal, and inquired what had been done in the Council. " ' Nothing to speak of,' came the answer, ' save that the bishop of Lincoln (Richard Fleming) recently in his nation made an intemperate attack upon the religious, especially the exempt : but to the joy of the whole of his nation he has fallen sick of a fever and has been obliged to drop his case . . .' which the abbot hearing, and understanding that nothing had been done in the Council nor was likely to be done because all were waiting for the Pope to come, decided to go to Rome and present himself in person to his superior and recommend to the Pope both him and his." So he left the Council, which his own fellow-countrymen were by this time preparing to undermine, had an audience with Martin V in Rome, and secured from the Pope a number of privileges for the abbey, including one to limit fasting in Lent. In Rome he fell ill again and thought that he was going to die, but St. Bernard appeared to him and promised him life " if henceforth he would read his books and study them carefully." A little study of them could not have harmed John Whethamstede, for Bernard was precisely the saint to tell him *scriptis gentilium se non tradere, sed potius accommodare*. Hard counsel for the maker of classical dictionaries.

After recovery the abbot returned to Siena, and upon asking whether anything had happened in his absence, he was told not; only some minor ordinances had been passed for the government of the Council. During the past weeks he had been much incensed with his convent for not replying to his frequent letters; finally, when news came, it was to the effect that dissensions had broken out in the abbey: that " the peace that passeth all understanding, that binds together the affections of neighbours more tenaciously than glue, had not perfectly kept the hearts of the brothers or the intelligences of the villeins." It was time for him to be off. Ill-health was the excuse that he pleaded to the president of his own delegation (which he had treated with the most complete indifference), and the president urbanely, and with an obvious twinkle, told him that of course he must go in those circumstances. So Abbot John went, but was none the less minded to stay seven weeks at Cologne, and he was back in England on 9 February 1424, after being away a little less than a year. He asserts that when he reached Barnet on his way back to St. Albans, the villeins came out to greet him crying " Hosanna, blessed is he that cometh in the name of the Lord." [1]

Obviously the abbot was not a typical English representative at a General Council. He was of no use to his delegation, and took little interest in the proceedings; his account is genuine *flores Sancti Albani*, somewhat full blown. Yet much is to be read between the lines: the suspicious dread felt by the exempt religious for the reform of the regular orders; the successful tactics of Martin V in using delay to exasperate and defeat his opponents; and the use that could be made of a General Council for purposes far other than strictly Conciliar. Such considerations seem far removed from Conciliar theory, from those lofty principles which, we read, were advocated before an impressed Europe by university dons. Historical emphasis changes with the years, and of late Conciliar scholarship and study have not been so exclusively concerned with the deeper theoretical issues that made the Birkbeck Lectures of Dr. Figgis [2] so absorbing. The realism of Valois and Finke has led their disciples to regard the Conciliar Movement not so much as a phase of European liberal thought nor as an episode in the history of representation, but as a stage, indeed a formative stage, in the diplomatic relations of the Western powers, wherein the parts played by Aragon,[3]

---

[1] *Annales monasterii Sancti Albani*, i. 118–183.

[2] *From Gerson to Grotius*, Lecture II, " The Conciliar Movement and the Papalist Reaction."

[3] For the attitude of Aragon and Castile to the Council see Finke, *Acta Concilii Constanciensis*, especially iv., 1 Abschnitt, pp. 1–200. For Anglo-Aragonese relations during the Schism, E. Perroy, *L'Angleterre et le grand schisme d'Occident* (1933), Ch. vi. For Aragon after 1417, K. A. Fink, *Martin V und Aragon* (Ebering's Historische Studien, Heft 340, Berlin, 1938).

Savoy, and the Italian city-states,[1] are now coming to be more fully realized. The last large-scale work bearing on the Councils, *Les Origines du Gallicanisme*, by Father Victor Martin of Strasbourg, in the volumes he has so far published, is a study of the interaction of Conciliar thought and national idiom, a felicitous balancing of theoretical considerations and practical politics. This is the result of the material published since Finke began his reasearches in the Vatican and Barcelona Archives, and systematic study of the sources used by Hermann von der Hardt for his great document-book on the Council of Constance was undertaken. With the publication of the chronicle of John of Segovia and of the notaries' manuals at the Council of Basel, it was inevitable that similar realistic views should prevail with regard to the later period of the Movement. At the same time the mass of data and materials now published upon the administration and economic working of the Papal Curia has provided the background necessary for appreciating the difficulties in the way of reform. The new realistic standpoint does not, in actual fact, supersede or render obsolete the earlier concentration upon the more ideological aspects of the Councils : it rather heightens our appreciation of what was really serious and constructive in Conciliar thought and provides criteria for distinguishing, in the sermons and tractates of the age, between good sense and mere rhetoric.[2]

Let us take an example of the two methods, the older and the more modern, from the Council of Constance, and begin with a summary statement of fact as it might have been written some fifty years ago by an Anglican *magister historiarum*.

" At the time when our story opens (1414) there had been schism in the papacy for thirty-six years. There had been two Colleges of Cardinals, two separate curial mechanisms for chancery, fisc and papal law-court, and now during the last five years a third Pope and practically a third obedience had been added as the unforeseen result of the Council of Pisa. In England, and to a greater degree in Bohemia, orthodox believers were alarmed by the prevalence of doctrine that struck at the root of authority in the Church : the notion of a purely spiritual society, severed from the world, whose principle was found in Wyclif's assertion that ' the law of the gospel is sufficient by itself, without the civil or canon law, for the perfect rule of the Church militant.' From many parts of Europe were coming protests against corruption in the Church of Rome, and abuses and indiscipline among the clergy, and appeals for

[1] M. de Boüard, *Les Origines des Guerres d'Italie* : *La France et l'Italie au temps du Grand Schisme d'Occident* (Bibl. Écoles françaises d'Athènes et de Rome, No. 139), *passim.*

[2] This is characteristic of Dr. Paul Arendt's *Die Predigten des Konstanzer Konzils* (1933).

reform of the Church in head and members were growing in intensity. Schism, heresy, material and moral disorder, to reflecting minds evils mutually connected, were calling to be rectified. This, in simplest terms, was the three-fold task of the Council that held its first session on 16 November 1414 and its forty-fourth and last on 22 April 1418. By the latter date the three contending Popes had been set aside, two having been deposed, and one having resigned, and an indubitable successor had been chosen. The works of John Wyclif had been sentenced to burning, his more offensive theses had been literally and specifically condemned, and two leading Czech preachers had perished in the flames. Three successive committees had considered the problem of reform, which had been burked at Pisa, and had drawn up resolutions which, while never approved *en bloc* by the Council, were none the less to form the bases of agreements made by individual nations with the papacy ; and decrees had been passed that provided against the recurrence of a dual election, continued Conciliar action in the Church at stated intervals, and proclaimed the superiority of the representative General Council over any and every authority in certain clearly defined spheres of the Church's life. The Council stands as an example of the representative principle applied, on the largest possible scale, to a body which had been growing increasingly centralized and bureaucratic since the middle of the thirteenth century."

Owing to its concentrated form such an account can, of course, barely indicate the points treated at length by earlier historians of that date : the Schism as a moral and intellectual problem ; the Bohemian situation as the aftermath of Wyclif ; the three clearly marked stages of reform and the three corresponding commissions, as Hübler too neatly arranged them ; the theoretical importance of the Council's declarations and the practical importance of its challenge to papal authority. Two more considerations of method must be added, which we are inclined to overlook : the interest of the earlier Conciliar scholars, from von der Hardt down to Creighton, in the personalities of the Council, an interest which, because it is so personal, is very illuminating and never to be left out of account amid the less picturesque methods of modern legal and constitutional analysis ; and Creighton's brilliant realization, expressed in one of his letters, of the vital importance of curial administration as the principal obstacle to reform.[1]

And now for more recent days. What an earlier historian was not in a position to describe, even in the briefest terms, was the tissue of negotiations which for nearly four years made the city of Constance the diplomatic as well as the religious centre of Christendom. (Perhaps

---

[1] *Life and Letters of Mandell Creighton*, i. 266 (to Mrs. J. R. Green).

Max Lenz in his booklet on *Kaiser Sigismund und Heinrich V* came nearest to recognizing their complexity.) Never before in the history of the Western Church, save for two years of Otto III's reign, had the Imperial Chancery and the Roman Curia settled down together for any length of time. Here were the two swords—or, perhaps mightier, the two pens—at peace for a while, and the *De Monarchia* had become a prophecy rather than an epilogue. Through the various royal embassies that spent prolonged periods in the city alongside of the ecclesiastical delegations, and quite as often through the national delegations themselves, Constance was in touch with London, Paris and Barcelona. Almost every German court of any importance was represented there ; and even if the Church had, after John XXIII's deposition, no official head, the great curial departments received their quota of visitors and impetrants. The stream of petitions continued, even if the Vatican Registers of Supplications do not start again until the election of Martin V.

The Council was a valuable organ for the dissemination of propaganda. Henry V used it thus against his " adversary of France " ; conversely, the diplomatic regrouping of the powers in the summer of 1416—if we may thus refer to the Anglo-German alliance cemented by the Treaty of Canterbury—had a profound effect upon the causes sustained by the English and the German nations in Council. The new axis led to the counter-creation of a strong Latin *bloc* under the inspiration of Peter d'Ailly, to the drawing together of the French, the Aragonese and the Castilians, and Italy against Anglo-German reforming idealism. The Council, reacting quickly to the Anglo-French struggle, both helped to mould and was in turn sensitive to the opinion of the greater national groups. It was by no means a predominantly academic body, whether by this term we describe its personnel or the nature of its resolutions. Universities were indeed represented, most of all the University of Paris, but the Council was not directed by academics. At all medieval Church Councils doctors and masters proffered memoranda (*cedulae*) and drafted resolutions, because their training in law or theology fitted them to do so ; yet at any given moment when the Emperor Sigismund was in Constance there were more laity of standing than there were clerks in the city.

Conclusions such as these are suggested by the diaries and reports of those present ; and it was the great achievement of Heinrich Finke that he was able to publish, in the *Acta Concilii Constanciensis*, the accounts of eye-witnesses as well as the projects, memoranda and sermons of propagandists and preachers.[1] Yet conclusions is scarcely the right

---

[1] For a bibliography of Finke's work cf. J. H. Beckmann in *Historisches Jahrbuch*, No. 55 (1935), 466–477, and his analysis of the work of Finke's pupils both there and in the list he printed in 1935 (published by Herder, Freiburg i. B.).

word ; what we have is rather the suggestive material for fresh study, and at present we can only discern its general direction. And what is true of the diplomatic is also true of the constitutional aspects of the Council. There are important questions of its internal organization to which Finke's studies, the documents he printed, and the theses of his pupils are the indispensable introduction : for instance, the relation of the Sacred College to the nations as well as to the Standing Committee of the nations is a crucial point ; equally worth investigating is the laborious process by which those cardinals, far from united in the early days, acquired an effective organization, recovered their lost ground, and ultimately stood as a force to be reckoned with. Again, in the more psychological sphere, no historian save the contemporary Ulrich von Richenthal has adequately depicted the physical conditions and the mental and moral atmosphere in the very moderate-sized city on the lake,[1] where so much dignity, learning, subtlety and emulation were confined in an alarmingly small radius, and where a rumour took only an hour or two to disseminate. A walk of less than five minutes could bring any one delegation to the headquarters of another. From the lodgings of John Hus to the Dominican convent at the other extremity of the town it is no more than eight. The Pope, while he was still there, and the cardinals (who complained that, officially, they were starved of information), heard and knew everything that was being said, and privacy in debate was not easy for a nation to secure. Lastly, the sermons and the various broadsheets and memoranda submitted to the Council demand to be studied in relation to what we already know about Conciliar thought and argument. Thus we have only lately come to realize that the greatest writer and publicist of the Council was not d'Ailly, still less Gerson (to whom much is still uncritically attributed), but a Westphalian member of the Papal Curia, Dietrich of Niem.[2] This is very important, since it shows that criticism of abuses (particularly under Boniface IX) had touched the curial administration and affected the Chancery officials, to say nothing of the cardinals. Of the latter a group came to Constance determined that reform *in capite* should be carried out with all speed, and it was the combined attack of these brave men, together with the immensely effective propaganda of Dietrich, that made John XXIII's position so grave. It fell to the English delegation to close the door of escape by persuading the French to adopt their proposal of voting by nations.

This is not a digression ; for to understand something of the realistic

---

[1] Except perhaps Finke in his delightful *Bilder vom Konstanzer Konzil* (Heidelberg, 1903).

[2] Cf. Heimpel, *Dietrich von Niem*, pp. 287–303.

orientation which Conciliar study has received in recent years will enable us better to grasp both the achievements and the failures of this country in the General Councils. Normally, the doings of the English delegations excite little interest among historians, because it is thought that the assemblies were occupied with remoter ecclesiastical issues and that the results were meagre. It is, however, unnecessary to go farther than M. Perroy's illuminating *L'Angleterre et le Grand Schisme* to realize that this point of view can no longer be seriously maintained, England had, indeed, its own way of regarding Papal finance which to many seemed in urgent need of reform : but its idiosyncrasies, and its consequent caution on many of the larger issues of reform, did not thereby curtail its interest in the success of the first two Councils. Certainly this country did not take the lead in advocating a Council as the means of healing the schism. It was only gradually forced to that position by the utter mishandling of Anglo-papal relations by Boniface IX in a pontificate that ruined the interests of the Roman competitor, who, had always been able to count on English support. Yet, unlike France in 1398, there was no withdrawal of obedience on the part of this country ; for the situation as regards Rome was in reality highly complex, and its problems were not to be solved by taking a leaf out of the book of Gallicanism.

To official circles—and the English government was essentially lay in temper, supported by an episcopate largely trained in the civil service or employed in diplomatic work by the Crown—two things mattered : first, the maintenance of a system of alliances, bound together in a single obedience to an (it was hoped) accommodating and somewhat dependent Roman pontiff, which would serve to neutralize French and especially Avignonese influences in Europe, not least in the Mediterranean ; France and the French king, *adversarius noster de Francia*, were to England what Russia was to certain English statesmen during the last century, only much nearer and more provocative. (It was to Richard II's credit that he tried to break through this frosty conservative attitude.) Secondly, it was important that the king and—a long way after him—private patrons should be able to present the clerks they considered suitable to the benefices that seemed appropriate for their maintenance. The appointment to ecclesiastical benefices of the higher grades, particularly canonries and prebends, was a vital matter to the Crown in the fourteenth century and the subject of various agreements and compromises with the Curia, which continually sought to make provision for the cardinals from this particular source. As the general reservations were pressed from Avignon, England stood more firmly than ever on its old ground —that the right of presentation was a matter for the king's court, and must not be discussed in papal tribunals. This attitude underlies the so-called " anti-papal legislation " which was not anti-papal so much as English and customary, allowing the king, till 1390, to admit or refuse the papal provisor *pro libito voluntatis*. Even when the Act of 1390 closed the door to the issue of royal licences out of the statute, it was occasionally possible for the universities to petition the Pope for the advancement of their graduates. This appears to have continued till 1405 or 1406, though the evidence for such a statement can only be indirect. At the same time it was natural that the Pope should treat with a certain caution and lack of enthusiasm the churchmen of a nation which was not disposed to admit the general reservations and had Provisors and Praemunire on its statute roll. And when it came to Martin V, an indubitable Pope, caution turned to positive resentment and the papal assault on this country began.

These facts explain why, on the primary question of reform *in capite*, English delegates in the General Council were backward and temporizing. However loudly English prelates might grumble at the *servitia* and church-men of lower rank abuse the papal collector and the system of annates, their delegates were not officially concerned with Papal collation, as Dietrich of Niem was.[1] There was no need to be. Other points for reform were indeed discovered and abundantly discussed, particularly appropriations and dispensations for non-residence and pluralities ; and, whatever may be thought of the results, it is far from accurate to dismiss the English *Concordat* with the papacy in 1418 as insignificant, when matters like appropriations and dispensations which it raised were of general concern to the English Church. Yet the fundamental matter for reform was the complex legal and administrative structure that had grown up out of the originally simple act of petitioning the Pope for a benefice, and no English delegate, whatever he felt privately, was minded to advocate changes that his master the king, who had to stand by the Provisors Statute of 1390, would think it otiose to discuss. The Eng-lish had other concerns. In this country a peculiarly dangerous form of heresy was rife ; the first concern of *Ecclesia Anglicana* in the General Council, after due steps had been resolved upon or taken to secure one undoubted head, was to vindicate its orthodoxy and re-establish the purity of its faith above all suspicion. Hence the bitter, even passionate opposition of English delegates to Hus at Constance, and to the renegade Peter Payne at Basel. To English eyes unity and orthodoxy were of greater significance than reform. Not only from the governmental angle did reform raise dangerous fiscal issues, and threaten to rob the

---

[1] *Dietrich von Niem, Dialog über Union und Reform der Kirche*, 1410 (ed. Heimpel), pp. 45-50, 102-104.

royal nest of its eggs by upsetting a useful statute ; from the side of the religious orders it was full of perils, since it was inevitable that the privileges of the exempt houses would be assailed. The Convocation of Canterbury had discussed the matter in 1414, and even so cautious an ecclesiastic as Archbishop Chichele had urged Bishop Robert Hallum at Constance to press for the curtailment of exemptions. Yet in the English Concordat not a word was said on the subject, however strong may have been English representations upon it in their Avisamenta. I do not wish to imply that the English delegations at Pisa and Constance lacked religious who were friendly to reform. Spofforth, abbot of St. Mary's, York, who later became bishop of Hereford, was a whole-hearted reformer, and Thomas Chillenden, Prior of Christ Church, Canterbury, was no reactionary : I refer rather to the policy and achievement of the English delegation as a whole.

In his Papsttum und Kirchenreform Dr. Haller plainly under-emphasizes the reforming current in the English Church ; yet, as I have shown elsewhere,[1] that current was personal, individualistic rather than organized and controlled. There were keen men who felt deeply about abuses—Chichele and Hallum at Pisa, and Hallum again at Constance— yet how few of the Oxford "Articles touching the reform of the Universal Church " (1414) were they able to import into the Concordat of 1418 ! And after Constance reform is not a leading issue for the English, save as a disingenuous pretext for hastening on the Council urged (for political reasons) on Martin V in the interim between Siena and Basel ; a weapon in the hands of the arch-politician Bedford. How is this timid attitude to be explained ? And why, after 1418, are the English so backward in furthering what ought to be a principal aim of a General Council ?

It is difficult to give an adequate explanation ; the reason may lie not only in the facts suggested above, but also in the English idea of what a "nation" should be and do in the Council. It was the English who at the Council of Constance introduced the natio as a voting unit as against the diocese or the province. To them a nation reflected more than ecclesia Anglicana, it also represented regnum Angliæ. It was a microcosm of Church and State in one. It meant a great deal more than the social and disciplinary organization at the University of Paris and elsewhere. If the university supplied the form, political experience and a highly skilled monarch suggested the content. Size did not matter ; hence the bitter complaints of the French and the Aragonese against the paucity of the English nation and the smallness of the country it represented. It was a unit of imperium, reflecting the sovereignty of its master, and this can clearly be seen from the instructions given to the

[1] Infra, p. 154.

English delegation in 1416 and 1417, as well as from the proceedings at the Council of Basel. After the Treaty of Canterbury between Henry V and Sigismund, both English and German nations at Constance were ordered to vote as one. In a letter to the German nation written just after the Treaty, Sigismund bids them concur with the English :

> For, as you know, it has thus been provided by us and our dear brother the king of England, who in his letters has given strict instructions to the prelates and others of his kingdom that in all and sundry matters to be transacted in the Council they shall concur with you and agree in mutual harmony, and so we charge and require you that you shall be at one with them and vote together and hold yourselves firmly allied.[1]

When that co-operation grew embarrassing and no papal election could take place because the Anglo-German block insisted on reform first, it was Henry who in the autumn of 1417 called his nation off : at his command the nation *dimisit in illa materia regem Romanorum*,[2] as Fillastre very pertinently says. The delegation obeyed its royal master. It was the reversal of this policy of giving the separate nations separate voices in the General Council that led to the emphatic protest of Henry VI (i.e., the English Council) made by Lyndwood, keeper of the privy seal, to the Council of Basel. Henry told the fathers that voting by nations had been the method of procedure in the General Councils of Siena, Constance and Pisa, and that all had consented to it. He was prepared, he said, " so to proceed and do, on the part of himself and his subjects and lieges and the three estates of both his kingdom and domains." In other words, he claimed that his delegation should represent both England and France—not the France of Charles VII, but of Henry VI. The nationalist doctrine of the nation in the General Council could not be more clearly stated.

The Council of Siena (1423) presents remarkable contrasts to that of Constance. We have the spectacle of an English delegation under the presidency of the bishop of Carlisle which included distinguished men like Richard Fleming and Abbot John of Whethamstede, using tactics which can only be called obstructive and even wrecking, in favour of Martin V ; this, too, after Henry VI had pressed strongly, in the interests of reform, for a General Council. The English spokesmen who had visited Martin before the Conference had been most emphatic on the need for its summons. Hence the anti-climax. The point was very carefully discussed by M. Valois, whose suggestive conclusion in his *Pragmatique Sanction de Bourges*[3] has not yet been disproved : that the English at Siena acted as directed by the regent, the duke of Bedford,

---

[1] Finke, *Acta Concilii Constanciensis*, iv. 468–469.   [2] *Ibid.*, ii. 147.
[3] Pp. xxi–xxvii.

who was doing his best after the death of Henry V to secure a favourable ecclesiastical settlement in the conquered French provinces. His aim was to get into his hands as much of the collation of benefices as he could. At the same time he must humour Martin and prevent him from renewing his attack upon the Statute of Provisors in England. He had to squeeze the Pope very warily ; just enough pressure, but not too much. The English delegation and the representatives of the new Anglo–Burgundian University of Paris were instructed to support Martin in his distant and unfriendly attitude towards the Sienese, to report to him quickly if the conditions in the city were regarded as dangerous or impossible for the Council to be held, and to use all efforts against more radical proposals for reform. It is a remarkable spectacle, but the words of John Whethamstede which I have already quoted puts the position completely. Nothing of importance was done at the Council of Siena, because Martin and Bedford decided that nothing of importance should be done.

This failure of the English to support the Council, a complete contrast from their early attitude, is best witnessed at the Council at Basel. At this remarkable assembly there were many complicating factors : two in particular affected the English attitude towards the Council. In the first place the Pope, when he found that Cesarini had not taken his hint but had insisted upon going on with the Council, issued a bull of dissolution and transference. This proved a great difficulty, because the English at the urgent request of the promoters of the Council had already sent a small number of prelates over to Basel. The question which arose in the course of 1433 concerned the validity of this dissolution. Ought England to abide by it ? This problem was made worse by a second factor, the procedure of the Council of Basel. No longer was there a convenient system of voting by nations. Members of the various nationalities were now mixed up in the four deputations into which the Council was organized, and in those deputations voting went by heads, so that a simple master of arts could have a vote equivalent to that of a resplendent prelate. When Archbishop Chichele consulted Convocation on the matter this was one of the *dubia* or problems which he raised.

The dissolution and the method of voting both prejudiced the English against the Council. On the other hand, as Zellfelder pointed out,[1] it was particularly unfortunate that the arrival of the English delegation synchronised with that of the papal presidents who were appointed to sit beside Cesarini after the Pope had reluctantly recognized the Council. Hesitation and dislike of being incorporated in the Council under such a

[1] *England und das Basler Konzil*, p. 25.

system of voting made the English appear supporters of the papacy
and opponents of the aims of the Council.   This impression was height-
ened by their passionate opposition to the Hussites, in particular to
Peter Payne, the former Oxford Master, who was a protagonist of the
Hussite position.   None the less it was thought worth while to reinforce
the delegation during the course of 1434, and it was in this year that the
great chance of solid peace with France was permanently lost, and lost
very largely through the tactics of the English delegation.   Their aloof-
ness and opposition to Charles VII being represented at all at the Council
of Basel, their claim that in fact Henry VI was master of England and
France to the exclusion of Charles VII, was in part responsible for drawing together, under the aegis both of the Papacy and of the Council,
the duke of Burgundy and Charles VII.   The determining fact in the
position was that the duke of Burgundy was frightened of the Emperor.
He was in a particularly vulnerable position, with the Emperor on one
side, and France, that is the renascent France of Charles VII, on the other.
That he chose to leave the English alliance and to make it up with Charles
was at the bottom due to his suspicion of Sigismund, and to his feeling,
which had been growing since the coronation of Charles VII, that the
English were no longer to be masters in France.   The Peace of Arras was
prepared by the negotiations and efforts of the Council on one hand and
of Eugenius IV on the other, each trying to outdo the other so as to
gain the diplomatic triumph of bringing the two estranged parties
together.   Had the English been sufficiently watchful and conciliatory
in the Council, had they, in the days before the Conference of Arras,
refrained from pressing the claim of their master as against that
of Charles VII, they might have done much to prevent the landslide that
was ultimately to send them out of France.

It is a strange contrast, the frigid attitude of discouragement and
intransigence that succeeds to English enthusiasm and adaptability in
the period 1408–1418.   It points to a decline of policy and tactics in the
king's council, to an insularity, we must admit, on the part of Archbishop
Chichele, and to a somewhat provincial readiness on the part of the
English delegation itself to incur isolation as the alternative to the acceptance of its plan.   It is, then, in the later days of the Great Schism and
the earlier period of the Councils that English interest is greatest and
English activity most clearly to be traced : the period lying approximately
between 1390 and 1418.   To this we may now turn.

CHAPTER IV

ENGLISH CONCILIAR ACTIVITY, 1395–1418

THE Great Schism had dragged on for thirty years. "We in England," said Archbishop Arundel in 1408, "have till now taken little pains to work for union, by reason of which our prestige is manifestly weakened." In broad outline this statement from his writ summoning the July Convocation appears depressingly accurate. It was echoed with polite similarity five days later by the official of the Court of Canterbury, Master Henry Ware, in announcing the decision of the two committees which had been debating the matter. "It has long been incumbent upon Englishmen, especially upon us prelates and clergy, to restore and unify the seamless garment of Christ . . . Yet we are said to have done little or nothing, and the result is to diminish the conspicuous good name of England." [1] It may have been characteristic of English conservatism or, perhaps, of English inertia, that the Roman, as against the Avignonese, pontiff was supported right down to the summer of 1408 : that there was no withdrawal of obedience, like that of France in 1398, nor declaration of neutrality. Collectors like Lodovico of Volterra came, nuncii like Carlo Brancacci drew their due procurations with official support ; Boniface IX might even revoke his privileges and indulgences and call down upon himself (little as he would be affected by it) the indignation of the St. Albans Chronicler, [2] but the working, if at times uneasy, compromise between the English monarch and the Roman Pope had continued. As long as Boniface IX or Gregory XII did not press too hard for the revocation of the Statute of Provisors (1390), or challenge what Henry IV described later as " the statutes and ordinances of the Kingdom, issued by the assent of all the estates (*statuum*) and hitherto observed," [3] nothing serious seemed to occur. Yet if English minds moved slowly before 1408, they did at all events move. Behind official correctness there was a good deal of genuine alarm at the obvious scandal of the situation, and to suppose that there was no constructive thinking on the matter would be erroneous. It may be worth asking whether Master Ware's *modicum aut nichil* was

---

[1] Wilkins, *Concilia*, iii. 307, 309.

[2] *Annales Ricardi Secundi et Henrici Quarti* (ed. Riley), p. 350 ; for the revocation, see E. Ottenthal, *Regulae Cancellariae Apostolicae*, Boniface IX. no. 68 (22 Dec. 1402) ; *Cal. Papal Letters*, v. 535, 583, and vi. 89.

[3] Add. MS. 24062, fo. 155 v. (1409). For the expression " the lords and other estates in Parliament " used as early as 1407, cf. *Proc. Privy Council*, i. 301.

not rather too despairing an account of the general attitude of the English Church.

From a metropolitan's point of view, to judge by later events, it was probably not. The clergy were slow either to pay or to pray. The January Convocation of 1409 voted 4d. in the pound for the expenses of the delegation about to start for the Council of Pisa (this to include the 1¼d. voted the previous July), the money to be paid before next St. Gregory's Day to Master Richard Brynkley, dean of St. Mary Arches, and Master John Perche, Registrar of the Court of Canterbury.[1] The writ ordering the collection of the balance was dated 31 January 1409. From his London dwelling Bishop Robert Hallum of Salisbury gave orders some ten days before his departure with the Pisan delegation[2] for the money to be collected by archdeaconries in his diocese and paid to the collectors. At the beginning of May 1409, Adam Mottrum, Hallum's vicar-general, received, via the Bishop of London, Arundel's mandate to expedite the collection.

> The negligence of our suffragans and their sloth over the collection of the subsidy is plain and manifest to all. Two months have passed beyond the term of payment and scarce has one penny in seven been paid (et vix septenus denarius est solutus); wherefore, we wonder greatly that, as it seemeth to us, they hold God's cause so cheap.[3]

Two months is not serious arrears for a medieval subsidy. It is another story when we find in January 1416 Archbishop Chichele declaring, in connexion with a new subsidy of 2d. in the pound for the delegates at Constance, that of the earlier 4d. in the pound payable to the Pisan delegates some was still in the hands of the collectors, whilst numbers of the clergy had not paid at all.[4] In the spring of 1417 a letter addressed by the archbishop to Robert Hallum at Constance ends with a striking sentence :

> In the matter of the money owed you from this province, God knows, my brothers and the vicars of those absent, whose duty it is to raise the sums required, are behaving with negligence, although I have requested them both personally and through my officials ; as soon as they send in the money, it shall be paid to you without delay.[5]

No doubt ecclesiastics had observed with what foresight the Commons

---

[1] Concilia, iii. 312 ; for July, ibid., 310, and Reg. Roberti Mascall, p. 66.
[2] Which took place round about 16 February.
[3] Reg. Hallum, part ii. fo. 25. (The expression " part ii " is used, since there are two successive series of foliations in Hallum's Register.)
[4] Supra. p. 44.
[5] Royal MS. 10 B. IX. fo. 59 v. : " De pecuniis vobis a clero provincie debitis, novit Deus, confratres mei et absentes (i.e. absentium) vicarii, quarum levacio est de

at the beginning of Henry IV's reign, when piously asking the king
to use his influence to unify the Church, had expressly stipulated that
this should involve " no great charge or cost." [1]   Nor were the clergy
or laity more profuse with their prayers.   In the register of Bishop
Hallum occurs a remarkable letter from the primate, complaining of
the lukewarmness of their devotion in carrying out his requests for
prayers and processions on behalf of the peace and unity of the Church
and for " the most Christian prince Sigismund, King of the Romans,
who has laboured and still labours fervently for the union of Holy
Mother Church and peace among kings and princes."   After giving
several examples of the power of prayer in history and commending
to their notice " the most confident hope that the serene prince and
king Henry [V] has in its efficacy," the archbishop gives instructions
for special suffrages to be said in the dioceses, until the prelates are told
to do otherwise, *donec aliud habueritis in mandatis* (an echo of the royal
formula).[2]

In academic circles, as in Paris University, the atmosphere was very
different.   The Conciliar Movement was partly a university movement.
Conciliar theory from Durandus onwards had had a long and predominantly scholastic ancestry ; [3] it was not confined to continental
studia, for the treatise of the Minorite Provincial Nicholas of Fakenham,
though written in 1395, shows clearly that the doctrine of *epikeia*, pro-

presenti, negligenter se habent, licet ipsos solicitaverim personaliter et per meos ;
quam cicius ipsas introduxerint, absque more dispendio vestris persolventur." The
date of this letter can be seen from the sentence " Celebrato festo sancti Georgii
[23 April] habitoque ultimo huius mensis die [30 April] apud R. consilio, rex versus
partes transmarinas exercitu copioso se divertit."   The Council foreshadowed here
was probably held at Reading between 7-15 May, 1417 : cf. *Cal. Patent Rolls*,
1416-22, 102-6. In the only records of these payments which I have been able to
find, the farmer's accounts for the New College living of Adderbury, the payments seems to have been made punctually. T. F. Hobson, *Adderbury Rectoria*
(Oxfordshire Record Society, 1926), pp. 2, 14, 16.

[1] *Rot. Parl.*, iii. 456 (10 March 1401).

[2] Reg. Hallum, part. ii. fo. 38 v. " Plurium tamen nostre prouincie subditorum
relacione concepimus quod circa premissa (the prayers) tam cleri quam populi
tepescit devotio que ad preces huiusmodi fundendas accendi debeat." This letter
is in *Reg. Chichele*, iv. 158-159. For his earlier request for processions and prayers
on Sigismund's behalf, see *ibid.*, iii. 435-437 and iv. 127. In May 1417 Chichele
sent out yet another mandate for prayers to be made, this time on Henry V's
behalf, since some, *tepiditate causante*, were " ceasing to pray for the King." *Reg.
Chichele*, iv. 167-168. Perhaps Henry V's warfare was not as popular as has been
made out.

[3] For studies of its development see Franz Bliemetzrieder, *Das Generalkonzil im
grossen abendländischen Schisma* (Paderborn, 1904), pp. 104-190 ; his valuable
Literarische Polemik zu Beginn des grossen abendländischen Schismas (Vienna, 1909) ;
and Andreas Posch, *Die " Concordantia Catholica " des Nikolaus von Cusa* (Paderborn,
1930), pp. 36-61.

pounded, among others, by Henry of Hesse at Paris, had crossed the channel and had been discussed.[1] Paris, as all know, was the main source of propaganda ; hers was the effort to mobilize opinion and end the Schism by securing the adoption of one of her " three ways." Her main approach to Oxford did not materialize until Richard II was negotiating over his second marriage, and the policy of *rapprochement* with France was being thought out in its various implications. The deterioration of Anglo-papal relations under Boniface IX suggested also that Richard's attitude towards the Roman obedience might be capable of modification.[2] In Paris the earlier Anglo-German Conciliar enthusiasm had received a setback from the strongly Gallican attitude of the Court and of the theologians and medicals, while the artists tended to be divided according to their nations. By 1395, in spite of the fears expressed by the cautious and moderate Gerson, the university was putting out all its forces to canvass the universities and courts of Europe in favour of *cessio*, the resignation of both pontiffs. In the autumn of that year its ambassadors crossed to England and sought out Richard II. They came, it seems, armed with a general epistle to " all Christ's faithful during the schism" (dated 26 August), and with a special covering letter addressed to Oxford. The embassy never saw St. Mary's. Richard kept its members at Westminster, fearing perhaps, as Valois suggests, that Anglo-French rivalries might lead to disturbances in Oxford, should the French appear in Convocation.[3] He sent on the " general epistle," and let the abbot of Mont St. Michel expound to him the whole case for resignation. This was printed by Du Boulay,[4] with the somewhat Gallican observation that the solution proposed by the University of Paris and " put down in writing by the Abbot of Mont St. Michel " was made the object of a destructive attack by the University of Oxford " not out of a desire to seek peace, but out of emulation and envy." [5] As the late Mr. J. P. Gilson noticed, Du Boulay did not print the " general epistle," to which the Oxford reply of 17 March 1396, transmitted to

---

[1] Printed by Fr. Bliemetzrieder in *Archivum Franciscanum*, i. 577–600 ; ii. 79–91. For *epikeia* see *supra*, p. 9. Nicholas says that he writes " ad excitandum filios matris nostre Universitatis Oxonie " (p. 91). He was evidently put on to the task by Richard II.

[2] On the English attitude before 1395, cf. E. Perroy, *L'Angleterre et le Grand Schisme d'Occident* (Paris, 1933), p. 365. M. Perroy (pp. 267–268) calls Fakenham " Falrenham."

[3] *La France et le Grand Schisme d'Occident*, iii. 76. The covering letter is printed in Bulaeus, *Historia Universitatis Parisiensis*, iv. 751–752. This certainly cannot be the " Epistola quaedam a studio Parisiensi elaborata . . . et multiplici racionum congerie roborata " of which the Oxford reply speaks. The " rationes " belong to the epistle analysed below.

[4] *Op. cit.*, iv. 755–772.

[5] *Op. cit.*, iv. 775.

the king, is the direct answer.[1] It seems probable that he thought it to have been substantially the same as the abbot's oration, but indubitably it is not, though it naturally bears a definite relation to the other document.

In the Royal Manuscript in which this "general epistle" occurs,[2] it is termed *Compilacio Universitatis Parisiensis*. It is a long homiletic appeal for the resignation of the contending Popes, as being *magis ydonea et compendiosa*, for four reasons : *ex parte vie* (because the other solutions are more hazardous and uncertain), *ex parte cause, ex parte contendencium*, and *ex parte sancte Matris Ecclesie*. The first of these emanates from a four-fold fount—*facilitas, securitas, perfectio*, and the preservation of the honour of the obediences. The difficulty of summoning a general council " from the remotest parts of the earth, practically from the vast circuit of the whole universe," is insisted upon : [3] a council might be a nest of intrigue and dissension ; under divine inspiration · it may, perhaps, be free from error in matters of faith, but if wrong information is given to it, it is certainly liable to be deceived.[4] The way of resignation, however, is not only more secure and involves less risk of *falsa suggestio*, it is also more to be recommended on moral grounds (*perfectior*), since the resigning parties would be following Christ's command and example.[5] It would allow the honour of the various nationalities (*decus regnorum principum et populorum*) to remain undamaged, " without the label of error or infamy " which might accrue where a council had resorted to deposition.[6] Moreover, what judge or judicial body could settle the quarrel ? A council could not sit in judgment upon one Pope or the other. From the standpoint of the contending parties, resignation

---

[1] *Catalogue of Royal and King's Manuscripts in the British Museum*, i. 153 (no. 22). The " emulation " would be more true of their letter in 1399 : see *infra*, p. 64 and n. 3.

[2] 6. E. III. fos. 77–80. This manuscript belonged to Magdalen College, Oxford, " ex dono magistri Ricardi Lagharun," once Fellow of the College. Compiled round about 1450, it contains among its various items a number of anti-Lollard tracts, the " De reformacione Ecclesiae " and the " De Potestate Ecclesiae " of Peter d'Ailly, and Richard Ullerston's treatise on reform (on whom cf. *infra*, pp. 79–81). For other MSS. see Valois, *op. cit.*, iii. 77, n. 2, and Perroy, *op. cit.*, p. 368, n. 3.

[3] Fo. 77 v. : " Quis enim est qui nesciat multo facilius esse duos homines per quos stat hoc s[c]isma iuri suo propter pacem, si filii pacis sunt, cedere, quod in momento temporis solo utriusque verbo eodemque breuissimo factum esset, quam concilium aliquid generale de distantissimis terrarum partibus et tocius pene orbis vastissimo circuitu convocare . . ."

[4] *Ibid.* : " Est namque multorum opinio, quamquam impossibile sit in illis que fidei sunt generale concilium ab errore, sacro ipsum dirigente spiritu, [falli], in hiis tamen que facti [*sic*] sunt ex falsa suggestione aut mendacibus testibus, falli aut errore [*rectius* errare] posse, ipso scilicet spiritu veritatis propter mendacem spiritum prevalentem deserente."

[5] Fo. 78.   [6] Fo. 78 v.

would confer eternal glory upon those who consented to it ; [1] it would put an end to war in Christendom, to this madness in our own household that turns citizen against citizen and the members against the head.[2] Lastly, the Church calls for a remedy for her desolation ; and the letter ends with a florid address of the mother to her children of every age and degree and sex, bidding them have pity on her dejection, her pallor and misery : an appeal which, its writers declare, " is being heard and taken up by all circumcised hearts and ears," so that " their consent and the universal cry of the faithful for this way (of cession) seems in a sort equivalent to a general council.[3] Convocation did not think so : *nobis videtur longe aliter sentiendum* was the view taken at Oxford. The reply which the university forwarded to the king began with a detailed criticism of the Parisian thesis. That the way of resignation would be " easier," the Oxford masters wholly deny : it is a common saying, they remark, that the anti-pope, though elected only to resign under certain definite conditions, has no mind to give way. Resignation, too, unaccompanied by conditions (*nuda*), does not heal the dissension and perplexity in the Church ; there would have to be in addition a council, whether general or particular, or some method of compromise discovered, unless it is intended that both obediences should also resign with their respective pontiffs ; but in that case how would the Church elect a new Pope ?[4] Nor is resignation a " safer " method : the spirit of dissension would remain long afterwards, harming men's consciences and generating remorse or disquieting scruple. Only free and unfettered discussion in public can quieten and reassure men's minds ; the stifling of grievances is the worst source of trouble, and the way of resignation would make no provision against such inhibitions. Further, there is no reason why a council should be more easily corruptible than any other of the methods suggested.[5] If resignation is urged on moral grounds, is it not necessary to prove that both the parties are creating a scandal and an enormity by retaining the papacy ? And can this be justly said of Boniface ?[6] Nor can the texts from the Sermon on the Mount be legitimately employed in this context. Humility and surrender

---

[1] Fo. 79 : " O felices et fortunatos homines quorum iam in manu est per vocis significacionem brevissime paradisum promer[er]i, vitam eternam habere, quin et bonos esse."

[2] Fo. 79 v. : " Et certe bellum plus quam ciuile, quod si quis apto nomine velit appellare, domesticum furorem dicere poterit."

[3] Fo. 80 : " Ymmo consensus idem et universalis clamatio fidelium pro via ista videtur equiparari quodammodo concilio generali."

[4] Bulaeus, *op. cit.*, iv. 778.   [5] P. 779.

[6] *Ibid.* : " neque enim dicendus est in Ecclesiae perniciem praesidere qui iuste intronizatus non praeesse desiderat sed prodesse, timens suae dignitati renunciare, ne forte Ecclesia maiori exponatur periculo et graviori incursione turbetur."

of one's goods, when it involves danger to one's subordinates (*preiudicium subditorum*), is not to be justified. To refuse legal means of defending oneself and patiently to suffer injury was not St. Paul's way : he appealed to Caesar ; and we have as an example the attitude of Gregory the Great to the text of St. Paul which has been quoted as a justification of such passivity : "The Apostle has given us warning that we shall preserve humility in our minds and yet maintain the dignity of our order in all honour ; so that we shall not display an affected (*tumida*) humility nor an overweening presumption." [1] The example of Christ laying down His life is equally irrelevant. If the shepherd has to renounce his dignity for the salvation of his flock, why should he not equally be bound to retain it for their salvation ? These biblical citations are, in fact, capable of other explanations. The constructive part of their letter Convocation left till the end. The way we offer, they say, is one that not only brings back peace but corrects the errors that abound in the Church ; subject to Pope Boniface's approval and the consent of Catholic prelates and princes, it is that of a General Council. This has scriptural and historical justification, as Gregory the Great's example shows us ; [2] it is superior to the other methods in dignity, authority and in conformity with the demands of the situation (*factorum factis conformitate*). How otherwise can an end be put to this impossible position, unless a new type of remedy is applied, and one that will deal not merely with the fact of the Schism, but with the whole background of doctrinal error and administrative misgovernment ? *Sed difficilior . . . sed timendum*, opponents say. Is this any reason for thinking that we should take the narrow path leading to destruction or imagine that there will be nothing but disagreement in such a body as the Council ? In a General Council people are more sincere in their zeal, less partisan than at other times, and, above all else, the grace of the Holy Spirit co-operating with them is more effective. The difficulties raised by Paris against the Council are best met when they are actually encountered ; those which are not provided against by canon or by precedent might best be discussed by the leading churchmen of the Province (*seniores provinciae*). What is above everything else necessary is that the parties should come together for mutual discussion, which is the foundation of any further measure, whatever that may be. [3]

[1] P. 780 (printed as 788).
[2] P. 783 : "patet ex hoc quod magnus sanctus et doctor Gregorius venerari se quatuor Concilia generalia tanquam quatuor evangelia profitetur."
[3] P. 784. M. Perroy (*op. cit.*, p. 370) is rather sceptical of the conviction behind Oxford's advocacy of a General Council : "En dernière analyse, la méfiance pour tout ce qui vient de la cour des Valois, bien plus qu'une conviction profonde, a dicté la réponse d'Oxford."

The university did not depart from its view on the second occasion of its consultation. In 1398, after the formal withdrawal of obedience by France, another effort was made, this time by the French Court in conjunction with the University of Paris, to secure a French-English-Castilian agreement in favour of the voluntary abdication of the two Popes. Richard II was out of sympathy with the line taken by Oxford ; he leaned, like his new French allies, towards *cessio*. His ambassadors had urged it at the Frankfurt Reichstag in July 1397 ; [1] but he had still got to overcome the resistance of the university. At the end of 1398 Paris sounded him again, [2] with the request that he should go further and follow the French example in withdrawing obedience. The king was not slow in asking Oxford for its reply. The Regent and non-Regent Masters met in St. Mary's on 5 February 1399. Their answer, preserved in a Bodleian manuscript, shows that they realized the gravity of the step, but could not commit themselves to taking it. [3] After maintaining the canonicity of Boniface IX's election and stressing the need for discipline and obedience to authority in the Church, [4] they set forth at some length the arguments for a General Council. They were ready to send twelve chosen doctors, novices by comparison (*de nostris tironibus xii doctores electos*), to uphold their thesis against that of their Paris colleagues. [5] That the suggested negotiations ended fruit-lessly appears from another letter from Oxford to Richard II, written, it seems, in reply to further solicitations from the French university. This document, preserved among the Vatican documents upon the Schism, betrays more than a touch of irritation at the renewed initiative on the part of Paris. The French masters think that all must do as they desire and " practise as they practise, as if there was no *studium* anywhere but with them " : " that in no other place can the water of life-giving wisdom be drunk from Jacob's well, since it is deep there, nor disputation can be held beneath the shade of any other mountain save their own Parnassus." Boniface IX has offered to summon a General Council. This offer should be accepted, rather than the Paris proposal. They ask Richard II to remain loyal to Boniface " in the obedience which you have undertaken in full parliament with your clergy and people subject to you, and which you and your prelates, lords and commons have

[1] *Deutsche Reichstagsakten*, ed. Weizsäcker, ii. 460–461.

[2] For the French embassy, sent by Charles VI, *see* Valois, *Schisme*, iii. 291–292.

[3] Bodleian Library, MS. Digby 188, fo. 49 v. : " Nobis tamen sepius visum est quod medium negacionis obediencie tanquam sanctius iustius et breuius iam oblatum viam cessionis ultronee alias speculatiue discussam omnino reddit infamem, nichil penitus bonitatis in ea relinquens."

[4] *Ibid.*, fo. 47 v., 48.

[5] *Ibid.*, fos. 61, 61 v.   Cf. Anthony Wood, *History and Antiquities of the University of Oxford*, i. 534–535.

unanimously sworn to maintain." Richard is exhorted not to support the schismatics : " let your royal purity shrink in horror from providing fresh incentive to the Schism ; for your royal majesty does not waver in the matter of the faith, which itself touches the head of the Church." [1] The allusion is, of course, to Lollardy : but the implication of wavering in other matters of ecclesiastical politics is obvious, and may not have been lost upon the Francophil Richard.

At present we do not know to what extent the Conciliar views of Oxford were shared by the English clergy, regular or secular, before 1400. It is possible that many still clung, in spite of provocation, to the Roman pontiff, and believed that the anti-pope must be made to resign. A figure like the Avignonese-minded John de Ayton must have been an exception. The house of St. Alban was nothing if not orthodox in such matters. We are fortunate enough to possess among the treatises and *quaestiones* of its archdeacon, Nicholas Radcliff, a determination upon the attitude which in his judgment this country should adopt towards the contending parties.[2] The form of his arguments, the way in which he uses the identical scriptural quotations that occur in the Paris epistle analysed above and the character of his references to Boniface IX lead one to suspect that this particular *quaestio* was written not long after 1395, and probably before 1399, since he alludes to John of Gaunt in a manner to suggest that the duke was still living.[3] The manuscript containing the work bears the arms both of St. Albans and of Tynemouth (gules, three crowns, or) on its illuminated title-page, and the fact that the last treatise, *Contra querelas fratrum*, is, apparently on Bale's authority, attributed to Uthred of Boldon,[4] suggests that the book may later have been lent to the abbey's northern cell. Nicholas was prior of Wymondham before he came to St. Albans to be archdeacon ; he may have become prior of St. Albans into the bargain, for in Wyntershulle's Formulary at Cambridge, the majority of which seem to have been written between 1382 and 1386,[5] there are several

---

[1] Raynaldus, *Annales Ecclesiastici* (Lucca, 1752), viii. 34-35. Of the withdrawal of obedience the Oxford masters speak with caution : " nec damnamus nec simpliciter improbamus."

[2] Royal MS. 6 D. X. fos. 277 v.–281 v. On the fly-leaf are the words : " Hic est liber de conventu monasterii sancti Albani quem quicunque alienauerit a dicto monasterio vel titulum deleuerit anathema sit amen." For other pamphlets of a similar nature, cf. Perroy, *op. cit.*, pp. 371-376.

[3] In addressing the anti-pope he speaks (fo. 281) of " tue litere quas propria manu scripsisti et Regi Aragonie destinasti . . . Has literas dux Lancastrie me audiente asseruit se vidisse et in eisdem literis se legisse quomodo certificasti dominum regem Aragonie quod dominus Urbanus sextus erat canonice electus in papatum."

[4] *Catalogue of Royal MSS.*, i. 150.

[5] Cambridge Univ. Library, MS. Ee. iv. 20, fo. 1 : " Registrum de diversis commissionibus, procuratoriis, mandatis aliisque literis multum necessariis et in com-

commissions to " Nicholas the Prior," though, naturally enough, the latter's identification with Nicholas the archdeacon must remain uncertain in default of better evidence. Our writer was evidently *malleus Lollardorum*. The two *quaestiones* which precede the one with which we are concerned have a direct bearing on the issues raised by that sect: whether vows of religion, chastity, and virginity introduced by the fathers and approved by the Church *praeter legem evangelicam* could lawfully and worthily be observed ; and whether it was lawful for a Christian to reverence and adore images of the Crucified and His most pious Mother and other Saints.[1]

The third *quaestio* asks whether to compose the scandal of the schism Pope Boniface together with the anti-pope is bound to resign : but before the replies to the *arguitur quod sic* are finally made, a second problem is raised and settled : whether Pope Boniface is bound to consent at all to any one of the " three ways," resignation, compromise, or General Council, in order to stop the schism. The answer to this query being found emphatically in the negative, the earlier *quaestio* can be resolved in favour of Boniface's remaining and the anti-pope resigning. The argument in favour of resignation is presented on eleven grounds : the most prominent of these are the general utility of the Church, and the need for self-sacrifice on the part of the supreme pastor, supported by numerous biblical citations and examples ; e.g. Christ, although He was Son of God, the creator of the whole mechanism of the world (*tocius machine mundialis*), although He was *summus pontifex ac pastor ecclesie militantis*, yet laid down His life : Boniface is Christ's representative, *ergo—*. Charity seeketh not her own : the popes should have greater charity than others, since, as Fitz Ralph (*Armachanus*) says, St. Peter deserved the papacy through his burning charity, and it follows that Charity does not retain what she has got, if it is to the scandal of others.—Matt. v. 40, " And if any man would go to law with thee, and take away thy coat, let him have thy cloke also " : the doctors of the Church show that the ideal Christian (*quilibet vir perfectus*) will prefer to suffer the loss of his property by robbers rather than resist to the scandal of others.[2] Boniface is certainly *vir perfectus* and should follow the Saviour's command. These and other points are met at the end, after the subordinate *quaestio* has been settled, by the contention that

munem usum in dies convolantibus editum per fratrem Willelmum Wyntershulle, domini Thome Abbatis capellanum, anno domini millesimo tricentesimo octagesimo secundo." The section on the *dictamen*, fos. 152–177, is in a later (fifteenth-century) hand. On Wyntershulle, cf. V. H. Galbraith in *St. Albans Chronicle*, p. lvi.

[1] Fo. 299 f. The Lollard attack upon images was the cause of a number of treatises *de adoracione et veneracione ymaginum*, e.g. Royal MS. 6 E. III. fo. 59 ; Merton College, Oxford, MS. CCCXVIII. fo. 118 v. (John Deverose).

[2] Fo. 277 v. to 278.

Boniface is not morally bound to give up his dignity, since he did not originate the *schismatica pravitas* ; nor is it necessary for him to lay down his life for the sheep, since the Schism is not detracting from the true fold : it perplexes and disturbs the sheep of Boniface, but does not seduce them from the unity of the Church.[1]

The argument against resignation—and it should be noted that although according to its wording the *quaestio* envisages the resignation of *both* Popes, it is more frequently Boniface's resignation that the author is examining—is primarily based upon Boniface's valid and canonical succession, and upon the chaos and confusion which would arise if his title were doubted. His indulgences would go by the board, ordinations would be a matter of doubt, all who had confessed in hope of the remission of their sins would be thrown into uncertainty and perplexity.[2] If both resigned, then general doubt would be cast upon promotions to the cardinalate in either quarter ; [3] moreover, if Boniface were to synchronize his resignation with that of the anti-pope, the latter's party would certainly meet in conclave and elect another Pope, so that the last error would be worse than the first. Furthermore, if both resigned and a single new election took place, only the cardinals who survived from pre-schismatic days would be legally entitled to elect the new Pope ; the rest would be disqualified.[4] But is Boniface bound to take any one of the *tres viae* at all ? In order to compel him to do so it would be necessary either to impugn his title or establish the right of certain determinate human persons to sit in judgment upon the supreme pontiff. The second point Nicholas takes first. It is argued, he says, that bishops to-day (*moderni*) have as much power as the apostles, since they are their legitimate successors ; but the apostles had the same power as Peter, neither more nor less ; " since therefore the Church of Christ has greater power than any of its bishops, it would seem to follow that the power of the Church is greater than that of the supreme pontiff and that the power of Pope Boniface is liable to coercion." [5]

[1] Fo. 280 v.

[2] Fo. 278 v. : If Boniface's title were doubted, then " omnes cardinales, episcopi, rectores et vicarii ab eo graciose promoti et omnes quibus ab eo concesse sunt indulgencie in extremis et [qui] in ultimo jubileo putabant se plenarie remissionem suorum consequi peccatorum de suis gratiis fluctuarent. Item omnes presbiteri, diaconi et ecclesiastici ab huiusmodi episcopis ordinati de suis ordinibus hesitarent, necnon et omnes tam literati quam laici ab huiusmodi presbiteris confessati de remissione suorum peccaminum incerti fierent et perplexi."

[3] Fo. 279 : " presumpcio magna foret de eorum cardinalibus creatis ab eis post inceptionem scismatice pravitatis quod non habuerunt verum titulum sui status."

[4] *Ibid.*

[5] Fo. 279 v. : "cum ergo ecclesia Christi maiorem quam aliquis episcoporum habeat potestatem, sequi videatur quod potestas ecclesie maior est potestate summi pontificis et quod potestas pape Bonefacii cohercibilis est."

Moreover, it might appear from the circumstances of Matthias' election in the *Acts* that all bishops were equal ; and we read that when Stephen and six others were chosen, the multitude of the faithful set them before the twelve apostles and they laid their hands upon them. To these arguments the reply is made that in law, except for heresy, the Pope need submit to no court save the *forum poenitentiae* or unless he volunteers to purge himself of any charge. He is not bound to submit the question of his election to examination or to have his title discussed. But it would be simplest, say Boniface's opponents, if a General Council, " collected from the remotest parts of the earth and the vast circuit of the whole universe " (here is the phrase again) were summoned. The other *viae* are long and contentious. This would be the best way of quieting men's consciences and of tearing up the Schism by the roots.[1] But, replies Nicholas, if this general assembly is held, the same radical division is bound to make itself felt there ; moreover, a council is not in itself a quicker way than resignation or compromise ; and what need is there in reality for any of these methods ? The title of Boniface is so conspicuously clear that it removes all doubt, and his conduct supports the verity of his title ; the anti-pope has with his own mouth admitted that Urban VI was canonically elected, and Boniface is his true and canonical successor. The work ends with a perfervid exhortation to the anti-pope to admit his schismatical guilt and submit to the powers of Europe, not to allow Christ's seamless tunic to remain in pieces, and to " the pillars of the Church," prelates, doctors, masters, professors of evangelical truth to unify her and to give the right answer to the Lollards, who oppress her. Finally, a similar appeal is made to those who are *speciali privilegio filiacionis aliis prerogati*.[2] Are these the Benedictines ?

The *quaestio* does not show Nicholas as a constructive thinker. Most of his arguments could be utilized by the anti-pope's party against Boniface. Nicholas cannot admit that Boniface's title might be called in question ; he cannot conceive of any mitigation of the rigour of canon law. One may imagine with what despair Gerson or Robert Hallum would have regarded such conservatism. Still, it must be remembered that we are yet in a comparatively early stage of conciliar speculation, and it does not do to anticipate. The references to the consequence of resignation upon the obediences and upon the validity of ordinations suggest that the treatise belongs to the early period of

[1] Fo. 281 : " Hec insuper via est plana et directa, nullis prorsus scopulis seu sentibus impedita : alie vero vie difficiles sunt et longe atque perplexe et perplurimos affectus ad exitum producentes. Hec etiam via est securior eo quod per eam magis quam per aliam quietabuntur hominum consciencie utrobique et scisma cessaret radicitus exstirpatum."   [2] Fo. 281.

nuda rather than of *practicata cessio* ; that is, to the time when discussion
turned upon resignation without mitigating provisions or safeguards
against the difficulties that might arise therefrom ; it advocates for one
of the contending parties a course which the Paris intellectuals after 1395
rejected as, in its simple form, too rigorous and detrimental for the
Church. That this view about the English method of interpreting
cessio was taken in France appears from two Paris treatises, both belonging
to the controversial literature of 1398 or thereabouts.[1] Copies of these
are preserved in Balliol College MS. 165 B, a collection of treatises and
extracts from the literature of the Schism, in a variety of hands, brought
together, I should conjecture, somewhere about the time of the Council
of Basel.[2] To judge by the amount of material included upon the
Spanish Pope, this fifteenth-century editor's main interest here has been
in Benedict XIII. The treatises, " Anonymi cuiusdam doctoris Parisiensis Allegationes in materia et facto subtractionis " and " Allegationes
pro subtractione ab obedientia concertantium de papatu," carry their
aim upon the surface, but their interest here lies in their similar report
of the attitude taken in Paris towards the criticisms conveyed in the
Oxford letter of 1396 : the *cessio* envisaged in that letter, some had
urged, was not the resignation which might be contrived along the
lines suggested by the French prelates. The Oxford letter " speaks
only of *simple* resignation, and there is no mention in it of a negotiated
settlement." The negotiations now suggested by Paris were that the
two contending parties should meet in some safe place accessible to
both, such as Genoa, and then, with their cardinals in attendance,
" solemnly revoke all processes made by the one against the other and
by their adherents, and absolve each other as best they can : and after
that let them confirm the collations of benefices and the promotions
made by either side ;[3] in the case where there are two bishops claiming

---

[1] On which see Valois, *op. cit.*, iii. 266–272. Valois does not mention these
particular works.

[2] They are edited with marginals and occasional headings in a mid-fifteenth-
century hand ; but the script of several of the quires seems earlier and more contemporary with the events described. The watermarks, which Mr. Mynors has
kindly traced out, are probably French, contrasting with the predominantly South
German origin of those in Balliol College MSS. 164, 165A and 166. Probably it
was possible to buy Conciliar treatises and sermons or to acquire them through the
copying services of booksellers (cf. in this connexion the Florentine Vespasiano
Bisticci who got books copied for William de Grey). They could then be bound
up together, as was sometimes done very unsystematically, to serve as exemplars.

[3] Balliol College MS. 165 B., p. 77 (cf. p. 109) : " Nec obstat quod dicitur de
epistola Oxonensis studii quia nuda cessio nisi bene patricata [*sic, for* ' practicata,'
written above the word, ' patyicata '] non sufficeret ad sedacionem scismatis ut ipsi
dicunt respondendo ad epistolam Universitatis Parisiensis [*analysed above*, pp. 61–2],
que epistola solum loquitur de cessione et non sit in eadem mencio de practica ; sed

one Church, he who is in possession of the Cathedral city shall remain bishop, while the other shall draw a pension assigned to him out of the episcopal revenues." [1]   Certainly *practica* had something to be said for it, as the fifteenth-century editor of the Balliol volume showed in his marginal comment,[2] and it is also true that Englishmen were inclined to make *cessio* rather too simple a process and to attack it on those grounds. But Oxford had at all events a shrewd sense of the difficulty of securing concerted resignation, and its unwavering determination to secure both unity and reform through a General Council is one of the more striking features in its history.   The grounds of this decision were, as the careers of Robert Hallum and Richard Ullerston show us, grounds of principle rather than of tactics.

II

From Wylie,[3] Valois,[4] and Junghanns [5] we know something of the fitful attempts made by Henry IV's diplomacy to unify the Church. The correspondence with his ally, Rupert of the Palatinate, who had married his daughter, Blanche, shows the two powers tentatively drawing together and promising to assist one another in restoring unity.[6]   On 30 November 1402 Bishop Edmund Stafford of Exeter was able to tell Parliament somewhat optimistically that the desired consummation was in sight, only to receive the characteristic reply that such efforts were to be welcomed as long as they involved no expense.[7]   But the government's preoccupation with rebellious movements and the concentration of churchmen upon the pressing problem of Lollardy diverted attention from the main European question till the death of Innocent VII roused Henry IV to instruct Sir John Cheyne and Dr. Henry Chichele, his ambassadors at Rome, to bring influence to bear upon the cardinals of the Roman obedience not to elect a new pontiff, but to hold their

practicata per modum deliberatum per prelatos Francie sufficit melius ad cedacionem [sedacionem] scismatis. . . .   Praticetur ergo via cessionis sic : conveniant ambo concertantes in uno loco medio et bene tuto sicuti Janue : et in isto cum suis cardinalibus et ipsis ibidem simul convenientibus revocent [sic] quilibet eorum processus quos fecerint unus contra alium et eis adherentibus et absolvant se ad inuicem modo quo fieri potuerit meliori ; et postmodum confirment collationes beneficiorum [et] promotiones hinc et inde factas."

[1] Balliol College MS. 165 B., p. 77 : " Ita tamen quod ubi sunt duo episcopi ad unam ecclesiam, ille remaneat episcopus qui civitatem possidet, assignata alteri pensione super proventibus episcopatus."

[2] " Practica remedium contra schisma."

[3] *History of England under Henry IV*, iii. ch. lxxxi.

[4] *Op. cit.*, iii. 478 ; iv. 9.

[5] *Zur Geschichte der Englischen Kirchenpolitik von 1399–1413* (Freiburg i. B., 1915), which should, however, be used with caution.

[6] Junghanns, *op. cit.*, pp. 6–10.   [7] *Rot. Parl.*, iii. 485, 492–493.

hand and concert measures for terminating the Schism.[1] Henry's recommendation expressed in a special letter to the cardinals,[2] bore little fruit, since it came far too late.[3] But at all events it was sent. There is probably some truth in Junghanns' suggestion that Owen Glendower's understanding with Benedict XIII, involving the revival of the ancient claim to make St. David's a metropolitan Church, the establishment of a Welsh University and the proclamation of Henry IV as a usurper and a heretic, may have aroused the king to the dangers of the situation.[4] Certainly it was not till early in 1407, in the king's letter of 8 January to the College of Cardinals and his instructions (18 January, cited above) to his envoys at Rome, Cheyne and Chichele, that the interesting and important series of diplomatic letters and acts ending in England's support of the Council of Pisa begins to run. We can gather from a letter of Archbishop Arundel, dated 2 February 1407, that Gregory's movements were being very carefully watched by Churchmen in England.[5]

To 1407 belongs the remarkable letter of "Richard, Bishop of Rochester," to the Roman Curia.[6] This prelate has generally been thought to be Richard Young, who was translated from Bangor to Rochester in 1404, though he did not take formal charge of his diocese till 2 May 1407.[7] On the strength of the dating, "London, 1407," and the fact that Richard Clifford became bishop on the 27th of April that year, Junghanns attributed the letter to Clifford ;[8] but he ignored a passage within the letter narrating the writer's gift to Boniface IX and the cardinals of "a sext of six folios, containing a series of legal arguments (on behalf of Boniface), *prout in numero hinc concurrebant sub correctione sociorum et maiorum meorum Cardinalium*. This "sext,"

---

[1] 18 January 1407 : MS. Cotton Cleopatra E. II. fo. 249. Valois (iii. 478) corrects the date given in the Cottonian Catalogue (p. 587). Chichele's first commission to Rome was not dated July 1405, as stated in *Dict. Nat. Biography*, X. 227, but July 1406 (*Foedera*, Hague ed., iv. i. 100). Except for missions to Charles VI and to Gregory XII at Siena, he appears to have remained in Rome, and to have taken the place of the bishop of St. David's on a second commission (with Cheyne), issued on 26 April 1407 (*Foedera*, iv. i. 113) ; on April 3 1408 the mandate for the restitution of his temporalities as bishop of St. David's speaks of him as having been " in the King's service in the Court of Rome for the space of a year and a half " ; *Cal. Pat. Rolls*, 1405-1408, i. 426. The chronology of these years is given in my Introduction to *Reg. Chichele* (i. xxv-viii.).

[2] Cotton, Cleopatra E. II. fo. 250 (wrongly dated in the Cottonian Catalogue).

[3] Valois rightly comments on the slowness of the cardinals to inform Henry of the new election : iii. 478.

[4] *Op. cit.*, pp. 11-15.   [5] Wilkins, *Concilia*, iii. 302-303.

[6] Printed in Martène et Durand, *Amplissima Collectio*, vii. 748-750. It was to be found in the Chauvelin MSS. which before the Revolution belonged to Harlay (cf. L. Delisle, *Cabinet des manuscrits*, ii. 100-103) ; now, it would appear, in Bibl. Nat., MS. Latin 12542.

[7] Wylie, iii. 141. Wylie and Valois both accept Young's authorship.

[8] *Zur Geschichte der Englischen Kirchenpolitik*, pp. 28-29.

described as by Richard Ingh (i.e. Young), has survived in a Vatican
Codex (Lat. 4153, fos. 95-98 v.) and contains arguments similar to those
in the letter. Moreover there does not seem to be any evidence that
Clifford, the great administrative clerk, the former keeper of the privy
seal, was ever at Rome in the time of Boniface IX ; his English employ-
ment kept him too busy.[1] There is, on the other hand, positive testimony to Young's being in the Curia in 1395.[2] He had been an Auditor
of the Sacred Palace, which surely explains the *correctio sociorum* of our
text ; and it is quite clear from his discussion of the part alleged to
have been played by *metus* or the influence of fear in the election of
Urban VI that the author was a canonist, which we know Young to
have been. The interest of the letter, however, lies in its mixture of
Conciliar and anti-French tendencies. Young says that he has heard
how Gregory XII and Benedict XIII both have resignation in view :
God grant that the French do not use the occasion to wrest the papacy
to themselves, as has happened before. If it happens that such resignation is impeded in any way or fails to materialize, Gregory XII should
convoke a General Council, since it is his prerogative to do so.[3] This
Council both the anti-pope and the king of France are bound to attend.
If they do not, they will be guilty of contumacy, and the whole power
of the Church will revert to the Council, the contumacious parties being
bound to uphold whatever is done there. If the French king absent
himself, he should be threatened with deposition and à Crusade should
be undertaken against his lands (they shall be open, he says, *spoliis Christi
fidelium*) : his kingdom should then be assigned to the king of England
to fortify his title thereto. Probably neither the French monarch nor
his adherents will expect so sharp a stroke (though the Council can do
more than this), nor can they defend their obstinacy as the Greeks do,
for the Greeks are on the borders of Christendom, whereas the French
are in its very heart. It need not be a matter of great difficulty to summon
the clergy to such a Council : there were Councils in the past on the
matters of heresy, while here it is simply a question of the right of two
mortal persons, which certainly can and should be decided, even if the
despoiled Pope (*papa spoliatus*) petition to be restored. This " way "
is the safest method of ensuring the preservation of the sanctuaries in
the City of Rome, which to the laity are a sign of our faith, and also of
safeguarding the whole patrimony of St. Peter. The author was

---

[1] On his career, see T. F. Tout, *Chapters in Medieval Administrative History*,
iii. 430, 464 ; iv. 49, 385 ; v. 53-54.

[2] Wylie, iii. 140. He was there in 1393 ; *Cal. Papal Letters*, iv. 479.

[3] *Reichstagsakten*, ed. Weizsäcker, vi. no. 202 (Henry IV to Rupert), shows that
Henry took this line : " Sicut a valde peritis audivimus, ad prefatum dominum
Gregorium spectat convocare concilium generale."

evidently drawing upon his own experiences of the disturbed condition of the Roman neighbourhood ; one can see that he is a nationalist at heart, a man who would have been acceptable to Henry V, showing no realization of the deeper issues beneath the contest of two " mortal persons." It is particularly interesting, therefore, to note that Henry IV displayed a somewhat wider vision than this, when once he felt justified in forsaking Gregory.[1]

It is not our purpose to narrate the events of 1408, which led clergy and king to their decision : Gregory's creation (9 May) of new cardinals, the coming of Richard Dereham, the Cambridge chancellor, to England (8 July), with messages from the outraged cardinals at Pisa, the July Synod at St. Paul's, and the reinforcement of Conciliar policy by the advocacy of the abbot of Westminster, the bishop of Carlisle and—more important than any—Archbishop Uguccione of Bordeaux.[2] Private information, sent by a man like bishop Henry Chichele, may have had as much effect in determining influential minds on the course of action to be followed as the official appeals of the Pisan party.[3] The point we would emphasize is that once Henry had brought himself to accept the Conciliar solution and had forsaken Gregory XII, he was not content with the formal restoration of unity in the person of Alexander V, but was anxious that the Council should be continued for the purposes of reform. Our evidence for this comes from the remarkable letter-book of John Prophet,[4] dean of York, at first senior clerk (*secundarius*) in the privy seal office and later, on Richard Clifford's departure, keeper. Since 1389 Prophet, as clerk to the Council, as well as " secondary " in the privy seal office, must have had most of the important diplomatic correspondence through his hands. Correspondence with the Curia was regularly conducted under the privy seal, a practice that seems to have become normal during Edward III's reign : and now that such business has disappeared from the dorse of the Close Roll, where we should find it in the thirteenth century, it is to formularies and letter-books that

---

[1] Which was not to be done without the fullest warning : *Reichstagsakten*, vi., *loc. cit.* : " Videtur nobis (Henry IV) huiusmodi subtraccio a vero papa, saltem ante requisicionem de qua supra fit mencio, reos scismatis arguere subtrahentes." The standpoint of Young is very like that of the anonymous clerk who made the curious suggestion for the spiritual outlawry of Charles VI, contained in Harleian MS. 431, fo. 115 ; on whom, see Valois, iii. 77.

[2] On which, see Wylie, iii. 363–366 ; Junghanns, pp. 31–32. The sermon preached by him before the king early in November 1408, a summary of which is in the Latin Register of the Metropolitan Church of Bordeaux (Lopès-Callen, *L'église metropolitaine et primatiale Sainct André de Bordeaux*, i. 283–285), is given in MS. Bodley, 462, fos. 292 v.–295 v., printed by V. H. Galbraith, *The St. Albans Chronicle*, pp. 136–52 ; *supra*, p. 4.   [3] *Reg. Chichele*, i. xxviii.

[4] Harleian MS. 431. On Prophet, see Wylie, ii. 484 n., iii. 295 n., 351 n., and especially Tout, *op. cit.*, v. 52, 97, 102, 106.

F

we must resort for missives of importance from this office.[1] Prophet's volume is more of a letter-book, a *copiale*, than a strictly classified formulary containing examples of the various types of letters emanating under the privy seal.[2] He has thought it worth while to insert the cardinals' statement of their intentions at the election of Innocent VII, together with the notary's certificate,[3] and the important " juramenta et vota cardinalium in ingressu in conclavam ante eleccionem Gregorii " [XII].[4] (In the margin he has drawn a pointing hand with the censorious remark " nulla excusatio Gregorii.") He has copied here in full the charges made against Peter de Luna at Pisa with the names of the witnesses in each case,[5] and, at the end, a number of " doubtful points " that might be raised in the anti-pope's favour.[6] Thus he has sketched in the papal diplomatic background, to enable a reader to understand Henry IV's letters more fully.

Henry, as Wylie pointed out, took a long time in recognizing Alexander V ; not, in fact, till 17 October 1409, though the news of the election came through in July.[7] Once recognized, he was regarded by Henry as something more than the product and symbol of unity ; as an instrument of reform. The English king's letter, written after the return of the greater part of the delegation, is worth quoting in some detail :

> Truly, blessed father, when the Council was over, our ambassadors on returning brought us in their account of its termination such good hope for the future that we overflowed with happiness and jubilation, watered, as it were, with honey-flowing streams. Yet we have heard to our great sorrow that certain Christian Kings and princes of secular importance have refused to acquiesce in its findings, and still adhere to one or the other sides in the ancient dispute, so that unless the Lord of Mercy has compassion on his people, the spark will become a flame not easily extinguished. I beseech you, therefore, to persist with the Council ; for if it is continued, we have hope in the Lord that through its meeting the universal good of the Church may be re-established, and certain detestable abuses cease through the worthy

---

[1] Witness the use made by Wylie of Hoccleeve's formulary (Add. MS. 24062), in which also occur a number of the letters given in Prophet's book, under the section " missives," fo. 145 f. This admirable formulary is very systematically constructed, e.g. fo. 95, " As capitans des Chastelx " ; fo. 101, " As Seneschalx, Receuers, Fermers et Auditores " ; fo. 115, " As diverses estatz en Guyenne " ; fo. 121, " Omne gadrum " (" omnium gatherum," a large miscellaneous class of letters). For Hoccleeve as a clerk of the privy seal, see Tout, *op. cit.*, v. 75, 106–110 ; for the privy seal diplomatic, pp. 120 f.

[2] Although at the end (fo. 99) are a great many specimen endings (*conclusiones*) from letters addressed to important personages.

[3] Harleian MS. 431, fos. 49–50 v.

[4] *Ibid.*, fo. 50 v.   [5] Fo. 73 f.

[6] Fo. 95 : " Quia fide attestante minus feriunt iacula que preuidentur."

[7] iii. 387.

reformation of many errors, by God's will. In this event we propose to send ambassadors to give clear answers upon the matters expounded to us discreetly and elegantly by the envoys of your holiness, after first taking mature counsel, as right and fitting, with the nobles and estates of our realm in our parliament to be summoned especially on that account ; without the calling of which or the assent of the estates aforesaid, since it touches their interest, no statutes or ordinances previously made can be revoked or changed.[1] But if your holiness (as we hope will not be the case) at any one's instigation or suggestion decide to forego this pious and sacred project of celebrating a General Council, then the effect upon the Kings and princes zealous for the Universal Church is specially to be feared, and the great dangers that may arise will be particularly formidable, and every care will be needed lest the author of the schism [the Devil] renew his attack and tear men away from the root of unity in the Church.[2]

What were the matters expounded by Alexander's legates ? The mention of parliament and the revocation of statute and ordinance suggests that it was the old question of Provisors that Alexander had so early in mind. That this was so seems probable from another un-dated letter, also copied into Hoccleve's formulary, in which Henry, in replying to Alexander's announcement of his election, stated that he had great confidence in Alexander's not attempting anything against the statutes and ordinances published by the consent of the estates, nor " trying any novelties which will be derogatory to our crown or the *regalia*," and requesting him, if he was meditating anything of the sort, to let the matter rest till the General Council " shortly to be summoned."

Did not Henry's caution over existing statute—and it is interesting to observe his insistence upon the assent of the estates—when combined with his protestations in favour of reform in reality constitute an illogical attitude ?   Could desire for reform in the Universal Church harmonize with national-mindedness upon the vitally important matter of the collation of benefices ?   Dr. Haller's opinion is that England cared more for unity in the head than for amelioration.[3]   While one recognizes the substantial justice of the remark, it is impossible to overlook the other side.   We have clear evidence, a small part of which was discussed above, of the reforming zeal of a number of Oxford Conciliars ; we have a letter from Chichele to Robert Hallum at Constance strongly

[1] Note 2 : " habito primitus ut est opus et congruit superinde cum proceribus et statibus regni nostri deliberacione matura, praesertim in parliamento nostro propterea celebrando, sine cuius vocatione et statuum predictorum assensu, cum illorum in premissis interesse versetur, nulla statuta vel ordinaciones in ea parte prius edita reuocari poterunt aut mutari."

[2] Harleian MS., 431, fo. 42.

[3] *Papsttum und Kirchenreform*, p. 463 : " So geht die englische Kirche hinsichtlich der reformatio in membris ihren eigenen Weg und braucht sich auch um die reformatio in capite, an der sich das Konzil zu Konstanz vergeblich abmüht, und das Konzil von Basel sich erschöpft, nicht weiter zu kümmern."

protesting against the exemptions that undermined the authority of prelates ; [1] and above all we have the sermons and the leadership of Hallum, head of the English delegation both at Pisa and at Constance, to provide the exceptions. When Hallum's career, especially in the Oxford period, has been more fully studied and brought into relation with the reforming efforts of his time,[2] it will be understood why his death in September 1417 was nothing short of a tragedy ; for, apart from the loss of administrative leadership in the Council, which the bishop shared with the Patriarch of Constantinople, it robbed that body of just that element of firmness and moral purpose which it most needed : refusal to be deterred by nationalist passions or irrelevant issues or the weariness that was increasingly prompting the delegations to make a formal election and return to their closes and homes.

There is nothing of the extremist and very little indeed of the academic theorist about the Lancashire man who had left the chancellorship of Oxford to become Arundel's archdeacon before his promotion to Salisbury. He could argue with Hus in his rooms in Gottlieben Castle, he yielded to none in his abhorrence of Lollardy,[3] though, characteristically, he would not have the death penalty inflicted for heresy. We can almost hear him with his compatriots, as Ulrich von Richental depicts them in his chronicle, singing mass so sweetly as to provoke the wonder of the people of Constance. A lover of Dante—Giovanni da Serravalle did a Latin translation of the *Commedia* for him while he was at Constance [4]—he had a capacity for poetic diction that reveals itself in his sermons and even in his formal announcements : a capacity transcending the euphuism of a stylistic age, a certain quality of expression by which the man himself shines through the edifice of words. His indulgence for visitors to the shrine of St. Edward at Shaftesbury is a fair example, just as it also portrays his idea of a Christian prince :

> To all sons of Holy Mother Church that see or hear these letters Robert by divine permission humble servant and minister of the Church of Salisbury

---

[1] Royal MS. 10, B. ix. fo. 59 : " Assurgite propterea, queso, frater carissime, et manum extensam adhuc extendite, ut non solum uniri, quin pocius poterit reformari mater nostra, et ad suum honorem . . . virilius redintegrari. Quod idcirco dixerim propter exempciones quamplurimas, que importunis instanciis, nedum pecuniis, obtinebantur, ex quibus prelatorum vilipenditur auctoritas, et regularis emarcuit obseruancia discipline." This matter had come up before the Michaelmas Convocation of 1414, " in quo tractatum est de privilegiis exemptorum per Romanos Pontifices indultorum, quibus gavisi sunt hactenus, annullandis. Hoc initium signorum fecit novus metropolitanus [Chichele], ut manifestaret bilem suam " : Walsingham, *Historia Anglicana* (Rolls Ser.), ii. 302.

[2] A beginning has been made by Mr. F. D. Hodgkiss, in his M.A. dissertation (Univ. of Manchester Library), " Robert Hallum, bishop of Salisbury."

[3] Reg. Hallum, part ii. fos. 37, 38, 50 v.

[4] Cf. W. Schirmer, *Der Englische Frühhumanismus* (Leipzig, 1931), pp. 16, 17.

greeting in Him who from the garden of his Church Militant gathers roses in war, lilies in peace, and sets them before His face to behold. The saints of God, gathered from the earth to be partakers of their Lord's inheritance, who have received from His hand the wreath of Heavenly benediction and are now in the realm of perpetual praise and glory, should be honoured by all nations of the earth with devoted service, extolled with eulogy of song, and venerated with reverent ceremony. . . . Among them the glorious martyr Edward, God's chosen athlete,[1] once the illustrious king of the English, has merited special veneration and peculiar honours at the hands of Englishmen, for that in the choir of the blessed he shines with intenser brilliance than others, and in life as well as in death made the kingdom of England illustrious by his fame. . . . He it is who, of royal birth and lineage, when on his father's throne grew daily to greater splendour through his admirable intelligence, his gift of mercy, and his high and gracious humility ; for from his earliest manhood, as he trod the path of truth and laid low with the sickle of virtue those blandishments whereby human frailty is often deceived, to all men he showed himself gentle, friendly and devotedly kind ; by his chastity to be worthy of praise, by the charm of his character a man of distinction, by his mercifulness one of good will, by his compassion one of mercy, nor ever in the rigour of justice hard-hearted. He it is who lifting his heart aloft to God and by his life looking forward to Him (*sua in ipsum vita prospiciens*), never ceased to search for Him and mentally to hold Him fast, wakeful to His commands, a keen worker and a ready. Strenuous and devoted alike in his military prowess and in settling the business of the Church, enemies and men of evil life he treated with a certain asperity, while those of virtuous life, especially if they were in holy orders, he protected from all molestation, as his pious father had instructed him. He it is on whose account there was great happiness in England then, great continuance of peace, great abundance of wealth ; who of his bountiful nature made it his daily rite and custom to nourish the needy, to give refreshment to the poor, to clothe the naked, counting as great gain whatever he expended on such works. He it is to whom faith gave moral stability, hope uprightness, love of God and neighbour breadth of soul ; to whom prudence lent circumspection, temperance a balanced nature in all things, righteousness an innocence of mind, and bravery initiative and vigour. His life was fragrant with the balm of all the virtues, like a store-chamber filled with all the Lord's spiritual gifts.[2]

In this conventionally idyllic picture of a pre-conquestual saint and king, behind formal antithesis and the elegances of the " flowery " style, certain phrases hold the mind ; the Gardener gathering the blood-red and white flowers of His Church : *sua in ipsum vita prospiciens* : the store-chamber full of *charismata*. The same is true of the best known of his sermons, that preached before the Council of Constance upon the second Sunday in Advent 1415, to which we shall shortly refer ; it is true also of other documents preserved in his register. Perhaps this note of distinction and a certain elevation of mind which it reflects

---

[1] This was one contemporary description of Henry V.
[2] Reg. Hallum, part. ii. fo. 56 v.

derived from the atmosphere and conversation of the group of men living hard by St. Osmund's cathedral and walking in the cloister built by Elias de Dereham. Fortunately both the episcopal and the chapter registers of Salisbury for this period are preserved. They reveal to us —though naturally the information has to be extracted mainly from the daily routine of administration—a society of considerable learning and eminence, at one in the service of the English saint associated in their minds with the use and form of worship that has made Salisbury the spiritual home of English liturgiology. The Act-books of the notaries Viringe and Pountney, which record the acts of the chapter while John Chaundler was dean, have many points of great interest to all ecclesiastical historians, and are of particular importance in two directions connected with our own inquiry : they throw light on the composition and prestige of the confraternity of Salisbury, and supplement our knowledge of the canonization of St. Osmund, a process taken up once more by Bishop Hallum in 1412, the main record of which is the parchment *Registrum in causa canonizationis beati viri Osmundi olim Sarisberiensis Episcopi in Anglia.* This is preserved, like the notaries' registers, among the muniments of the dean and chapter.[1] The majority of this register was printed by Mr. A. R. Malden in a (now) scarce book, *The Canonization of St. Osmund.*[2]

If we are to understand something of Hallum's status in influence, the position and policy of his Cathedral Church cannot be left out of account. The Salisbury *confratres* had long been a distinguished body,[3] and in the early fifteenth century the tradition was maintained and, if anything, strengthened. The Prince of Wales and his brother Humphrey, duke of Gloucester, were admitted (Humphrey in person) into the fraternity on 15 September 1409,[4] and Queen Joan with the ladies and gentlemen of her household a year later.[5] The fact may bear testimony to Hallum's influence at Court ; though whatever part he may have played in the matter, it is more likely to represent a move on the part

---

[1] The volumes were utilized both by Dr. Christopher Wordsworth for his *Salisbury Ceremonies and Processions*, and by Mr. W. H. Rich Jones for his *Fasti Ecclesiae Sarisberiensis.*

[2] Wilts Record Society (Salisbury, 1901). For a description of the register of St. Osmund's canonization, see p. vi.

[3] See the series of admissions given in Dr. Wordsworth, *op. cit.*, pp. 148–149. For the method of admission, cf. the " Modus recipiendi aliquam honestam vel nobilem personam in fratrem seu sororem Ecclesiae Cathedralis Sarum " in Malden, App. III. p. 243.

[4] Muniments of the Dean and Chapter of Salisbury, "Viringe " Act-book, fo. xvii. (later pagination, 33).

[5] *Ibid.*, fo. xxv (p. 49). Her knights included Hugh Lutterell and William Cheyney.

of the chapter towards securing powerful support in the future campaign for the canonization of St. Osmund. In 1409 the chapter was sufficiently distinguished to attract important personages. Among its members, in addition to Chaundler, were Thomas Polton, in the future to be successively bishop of Hereford, Chichester and Worcester ; [1] Simon Sydenham, who was to represent his country at Constance, and later became dean and in 1429 bishop of Chichester ; the precentor and former archdeacon of Ely, Adam Mottrum, and Geoffrey Crukadan (both of these acted as Vicars-General for Hallum while at the General Councils) ; Robert Brown, later well known at court, and George Lowthorp, who was to become treasurer for the canonization, while but lately Henry Chichele, now bishop of St. David's and evidently in high favour for his diplomatic abilities, had been Chancellor, and Nicholas Bubwith, archdeacon of Dorset. In 1416, when the campaign for canonization was well under way, the most significant figure of all came to take up his residence in a canon's house hard by his friend's palace—Richard Ullerston, [2] like Hallum, both a Lancashire man and Chancellor of Oxford (1407-1408), the author (at Hallum's instigation) of the " Petitiones pro Ecclesie militantis reformatione " [3] that bear a definite relation to the Oxford memorandum upon reform (1414) which

[1] " Viringe " Act-book, fo. ij v. (p. 4), 9 July, 1408, for his admission to a canonry. It is doubtful whether he resided.

[2] " Pountney " Act-book, fo. xxij v. (17 Dec. 1416). Ullerston was to have as much as " aliquis alius canonicus habuit in residencia sua iuxta statuta et consuetudines ecclesie memorate ; pro qua residencia sua soluit ibidem per manus magistri Henrici Harborough precentoris summam XLV librarum que summa fuit deliberata dominis G. Louthorp et W. Workman ad usum opus et utilitatem canonizacionis beati Osmundi receptoribus firme et introituum Canonicorum inibi, faciendo residencias per capitulum specialiter deputatas per septennium duraturas prout patet in actis beati Osmundi (cf. W. H. Frere, Use of Sarum, i. 11). Insuper idem Ricardus petiit sibi aliquas domos canonicales ad faciendum residenciam suam et inhabitandum in eisdem sibi assignari. Et quia domus canonicales iuxta palacium Episcopi steterunt vacue que fuit [sic] magister Johannis Harlegh in quibus nullus inhabitauit ideo decanus easdem sibi assignauit, decernens ipsas domos canonicales iuxta portam sancte Anne, in quibus ex gracia capituli ipse alias inhabitauit, fore vacuas." These houses are nos. 46 and 39, respectively, in the plan published by Dr. Kathleen Edwards, " The Houses of Salisbury Close in the Fourteenth Century," Journal of the British Archæological Association, 3rd Ser., Vol. iv. (1939), opp. p. 73. On Ullerston, cf. Malden, p. 236, n., Dict. Nat. Biography, and the full treatment in A. H. Wood, " Richard Ullerston, Canon of Salisbury " (M.A. diss., Univ. of Manchester Library, 2 vols., 1936). He was collated to the prebend of Axford on 25 March.

[3] Printed by von der Hardt, Magnum oecumenicum Constantiense Concilium, i. 1126-1170. This important statement of the needs of the Church contains sixteen points to be laid before a General Council. It must have been written later than June 1407, since the preface is addressed to Hallum as bishop of Salisbury, and on the eve of the Council of Pisa, of which he speaks (p. 1128), as " praesens concilium."

Wilkins fortunately printed.[1] It is not difficult to imagine with what pleasure Hallum, far away at Constance, would view his learned friend's accession to the chapter ; the dean certainly appreciated it, since he got the newcomer to preach a special sermon seven months before he was formally admitted to his full canonry. Early in May 1416, a chapter was summoned to consider ways and means of expediting St. Osmund's canonization ; for it Ullerston preached on the text *Exaltent eum in ecclesia* (Ps. cvi). His manuscript, on paper and in a small and beautiful hand,[2] is inserted in the Pountney Act-book. Mr. Malden rightly observed that there cannot be many instances of a sermon nearly five hundred years old existing in the original manuscript of the preacher.

The sermon [3] sets forth the merits of St. Osmund and his claim to be canonized. After an exposition of other scriptural passages parallel to the text chosen, Ullerston inserts a special bidding prayer :

> Therefore before we proceed further, let us ask the governor of the universe, the bestower of all grace, *who maketh the desert a standing water and watersprings of a dry ground*, to moisten the desert of our hearts with his heavenly rain, that I may be able to say something which may stir you to bring forth the fruits of a better life, praying moreover, as our custom is, for the estate of the whole orthodox Church, and chiefly for the happy issue of the General Council now in progress, and especially for our lord bishop of this diocese, who has borne more labours and greater for establishing unity in the Church than any other prelate in all the world, as is fully known ; and not only for him, but for our dean and for all members of the confraternity and all ministers of this Church. And on the temporal side, ye shall specially remember in your prayers Sigismund, most Christian King of the Romans, who like another Maccabæus is standing zealously for the Church. Ye shall pray moreover for our victorious King of England, Henry V, faithful soldier of Christ and strongest striver after peace, that the Lord may go with him and strengthen him in his pious intentions.[4]

The bedes bidden (and in them we can see the interest of the chapter in Conciliar events as well as the fulfilment of Chichele's mandate), Ullerston develops four reasons why Osmund should be canonized : his foundation of Salisbury ; his munificent endowment of the Church, the sacred ritual he prescribed for it (*sacram eius institucionem*), and his holiness attested by many miracles. Osmund was both the elm and the vine : he made others fruitful and was himself fruitful too. He was set over the Lord's vineyard not only to bear fruit himself, but to sustain the whole vineyard.

---

[1] *Concilia*, iii. 360–365. Cf. Haller, *Papsttum und Kirchenreform*, pp. 463–464.

[2] Mr. Malden was correct (p. iv) in considering this to be the original draft. The corrections and additions to the text, in the same hand, are not those of a copyist nor of a scribe working to dictation. The insertion of a contemporary paper document in a vellum register is further confirmation.

[3] Printed by Malden, App. II. pp. 236–242.   [4] *Ibid.*, p. 238.

Nor is it true to say, as certain madmen in our time do, that doctors of the Church who live upon such endowments (as St. Osmund provided) have sinned by so doing, for the four doctors of the Church drew their sustenance from such. . . . And if that is not enough, hear Christ himself, what he saith : for Christ saith to St. Bridget according to her account in the Sixth Book of Heavenly Revelations made to St. Bridget : " I " he saith, " and my friends have endowed my Church that clerks shall pray with the more quiet therein." [1]

Naturally we shall be most interested in his account of the *sacra institutio*. This is the Use of Salisbury, " incomparable in the world, though latest in time of the various observances in the Church." Its lateness should not be thought to detract from its value, since like the philosophy of Aristotle it eliminated earlier error, extracting the marrow of all that went before (*medullam summarum*).[2] As Aristotle, " so did this keen servant of God : for scrutinizing many uses of greater reputation he chose the stronger, the more graceful and the choicer elements in each, arranged them in excellent form and gave them into the keeping of his Church." In such a practice could be found an argument to prove that the rites and observances of the English Church are more perfect than in any other country within the Christian Church ; and Ullerston quotes Gregory's letter to Augustine bidding him collect " ex singulis quibusque ecclesiis que pia, que religiosa, que recta sunt . . . et hec quasi in fasciculum collecta." • If the English observance is pre-eminent among them, it follows that our " Use of Salisbury is the chief among other Uses in the whole world." [3] Thus is the English rite praised for its eclecticism.

The canonization of St. Osmund may well have been a move to generalize the Use of Salisbury in England. The campaign was not immediately successful, and it took the combined efforts of William de Grey, Nicholas de Upton and Simon Houchyns to secure the desired consummation between 1452 and 1456. It should be noted that the aid of the important William de Grey was sought on the strength of his being " frater ecclesie " ; [4] this may throw some light on the policy pursued in 1409-1410. But the main point which I would especially emphasize here is that in a period to which the virtues of zeal and energy are only grudgingly acceded, we find an important English chapter being recruited from some of the most progressive minds of the day, keenly interested—the names and careers of its bishop and of Ullerston and Sydenham show it—in the success of the universal Church in council,

---

[1] Printed by Malden, pp. 239-240.
[2] This does not, I think, refer to *summae* in the technical sense.
[3] *Ibid.*, p. 241.
[4] See the English letter from the dean and chapter in *ibid.*, pp. 118-119.

and pressing forward with influential help the claims of its ritual and the example of its founder upon a Church that needed the reinforcement of such enthusiasm and devotion.

But it is only too easy for sophistication to seek political motives. We may be pretty certain that for Hallum the glory of St. Osmund and of Salisbury would less be the aim of his life than, if it so came about, the happy result of his efforts in an even higher cause. That those efforts were devoted unremittingly to reform, both his register and his sermons make clear. In the former he stands out as a firm disciplinarian. We can see him reproving his own dean for not correcting abuses in one of the prebendal churches,[1] zealous for the good order and efficiency of his diocese,[2] dutifully recording and quickly acting upon the mandates of his metropolitans [3] or of papal collectors,[4] and, except for his visits to Pisa and Constance, resident to an unusual extent within his see. Above all he appears to us as a man filled with a high sense of a prelate's responsibility, and we know that he shared Ullerston's admiration for " Lincolniensis "—Robert Grosseteste. From one sermon especially we receive an unforgettable picture of Hallum's earnest and responsible outlook : the much-copied *Et erunt signa in sole*, extracts of which are given by Dr. Finke,[5] and which occurs in a number of manuscripts abroad, has apparently its sole English exemplar among the manuscripts of Jesus College, Oxford.[6] It was preached before the fathers at Constance on 8 December 1415. The sun, he says, has four characteristics or properties which are applicable to the papacy and the episcopate alike—" nobilitas conditionis, sublimitas positionis, utilitas operationis et volubilitas regirationis." The sun, " a marvellous instru-

---

[1] Reg. Hallum, Part ii. fo. 8 v. : Monition to Chaundler to remedy the serious abuses in the prebendal Church of Beer, which " sub male recte iurisdictionis umbraculo divinam maiestatem offendunt " ; cf. fo. 7 v., where he reproaches the archdeacon of Dorset for an inadequate certificate upon the vacancy of Winterbourne Came.

[2] See e.g. (Part i. fos. 19, 19 v.) the process against the rector of Stalbridge : the " littera ad compellendum presbiterum ad deserviendum cure " (Part ii. fo. 4) ; the commission to the sub-dean of Salisbury warning him and all incumbents and chaplains in the place " contra non observantes dies dominicos et festiuos (*ibid.*, fo. 4 v.) ; the commission to hear and correct defects in the nunnery of St. Mary at Kington St. Michael's (*ibid.*, fo. 5 v.) ; and the careful way in which he inquires into losses of furniture and ornaments in parish churches (*ibid.*, fos. 9 v., 12 v.).

[3] E.g. *ibid.*, fo. 25 v. (collection of 4*d.* in the pound for the Pisan delegates) ; fo. 53 v. (publishes constitutions of Archbishop Arundel) ; fos. 37–38 (publishes constitutions of Chichele on heretics and on wills).

[4] E.g. *ibid.*, fo. 14 v. (Marcellus de Stroziis in letter dated London, 19 March 1410).

[5] *Acta Concilii Constanciensis*, ii. 424. On interpretations of this text, cf. Paul Arendt, *Die Predigten des Konstanzer Konzils* (Freiburg-im-Br., 1933), p. 112. He had also preached on 22 Jan. 1415 ; Finke, ii. 393.

[6] Jesus College Oxford, MS. no. XII. fos. 203–220.

ment, the work of the most High," turns its whole face in ardour and labour towards God, and so, by imperceptibly generating virtue in things below, changes potentiality into actuality, the hidden into the manifest.[1] In such manner the Pope and the bishops are brought forward to the knowledge of all, postulated by the Church, elevated to their dignities and confirmed in their stations. The sublimity of the sun's position should signify the distance of the Pope and the bishops from avarice and secular preoccupations, and their power of shining with pure lives and healthy warmth of doctrine from on high. The utility of the sun's working should portray their zeal in reproving sin and heresy, and its constant revolution round the earth (*volubilitas regirationis*), their rise to the splendour of the meridian through justice and charity, and their retreat again (as night comes on) into their own consciences where they keep themselves in all humility.[2] The sun, too, may suffer eclipse, when the high office in the Church is acquired venally and corruptly. Money gets round all obstacles to promotion.

> If you say that the candidate for promotion is of humble birth, Simon (Magus) replies that Peter himself was not a patrician nor of distinguished ancestry, but a fisherman of low degree : if it is objected that he is still a boy, Simon shows that the elders of the people were condemned by Daniel as a child ; if he is alleged to be illiterate, Simon answers that we nowhere hear of the apostles attending school ; if married, the reply is the apostle (Paul) was married too, and prescribes that the man to be elected bishop shall be the husband of one wife.[3]

It was a custom to inveigh against worldliness and self-seeking ; most of the preachers at Constance did so, and Hallum is with them in drawing a grisly picture of the retribution that will follow at the end ; [4] but more clearly than they he sees how sharp is the moral issue between the old order and the new discipline that is needed. The Church cannot contain both types. In the book of Kings we read, " *The Cloud filled the house of the Lord so that the priests could not stand to minister because of the cloud.*" The cloud is not the glory of the Lord, but the thick mist of worldly lusts and imaginations. It is this that leads to the present vilification of churchmen, to the laughter and scorn of the laity, even

[1] Fo. 205.

[2] Fo. 205 v. : " Sol enim oritur quando vita boni pastoris vere lucis operibus populo declaratur : occidit quando se subtrahens principis aspectibus lectioni, meditacioni, oracioni et contemplacioni totius mundi incumbit. . . . Sed tamen sol spiritualis ad locum suum revertitur quando ingressus propriam conscientiam flectitur ad aquilonem dum humilitate se custodit." The last phrase is characteristic of Hallum.

[3] Fo. 207 v.

[4] Fo. 208 v. : " in morte apparebunt tibi demones horribiles, expectantes, delaturi tuam animam ad Gehennam. Ubi tunc divicie et delicie ? "

at this present Council.[1]   At the end, however, after further developments of his metaphor, Hallum is able to look forward to the day when
the sun will again break through.   " Igne quodam spiritus sancti sese
cunctis communicabit per liberalem conpassionem, mentes unificabit
per actualem dilectionem, ac corda et corpora purificabit per criminalem
abstractionem, et tandem per septem dona spiritus sancti, tanquam per
septem gradus rectissimos, suis gregibus ducatum praestabit ad eternalem
remuneracionem. . . ." [2]

These examples of Conciliar zeal and activity on the part of Englishmen, if they are insufficient to disprove Stubbs's implication that the
country as a whole was not interested in the movement, at least suggest
that something more was done than piously to deplore the schism and
to seek formal unity but nothing else.   England produced no great
conciliar theorist : yet there were some who had the imagination and
the intuition [3] to grasp what a Council might do, and to say so a good
while before that course became the official French policy.   In the earlier
stages its advocates might not be able to convince the great men of the
University of Paris ; yet on its way to Pisa the English delegation received
in 1409 from Gerson a handsome welcome that showed that the bygones
of the previous century were bygones ; [4] for it was the united action
of Paris and Oxford that year which in reality made Conciliar action,
for a time at any rate, the future road for the Western Church.

[1] Fo. 210 v. : " Pace vestra loquor, sanctissimi patres, si ista solerti studio
curassemus [the avoidance of torpor and luxury], non tam horrenda et tam abhomina-
bile de ecclesiasticis personis predicaretur in mundo.   Taceo quod nec multis est
corona patens, nec tonsura conveniens, quia in veste lascivia, insolencia in gestu,
turpitudo in verbis . . . loquuntur insaniam.   Praeterea in divinis officiis quanta
sit negligencia cum sepius a sacra missarum solempnia [sic] pocius ad ridendum,
ludendum et confabulandum quam ad psallendum et orandum congregari videntur.
Dicam, dicam boni lugent, mali rident : dicam dolens."

[2] Fo. 220 : Earlier (fo. 204 v.) he quotes St. Hilary of Poitiers to illustrate the
perpetual resilience and recuperative power of the Church : " hoc habet ecclesia
proprium quod tunc vincit cum leditur, tunc intelligit cum arguitur, tunc obtinet
cum deseritur, et post pauca dominum prosequitur, floret dum contempnitur . . .
vincit et tunc stat cum superari videtur."

[3] That Englishmen were not devoid of these qualities appears from a story of
Gerson, who remarks that their imaginativeness was once somewhat unfavourably
commented on to the duke of Burgundy by " the duke of Lencastre " (John of
Gaunt), rather surprisingly to our modern ears : " Habemus in Anglia viros sub-
tiliores in imaginationibus : sed Parisienses veram habent solidam et securam theo-
logiam."   Opera, ii. 149.

[4] In his " Propositio facta coram Anglicis," Gerson, Opera, ii. 123–130 ; cf.
especially p. 127 : " Et hec non est parva congratulationis materia, quod in unam
conventum est sententiam per duas Universitates toto orbe celeberrimas."

CHAPTER V

OCKHAM AS A POLITICAL THINKER

THERE seems to be no way round Ockham. Sooner or later he confronts every worker in later medieval history. In Conciliar studies, for instance, we are frequently told that this or that view " is to be found in Ockham," and there the matter is unsatisfactorily left. In this country only very few care to explore the mountain range that seems to lie across the intellectual history of the fourteenth century, profoundly influencing the studies of generations. Because it is so vast, I may be forgiven for trying to indicate one or two of the approaches to this *massif*; not the normal, though difficult, paths of logic or metaphysics, but some that may have a bearing upon topics of interest to students of fifteenth-century political thought and doctrine.

There is an excellent biographical sketch of Ockham by the late Dr. R. L. Poole in the *Dictionary of National Biography*; [1] but since it was written, it has become more than a little uncertain that he ever went to the University of Paris after taking a B.D. at Oxford, or that he met there Marsilius of Padua. Ockham must have been born in 1288 or 1289; for a William of Ockham, O.F.M., was ordained subdeacon by Archbishop Winchelsey in St. Mary's, Southwark, on 26 February 1306, [2] and there is every likelihood that this is our Ockham. Hofer's suggested date for his birth (1290) would make him too young then for the subdiaconate. He seems to have spent his early university years at Oxford only, where he joined the Franciscans. In later years he was known as *inceptor Oxoniensis*, which means that he had qualified for, but not actually taken, the degree of D.D. The first certain date in his life is 1324, when he was summoned to the Court of Avignon. The cause was alleged heretical statements made in the first book of his *Commentary on the Four Books of the Sentences*, which he had written

[1] XIV. 802–806; for bibliography, cf. Ueberweg-Geyer, *Geschichte der Philosophie*, ii. (11th edition, Berlin, 1928), 572–574. Modern accounts are J. Hofer, " Biographische Studien über Wilhelm von Ockham," *Archivum Franciscanum Historicum*, vi. 209–233, 439–465, 654–669, and F. Federhofer, " Ein Beitrag zur Bibliographie und Biographie des Wilhelm von Ockham," *Philosophisches Jahrbuch*, xxxviii. 26–48. On the contemporary background Georges de Lagarde, *La Naissance de l'Esprit Laique au déclin du Moyen Age* (2 vols., 1934); J. Hashagen, *Staat und Kirche von der Reformation* (1931); and Otto Bornhak, *Staatskirchliche Anschauungen und Handlungen am Hofe Kaiser Ludwigs des Bayern* (1933), are particularly useful.

[2] Attention was drawn to this by the editors in *Guillelmi de Ockham Opera Politica*, i. (Manchester, 1940) 288, citing Reg. Winchelsey, fo. 116 v. (ed. R. Graham, Cant. and York Soc., p. 981).

at Oxford ; the publication of the investigation shows that the charges were purely theological and philological.[1] It was while he stayed at Avignon that he made the acquaintance of Michael of Cesena, then general of the Franciscan Order, and Bonagratia of Bergamo. These two prominent Franciscans were at the Papal Court defending their opinions on the vow of Poverty. Ockham was won over to their position, and was excommunicated along with them in 1328, not as the result of his earlier opinions, but for maintaining the views upheld by the general of the Order. The three men escaped from Avignon at the end of May 1328, to seek the protection of Lewis of Bavaria, who had broken with John XXII. Marsilius of Padua and John of Jandun had already joined the emperor. During the next eight years, which saw a great deal of pamphleteering in the imperial cause by the supporters of Lewis of Bavaria, Ockham and his friends settled at Munich. After Michael of Cesena's death in 1342, Ockham acted as vicar of the Franciscans who did not recognize the authority of Avignon. He seems to have held the seal till 1348, when it was sent to William Farnier, general of the opposing group. This was probably the year before his death.

> I confess openly, and it can be objected against me with truth, that I am withdrawing myself from the obedience of the Church of Avignon, and from the society of the multitude of friars minor, for no other reason than that the said Church of Avignon maintains errors and manifest heresies, pertinaciously approves, defends, and does not cease to commit grave and enormous injuries and acts of injustice against the rights and liberties of the faithful, great and small, laymen and clerks, to the danger of entire Christendom. Many of the said errors, put into writing, have been sent in the form of bulls to different parts of the world, to be inculcated as matters of firm belief into the ears of all Christians.[2]

Ockham wrote this in one of the latest of his treatises, the *De imperatorum et pontificum potestate* (1347). For the past nineteen years he had been engaged, when not occupied with logic and metaphysic, in the battle against Avignon ; and now, he says, I am prepared to render account for all I have done, written and said ever since I submitted myself to the rule of St. Francis, " that all the faithful may see whether anything can be proved against me by reason of which I ought not to be counted

---

[1] Auguste Pelzer, " Les 51 articles de Guillaume de Ockham," *Revue d'histoire ecclésiastique*, xviii (1922), 250 f. One of the charges against him (p. 252), was that of Pelagianism : he had made the statement, " Deus potest aliquem existentem in puris naturalibus primo acceptare tanquam dignum vita eterna et sine omni sui demerito reprobare " ; the committee examining his views fastened on the word *dignus*, which, they said, was erroneous, since it would make a man in his purely natural condition equal to one who is in a state of grace.

[2] R. Scholz, *Unbekannte kirchenpolitische Streitschriften aus der Zeit Ludwigs des Bayern*, p. 454.

among the sons of light." [1] He had been feeling a certain isolation ; the attacks made upon him by Conrad of Mengenberg, and the official disapproval of the Church (he had been under the ban since 1328) had not left him unscathed. There is a certain defiance, perhaps a certain loneliness, in his tone when he compares himself to Popes Damasus and Leo, or to Athanasius and Jerome who were similarly assailed. " I shall be more moved by one evident piece of reason or by one passage of scriptural authority, soundly understood, than by the assertion of all the universe of mortals."

The conviction that the Vicar of Christ, the successor of Peter, had incurred the guilt of heresy colours much of Ockham's political thought. The point needs emphasis, since there still is a tendency in some quarters to think of the great Franciscan only as an aloof, detached mind, a philosopher of first principles, rather than as a figure deeply involved in the controversies of the age.[2] The moderation of the *Dialogus* might easily lead one to regard him as a hesitant academic, in strong contrast to the radical Marsilius of Padua. This is how Mr. Sullivan depicted him in a comparison of the two philosophers,[3] and indeed there are sections of the *Dialogus* which might confirm one in this impression. But against this massive work of careful deliberation must be set the controversial treatises printed by Dr. Scholz, who reaches conclusions very different from those of the American scholar. The latter was inclined to see in Marsilius rather than in Ockham the thinker that influenced later medieval political thought in a radical direction ; Dr. Scholz, on the other hand, considers that the treatises of Ockham did much more than the *Defensor pacis* to change people's views about the nature of the spiritual power and to shake the papal system at its very foundations. No later reformer is uninfluenced by his ideas.[4] Yet it is perhaps an exaggeration of Ockham's controversial proclivities to judge him almost entirely on the *De imperatorum et pontificum potestate*, as Professor McIlwain has done.[5] True, Ockham himself speaks of this work as a compendium, a shortened version of the *Dialogus* ; but he does not say that his *conclusions* would be found in the larger work ; he merely observes that there the matters would be found discussed with care and elaboration (*exquisite*).[6] We

[1] Scholz, *op. cit.*, p. 453.

[2] The more correct view was stated by S. Riezler, *Die literarischen Widersacher der Päpste zur Zeit Ludwigs des Baiers* (Leipzig, 1874), still a work of great value for the background of controversy.

[3] J. Sullivan, " Marsiglio of Padua and William of Ockham," *American Historical Review*, ii. (1896–1897), 417–426.

[4] *Op. cit.*, p. 141.   [5] *The Growth of Political Thought*, pp. 293–297.

[6] " Sane que in hoc compendio perstringuntur, in aliis operibus, praesertim in quodam dyalogo quem incipi, qui habuerit, discussa inveniet exquisite." Scholz, *op. cit.*, p. 455.

should do well to understand the differences between the tentative, ponderous, composite *Dialogus* and the more hard-hitting, integral and unified *Streitschriften* of the later years, and not to think that either body of work alone is sufficient for a true estimate of Ockham's views.

There is one obvious reason why it is so difficult to form a critical judgment of Ockham as a " political thinker," if these words can ever be applied to one who was first and foremost a theologian and philosopher ; the *Dialogus* (to take his most famous political treatise) is a work of prodigious length, great comprehensiveness, and no little obscurity, and often the discussions seem to leave the reader in the air. This may be partly due to actual mistakes in the printed text, which has still to be read in the edition of Goldast, when a drastic overhauling by means of a new collation is obviously needed ; but it is partly deliberate, and I would venture to agree with Riezler [1] as against Dr. Haller, that the inconclusiveness cannot be explained away or the text made to mean something that it does not state. I think that we have frankly to face the length, the inconclusiveness and obscurity which have very reasonably daunted scholars, and to try to appreciate the subtleties of the method before we look for conclusions. This can be better done now that the *Octo quaestiones de potestate Papae* are available in a modern critical edition, to be followed soon by the greater part of the *Opus nonaginta dierum*.[2]

For Ockham is essentially a scholastic, brought up on Aristotle, Aquinas and Scotus. To most people he represents, in the late Dean Rashdall's words, " the culmination of all scholastic thought." Mention him to the casual philosopher, and out will come the celebrated " razor," which he is thought to have used against an unnecessary multiplication of entities—though in point of fact Richard of Meneville was before him in the desire to avoid them.[3] To most historians of philosophy he is the sceptic who used his powerful dialectic to attack Aristotelian metaphysics and realism in science, a precursor of the modern empirical and experimental point of view. Whether this commonly held opinion is, as Mr. Moody has recently argued, erroneous,[4] or sound, does not for the moment matter ; what matters is the fact that in an examination of the foundations of the spiritual power Ockham does not proceed by dogmatic definition, as Marsilius did at the beginning of Dictio II of the

[1] *Die literarischen Widersacher*, p. 250.

[2] Edited by J. G. Sikes, in *Guillelmi de Ockham Opera Politica*, I. This volume includes chs. i.–vii. of the *Opus nonaginta dierum*, the remainder of which will constitute vol. II.

[3] Cf. D. E. Sharp, *Franciscan Philosophy at Oxford in the Thirteenth Century*, p. 287 n.

[4] *The Logic of William of Ockham* (1935), especially ch. i. and his all too summary criticism of Michalski's method, p. 2.

Defensor pacis, nor by mystical analogies, like the theorists of the Investiture controversy, but by an exhaustive balancing and comparison of rival positions : an immense variety of discrepant views are made to face each other and are subjected to profound and acute criticism ; and we might say of the *Dialogus* in relation to medieval politics what Mr. Moody has said of scholasticism in general :

> Though the language and background of these discussions are not ours —so that we often fail to recognize the philosophical problems with which we are familiar in our modern discussions—once the barrier of language and terminology is crossed, and the translation of problems from one set of terms to the other accomplished, it is hard to find any important philosophical question that was not raised and subjected to thoroughgoing analysis, in the literature of scholasticism.[1]

The contrast with Marsilius of Padua is illuminating. On Ockham's side it springs not only from his scholastic method of thought, but from a background of political experience that made him more circumspect and balanced in judgment than the brilliant and revolutionary Italian. To Marsilius the Church was a department (*pars*) or organ of the State. This was the theory inspiring the proceedings of Lewis of Bavaria in his visit to Rome in 1328. The views of Marsilius on the power of the Emperor to depose the Pope (*Defensor Pacis*, Dictio 2, c. 25) which the Italian thinker derived from accepted histories, especially that of Martin of Troppau, there found its exemplification.[2] But when it came to dealing with the higher German clergy, Lewis, though he was able to make full use of the powers granted to the Emperor by the Concordat of Worms, 1122, though he might insist on elections to bishoprics being held in his presence, or upon his power to decide a disputed election,[3] was by no means master of the higher German ecclesiastics. Here, especially in matters of taxation, prescriptive right had to be respected.[4] And there is a contrast between the Emperor's high claims and what in practice he was able to effect. Ockham's arguments are not unaffected by the older, historic claims of a deeply-rooted religious society. To take a later analogy, he is in some respects nearer to the principles upon which Nicholas of Cues acted in his reforming legation in Germany (1451–1452) than to the more drastic methods of treating the clergy suggested by Marsilius. So, too, in his attitude to the papacy, Ockham is nearer to the *De concordantia Catholica* of Cusanus than to the radicalism of the *Defensor*. There is much in him of which Dante would have approved. He represents, in fact, a sort of half-way house between conservatism and radical reform. And he was flexible : he was indeed prepared for the

---

[1] Moody, *op. cit.*, p. 13.
[2] Bornhak, *op. cit.*, pp. 16–17.
[3] *Ibid.*, pp. 72 f.
[4] *Ibid.*, pp. 103–104.

Emperor to act in cases of " urgent need or evident utility " ; in the famous dispute over the marriage of his son with Margaret Maultasch of the Tyrol, when Lewis assumed the power of declaring her marriage with John Henry of Luxemburg null and of dispensing with the impediment of affinity, Ockham did not hesitate to justify the Emperor's action on grounds of Roman law, when a strict canonist would have denied that competence altogether ; he defended it on the ground that the Emperor was the successor of the Roman Emperors and that needs of State demanded it.[1]   Such facts serve to illustrate the difficulty of making hard and fast generalizations about Ockham, as indeed about any true casuist.

Ockham began his career of political controversy with the lengthy *Opus nonaginta dierum* (*c.* 1332).   This was the result of his association with Michael of Cesena, who had originally been at one with John XXII in suppressing the Franciscan spirituals, but had been forced into opposition by the Pope's condemnation of the doctrine of Evangelical poverty, had protested, and had been deprived of his office for disloyalty (8 June 1328).   In defence of Michael, Ockham wrote the *Opus*, a criticism of John's bull, *Quia vir reprobus*, in which Michael's views had been stigmatized as uncatholic.   In the *Opus*, the bull is taken section by section and the points at which the papal statement misunderstands Franciscan doctrine are tellingly brought out.   In doing so, Ockham, as his recent editors have remarked, has given " a complete account of the Franciscan teaching on the subject of poverty." [2]   In his closely reasoned defence of this, Ockham opposed the papal admonishing of Michael, and upheld the Minister-general's attack on the three papal pronouncements against Evangelical poverty, the *Ad conditorem canorum, Cum inter nonnullos*,[3] and *Quia quorundam*.   These Franciscans, whom he defends, are termed the *impugnatores* (of John XXII), and the views he expresses are placed in their mouths, while at the end of each chapter he explains, in lecture fashion, the meaning of individual phrases in the papal text.

The fundamental papal contention, expressed in Michael's condemnation, was that to draw a sharp distinction between use and ownership was meaningless ;   so far as consumable goods were concerned, neither in fact nor in law could use be separated from ownership or dominion.   It was absurd to say that you could have use in practice (*usus facti*) and not in law, for the power to use must involve some legal

---

[1] " Consultatio de causa matrimoniali " in *Opera Politica*, i. 280–284.

[2] *Opera Politica*, i. 290.

[3] Michael of Cesena had argued that this bull violated the earlier teaching of the Church about apostolic poverty, since it ruled out any interpretation that did not make Christ and His Apostles the actual owners of property in common.   Christ could have possessed no legal rights, since He was in no way subject to the Civil Law.

right. It was John's characteristic method to regard the spirit rather than the letter of the biblical texts cited against him by Michael; to him " the perfection of the Christian life consists principally and even essentially in charity," not in the renunciation of possession; [1] it was Ockham's method, on the other hand, to analyse with critical care and subtle distinctions the meaning of words and expressions dominant in the controversy : *usus juris, usus facti, res consumptibiles.* His contention was that in consumables it is perfectly possible to have use without legal ownership. For instance, to eat bread and to drink wine is to use either, but this constitutes no legal ownership in the bread or wine. Franciscans, he says, are " simple users " : *utuntur rebus nullum habentes ius quod valeant in iudicio litigare.* That was just the point at issue. The papacy, as guardian or trustee of the goods and possessions of the Order, was constantly being involved in litigation or disputes in which Franciscans were involved,[2] and the plea of Evangelical poverty might be used to escape liability for acts for which, in papal eyes, they ought to have been held legally responsible. Hence the desire of the Pope to divest the Holy See of responsibility in this quarter; hence the long discussions of the meaning of *usus* or of *res consumptibles* which fill so much of Ockham's work. But with the detail we shall not be so much concerned as with the general results of the controversy : the attack on Michael and the papal brushing aside of the Franciscan objections, brought prominently to the forefront of Ockham's mind the solution of a general council to which Lewis of Bavaria had in the earlier part of his struggle with John XXII appealed at Nuremberg in December 1323; [3] and secondly it was through the discussions of Evangelical poverty that Ockham was brought face to face with the problem of private ownership and so ultimately to political dominion. Franciscan controversy inevitably led him to the even larger questions discussed in the *Dialogus, the Octo quaestiones de Potestate Papae* (1340–1342), and the later *De imperatorum et pontificum potestate.*

The *Dialogus* is a discussion between a master and his disciple. Ockham may be taken to represent the master, whom the pupil questions on his opinions. Now in the Prologue the disciple is made to ask his teacher not to mention proper names of persons engaged in the controversy under dispute, and, further, not to confine himself to one opinion, but to give several, without revealing to the pupil which is his own. He is to state a *conclusio*, but not to say that it is his; and the

---

[1] Nowhere does this appear more clearly than in his introduction to the famous text *Ecce reliquimus omnia*, ch. xxiii.

[2] Decima Douie, *The Nature and the Effect of the Heresy of the Fraticelli*, p. 160.

[3] Bornhak, pp. 31–34.

reason for these requests is twofold. In the first place the disciple attaches so much weight to his master's views that if he knew that this or that opinion was the one favoured by the teacher he would not be able to decide impartially about it ; and secondly, the absence of names will ensure an unprejudiced verdict (*remotis zeli oculis*) upon the views discussed.[1] Throughout the *Dialogus* the disciple put the *quaestio*, and the master replies ; but almost immediately the mere statement of *rationes* for this or that opinion given by the master does not prove satisfying to the disciple, who asks for a *responsio* to each of the *rationes*. To this at first the master objects that he had been asked for a statement of various opinions on the matter discussed rather than for his own views on those opinions ;[2] but the disciple gets his way (greatly to the lengthening of the dialogue), and the master consents to indicate his view. He does so, however, with the utmost caution and tentativeness, and his opinion is often submerged in the long sequence of reply and counterreply. All this caution, one might almost say obfuscation, is therefore deliberate. It is deliberate not merely for the reasons given by the pupil, but because the opponent of Avignon must know what arguments will be developed by the supporters of John XXII and how to meet them in the best academic tradition. For in spite of the academic setting, the *Dialogus* is an amalgam of the ephemeral and the permanent. By "ephemeral" I do not mean matter that is unimportant, but rather the product of current controversy ; and this can be seen from the arrangement of the work.

It was put together gradually. According to the latest calculation, the *Dialogus* proper was begun at the end of 1333 or the beginning of 1334, and the first part was finished before 1334 was out. The third part was begun in 1337 or 1338 and, as far as we can see, was never completed. The present second part was substituted for this uncompleted third section. In content, the main building, so to speak, is concerned almost exclusively with heresy. To whom—theologians or canonists—does it pertain to define which assertions are catholic and which heretical ? How are such assertions to be distinguished ? By what procedure should persons be convicted of pertinacious and heretical opinion ? And how are heretics (the Pope included, if he becomes one) to be punished ? How are their followers to be dealt with ? From these problems we pass to an examination of the heresies of John XXII, particularly his statement that *the souls of the departed after they have been purged do not see God face to face until the day of Judgment*—the "heresy" of the beatific vision. The third part of the *Dialogus* is headed *De gestis diversorum Christianorum*, and

---

[1] Dialogus, in Goldast, *Monarchia Sancti Romani Imperii*, ii. (1614), 398 (Prologus).
[2] *Dialogus*, I. iii. 401. (The third figure refers to page in Goldast, vol. ii.)

is divided into nine treatises, each subdivided into books. This is the most controversial part of the work, one that sets forth the powers of the Pope and clergy, and purports to give biographies of John XXII, Lewis of Bavaria, Benedict XII, Michael of Cesena and others, including master William of Ockham himself. In actual fact Ockham does not get farther than John XXII, for when, after long preliminary considerations upon Pope and emperor, he reaches the pontiff who is the main target of his attacks, he inserts a lengthy *compendium errorum Papae* and breaks off the *Dialogus* abruptly at this point. In the text printed by Goldast, the *Opus nonaginta dierum* then follows : but, as we saw above, it is a separate, and earlier work.

It is important to bear Michael of Cesena in mind, since his challenge to the papacy raised the question of the legality of John XXII's action, and the relation of the Pope to the law of the Church is the fundamental topic of the *Dialogus*. If there is any need to point out the manifest difference between Ockham and Marsilius it could be done over this very point. Marsilius, the totalitarian, has scarcely any conception of the Church as a self-governing body with its own law and jurisdiction reaching beyond the sphere of the *forum internum* ; and it follows that the Conciliar theory in the *Defensor pacis* is of a very rudimentary order. But Ockham in his treatment of the spiritual power is far closer to the Gelasian tradition, or even to Dante's re-statement of it, than his radical colleague. He has a high notion of the spiritual authority. If, like Dante, he is bitterly opposed to the contemporary Canonists, he is as strong a believer as the later Conciliar thinkers in the conception of the Church as a society governed by a law that cannot be arbitrarily varied by an individual pontiff, and as a body whose *ethos* is based upon the primitive tradition of apostolic times. It was his belief in early Church organization and practice that made him so acceptable to Conciliar statesmen like d'Ailly, who made an abbreviation of passages from the *Dialogus* relevant to the situation at the Council of Constance.[1] It is well also to remember that in the thirteenth century the Franciscans had been prominent in proclaiming the supremacy of law, binding even upon the monarch, in the secular state : this is one of the main themes of the Song of Lewes, and inspired a number of the " constitutional " interpolations in the text of Bracton's *De legibus Angliae*.

And now look at some of Ockham's responses in detail. In the first or original part of the *Dialogus*, where the master is at pains to distinguish Catholic doctrine and heresy, it is the method of determination which is the subject of the pupil's inquiry. The people to do it, argues the

[1] Agnes E. Roberts, " Pierre d'Ailly at the Council of Constance," *Trans. Roy. Hist. Soc.*, IV ser., xviii. 135.

master, are not the canonists, but the theologians of the Church. The canonists may indeed frame the *libellus* or statement of the charge ; they know the formulae of accusation, how to proceed against, how to defend the accused ; they know the decrees ; but to the theologian it belongs " to know more deeply " (*profundius cognoscere*) what is in the canons, for theology is the *scientia superior*. The " superior " science deals with the general and permanent principles of morality, not *moralia particularia* where the specific application of those principles is required.[1] In a similar fashion custom must give way to the superior code of natural law ; to quote Gratian, *dignitate . . . ius naturale praevalet consuetudini et constitutioni*. This " deeper " knowledge is therefore a knowledge of principle ; the theologian alone can appreciate whether the statements made are consistent with orthodoxy, and how deeply grounded is the conviction of the person accused that his opinion is right. The canonists are but concerned with the penalty.[2]

The next step is to show what is meant by orthodoxy, e.g. whether conformity with the canon of holy scripture is enough to warrant a statement being termed catholic. Ockham appears to admit five guarantees of truth : holy scripture ; tradition that has come down from the apostolic age ; reputable chronicles and histories ; conclusions to be drawn from the truths established in the foregoing categories ; and the inspired writings of persons whose work has been accepted as such by the universal Church.[3] The truths proclaimed in the Christian faith are immutable, and immutably catholic. " No truth is catholic, unless it has been divinely revealed, either through its being inserted in the scriptures or because it has become known through the certainty of the Universal Church." It follows that no new truth can be made by the Pope ; he cannot add, like a legislator, to the sum-total of *catholica veritas* ; he cannot make a new article of faith, though he may give his approval to doctrines that have generally come to be con-

---

[1] *Dialogus*, I. xii–xiii. 407–408.   [2] I. xiv. 409.

[3] II. v. 415–16 : " *Magister* : Tenent isti, quod quinque sunt genera veritatum, quibus non licet Christianis aliter dissentire. Primum est earum, quae in Scriptura sacra dicuntur, vel ex eis argumento necessario possunt inferri. Secundum est earum, quae ab Apostolis ad nos per succedentium relationem vel scripturas fidelium peruenerunt, licet in Scripturis sacris non inueniantur insertae, nec ex solis eis possunt necessario argumento concludi ; tertium est earum, quas in fide dignis cronicis et historiis, relationibus fidelium inuenimus. Quartum est earum, quae ex veritatibus primi generis et secundi tantummodo, vel que ex eis vel alterius earum una cum veritatibus tertii generis possunt manifeste concludi. Quintum est earum, quas Deus praeter veritates reuelatas Apostolis aliis reuelauit, vel etiam inspirauit, ac nouiter reuelaret, vel etiam inspiraret : quae reuelatio vel inspiratio ad vniuersalem ecclesiam absque dubitatione peruenit, vel etiam perueniret." It is worth noting that the master says no more than "tenent *isti* " ; and the careful choice of tenses at the end of the sentence is characteristic.

sidered as catholic and true. Can he then say that such and such an opinion is heretical and condemn it ? On what authority, asks the disciple, does the pontiff rely ? The master recognizes that this is a very difficult question. Some, he replies, say that the Pope is himself of such great authority that he can at will declare any assertion to be heretical ; but this, interjects the disciple, is to imply that the Pope cannot commit heresy himself. Another opinion, resumes the master, is that the Pope or the General Council, when they condemn an assertion, do so on one of three grounds : that it is not founded upon Holy Scripture, on which the principal General Councils relied ; that it is contrary to Apostolic tradition ; or that it goes against revelation or inspiration. What then, the disciple asks, if the Pope or the Council claim to be inspired ? The wicked base their claims on miracles as much as do the good. The answer given is that the miracle was generally judged to be true ; and after giving the arguments for and against the various opinions about the Pope's power to approve or condemn a position, the master concludes that he must not rely on the wisdom or science of men, but on divine authority or manifest miracle only.[1] He quotes St. Paul, 1 Cor. iii. 1 : " my speech and my preaching was not with enticing words of man's wisdom, but in demonstration of the Spirit and of power : that your faith should not stand in the wisdom of men, but in the power of God." Miracle or catholic authority must be the test of orthodoxy, not papal theology or the prompting of the canonist. The speakers then proceed to discuss the belief of the laymen, especially the meaning of the expression *credere implicite*. There is no need to linger over the long technical discussion of the modes of belief or with the *modi pertinacie*, of which nineteen are enumerated, beyond noting that under the sixteenth of these the master manages to include a Pope who continues to assert an error contrary to the faith,[2] and under the seventeenth all who assent to that Pope's opinion.[3]

In the fifth book he replies to an important question put by the disciple. The younger man has stated the query thus : Christians generally appear to think that the whole collectivity of Christians cannot commit heresy ; some maintain, secondly, that the General Council cannot ; others, thirdly, that the Roman Church cannot ; others, fourthly, that the College of Cardinals cannot ; and others, fifthly, that the Pope cannot. What does the master think about these views, and especially the fifth ?[4] The master maintains that those holding the opinion that the Pope's authority in matters of faith is absolute err, since a canonically

---

[1] *Dialogus* II. xxx. 431 (the second occurrence of this page-number).
[2] IV. xxix. 466.   [3] IV. xxx. 466–467.
[4] . i. 467.

elected Pope *can* go astray.[1] Any that occupy their days with medieval theological controversy will be prepared here for arguments from the careers of Popes Symmachus and Leo, and Ockham will not disappoint them. The master goes on to explain that not only may the Pope commit heresy : the College of Cardinals may be defiled with it also ; [2] and on such heresy the rest of Christendom has the right to sit in judgment. If the Pope or the cardinals are heretical, the rest of the Church may none the less be sound. This gives a foretaste of the argument in the extremely important chapter xxii of the same book (V), wherein the master argues that the Roman Church, which is distinct from the whole congregation of the faithful,[3] *can* err in matters of faith ; but then not only may a General Council, but the whole collectivity of Christians err in these matters. No section of the Church, not even the " whole multitude " of believers itself, is exempt from taking a wrong line and falling into heresy.[4] Here we have the distinction, familiar to readers of Dietrich of Niem, drawn between the *Roman* and the *whole* Church. Dietrich uses it to argue that the *whole* Church, the *genus*, has the right to correct, by means of a General Council, the Roman *species*. Ockham, on the other hand, is far more sceptical and does not fail to emphasize the human and fallible nature of the Church in all its organized forms : no section of the Church, not even the totality, is free from the capacity to err. We should do well to contrast with this the views of Gerson, some seventy years later, in his *De auferibilitate Papae ab ecclesia*, where he argues that the bridegroom, Christ, can never be separated from His Church, His bride, and is to her a constant spring of inspiration, sustaining all ranks and grades in the Christian society.

None the less, when the Pope is a heretic, he must be punished, and the authority to do so is a General Council. This can be convoked by other authority besides the Pope ; it can be summoned by the bishops, or, if they will not do it, by kings and princes ; in the last resort, by all Catholic men and women.[5] The disciple is somewhat surprised to hear the master maintain that the Council could be summoned without papal

---

[1] V. ii–iii. 469–473. The objections to the fifteen demonstrations of this are stated in ch. iv. They all come under the general proposition that a canonically elected Pope cannot be a heretic as long as he remains Pope.

[2] V. viii. 478–479.

[3] V. xxii. 489. " Romana ecclesia, quae est distincta a congregatione fidelium, sicut caput a corpore."

[4] Ockham obviously realizes the very controversial nature of these assertions, since he is careful to state the arguments for and against very fully ; he represents the *disciulus* as being appropriately surprised at their tenor. This statement of the fallibility of churchmen in their several degrees is very characteristic of Ockham's outlook : but he never says *ecclesia potest errare* : he uses the expression *tota multitudo virorum et clericorum et laicorum ; tota multitudo fidelium.*

[5] VI. lxxxiv–v. 602–604.

authority ; he argues, much as the orthodox canonist after 1378, that such a thing is impossible. The master, however, replies that there is good precedent : a *particular* Council can be summoned without the Pope's authority, to decide which is the true Pope in case of schism, as has happened at times in history. The bishops who assembled to judge Pope Marcellinus on account of his idolatry or to condemn Pope John XII constituted a *particular* Council : *a fortiori* a General Council can be called to sit in judgment on a pseudo-Pope, if suspected of heresy.[1] In such a Council kings, princes and other members of the laity may appear : it is not confined to Churchmen. The Emperors were present in the early Councils, and kings may come unbidden ; for matters of faith touch not only the clergy, but the laity.

It will be noted that the primary object of the General Council, as Ockham sees it in this part of the *Dialogus*, is to deal with a Pope who is guilty of heresy. So far the problem of a papal heretic has dominated the work. It is not until we reach the *Pars tertia*, entitled *De gestis diversorum Christianorum*, that the discussion leaves consideration of theological error, and comes to more general topics ; and even here we have first to traverse a section on the dogmas of John XXII. The *De gestis* was intended to contain nine treatises, only two of which appear to have survived. The first of these, headed *De potestate papae et cleri*, is an exhaustive discussion of five opinions commonly held concerning the power of the Pope. These are the following : (1) That both in spiritual and in temporal matters the Pope has such plenitude of power from Christ's ordaining that he can do, as a matter of course (*regulariter*) and in any event, everything that is not against the law of God or the law of nature ; (2) That he has, of divine right, such plenitude of power in spiritual, not in temporal things ; (3) That he has this plenitude of power (both spiritual and temporal) partly from Christ's, partly from man's ordaining ; (4) That neither from divine nor from human agency does he possess any such plenitude ; (5) That he can exercise his power in single instances ; not as a matter of course, and not of divine nor human right, but as individual occasions require (a theory of ' casuality ').[2] It would be impossible to follow the discussion of these in detail : but the more important of Ockham's conclusions may be indicated. Here again it is necessary to emphasize the caution shown by the master. *Dicunt : praefati opinantes dicunt : illa sententia tenet ; ponunt ;* and so forth.

The Pope does not possess the plenitude of power in temporal

[1] VI. lxxxiv. 602.

[2] *Dialogus*, " De gestis diversorum Christianorum," Tractatus primus, c. i. Goldast, p. 772.

matters ; for if he was above all positive law (*legibus positiuis solutus*), as the plenitude in temporal matters would imply, this would reduce Christian law, which is the law of freedom, to the position of a law of bondage (*lex seruitutis*).[1] All Christians would then become the Pope's slaves (*serui*) ; it would mean that he could deprive kings, princes and laymen of their possessions, and the result would be an infinity of dissension and strife. In such a case Christian law would be one of greater servitude than the Mosaic law. Christians are not the *serui* of the pontiff : [2] they can exercise ownership and lordship over temporal goods and property, for otherwise they could not make donations to churches and their gifts and conveyances would be invalid. The power which the Pope exercises is purely spiritual ; and this is partly from Christ, partly from human ordinance. Much of it he receives in virtue of canons made by General Councils ; and it follows that such Councils do not derive their authority from the Roman pontiff, but that the pontiff derives his from them. For, too, the Pope's coercive power (*potestas coactiva*) he draws not immediately from Christ, but, mediately, from the faithful. In chapter xvii the problem of the spiritual and temporal plenitude of power is thus met :

> It is asserted that Christ made the blessed Peter head, prince and prelate over the other Apostles and all the faithful ; granting him in all things to be done or omitted that relate to the governance of the community of the faithful as regards morals and every sort of spiritual necessity, all power in such matters as could without danger, providently and to the common advantage, be entrusted to one man ; and freedom and coercive jurisdiction, provided that these did no notable harm or caused no extensive loss to the rights of the Empire, of kings, princes and any others, clerks or laymen, which belonged to them by the law of nature, the law of nations or the civil law after the institution of the law of the gospel. But in temporal matters he gave them [the successors of Peter], as the normal rule, only the right of seeking temporalities for their sustenance and the fulfilment of their office. All power, however, which the Roman pontiffs have possessed or still possess in the ordinary course beyond that just specified, they have secured and now hold as the result of human action, whether condition, concession, spontaneous submission ; or consent, tacit or expressed ; or because of the powerlessness, negligence or malice of other men ; or through custom or some other human right.[3]

The almost painfully careful wording, and the emphasis laid upon the gradual historical evolution of the papal prerogatives, are worth notice. In the foregoing chapters Ockham does not actually deny to the papacy the plenitude of power in spiritual things. He lays down four reasons for it, and without recording a definite view passes on to consider it in

---

[1] *Dialogus*, " De gestis diversorum Christianorum," Tractatus primus, *c.* v, 776.
[2] *Ibid.*, *c.* viii, 780–781.　　　　[3] *Ibid.*, *c.* xvii, 786.

temporal matters. The passage quoted above seems the clearest record
of Ockham's opinion on the source of papal power discoverable in the
Dialogus ; but in the later *De imperatorum et pontificum potestate* has been
forced to use clearer language. To that I will come very shortly.

Ockham's *Octo quaestiones de potestate Papae*, written shortly after
1314, is probably the most comprehensive existing treatise on the relation
of Pope and Emperor. It was composed, he says, at the request of
some individual whom it has been usual to regard as Lewis of Bavaria
himself. The impersonal method is again adopted ; Ockham describes
himself as preceding *solummodo recitando et allegando* ; but the late Mr.
Sikes, in his edition of the work, has shown that the *responsiones* at the
end of each *quaestio* bear a notable correspondence, often verbal, with
Ockham's more crisp and definitive *Breviloquium* [1] in which the imperial
point of view is defended.

It is indeed a treatise written in the fulness of time, when propagandists were familiar with the main arguments on either side : whether
one man can rightfully hold both the supreme spiritual and the supreme
lay power ; whether secular authority is derived immediately from
God or from His vicar, the Pope (the question asked in the third book
of Dante's *De Monarchia*) ; whether from Christ's institution the Pope
and the Roman Church have the right to grant secular jurisdiction to
the Emperor and to lay princes. Ockham observes that problems of
this kind need far more space than he can give them : [2] a modern reader
might think the allowance liberal enough, for the arguments on either
side are set out with astonishing fulness. Students of medieval Germany
will be more interested when Ockham asks whether imperial election
confers full powers of administration on the German king,[3] or inquires
what rights the Church possesses in view of the fact that its bishops
anoint and consecrate kings who hold their thrones by hereditary right.
On the first of these issues, he notes the opinion of those who allege
that election as king of the Romans gives the king full administration
in Italy and the other lands and provinces subject to Charlemagne before
his imperial unction and consecration,[4] but not elsewhere, a point raised
by Lupold of Bebenberg, whose *De Iure Regni et Imperii* Ockham chal-
lenges elsewhere.[5] Here his contention on the general nature of secular
authority, advanced in the second *quaestio*, comes in to decide the matter.
All lay power is had immediately from God ; though with regard to

[1] *Opera Politica*, i. 3.   A summary of the *quaestiones* is given in R. W. and
A. J. Carlyle, *A History of Medieval Political Theory in the West*, v. 48–51.
[2] *Opera Politica*, i. 56 : he speaks of the " brevitas . . . istius opusculi."
[3] *Ibid.*, pp. 126 f.   The question is whether there is any distinction between
regnum and *imperium*.
[4] *Ibid.*, p. 149.   [5] *Ibid.*, p. 128.

actual administration, the supreme power of the king of the Romans is more fully exercised in the lands immediately subject to the Empire than elsewhere. In those lands election as king of the Romans, it is argued, gives as full power as imperial coronation and consecration. The question therefore of exactly what is conveyed to the monarch by unction and coronation must arise, especially when a king succeeds not by election, but by hereditary right. Is unction of no great importance ? Unction and crowning, Ockham replies, give no power over temporalities, for queens are also anointed and crowned, yet receive no such capacity. Nor do such ceremonies confer any *donum spirituale* : the kings of England and France who touch for the scrofula do not cure people because they have themselves received unction, for other anointed monarchs have not the same power—it must derive from causes outside our ken. Yet unction and coronation may have a helpful spiritual effect, if received with good intention, like the ceremonies at the conferment of knighthood, nuptials, enthronement of prelates and so forth.[1] Ockham would not belittle the symbolic act, but is careful not to exaggerate its significance.

From such a conclusion it may be anticipated what answer he will give to the question whether coronation of the *Rex Romanorum* by some other archbishop than the one who normally performs the rite is valid. (Lewis of Bavaria, after the double election of 1314, was crowned by the archbishop of Mainz, not by the archbishop of Cologne, the right archbishop, who crowned his rival, Frederick of Austria.) But he reaches his affirmative conclusion, not by minimizing or restricting the importance of the coronation ceremony, but by asking, characteristically, whether the Emperor incurs guilt (*culpa*) by such an apparent contravention of the normal practice. Such a practice, he claims, must be founded either upon " pure grace " or upon right. If upon grace—the favour of the Emperor or of the *populus*—it can be varied without guilt by an Emperor not prepared to follow the practice of his successors ; if upon right, there may indeed occur cases where deferment of coronation and consecration because the right archbishop is not available would seriously endanger public security,[2] and be contrary to *ius*. The implication is that 1314 was such an example. Ockham is, however, careful to add that the king would incur guilt if no reason could be given why the services of the right archbishop were not retained.[3]

The cautiously distinguishing academic was capable of making clearer and more unequivocal statements.

Let us look at some of these. Probably during the last quarter of 1338 Ockham, from abroad, wrote a treatise supporting Edward III's

[1] *Opera Politica*, pp. 155–156.   [2] *Ibid.*, p. 166.   [3] *Ibid.*, pp. 172–173.

request for clerical subsidies in the war with France : *An princeps pro suo succursu, scilicet guerre, possit recipere bona ecclesiarum, etiam invito papa.* Could Edward receive clerical contributions when such grants were regarded with disfavour by the papacy ? Here a strongly erastian note is sounded in the proposition that the English prelates are bound to aid their king in a just war ; since " The prelates and clergy subject to the King of England do not possess their temporal possessions, especially those which they have in abundance, by divine right, but by human right which emanates from the king " (*jure humano ab ipso rege manante*), and Ockham goes on to interpret the intention of kings and other pious benefactors of the Church :

> It was the will and intention of the kings of England and others of their subjects who conferred temporal goods on the Church that temporal goods should be expended upon pious causes, especially those which might re- dound to the common utility of all in the dominions of the same kings. . . . But among pious causes the defence of one's country and of the rights of the kingdom must not be accounted the least. . . .[1]

An essential point made by Ockham is that the kings and other bene- factors of the English Church were the original owners of the property so donated, not the Pope :

> therefore when they gave their gifts to English churches, they were able to ordain how those goods were to be expended and how much power the clergy and the Pope should have in them ; nor has anyone any power over them except what the kings of England have conferred upon the donees. Wherefore if the kings of England neither tacitly nor expressly gave the Pope any power over those goods, the Pope has in the ordinary course no power over them at all.[2]

It would be interesting to know how far this argument was " inspired " by Edward III, at that time in close communication with Lewis of Bavaria.

It is unlikely that views such as these added much to Ockham's unpopularity with the Curia at Avignon ; much more dangerous, in the eyes of the orthodox, was the treatise he put out at the end of 1347 or early 1348, directed against the declaration which Clement VI made obligatory upon all persons about to be promoted to higher office in the Church (*quilibet notabiliter promovendus in ecclesia*). The occasion was the succession to the Empire of Charles IV, the " Emperor of the priests," in the room of Lewis of Bavaria. Clement's formula, issued

---

[1] *Ibid.*, p. 258. Dr. Scholz, *op. cit.*, p. 170, dates this treatise " between 1338 and 1340 " ; but its editors in *Opera Politica* convincingly narrow the limits from between August 1338 and the end of 1339 (i. 225–7).

[2] *Ibid.*, i. 261–2.

29 November 1347, consisted of three undertakings. The prelate-elect
was to confess the Catholic faith

> and believe and hold, as the Church holds, that it does not belong to the
> Emperor to depose the supreme pontiff or to elect or create another ; he
> was to swear that he would obey the decisions of Pope Clement and the
> Roman Church in dealing with the former supporters of Lewis of Bavaria ;
> and to promise faithfulness to the Pope and obedience to Charles as Roman
> king approved by the same Church.

Ockham observed that the letter was a letter of abjuration and confusion rather than one of "good confession," and that it had sown
schism and discord.[1]   Under the first head, he argued that no pope who
was a firm and proper pastor would ever be proceeded against by an
Emperor ; such action had never been known.   If the Pope deviates
from the Catholic faith, he ceases to be a prelate of the Church, and can
be proceeded against by the Emperor.   It is absurd to say that the
Empire, which is from God alone, lacks the authority and power to
denounce the Pope and to depose him when he goes astray from the
faith or errs in morality.   On the second point, there is serious doubt
whether Clement, a man of irregular life, has not entered the sheepfold
by the wrong way.   He is a hireling rather than a shepherd.   His
character and morals suggest that he is no true Pope, and his support of
the errors of John XXII proves it.   On the third, Charles cannot be
admitted as a true Emperor because he is a Luxemburg, a descendant of
Henry VII who was excommunicated by the Church, and, because of
this, can only be legitimized by the grace of Avignon.   He is no more
than *rex clericorum*, the clerks' king, the stipendiary of the Avignonese.

It was this treatise that aroused the wrath of Ockham's most vigorous
opponent, Conrad of Mengenberg, the anti-Franciscan author of the
Planctus ecclesiae, who in 1354 sent Charles IV, through Bishop Frederick
of Regensburg, a tract against William of Ockham.   He composed it,
he said, when he was waiting in Nuremberg for an occasion to present
to the Emperor his book on the *translatio imperii a grecis in Francos et
Germanos*, for in that city a *quaternulus quidam* that professed to be written
by Ockham came into his hands.   His opinion of the Englishman is interesting.   Ockham had, he thought, captivated so many philosophers that
a third of those now engaged in that study had "apostatized from solid
philosophy."   Conrad compares Ockham to the dragon of the Apocalypse,
the great enemy of the Church and the corruptor of youth.   He is the
heresiarch of his age, and from Clement VI he repeats the statement that
Ockham was the teacher of the abominable heretics Marsilius of Padua
and John of Jandun.   There is one curious personal touch.   Twelve

[1] Scholz, *op. cit.*, p. 348.

years ago, Conrad says, Ockham sent a fellow-Franciscan, an English-man, to ask him to avoid censorious expressions whenever disputing against Ockham.[1]   This means that the German was on Ockham's tracks as early as 1342 ; and from his *Treatise against William Ockham* can be gleaned evidence to suggest that Conrad knew the early part of the *Dialogus*.   " About all the cardinals and the whole clergy falling into error, I reply that it is impossible for all the prelates of the Church and the whole clergy to err in the faith, while the laymen walk in the right path."   The allusion to Ockham's view about the *tota multitudo* going astray is obvious.

Very nearly the last of his controversial works is the *De imperatorum et pontificum potestate* which Professor McIlwain has analysed so fully. This, as I suggested, contains a development of chapter xvii of the first Treatise in the *De gestis diversorum Christianorum*.   There is no *dicitur* here. The point of view is concise and Ockham's own.   Yet, in spite of the extreme bitterness which he feels against Avignon, he is never extreme. It is the view of a constitutional liberal, not of an anti-papal zealot, that demands our scrutiny.

The trouble in the Church, Ockham argues, arises from the fact that the Roman pontiffs have left their own province and stretched out their hands to what is not theirs.   They argue that they can do this because of Christ's commission to Peter ; but neither in temporalities nor in spiritualities did Peter ever have such plenitude of power as to be able to do everything not forbidden by divine law or the law of nature. Peter and his successors have, in fact, received a limited spiritual power and a carefully bounded temporal authority.   The principate instituted by Christ *nequaquam regulariter ad temporalia se extendit* ;[2] it does not extend to the rights and liberties of others, enabling the Pope to remove or disturb them, especially those of emperors, kings, princes and other laity.   And in spiritual matters, the *quodcunque ligaveris* must be under-stood " with its exceptions " ;[3] and one of these exceptions is character-istic of Franciscan argument.   The " principate instituted by God " has been so ordained for the good of its subjects, *propter bonum subditorum* ; it is a *principatus ministrativus*, a principate of service, rather than one of domination, which, to use a Greek name, is called despotic.   The minis-terial kind, being " in respect of free men," is much nobler and greater in dignity than the principate of domination (*qui est respectu servorum*).[4] Readers of Conciliar literature will recollect that to Cusanus the papal supremacy rests upon the fact that the Pope is *maior in administratione*.

Professor McIlwain very justly comments upon the height of

---

[1] Scholz, *op. cit.*, p. 366.   [2] *Ibid.*, p. 457.
[3] *Ibid.*, p. 459.   [4] *Ibid.*, p. 462.

Ockham's ideal for the papacy.[1]   In answering the question (ch. xiii) *wherein consists the sublimity of the apostolic principate*, Ockham gives a definition of the Pope's judicial supremacy which would have commended itself to Innocent III.   The papal supremacy, he says, is seen

> in the fact that the Pope by divine right can, as a matter of course or by way of a special case (*regulariter vel casualiter*), do all things which are necessary for the governance and regiment of the faithful, although in the normal course of events there are certain limits set to this power which he is not usually allowed to transgress ; and what these limits are is clear from what we said above, although it is not clear what are the cases in which lawful exercise is made of those powers that are not granted to him as a matter of ordinary routine.   And perhaps we cannot lay down any general rule about them ; but in dealing with them it is necessary to proceed with deliberation according to the discretion and counsel of the wisest men who love justice most sincerely without acceptance of persons, if such men are available, whether poor or rich, subordinates or prelates.   If such persons are not forthcoming, the case must be passed over, lest the Pope, out of ignorance (under which in fact he often labours), perilously transgress the ancient limits and decree sentences which by divine law are null.

Jure divino the Pope can do all things " necessary for the government of the faithful " :   in practice he should go circumspectly.   Here is the position, put in another way (ch. xii), and in the form of a reply to the orthodox papalist :

> The community of the faithful ought [the objector urges] to be subject to one head and supreme judge in all causes and cases arising, since otherwise it would not be best ordered, because it would have several heads, or lack a head, both monstrous conditions.   But none beside the Pope is the head of all the faithful in everything ; the Emperor no, since spiritual things do not belong to him ; therefore to the Pope, in every respect, the community of the faithful is subject.
>
> To which I reply that just as the archbishop in his archbishopric, and the patriarch in his patriarchate, are heads and supreme judges in spiritual things, though neither can take cognisance of the cases that come before their subordinates, unless by consent or some other legal way those cases are brought before them (Causa IX, Quaestio 3, ch. viii, *Conquestus*) ;[2] and therefore neither archbishop nor patriarch is regularly and ordinarily judge within his spheres, in every matter ;   so, though not all the faithful are immediately subject in all things to the Pope, nor is the Pope in many matters their judge, yet, because in the necessary definition of every case by a judge, whether in the ordinary course or on special occasion, by divine law there should be some one deciding authority, therefore we must concede that the Pope below Christ is head and judge of all the faithful.

In the last resort Ockham cannot escape from a unitary theory of papal

---

[1] *The Growth of Political Thought*, p. 296.   This is especially marked in ch. xii. (Scholz, p. 467.)

[2] *Corpus Iuris Canonici* (ed. Friedberg), i. 608–609.

sovereignty ; it was Marsilius who knew how to do that. The liberal tries to curtail the operation of the papal power ; the revolutionary does not argue about the *plenitudo*. He denies it altogether. It is, however, less easy to follow Professor McIlwain when he says :

> The part of his [Ockham's] thought most unusual and most noteworthy is his reservation of the ultimate decision even on the deepest questions of faith and practice to the Gospel alone, and the Gospel interpreted not by the Pope or apparently even by the clergy alone, but by " the discretion and counsel of the wisest men sincerely zealous for justice without acceptance of persons," etc.

If the first of these passages which I have translated above is carefully read, Ockham's meaning will be clear. He is not referring to the Gospel at all, but to the help of expert jurisconsults at the Curia, who will advise the Pope whether he can exercise his jurisdiction in a particular matter (*casualiter*). To make Ockham anticipate the claim to private judgment, " acted upon though disavowed afterward by the Protestant leaders of the sixteenth century," is to credit him with thoughts beyond even the power of the *inceptor venerabilis*.

Looking back upon these treatises, one has to admit that Ockham is very formidable : not because of the reservations, the delicate balancing of his mind, his philosopher's caution and circumspection—these we might expect ; but because of the frightening efficiency and comprehensiveness with which he enumerates every possible argument for the sides he is trying to represent. The case for and against the papacy has become so stereotyped, the accumulation of thesis one way or the other so vast, that one wonders whether the true spirit of secular or of ecclesiastical government has not vanished in this bloodless parchmented combat. The passion of Dante for a true world civilization under the power that should reconcile or moderate dissident wills ; the fierce longing of Peter Damiani for justice, nay righteousness, under the spiritual sword —where are such strivings now ? Reduction to formula seems to be sapping the freshness of the medieval world.

CHAPTER VI

SIR JOHN FORTESCUE AND THE LAW OF NATURE

ALL that took a prominent part in the government of England during the years 1437–1471 must at times have wished themselves burgesses of Bristol or prosperous woolmen of Northleach or Chipping Campden. Public life was a dangerous crust, the fires of private jealousy and dynastic dissension beneath ; and the cause of the peril, stated in its broadest terms, was nothing less than a great usurpation which had placed on the throne, at a time when notions of public law and of the extent of the royal prerogative were still in a state of primitive confusion, a dynasty insecure in its foundations. It is easy to make too much of the family broils and dissensions of this unquiet time ; it is equally simple to regard them as an irrelevance in the social and economic growth of England. Neither view is adequate, but the first comes nearest to the truth, however old-fashioned it may sound. Our history until the days of democracy, and perhaps even beyond, is the history of our families, of the local leadership that gave tone and life to the countryside and formed the opinion of our people. "With whom haldes yow ? " was the question asked by the rebels in 1381 : "Wyth Kinge Richarde and wyth the trew Communes." The families must hold with the king's person from which the attributes of royalty are inseparable. The intimate connexion of royal person and royal office, of the *persona* and *officium regis*—perhaps one of the very few constitutional doctrines generally accepted—shows us why this necessity was paramount. Those who have read Maitland's famous essay on the Crown as Corporation Sole will not forget the emphasis that he lays on the medieval king's person in its inherent connexion with the medieval State.

In 1399 Henry of Bolingbroke had made a comprehensive claim to the throne, doubtless in consideration of the varying views of what constituted a valid title. He claimed the Crown in virtue of being in the direct line of succession from Henry III, by the right of divine favour shown to him in his recovery of it, and—this by implication—by the right as well as the duty of removing a lawless king. This was to safeguard himself very carefully, and the lords spiritual and temporal and all the estates, we are told, " consented that the said duke should reign over them." Most scholars now accept Dr. Lapsley's contention that Henry was anxious to avoid a parliamentary deposition ; it was judiciously arranged, after considerable thought given to the matter, that Richard should convey his enforced resignation to an assembly that was not legally a parliament, and parliament, when it actually met, formally accepted the *de facto* revolution. Until 1406, the year after Scrope's condemnation, no attempt was made to secure the succession by statute. The lords and commons had ratified a *fait accompli*, and given no express opinion upon the grounds for the validity of Henry's title. But in this year the statute of VII Henry IV c. 2 was passed, entailing the kingdom and Crown upon Henry's sons. It may have been no more, perhaps, than a statutory declaration of existing law ; but, as Dr. S. B. Chrimes has pointed out,[1] it is the manner of the enactment rather than its provision that is significant. The speaker came before the king and lords in parliament, and prayed that the commons might have communication with all the lords, and the king granted the petition. After consulting with lords and commons, Archbishop Arundel, in their name, put forward a petition touching the inheritance and succession to the Crown, and prayed that the king would affirm it in parliament, and that it might be enacted and enrolled upon the rolls of parliament and held and proclaimed as a statute. Finally, it was assented by the king and the lords that the petition should be exemplified under the great seal, and also sealed under the seals of the lords and the seal of the arms of John Tiptoft, speaker of the commons, and in their name.[2] Now sealing as a part of the authenticating of statutes is sometimes mentioned in the year-books ; but this was something of deeper implication than the ordinary statute, for it required the great seal, the seals of individual lords and of the commons collectively. The importance of the Act could not fail to appear. Henceforth, there was to be a title to the throne by statute.

Could such a title withstand a claim of indefeasible hereditary right ? The statute of 1406 was directed against legitimism, the regular weapon of Henry IV's enemies ; it remained to be seen whether someone would have the courage to say that hereditary right was something so indelible that no statute could obliterate it. It took fifty-four years and a good deal of courage for this to happen, for the eventual claimant and his friends had been attainted in the Coventry parliament in 1459, and the remainder of the lords had taken solemn oaths of allegiance to Henry VI as King " by succession born to reign." The duke of York's *coup d'état* in June 1460 placed the earl of Warwick in control of the king's person, and the Yorkists in charge of the administrative offices. But the lords who had sworn to uphold the king were not to be rushed or treated

---

[1] *English Constitutional Ideas in the Fifteenth Century* (1936), p. 25.
[2] *Rot. Parl.*, iii. 580–581 ; *Statutes of the Realm*, ii. 151.

cavalierly.   They secured York's claim in writing, and had it read to them, as the pleading of a person issuing in the high court of parliament. Then they consulted the king, who asked them to state objections to the claim.   They accordingly turned to the judges, who declined to advise, because, as they said, it was a matter between two parties, the king and the duke of York, and in matters between party and party they could not give an opinion ; they were the king's justices and had only to determine such matters as came before them in the course of the law.   This, on the other hand, was a business for the lords of the blood and for the peerage.   The serjeants-at-law and the king's attorney were approached, and likewise excused themselves.   Everyone had wriggled out, and the lords could no longer evade the issue.   They felt compelled to remind the duke of York of the " grete and notable Acts of Parlements made in dyvers Parlements of dyvers of the King's progenitours, the which Acts be sufficient and resonable to be leyed ageyn the title of the seid Duc of York : The which Acts been of moche more auctorite than eny Cronycle, and also of auctorite to defete any manere title made to eny persone." [1]   That is to say, the statutes were stronger than any documentary proof of descent.

The duke of York replied.   He said that the oaths of allegiance were invalid in the face of God's law and commandment.   The nature of an oath was to confirm truth, and the truth was that the peers ought to help in assisting in truth and justice, notwithstanding any oath of fealty made by either of the parties.   He pointed out, with devastating accuracy, that there were no acts of parliament entailing the crown save that of VII Henry IV c. 2, to which we have just alluded ; and he urged that if Henry had legally inherited the title of king he would not have needed such an act or (assuming that they existed) any such acts.   The act in question was " of no force or effect ayenst hym that is right enheriter of the said Corones, as it accordeth with Godd's lawe, and all naturall lawes, howe it bee that all other Actes and Ordinaunces made in the said parliament and sithen been good and suffisant ayenst all other persones." [2]   Right might be in abeyance, but it did not decay, and would never perish—here he struck at the Lancastrian claim of pre-scription.   The lords, no doubt as they were meant to do, gave way ; but the point to observe is that, when in the last resort they bowed to superior force, they explicitly recognized the claim of God's law of inheritance to be valid, and not to be defeated by parliament.   The whole episode shows that there were no clear principles of public law on the question of the succession.

There is evidence for thinking that the chief justice of the King's

[1] *Rot. Parl.*, v. 376.   [2] *Ibid.*

Bench who declined to give an opinion on York's claim was our Sir John Fortescue, who was acting until the end of January 1461 ; [1] in the later enforced retractation of his Lancastrian principles he said that the matter of the succession, as the highest temporal concern ought " to be treted and declared by the mooste profound and grettest and lerned men that can be gotten tharto, and not by men of my simpleness that have not moche labored or studyed in any facultie except the lawes of this londe, in which the students lerne full lytell of the right of succession of kingdoms." His pen may have been no less active when after Towton he followed the Lancastrians into exile in Scotland. Between April 1461 and July 1463, if we accept Mr. Plummer's chronology, he wrote four tracts upholding the Lancastrian succession, which he was later to refute, together with a very important treatise, *De Natura Legis Naturae*, in which this defence was embodied : [2] but embodied on grounds that call for special notice, both on account of the author's method, as well as for the detailed contents. For it is a treatise that meets the duke of York on his own ground, and is not concerned with parliamentary title ; and it shows that Fortescue was by no means accurate in disclaiming a knowledge of jurisprudence, as we may term it, in favour of specialization in " the lawe of this londe." [3]

The first part of the *De Natura Legis Naturae* might seem the work of a clerk rather than of a knight, however lettered. Fortescue complains a little too pessimistically of the narrow curriculum pursued by the English student of law ; he speaks of the lucubrations of twenty years devoted to the technicalities of the English common law, with little attempt made to m ster the civil law, the laws of other countries, and the general principles of jurisprudence. He himself is a fair example of a different tendency. Those robust English lawyers Hengham and Bereford might, had they lived then, have thought that he went too far in the opposite direction ; though they would certainly have approved of the comparison he draws between the civil law and the English common law in his *De Laudibus Legum Angliae*,[4] and the way in which the prince in the treatise is made to commend the knowledge of the

[1] See the chronology of Fortescue's life in *Sir John Fortescue, De laudibus legum Anglie,* ed. S. B. Chrimes (1942), pp. lxv.–vi.

[2] Dr. Chrimes does not feel certain about this date : " It seems to me a very formidable and academic kind of work to have composed among the plots and alarums in Scotland, where he is supposed to have written it " (*Sir John Fortescue,* p. xcii. n. 2). I am inclined to agree with his suggestion that it may have been written on the continent at a later date, and that Fortescue—like the Marian exiles later—took his books of reference away with him.

[3] Sir Frederick Pollock (*Essays in the Law,* pp. 53–54) has called the treatise an " artificial performance " of " slight interest and no value."

[4] Chs. xix.–xxiii., in *Sir John Fortescue,* pp. 43–53.

elementary principles of jurisprudence.[1] The fact is that the clerical tendency of Fortescue's mind is the normal reflection of the academic, as opposed to the purely vocational phase of legal training given at the Inns of Court ;[2] while Bracton started from the Roman law of his time, the legal student of the fifteenth century, if he had had an adequate education, and had not come to Westminster straight from a grammar-master, began with the scholastic philosophy and the canon law. The "Dialogues between a Doctor of Divinity and a student of the Laws of England," by Christopher St. Germain, published between 1523 and 1530,[3] show, for example, that the law student of the later Middle Ages took his background of general notions from Gerson's *Regule Morales* (especially for the exposition of equity or *epikeia* there set forth). The Doctor in St. Germain's dialogue starts with a summary of the teaching of the eternal law, the basis of the order in the universe provided by God's will. He then passes, in the order of legal generalities, to an exposition of natural law, defining it either as the law of living beings or as the law of reasonable creatures, i.e., human beings. These matters were not "academic" in our limiting sense of the word : for the second half of the fifteenth and the early sixteenth century were times when the court of chancery and the ecclesiastical courts were often pitted against the common law tribunals. As Sir Paul Vinogradoff put it : "Long before the struggle of Coke against Ellesmere and Bacon, Common Law judges and barristers had realized the danger of their position in view of the encroachments of the Chancery." The common lawyers had to know the basis of the opponents' arguments. In the Latin version of the *Doctor and Student* the problem of conscience and equity is given a prominent place, and the doctor's definitions are those of a philosophical canonist. He begins his treatment of conscience as a source of legal decisions by a Thomist disquisition upon *sinderisis*. Now Gerson's discussion of equity or *epikeia* is likewise based upon passages in the *Summa Theologica*. *Tractans non recusat subsidia aliarum facultatum*, remarks Fortescue : the auxiliaries are all called up, and of these Aristotle and St. Thomas are the greatest.

It is clear that Fortescue had pondered deeply the famous *quaestiones* of the *Prima Secundae*[4] which translate St. Thomas's theory of primary

---

[1] Ch. xiv., in *Sir John Fortescue*, pp. 35-36.

[2] On which see in this connexion *Sir John Fortescue*, pp. 117-121, and Dr. Chrimes's notes, pp. 197-199 ; the observations of the late Professor Tout, " The Household of the Chancery and its disintegration," *Collected Papers of Thomas Frederick Tout*, ii. 164-166 ; and, for an earlier time, W. C. Bolland, " The Making of a Medieval Justice," *Cambridge Legal Essays*, pp. 57-70.

[3] " Reason and Conscience in Sixteenth Century Jurisprudence," *The Collected Papers of Paul Vinogradoff*, ii. 190 f.

[4] " Cf. the admirable summary in C. H. McIlwain, *The Growth of Political Thought in the West*, pp. 326-327.

and secondary causes into terms of the law governing the Universe.
To St. Thomas all laws manifest the divine reason, which is eternal and
through God's providence exists as the norm or rule for the government of His creatures.   Such eternal law is the source of all earthly
law, to which the whole creation is subject, and in which all parts of
creation participate.   A rational creature participates with God more
fully than an irrational in eternal reason, and by the light of natural
reason inclines towards the acts and ends that reason prescribes.   But
positive law derives from practical reason, and is promulgated for
the government of a political society.   What, therefore, is its relation
to the law of nature ?   St. Thomas Aquinas draws a parallel here between
the speculative and the practical reason.   He shows that in the speculative reason the results or conclusions of various branches of knowledge
that are not naturally known to us are discovered by a deductive process
through our reasoning from principles that cannot be demonstrated,
but are naturally known ; in like fashion, human reason has to extract
from natural law, as from certain general rules that cannot be proved,
the laws which apply to particular cases.   This is how human laws
should be derived : to be truly laws, they must be founded in the precepts of law natural.   Now Fortescue is especially concerned to show
the relation between law natural and law positive (*ius regis*) ; and his
concern is intelligible.   He is about to appeal, in his argument, to
the law of nature.   If there is any serious discrepancy between natural
law and royal law, if royal law is to take the foremost place and natural
law to be thrust into the background, the whole argument would
break down, and the arbitrary acts of a king have a validity that nothing
could shake.

Fortescue begins his treatise, the *De Natura Legis Naturae*, by the
practical question, " A king recognizing no superior has a daughter
and a brother, the daughter has a son.   The king dies without a son.
Does the kingdom descend to the daughter, or to her son, or to the
king's brother ? "   In other words, could the female descendants of
Lionel, Duke of Clarence, possess, and, possessing, transmit a valid claim
to the throne of England ?   Were Philippa and Anne Mortimer *coronae
capaces* ?   Fortescue begins by emphasizing the importance of the question.   *Omnia amamus, sed principari magis.*   Monarchy is the highest
prize of all, and therefore the problem of the succession is of the greatest
significance.   The question is a legal one, but involves other branches
of knowledge as well.   Theology and philosophy (he implies) have to
be brought in ; for its solution necessitates another law than the canon
or the civil.   The civil does not hold in England : the canon deals
with spiritual matters.   It is the Law of Nature which must decide.

This was the code that prevailed until the granting of the Mosaic law upon Sinai, a period which, according to Josephus and Augustine, had exceeded 3644 years. But it remained in operation after the new code had been revealed, and Our Lord Himself confirmed it and enjoined it by the commandment : " All things whatsoever ye would that men should do unto you do ye even so unto them, for this is the law and the prophets." The canon láw expressly declared this to be the Law of Nature, and Fortescue quotes with approval the great statement of Aquinas that it is " nothing else than the participation of the Eternal Law in the rational creature." [1] This law " all the laws of the Old and New Testaments have approved." It is " natural equity," and under it kingship first " burst into being " (prorupit). Fortescue quotes various examples of just kings in the Old Testament who lived under the Law of Nature ; but a difficulty here arises over the case of Saul. If it is true that the Law of Nature established the kingly office in its beginnings (regie celsitudinis primordia stabilivit), why did the children of Israel sin by asking them a king ? If Samuel is made to say that the King will come and take away their fields and vineyards and olive-yards, does this not imply that the King is breaking the Law of Nature ? Fortescue answers that if the people of Israel showed themselves un-grateful to God, they would not thereby denigrate the kingship. Be-sides, the people of Israel had God for their King, and stood in a special relation to Him : " peculiaris vero erat sibi populus iste." Furthermore, the law of the man who ruled over Israel was not the law of any king, but of a peculiar and particular individual. On this point Fortescue seizes the opportunity for a digression upon the famous distinction which occurs prominently in his work, and it must be admitted that the introduction of the theme is somewhat laboured. The particular individual, he implies, may govern either royally or politically. He appeals first to works of history and to practical experience, next to the teaching of Aquinas, his continuator Ptolemy of Lucca, and Giles of Rome, in classifying all dominium as either regale or politicum. [2] But with an English judge's experience, he maintains that in England the two are blended, or coexist, in a dominium politicum et regale, a political and regal dominion, in which the king's power is supreme save in certain spheres delimited by law and custom ; [3] for in this country the kings

[1] The Works of Sir John Fortescue (ed. Lord Clermont), I. v. 68, from Summa Theologica II. i. lxxxvi. 2.

[2] Professor McIlwain, The Growth of Political Thought, pp. 358–359, has well shown the importance of these references in interpreting what Fortescue really meant by dominium politicum. The theory and the difficult problem raised by Fortescue's own statements of his sources, are discussed by Dr. Chrimes in English Constitutional Ideas of the Fifteenth Century, pp. 309–324.

[3] Chrimes, op. cit., p. 339.

do not make laws nor impose subsidies without the consent of the estates,[1] and the judges are all bound by their oaths not to give judgment against the laws of the land, even if they hear the king's mandate to the contrary. This is "political" dominion ; "*id est plurium dispensatione regulatum.*" Mr. McIlwain has shown how important is this notion of plurality in Fortescue's conception of political rule. He points out that it is not the consent of the estates so much as the legal and organic nature of the kingdom which leads Fortescue to make this statement : not constitutionalism so much as respect for law and custom.[2] Fortescue terms those Roman Emperors "political" rulers who ruled the Roman state *ad plurium usum.* This is very important, for, in Fortescue's way of looking at it, the State is compounded of various parts or communities, each regulated by law or custom, which the king, though with their approval he may change or vary it, is bound to respect. Such is the notion that he attaches to the word "political." It comes, he quaintly says, from πολυς, "many," and. ικων, "administration," "as it were a system of government administered by many." At the same time, the ruler governing politically is also exhorted to govern royally. Not all cases fall within law and custom. The chastisement of criminal offences and the administration of equity, "which is a superlaudable relaxation of the strictness of the law,"[3] should lie entirely within the disposal of the ruler. There are other cases, too, where the political ruler will also govern royally : in a rebellion among his own subjects, or in a case of invasion from abroad. A king ruling politically is of equal power and liberty with one ruling royally,[4] for, like royal, political rule, Fortescue implies, springs from the Law of Nature. It is of the essence of the Law of Nature to give each person his right ; and respect for the rights of individuals and communities is (if we interpret him correctly) of the essence of *dominium politicum.* The *ius regis*, in fine, must be subject always to the Law of Nature, which is certainly the

[1] Fortescue had had plenty of experience in the Commons. He had been returned for Tavistock (1421, 1423, 1425), Totnes (1426, 1432), Plympton (1429), and Wiltshire (1436), so that his observations about the consent of the estates should bear the stamp of experience : cf. *Sir John Fortescue*, pp. lix, lx.

[2] McIlwain, *op. cit.*, pp. 359–363. Dr. Chrimes (*English Constitutional Ideas*, p. 339) would draw a sharp distinction between a "limited" (as here) and a "constitutional" monarchy.

[3] I. xxiv. 85 : "Epiches, ut dicit Aegidius Romanus, est indulgere super justum, natura namque humana semper supplicat pro venia. Haec virtus, ut dicit Philosophus V° Ethicorum, justum legale non diminuit : epickaia enim dicitur ab επι quod est *supra*, vel *laus*, et καλα quod est laxa, λ mutato in ι, quasi *superlaudabilis laxatio rigiditatis legis.*" This is, of course, a familiar theme in Gerson's moral, as well as Conciliar, writings. Cf. *supra*, p. 9.

[4] I. xxvi. 88. This is in effect the well-known constitutional theme of the thirteenth century : cf. Holdsworth, *Hist. Eng. Law*, iii. 253–254.

case with the law of a king governing politically as well as royally. Errors in royal law should be reformed by reference to the Law of Nature : so, conversely, errors in political, just as much as in royal government. For *ius* is born from *iustitia*, as in theology the Son originates from the Father ;[1] the Creator willed the Law of Nature as His rule and instrument for ruling the world and temporal things. Even after the Fall, when original justice had gone, natural justice never left. The *lex naturae* is the daughter of the Divine Law, and all human laws are instruments by which the Divine Law displays its virtues in human action : it stands to the Law of God as the moon to the sun.[2]

Having in this quasi-theological introduction told us something about the Law of Nature in general, Fortescue comes to apply it to the present case. He makes the three parties, the late king's daughter, her son, and the king's brother, approach and plead before Justitia. The proceedings are not without humour. The daughter claims that the king's grandson proposes to exclude her, against both nature and the divine law, from her lawful inheritance. To the first of these charges the grandson replies that this is not a case where the analogy of private law will help. " Human law does not treat public office like a piece of land, or a position in a household." True, nature does not forbid a woman to minister in a lowly office or in a private capacity : but the higher offices like those of Constable or Marshal " nature has separated (*sejunxit*) from the administration of women."[3] Private estates may be allotted to women " for their sustentation " : but not so public offices. Turning to the argument from divine law, the grandson shows that the kingdoms of Israel and Judah did not descend to women. The grandson has the right to rule while his mother is still alive, for the Magi asked, " *Where is he that is born King of the Jews ?* "[4] The king's brother then takes up his plea, beginning with the argument from nature. Physically, women are not made like men ; their anatomy, as Aristotle has shown, destines them for different tasks.[5] *Bellare et iudicare sunt officium regis.* Warfare is the highest exercise of his body, judging the supreme activity of his spirit.[6] Socrates and Plato did, indeed, allow that it might be in the interests of the State for women to fight (*sanccierunt esse politicum*) : but in the *Politics* Aristotle implicitly

[1] I. xxxvii. 100–101 : " cum sicut Deus Dei Filius est, Veritas Patris increata, ita lex naturæ a justitia genita est veritas justitiæ creata quæ mundum quem condidit Veritas eterna conditum jam regulat ipsa sempiterna."

[2] I. xlii, xliii. 106–109.

[3] II. iii. 117 : " non ut agrum, ita officium, nec ut privatum ministerium, ita et publicum regulat lex humana."

[4] II. iii. 120.   [5] II. viii. 121.   [6] *Ibid.*, p. 122.

condemns such an opinion, the canon law repudiates it also, as well as St. Thomas in his *De Regimine Principum*, when he points out that the nature of an object reflects the purpose for which it is directed by the infallible Agent : and woman is weaker and less rational than man. Then (a little unkindly) : " Who ever hunts for hares with cats ? Nature made greyhounds for the fields and the pursuit of hares, but cats to remain at home to catch mice. For shame ! He who takes a woman, fitted by nature for domestic cares, away from her home to govern people is like the man who hunts wild creatures with cats." [1] But the incapacity of the son to succeed *jure materno* is demonstrated by the law of succession in France,[2] as well as by the ordinary processes of the common law in England. In this country, if a testator, in making his will, gives his land to a man and his male heirs, and the donee has no son but a daughter, the land returns to the donor. The grant has the condition implicit, but not deliberately expressed. Even if the donee's wife marries after her husband's death and has a son, the son cannot claim that land ; and if a son is born to the daughter while the father is still living, the position is not altered. Such a limited grant in England is called a *donum talliatum*, an entail.[3] Suppose the older son succeeds to his father's inheritance (granted that the donee has two sons) : if the elder son has no male issue but only a daughter, who has a son, after the original donee's death the estate goes to the junior son, not to the daughter of the elder or to her son. " The writer of this knows these things well, who has studied and practised in the laws of that kingdom for more than forty years and for long has exercised the chief justiceship (*Judiciarium*), the supreme office of the land." How is this case in the land law different from the one about which the main contention has been raised ? How can a mother transfer to her son the right which she herself cannot possess ? It is a rule of law that no one can transfer to another more right than he himself is known to possess.

Fortescue is here making the king's brother depend upon the concept of the kingdom as real property : *reale est quod petimus regnum.* This is very similar to the argument which, in the same period, made the taxes voted by parliament appear as the profits of the king's court.[4] The next contention advanced by the *frater regis* comes from Scripture. Christ was not King of the Jews *iure materno* : it was Joseph who was

[1] II. ix. 123.
[2] II. xi. 124 : " In Regno namque Franciæ, cum reges dominia sua dederint in forma predicta, et donatarii post se filias reliquerint et obierint sine fetu masculino, reges regni illius dominia illa concito resumunt, et ea ex tunc retinent pristino iure coronæ suæ, nullo huic iuri unquam renitente."
[3] II. x. 124.
[4] See T. F. Plucknett, " The Lancastrian Constitution," *Tudor Studies*, pp. 164–165.

the true heir of the kingdom of the Jews, " of the house and lineage of David," though the kings of that line had ceased ; but it was not through Joseph that the kingdom descended : Our Lord did not say " My kingdom is not *in* this world " : He said, " My kingdom is not *of* this world." It would have been *of* and *in* this world if He had succeeded by the right of His mother, or by some other temporal right. On the contrary, He became king *divinae constitutionis iure*, for before He was conceived God gave Him the promise of the kingdom of Israel for ever : " that of His kingdom there should be no end." " Wherefore let us not think that so lofty a power proceeded from the temporal succession of men." [1] The purpose of St. Matthew's genealogy, a genealogy not of Joseph, but of Christ, is not to show that Christ had the right to the kingship through His mother, but that He was of the tribe of Judah : it was, as we might put it, to emphasize His Davidic descent.

Then follow the " replications " of the king's daughter and of her son to the foregoing argument. The daughter complains of the unequal struggle : she has to repel the arguments of two men against one woman, and one of those her own son. She maintains that it is unjust (" against the Law of Nature ") that a woman cannot succeed in her son's lifetime, and that she is debarred from the throne because she cannot make war or judge. With the point of law she does not really deal ; instead, she proposes to show that a woman is *capax regalis officii*. Before the Fall, natural dominion, which, as St. Thomas says, consists in the office of counselling and directing, was always administered by the wise (for, as Aristotle in the *Politics* observes, *regens in intellectu et industria est naturaliter dominus*). Admittedly, after the Fall it was not merit alone that determined who should succeed to the rulership ; but it is not necessary for the woman to go to battle or to give judgments personally : she can do her royal acts through vicars, as David through Joab and Justinian through Belisarius.[2] The grandson, in turn, claims not as his mother's heir, but as his grandfather's. " I should have succeeded," he says, " if my father had been my grandfather's own son : why should I not then succeed through my mother ? " He follows this up by arguing that the woman was made to be subject to man. The man has a double dominion, one in common with the woman over all living things on the earth (*animantia terrae*), the other a *praelatia* over the woman and over all living things.[3] The man is like the rector of a city state who is *praelatus*, not only over the domains of the city themselves, but over all the citizens within. As was observed by the Master of the Sentences, commenting upon St. Paul's solution

[1] II. xi. 126.   [2] II. xv. 129–130.   [3] II. xviii. 132.

to the question raised in I Corinthians, xi., whether women should cover
their heads or not : there is no doubt that man is made in the image of
God, not according to his body, or any part of the soul, but according
to the rational mind. From which we must understand that the first
man, the rational mind whom God set over all creatures, was master
over his own body, and so over the woman who was potentially within
him, for woman was made of man. The woman, indeed, told the
serpent that both she and Adam were bidden not to eat of the fruit of
the tree : but the actual command was given before the woman was
formed (*plasmata*) and by using the plural, " *we* were bidden not to eat
of the fruit," she recognized that she was in Adam and subject to him,
to whom alone the command had been given. Her name, *virago*,
itself implies subjection. A woman did not bring forth Adam or Eve.
A woman can, indeed, conceive and bring forth, but cannot procreate :
it is the work of a man to create in the image of God, since to rule the
world and to procreate are to be the *ymago Dei*. A woman, who is
not the image of God or made in His image, cannot rule the world.[1]
To sum up, *Mulier naturaliter subest viro*. Deborah, Judith, the queens
of the Messagetae, and Semiramis (whose example is not for imitation)
will not help the argument as historical examples of reigning women ;
for it is principle which corrects the facts ; facts never alter underlying
principles.[2] Only women subject to their husbands can rule men.
One cannot help recollecting that, not much later, facts did very extensively alter Sir John Fortescue's principles, at any rate as expressed in
writing.

The king's brother replies that it is not the infirmities of women
which debar them from the highest rule, but the defect of natural goods.
Their incapacity to rule is proved by Divine decree, and only secondarily
by natural reason, and he proceeds to show why he appeals to the *lex
divina*.[3] True enough, this law can only be discovered by discursive
reason : but when revealed, it is more stable than the *ratio discurrens*,
and cannot be shaken by the mobility of the latter. Original sin, he
argues, struck the woman more severely than the man ; and he draws
from the events in the garden of Eden an interesting comparison between
the qualities of the *lex naturae* and the *lex divina*. The Law of Nature
left the woman to be subjected to her lord at her own will : *ius divinum*,
when the woman refused, compelled her by another's will. The Law
of Nature sanctioned her obedience to her husband : the *ius divinum*,
when she abused this liberty, subjugated her to her husband. The

[1] II. xix. 134.
[2] II. xxii. 137-138. " Ratio est quae facta corrigit : sed facta nunquam mutant
rationem." [3] II. xxvi. 141-142.

former directed that she should be compelled and governed by her husband : the latter, when the woman made naught of it and sought to teach her husband, made him a more severe pedagogue than he was before.[1] The argument is that the Divine Law, to which the king's brother is now appealing, binds men more strongly than the Law of Nature. None the less, we must rely on the Law of Nature for the solution of our question, since Divine Law is infinite and surpasses all human understanding : there is no comparison between it and human law, and the only possible mediator between the two is Law Natural.[2] Later on, he turns back to secular law and shows the grandson that A cannot transfer anything to B unless A has got it to transfer.

> In the kingdom of England the son may endow his wife during his father's lifetime with his father's patrimony *ad ostium ecclesiae*, provided the father gives his assent : but the son cannot do it with another's patrimony, even though the other give his consent. And if any grandson seek in the King's court property so entailed, although his father die in the lifetime of his grandfather, the claimant will say that the property descended to his father from the grandsire.

The *regnum* as such cannot, therefore, descend to the female either by divine or by natural law.

After this come the " duplications " to the argument by the king's daughter and the grandson, but these add very little to what has gone before. Justitia then sums up. In the nature of the universe the woman is subject to the man. In the state of innocence, the first man had " prelacy " over the woman by reason of the virtues with which he was able to direct and teach her. These virtues are the moral virtues, prudence, bravery and temperance. The superiority of the man over the woman is like that of the soul over the body, the superior part of the reason over the inferior. After a number of such arguments, the judge gives the verdict in favour of the king's brother. Then comes a remarkable ending. Owing to the government of the kingdom being in suspense while such debates are on, and lacking a defender, the situation is likely to damage the Church through the disturbance of the peace that inevitably accompanies these circumstances. Fortescue therefore urges his treatise to go to Rome and submit to the examination of the Pope : " For to him, as is mentioned in the previous treatise, Moses remits any difficult and arduous judgment that may arise in the courts of man, wishing that whatever he judges or teaches according to the law of God all sons of men may teach." [3] Such a conclusion might have pleased Innocent III : it is doubtful whether Pius II would have welcomed it.

[1] II. xxvii. 143.   [2] II. xxix. 145.   [3] II. lxx. 183.

The three main arguments of the king's brother—from real property, from divine, and from natural law, as determining the woman's place in the universe—constitute an interesting comment on the chaos of contemporary ideas about the question of the succession. It is clear that there are no stable principles of public law to determine so important a matter. The whole treatise must be considered an illuminating comment on the weakness of parliamentary statute, and upon the continued prevalence of the scholastic notion of the legal norm or censor, to which appeal in doubtful cases may be made.

But Fortescue is by no means consistent in his demonstrations. He begins by repudiating the use of the courts and the civil law for settling the question at hand. Yet in the last part of the treatise the king's brother draws freely upon them,[1] and his is the winning cause. Law to Fortescue seems to have been a vestment shot with many colours : there is the law of the Church, the law of Rome, the appeal to principle, whether deep in the eternal mind or apparent to the eye of reason ; and there are *humana iura*, regulating the practice of the courts. There is no need to point out that these various materials are not of the same quality. The Law of Nature, throughout its long history, has never been capable of being treated as a code to which judges can turn. It has been, in Sir Paul Vinogradoff's words, " a most powerful ferment in the evolution of legal ideas." [2] By the practically-minded it may be represented that the appeal from written to unwritten principle is vague and unsatisfactory as well as tedious in statement. The moralizing historian will find contradictions between theory and practice, and assess the argument from nature by its practical efficacy, which he will not estimate very highly. It is, however, worth while pointing out that the theory, even for strict legal purposes, was not simply of academic interest. *Ius naturale* might be appealed to in the courts. In 1468 Yelverton, J., said in the Exchequer Chamber that in the particular case he was deciding they must, like the canonists and civilians, resort to the Law of Nature which is the ground of all law ; and five years later the Chancellor declared that a certain case *serra dètermine solonque le ley de natur en le chancerie*. The history of reason and conscience in Chancery pleading is a lengthy one, and even to-day, now that equity has become so stereotyped, it is noteworthy that fresh appeals are being made to the test of nature to decide marginal cases.

Apart from his theory of *dominium politicum et regale*, there is nothing particularly original in Fortescue's treatise. The arguments from St. Thomas, the pleading of the parties, and even the appeal to the Law of Nature to decide the matter of the succession, are in a good orthodox

[1] II. lv-lvii. 172-173.   [2] *Common-sense in Law*, p. 242.

tradition. On the last of these points, those who have read the treatises supporting Edward III's claim to the French throne will not greet Fortescue's appeal to *lex naturae* with surprise. It had been tried before. But this does not make it any the less interesting. That the Law of Nature should have been employed to support a title based on an act of the estates shows that the authority of the statute was not thought to be of so fundamental a character as the principles from which all particular statutes were, in the last resort, supposed to be derived.

CHAPTER VII

THE BRETHREN OF THE COMMON LIFE

AT various times in the history of the Christian Church there have arisen communities and brotherhoods whose purpose has been to live and work in the world, yet by common rules and a common discipline to safeguard themselves and others from its contaminations : groups of men and women with some clearly defined social or charitable or intellectual purpose, such as the guarding of pilgrims the care of the sick and needy, the pursuit of Christian knowledge—or simply prayer. The military orders, the Franciscan tertiaries, the various eleemosynary foundations of the later Middle Ages are obvious, if ill-assorted, examples. In many of them lay or quasi-lay elements played an important part ; in and through them the secular borrowed the advantages of the religious without dying to society.

The communities that form our subject now, the Brethren of the Common Life,[1] had an individuality of their own. They were not immediately blessed or welcomed by the Church ; they were essentially products of the medieval municipality, and the small municipality at that, where life flowed more peacefully than in the greater industrial towns. They were a northern movement, linked to the piety and the art of the Low Countries, the home of grave and sober men ; and, more successfully than other groups of devout people, they blended strict discipline and subordination of self to the community with an exceptional degree of spiritual freedom and inward happiness.

Later we shall have occasion to notice the devotion of the young

[1] See the bibliography in A. Hyma, *The Christian Renaissance* (Michigan, 1924), pp. 480–494. The main original sources for the early period are (1) the letters of Gerard Groote ; the main edition is by J. G. R. Acquoy (Amsterdam, 1857), other letters have been edited by G. Bonet-Maury in *Gérard de Groote, un précurseur de la Réforme* (Paris, 1878) ; J. Clarisse in *Archief voor kerkgeschichte*, iii (1831), 5–27 ; H. Nolte in *Tübinger theologische Quartalschrift* (1870), pp. 280 f. ; W. Preger, *Beiträge zur Geschichte der religiösen Bewegung in den Niederlanden*, pp. 29–61 ; (2) Thomas a Kempis, *Vita Gerardi Magni* and *Vita Florentii* in *Opera Omnia* (ed. M. J. Pohl, 7 vols., Freiburg, 1902–1921); (3) *Jacobus Traiecti alias de Voecht Narratio de incohatione domus clericorum in Zwollis* (ed. M. Schoengen, Amsterdam, 1908). Important secondary works are E. Barnikol, " Studien zur Geschichte der Brüder von gemeinsamen Leben," in *Zeitschrift für Theologie und Kunst* (Tübingen, 1917, Ergänzungsheft) ; W. Moll, *Johannes Brugman en het Godsdienstig leven onzer vaderen in de vijftiende eeuw* (2 vols., Amsterdam, 1854) ; M. Van Rhijn, *Wessel Gansfort* (1917) ; Hyma, *op. cit.*, and *The Youth of Erasmus* (Michigan, 1930).

Thomas a Kempis to Florence Radewijns, the friend and disciple of Gerard Groote.[1] Thomas never forgot the impression made upon him by that remarkable man in the home of the society from which he drew much of his inspiration. The home was Deventer, the Flemish town of dark-stained wooden roofs set in the valley of the Yssel, which, as Hyma has observed, always remained the geographical centre of the Movement known as the *Devotio Moderna*.[2] The *Devotio* had, as it were, two wings : the Brethren of the Common Life themselves, and the Augustinian canons regular of the Congregation of Windesheim (to which Thomas a Kempis at Agnetenberg belonged). The whole unquestionably originated in the life and work of Gerard Groote (1340–1384), and it came to an end in the sixteenth century under the pressure of the Reformation.

John Vos of Heusden, a leader of the *Devotio*, said when he was dying in 1424, " Groote was the first father of our reformation, the source and origin of the *Devotio Moderna*. He was an apostle in his country, who kindled the fires of religious fervour in the cold hearts of men and drew them to God." [3] In a letter to Urban VI, William de Sarvavilla, chanter of the University of Paris, described Groote shortly after his death, when his enemies had got the bishop of Utrecht to forbid deacons preaching in public, a sentence which had involved Groote :

> Truly he was the Great, for in his knowledge of all the liberal sciences, both natural and moral, of civil law, canon law and theology he was second to none in the world, and all these branches of learning were united in him. He was a man of such saintliness and gave so good an example of mortification of the flesh, of contempt for the world, brotherly love for all, zeal for the salvation of souls, effectual preaching, reprobation and hatred of wickedness, withstanding of heretics, enforcement of canon law against those that broke the vow of chastity, conversion to the spiritual life of divers men and women who had formerly lived according to the world, and of loyalty to our lord Urban VI—in all those things, I say, he gave so good an example that many thousands of men testify to the belief they hold that he was not less great in these virtues than he was in the aforesaid sciences.[4]

William was writing to uphold Groote against detractors, and his praise, for all its warmth, has a conventional sound. It scarcely conveys the secret of Groote's appeal, the intimacy with which he could speak to every heart. Groote never became a priest—his humility forbade. He was probably the greatest popular preacher that has ever appeared in the Low Countries ; and " popular " does not imply sentimental or anecdotal sermonizing, but the capacity for speaking directly to each

---

[1] *Infra*, p. 152.
[2] *The Christian Renaissance*, p. 3.
[3] In Hyma, *op. cit.*, p. 39.
[4] In Hyma, *op. cit.*, pp. 37–38.

individual in his congregations.   In the Carthusian monastery of Monnikhuizen (where he had been undergoing a novitiate) they saw it plain,
and no one can read the account of him written by Thomas a Kempis,
the *Vita Gerardi Magni*, without recognizing that the apostolate that
Groote undertook in 1378 was a matter of general expectation.   He was
discharged from the house to preach and convert, not because he found
it hard to live the religious life.   The successful master of Paris and
Prague, with his taste for science (he had studied astrology and magic)
and his prospects of preferment (he already had two prebends), left the
world to return to it in a new missionary guise.

Such a man inevitably draws friends.   His were the younger clergy,
like Radewijns, vicar of St. Paul's altar in the Church of St. Lebwin,
Deventer, or younger teachers like John Cele of Zwolle.   And the
theology they must have talked was not that of the schools, nor can it
have been in line with the difficult, sometimes almost pantheistic speculation of Groote's friend John Ruysbroek, but must have centred in the
cult of the inner life which is found in people like the Strasbourg mystics
of the fourteenth century,[1] later to achieve expression in the writings
of the Congregation of Windesheim : a language poetical, but never
recondite ; drawing plentifully on St. Bernard, and Hugh and Richard
of St. Victor ; full of echoes of these great masters of Christian prose,
unoriginal but compelling.   Some of the circle lived in Groote's own
house ; and to it were invited from time to time schoolboys and copyists.
The copyists were an important element in the circle.   In a recent study
of manuscript and text-book reproduction at the medieval universities,
M. Destrez has explained the system of copying from " exemplars " that
made possible the reproduction of lecture-notes and sermons on a considerable scale before printing (possibly more expensive in its earlier
stages) took its place.[2]   The workshops or studios of the copyists were
places to which the young clerk might go to support himself after his
schooldays, before he secured a benefice or to supplement his small
earnings elsewhere.   Some of these copyists lived in Florence Radewijns's
vicarage, and the story of how they formed a little community is well
known, but can be re-told.   One day Radewijns approached Groote :
" Master, what harm should there be in our uniting our weekly earnings
and living the common life ? "   " Unite your funds ? " replied Groote.
" Surely impossible, for the medicants would attack us for attempting
to found a new religious order." [3]   Groote's answer is easily understood.

[1] Cf. E. Vansteenberghe, " Le mouvement mystique a Strasbourg au XIVe
Siècle " (*Bull. Soc. des amis de l'Université de Strasbourg*, 1927).

[2] *La Pecia dans les manuscrits universitaires du xiiie et du xive siècle* (Paris, 1936).

[3] J. Busch, *Chronicon Windesheimense*, ed. K. Grube, *Geschichtsquellen der Provinz
Sachsen und angrenzender Gebiete*, xix (1886), 254.

Already he had composed a constitution for a sisterhood which had united funds in the effort to live the common life. This was in 1379, and in that constitution he had expressly-stated that he was not proposing to found a new order, but simply to provide facilities for pious women to live the devotional life.

The early sister-house, known as the House of Master Gerard (since he originally owned it), was not a nunnery. There were no vows, and any woman could leave, if she so desired. It was simply a hostel with two matrons who bought the supplies and saw that the daily tasks— dairying, sewing, knitting, weaving, spinning, and so on—were performed. This was evidently the model that Radewijns and his young friends had in mind. Groote felt that if there was to be a community for men, it had better be a convent built for the purpose and an Augustinian one. A group living together under no vows would run the risk of ridicule, and even of scandal. The project for a convent materialized at Windesheim : but Groote did not live to see the other, the truly characteristic type of brother-house, for though he provided the inspiration, and suggested, by his instructions to the sisters, the model, the actual foundation of the first community was due to Radewijns. Rudolf Dier de Muiden states that it was Radewijns who acted as treasurer for those who lived with him, and " seeing that they were fully converted to the Lord, and were of so reasonable and adaptable a disposition (*tam tractabiles et flexibiles*), amalgamated their resources and made one common stock out of the several sums ; and so thereafter they began to live in common." [1] Until 1391 the group lived at Radewijns's vicarage. In that year the " house of Florence " was built in the Enghe Strat.

The other original house of the Brethren was Zwolle,[2] where Groote's disciple Henry Foppens of Gouda bought a house to lodge poor school-boys, and in the adjoining tenement two laymen built a house for the first little nucleus of Brothers. The great attraction of Zwolle in the early years of the fifteenth century was the teaching of John Cele, rector of the city school, who, as Hyma states, succeeded in collecting as many as 1,200 boys at a time from districts far removed from the Yssel Valley.[3] In Zwolle, therefore, the Brethren, after acquiring a new house in 1396, had a large field in which to work. The first colonies of Deventer were Amersfoort and Delft. At the latter the magistrates heard of the work of the Brethren at Deventer, and being anxious to secure a similar society

[1] Scriptum de magistro Gherardo Grote, domino Florencio et multis aliis devotis fratribus," in G. Dumbar, *Analecta Daventria*, i. 13.
[2] For the school here, cf. M. Schoengen, *Die Schule von Zwolle von ihren Anfangen bis zur Einführung der Reformation (1582)*, 1 Teil, *Von den Anfangen bis zu dem Auftreten des Humanismus* (Freiburg, 1898), 63 f.   [3] *Op. cit.*, p. 93.

of copyists, asked the mother-town to send them a group of Brethren (1403). Zwolle's colonies were Albergen in Eastern Over-Yssel (1406) ; then Hulsbergen near Hattem (1407), and in 1424 's-Hertogenbosch. In 1425 the Brethren at Zwolle had to leave their house on account of an interdict, and moved to Doesburg, where a new community was established in 1426. Zwolle also founded the house at Groningen, the home of Wessel Gansfort, while Delft founded Gouda (1445) and Utrecht (1474). The colony of 's-Hertogenbosch was Nijmegen (1469). In Germany there were many houses ; the earliest was Münster (West-falen) in 1400. The house at Cologne dated from 1417, and from Cologne various houses were founded in the Rhineland. In the Southern Low Countries the movement spread to Ghent, Antwerp, Brussels, Cambrai, Liége and Louvain.

It was between 1395 and 1403 that the main characteristic of these communities made its appearance in the building of the *Domus pauperum* at Deventer. This was simply a hostel for the poorer pupils attending the cathedral school. Such was the origin of the dormitory system established in various places (especially at Zwolle). Later, at Deventer itself, Cardinal Nicholas of Cues established the *Bursa Cusana* for this purpose. It should be emphasized that in the earliest stages of the move-ment the brothers were not schoolmasters first and foremost, but what we should call " home missioners." Later, when the Brethren them-selves taught—and some were distinguished teachers—religious and moral instruction was always prominent.[1] The early organization was a nucleus of some twelve to twenty persons, priests, clerics, and a few laymen, living and working together in a single house, and attached to it or adjoining it, sometimes in the same building, a small youth hostel for young people attending the schools in the town.

The purpose of the Brethren is expressed in a document originally identified by Schoengen as the constitution of Zwolle, but since shown to be a statement of the routine and methods followed at the Florence House at Deventer.[2] It may, in point of fact, be taken to represent both places.

Our house [it says] was founded and endowed with its small rents and goods in order that, after the manner of the primitive Church, devout priests and clerks with a few poor laymen might live there in common from the labour of their hands, that is the work of writing (*opus scripture*), and from the returns from certain estates : attend Church with devotion, obey the prelates, wear

---

[1] Cf. the remarks on their activities by G. R. Potter, in *Cambridge Medieval History*, viii., esp. pp. 711–712.
[2] MS. 73, G. 22 of the Royal Library at the Hague. Printed Hyma, Appendix C, pp. 440 f.

simple clothing, preserve the canons and decrees of the saints, practise religious exercises and lead not only irreproachable, but exemplary lives, in order that they may serve God and perchance induce others to seek such salvation.

The way to this was through self-examination, humility and all spiritual exercises—prayer, meditation, reading, manual labour, watching, fasting. Meditation was to be not only " on such subjects as induce men to fear the Lord, such as sin, death, judgment and hell " ; but, " lest continued fear might engender dejection and despair," more hopeful topics were to be pondered, " such as the kingdom of heaven, the blessings of God, the life of Jesus Christ and his passion." Sombre and happier subjects were to alternate throughout the days of the week, but " at festival times we conform to the practices of the Catholic Church, forming our meditation and exercises from the matter of the feast." [1]

The Brethren rose between three and four in the morning for Matins, " in an alert and lively manner, shaking off sleep from our eyes," according to the text of Jeremiah : " Rise, give praise in the night at the beginning of the watch, pour out thine heart like water before the face of the Lord, lift up thy hands to him." And while prayer is being offered no one is to spit or cough or yawn ; nor is he to turn over and flutter the leaves of his service book, especially in the Lord's Prayer or in the Creed. A period was set aside for the reading of Holy Scripture, after the hours had been said ; in this time " we shall avoid useless discussions and obstructive business . . ." At daily mass " we do not stand or sit facing the people before the service begins, but go to places in the choir that are free from all distraction." [2]

Manual labour was enjoined daily. " Human frailty does not admit of men being continuously occupied in mental exercises," and " the work of our hands makes us free, lest it be necessary to gape after the contributions of others." Chief among manual work is the *opus scripture* or copying. On weekdays the three hours before lunch (8 to 11 a.m.) were given up by ordinary clerks to manual work, but priests did it for two hours only (8 to 10 a.m.). After lunch manual work was continued from 12 noon to 3 p.m. Vespers were then said, and tasks resumed at 4 p.m. " On fast days we work till eleven and after lunch begin at 1 p.m." Work was to be done in silence that might be broken by ejaculatory prayer. The celebrated Block Book, *Historia seu providentia Virginis Mariae ex Cantico Canticorum* (*c.* 1465), belonging to the John Rylands Library, shows in one of its illustrations a picture of a group of agriculturists wearing the habit, cutting and threshing grain, pounding it in a mortar, and grinding it in a hand-mill. In the background is a little oratory with two books open on a desk. Dr. Guppy has suggested

---

[1] Hyma, pp. 442–443. [2] *Ibid.*, p. 443.

that in this combination of agricultural work with study " may be seen an illustration of the daily work of the Brethren of the Common Life, to whom have been attributed the engraving and printing of the book," though, naturally enough, " their connexion with the book cannot be definitely established." [1]

Cooking and sewing was done by novices and juniors, who were instructed specially to look to the water supply, and in winter prevent the drinking water from getting frozen—*ne canale sine aqua inveniatur.*

> At table we must sit in silence, avoiding all noise, so that we may the more quietly and attentively hear Holy Scripture read there. And we must restrain our eyes, and not look about to see what is going on at table, unless it is someone's duty so to do. And we must not be dainty (*exquisiti*) or particular about the amount of food or drink served to us or the way of serving it. In drinking we hold the bowl or cup with both hands ; and we do not roll up our table-cloths until the rector rolls his.[2]

After lunch during the summer months a short nap was allowed, and the Brothers were woken by the reader at table when he had finished his own lunch. The reader held office weekly. He was permitted " to take some food before the brethren enter the refectory, as well as to quench his thirst before he reads." [3]

After supper (about 6 p.m.) each man went to his room and did then what he liked, either pumicing books or drawing the lines on the quires, or studying or speaking with someone for the edification of his soul, until eight o'clock. At this time strangers had to leave, and the doors were shut. Henceforth silence had to be maintained until the morning. From 8 to 8.30 the Brethren prayed or meditated, and then went to bed. During this half-hour the practice of having evening addresses (*collationes*) became general. On weekdays these were for the house alone ; but on Sundays and holy days the Brethren gave addresses to which outsiders and the laity might come, and these seem to have taken place in the 6 to 8 period. From such a practice the Brethren got their name of " Collacie Broeders," the " Sermon Brethren," under which certain groups of them were later known as printers. During these evening hours on ordinary days the Brethren were allowed to talk to people in their own private rooms, provided that no such conversation lasted longer than half an hour.[4]

---

[1] *The Beginnings of Printed Book Illustration* (Catalogue of an Exhibition of Printed Book Illustrations in the Fifteenth Century, Manchester, 1933), p. 60. These tasks of manual work and study were enjoined by St. Benedict, and the books may represent nothing more than the reading prescribed by the rule : but the Netherlands origin of the Block Book is plain.

[2] The phrase is " mensalia convolvere." The cloths were in long narrow rolls.

[3] Hyma, pp. 444–446.   [4] Pp. 447–448.

As the communities grew, the offices of rector, procurator, librarian, *vestiarius* or tailor, steward of the guests, and porter were defined. The rector is more like an elder brother than the head of a convent. Though he is *paterfamilias*, he has no authority of jurisdiction (*nulla jurisdictionalis auctoritas*) over the Brethren ; yet he is allowed and obeyed in the interests of order and peace. His work is mainly administrative and presidential, and he acts as chairman of a financial committee to manage the affairs of the house, on which sits the procurator, the bursar of the community. The procurator receives the income of the house, donations, and the property of the individual brothers contributed to the common stock. He is not to be monopolized or distracted in his religious life by his work. The rules instruct him not to go running here and there in pursuit of his office, but to do his bursarial work in between his spiritual duties.[1]

The chapters on the *opus scripture* and on the librarian are of considerable interest. Unhappily the manuscript is illegible in places, and the lacunae are not always easy to fill.

> Let one of the brothers be responsible for the writing and preparation of books and the custody of the parchment, so that all the brothers shall have enough to write upon and correct examples from which to copy. And, if it be possible, let him procure Latin texts for all. And let him not say no too readily to any man who asks that a good book be written for him, although at the moment there may be no one free to write it, but let him ask the client to wait just for a little. When someone asks for a book to be written for him, for which he (the brother in charge) has a writer ready, let him show the inquirer the hand of the writer and make an agreement with him quire by quire : but in the case of the more notable books let him not make an agreement with any man except by counsel of the rector. Let him make the contracts clearly, and, if need be, in writing, that it may not be necessary to dispute the sum. And where payment in ready money is not made along with the order, let him not hand over the book before payment has been made or reasonable security to pay has been given, especially with a new customer.[2]

The Brother in charge of the writing-room has also to see that the ink is properly brewed " and is good for our writers " ; and he has to give notice when the evening sermon is preached on feast days, " that on the second day of each solar month, if it is a weekday, each brother with his companion allotted to him correct, and write in the corrections, before any further writing is proceeded with." [3]

It is the task of the librarian (*Armarius*) [4] to look after all non-service books and to see that they are properly labelled ; and to watch for fading in the text or holes appearing in the parchment (*ne quid exesum*). He is

[1] Hyma, pp. 450–452.   [2] P. 454.   [3] *Ibid.*
[4] More strictly, " keeper of the book-cupboards."

to remind people who have books out that they must return them at a specified time, and to send a messenger to the offender, if they are not brought back. "And he must let no book go out of the town without the knowledge of the rector, but no brother must presume to let any book leave the house, without the knowledge of the librarian." He must look after the physical condition of the books, and not let them get dusty or dirty. The librarian must point out the passage for the lesson to the lector who reads at table. Once a year he must make an inventory of all books in the house.[1]

There are many other clauses of note in this very practical set of rules. They give a picture of a methodical and frugal little community. One dealing with the guest-master is worth excerpting. The guest-master is always to provide guests with a book, from which they can read for the good of their souls, "to provide occasion and matter for speaking about God and the edifying and salvation of the soul, which book he must always place upon the table before he places before them the first dish." He has to wash the feet of guests, or (more mercifully) "have them washed, when they come on foot from a distance, especially if they are religious and devout; or at least bring them hot water that they may wash them." The house has to be visited once a year by two priests who are rectors of congregations, "and on whose part we presume special fidelity to our house and estate." [2]

There was only one promise made by novices when being accepted as Brothers: the promise of continence. This is "the good custom kept in this house from the beginning." Without it no one could be received into the *fraternitas*.[3] There was no actual vow of poverty, but it was a clear understanding that all possessions must be surrendered to the common chest. *Sit communis bursa, sit communis archa, sit mensa et provisio communis, nisi quod provideatur unicuique, prout cuique opus existit.* "Moreover, we ought to take care that we should not become too much attached to the things which we are allowed to use ; but so shall we strive to restrain our affection from love of our household possessions (*rei familiaris*) that if anyone is sent by the rector to change his room, he shall do so at once, bearing away nothing with him, except what the rector assigns." [4] Even within the house the habit of *meum* and *tuum* was to be avoided.

After John Cele, the two greatest teachers associated with the movement, Hegius and Wessel Gansfort, were neither of them Brethren in the full sense of the word, but had spent years in the dormitories maintained by the Brethren, and were in harmony with moral and religious

[1] Hyma, pp. 454–455.   [2] P. 459.   [3] P. 463.   [4] Pp. 467–468.

ideas of the *Devotio Moderna*. To compare them, Hegius was the humanist, Wessel Gansfort the moral philosopher. Wessel is a sort of John of Salisbury in the fifteenth century : an itinerant scholar, but, unlike John, refusing preferment at the end, and, again unlike John, caustic and extreme, often shocking his listeners with paradox and violent opinion, " the master of contradictions " (as they called him in Paris). Both had a full measure of wit, but Wessel little of John's polish and moderation.

Wessel was born at Groningen in 1419 or 1420, and his body now rests there in St. Martin's Church. He appears to have gone to Zwolle in 1432, and to have remained seventeen years in the *Parva domus* or dormitory erected by the Brethren for boys attending the City School. It was during this time that he made the acquaintance of Thomas a Kempis at Agnetenberg, three miles away. Wessel became a teacher and gave lectures in the dormitory from 1440 to 1449. This instruction was probably of a religious kind. In 1449 he matriculated at Cologne, and took his Master's degree in 1452. In 1453 he was at Louvain, the following two years at Paris. To Paris he returned for eleven years in 1458, a very important time for him, since it was there that he became friendly with Ockhamist teachers of the generation after Gerson and d'Ailly, and with theologians who had listened to those great masters. Paris was no less distinguished, with masters like Marsilius of Inghen and Albert of Saxony teaching there, than in the classic period of the great Conciliars. In earlier days Gerson and d'Ailly had supported the Brethren, and had revered Hugh of St. Victor, a sort of patron theologian of the Windesheim congregation.

Then, after eleven years of medieval philosophy at Paris, Wessel went to Rome, and we hear of him there disputing about indulgences with two other graduates of the University of Paris, and being advised to keep his views to himself. In Rome he made friends with Francesco della Rovere, afterwards Sixtus IV, and with Bessarion. In 1470 he returned to Paris, where he met the German humanist, John Reuchlin, who, as Melancthon tells us, greatly liked and respected him. Melancthon has a story that in 1473 Wessel was expelled from Paris for having attacked the superstitious views of certain dignitaries in the Church. Whatever may be the truth of this, there is no doubt that at Paris Wessel was a great success. One scholar said of him that he was either a second Alan of Lille or an angel or something that he would not name. His outspoken views on the hierarchy and the administrators of the Church made him many enemies. Characteristically Wessel never asked for any honours or dignities, and preferred to remain a teacher to the end. His biographer, Dr. Van Rhijn, is inclined to believe the story that

Sixtus IV, after being lectured and exhorted by Wessel to see that his reputation should correspond with his name, told him to ask something for himself. " Well then," said Wessel, " I beg you to give me a Greek and a Hebrew bible from the Vatican Library." " These shall be given to you," said Sixtus ; " but, you foolish man, why do you not ask for a bishopric or something similar ? " " Because I do not need it," Wessel replied.[1]

On his way from Rome he visited Florence, where the Platonic academy of Lorenzo and Ficino was flourishing. It does not appear to have impressed him much. He expressed his views about universities and academies in his treatise on the Sacrament of Penance. Drawing a contrast between wisdom and knowledge, he says :

> There is a knowledge that may be useless and vain : such is all knowledge that follows truth out of curiosity. . . . There is a strong and weighty argument against universities to be drawn from the fact that Paul secured but little fruit at Athens, accomplishing more in the neighbouring city of Corinth and in Thessaly, which was then almost barbarous, than in the Attic city, at that time the fountain of Greek philosophy. It goes to show that liberal studies are not very pleasing to God.

Wessel, who knew many humanists, remained at heart a man of earlier ideals. It was natural, therefore, that he should gravitate back to the humble men of piety, to spend the rest of his life at Zwolle, Agnetenberg, and in the end Groningen.

Wessel was a great and stimulating teacher. He has been called by Hyma a mystic, but unless we use the term mysticism very loosely, there is little in his work that answers to that description. His writing is the work of a devotional spirit, who had read many truly mystical writers, and sometimes indeed borrows their terminology, but never goes outside himself or becomes rapt in the ecstasy of communion with God or receives illumination or revelation denied to others. His theory of knowledge is genuinely Augustinian, and might have been found in St. Bonaventura :

> Therefore what Aristotle calls the active intellect, I call the light of God's countenance. What he says concerning conscience and reason pleading the best things, I ascribe, not to any power of the soul or to the natural state of the soul, but rather to the breath of.life breathed into man by divine power, and to divine assistance not only for the will but also for the intelligence.[2]

Of Wessel Luther remarked, " If I had read his works earlier, my enemies might think that Luther had absorbed everything from Wessel,

---

[1] *Wessel Gansfort* (1917), pp. 104–105.
[2] " On the Sure and Benign Providence of God," in *Wessel Gansfort, Life and Writings* (ed. Miller and Scudder), ii. 90. On the theory of illumination, cf. E. Gilson, *La Philosophie de St. Bonaventure*, ch. xii., pp. 326–387.

his spirit is so in accord with mine." This is no proof of any " pro-
testantism " in Wessel ; critics of the hierarchy, of indulgences and, in
general, of the rather overweighted spiritual machinery of the medieval
Church in the fifteenth century were not uncommon in the Low
Countries, as Ullmann showed long ago, and Wessel is in harmony with
a man like John Pupper of Goch, who contrasted the legalism or Judaizing
tendency in the Church with the freedom of the gospel.[1] It was the
advanced, we might almost say the " modernist," position in the contemporary Church, that Wessel was adopting. As for Luther's statement, only one question need be asked. If Luther's spirit had been
genuinely in harmony with Wessel's, would the course of history have
been the same ?

This is not to deny that Wessel had convictions which must have
been disturbing to orthodox breasts.

> The Church's mediation of divine grace, a cardinal doctrine, had very
> little prominence in Wessel's thought. He conceived of the Christian's
> relations with God in the personal terms in which they are always being
> presented in the New Testament, and constantly refers to our Lord's dealings
> with His disciples and others as illustrating His relations with us.[2]

He was at one with the Brothers in the emphasis he placed on love as
the main precept of the Christian life. We must love our Elder Brother
and be brought back by him to the Father of Love : by the Elder Brother
Christ is meant ; and this love involves love of our neighbour. Wessel
affirms that we cannot love Christ except we love those whom He loves.

Dr. Miller has observed that the breadth of Wessel's religious sympathy is one of the striking things in his character : and he very rightly
draws attention to Wessel's treatise on the Communion of Saints.
One of the headings in the treatise makes its character clear : " Concerning the true Communion of Saints from which none can exclude another ;
in which none but God alone can make one share ; and in which every
man is retained, however much he may have been excluded."

> All men, from the beginning of the rational soul that is breathed into them
> even until death, are wayfarers, and all these share in the one common supply
> of the light that shineth in the darkness. But certain of the wayfarers hate
> this light that shineth in the darkness, close their ears in order not to hear
> the words of the Law, and corrupt their ways in order not to keep the Law.
> And for this reason, there is another and more brotherly fellowship among

---

[1] The will, John held, may exist in a twofold state : the state of terror under the
law, which the Apostle calls the spirit of bondage wherein works of righteousness
are done from fear of punishment ; and the state of love under the Gospel, which
he calls the Spirit of Adoption. Cf. *De Libertate Christiana* (ed. Cramer and Pijper,
Bibl. Reformatoria Neerlandica, 1918).

[2] *Life and Writings*, i. 126.

the wayfarers that walk in the ways of the Lord and hear what divine Wisdom speaks among them : for it speaks peace among them. And those who " not having the Law, do by nature the things of the Law, these are a law unto themselves, showing the work of the Law written in their hearts." All these have the right to become and to be the children of God. Hence their communion consists of a fraternal relation to each other in God. And none can exclude a man from this communion or make him share in it but God alone.[1]

The reference to excommunication is clear. Again :

It is not then the charters of the brotherhoods that make their members share in watchings and fastings, in discipline and in prayers ; but it is the union of brotherly love. . . . Every man shares in the watchings and fastings, the observances and prayers of all religious orders, if he greatly desires blessings for them, even if no prior or chapter has given him papers for this. Nay, more, if he desires such blessings for them with more fervent longing than they themselves, he himself will share in them more than they that engage in them.[2]

Then follows a sharp criticism of colleges and fraternities, who have the right to allow their members a share in the prayers of the body. None who has

touched upon the matter of brotherhoods and the distribution of the treasure of a monastic college among outsiders and benefactors, has seriously studied the question : How far the prior of a house has the right to allow a benefactor to share in this treasure ; whether it should be proportioned to the piety of the benefactor, or the favour of the ruling prior ?[3]

Prelates and ecclesiastical superiors, argues Gansfort, " as they possess no arbitrary power over the effect of the sacraments, so they have even ess over the merits of piety."

The prelacy can bestow no higher blessing than that for which it is established. And it was established in order to secure a peaceful and inoffensive life for the servants of God with one another, in so far as the foresight and care of human frailty, aided by God, can secure it. But a prelate has no power to make a man more and more pleasing to God, nor does his authority extend as far as this. Under the guise of piety, through wills, they lay claim to fields and houses. Thus, through the words of the saintly rector, and through their own benedictions, they obtain disgraceful gain.[4]

Other propositions of Gansfort's may be quoted :

the ruler of a monastery is neither master nor judge nor depository nor dispenser of either the collective or individual merits of its members.[5]

The possessions, the shares, the inheritances, the rights of the citizens of

---

[1] *Life and Writings*, ii. 253–254. The parallel with Cusanus' earlier definition of the Universal Church as a *fraternitas* (*De Concordantia Catholica*) will be obvious.
[2] *Ibid.*   [3] *Op. cit.*, p. 255.
[4] *Op. cit.*, p. 257.   [5] *Op. cit.*, p. 258.

Jerusalem are not like those of the Egyptians and Chaldeans in that one man possesses more as another possesses less.

Sharing with others in that heavenly Jerusalem which is built as a city, is peculiar in this, that it does not involve loss to any possessor.

We might, perhaps, wonder at the emphasis placed on the more technical, may I say, professional aspects of the Communion of Saints, until we recalled the fact that this is the fifteenth century, and that more than in any previous age people were concerned with the official mechanism of intercession. The almost universal custom of founding chantries, the multiplication of fraternities, the emphasis laid by artists on the perils of the soul and the saving help of the saints, all testify to the relevance of Wessel's strictures about the perils of externality in religion and of his desire, in his own splendid phrase, " to bring that participation (in a brotherhood) back to the merits of the participant and refer the distribution to God who knows and accepts him." [1]

As time went on, the independence of the Brethren suffered not exactly a change, but that modification and adaptation to contemporary institutions and currents of opinion which every religious group and order has to undergo when the pioneers are dead. As with the Franciscans, even in the earliest stages of the Common Life the Brethren had to meet the criticism and pressure of the religious orders, and the ultimate similarity of their aim was bound in time to react upon their methods, particularly in the religious and moral bent which they gave to their educational activities. To what extent were these to be reconciled with a free and critical humanism? In this connexion 's-Hertogenbosch is particularly interesting, since Erasmus wrote two accounts of his experiences with the Brothers there. The first is in his *Compendium Vitae* or his autobiography; the second is in a letter to Grunnius. Neither of these are at all favourable. They relate how, on the death of his father, he was sent, when he was already ripe for a university, to 's-Hertogenbosch : the guardians were afraid of a university, because they had decided to bring him up to religion.

Then he lived, that is to say he lost, nearly three years at the brothers' house, as they call it, in which Rombold then taught. This class of teachers is now widely spread through the world, a destruction of good intellects and seminaries of monasticism. Rombold, who was much pleased with the capacity of the boy, began to solicit him to become one of his flock ; the boy excused himself on the score of youth. A plague having arisen in the place, after he had suffered some time with a quartan fever, he returned to his guardians ; having by this time acquired a sufficiently fluent style out of some good authors.

[1] *Op. cit.*, p. 256.

In the letter to Grunnius he speaks of his

> being put out of the way into a company of *Fratres Collationarii*, who, having
> vested themselves everywhere, make a regular business of hunting up boys
> to be trained. Their chief care, should they see any youth of unusually high
> spirit and quick disposition (of which nature are almost all very fertile minds),
> is to break his spirit and humble him by blows, threats, scoldings and other
> devices, which they call " breaking in," and thus to fit him for the monastic
> life. For this work they are much esteemed by the Dominicans and Fran-
> ciscans ; for these latter admit that their orders would very soon perish, did
> not some such seminary as the above feed them. . . .   True, I think, they
> have among them some not ill-disposed men ; but since they suffer from a
> lack of the best authors and live in their own obscurity, spending their lives
> in the observance of rites and ceremonies, . . . I do not see how it is possible
> for them thoroughly to instruct youth.[1]

The letter to Grunnius is not altogether above suspicion ; but in the
dialogue of Erasmus between Leo and Ursus *On the correct pronunciation
of Greek and Latin*, Ursus gives his experiences with the Brothers of the
Common Life. He says :

> I was educated by these brethren at Deventer, when I had not yet finished
> my fifteenth year. The procurator of their house tried everything to induce
> me to join the order. And I was a boy inclined towards piety. When this
> excellent man noticed that his work availed nothing, he tried exorcism.
> " What did he do, pray ? " asked Leo. " He took down a Crucifix and
> entreated me, as I was crying." " Don't you know," he said, " what has
> been suffered for you ? " " I don't know," I replied. " I testify that through
> this," he continued, " you will not do something to render this death in vain,
> but you will follow my counsel lest you die eternal death with the world."

A passage that might have come out of a novel by Father R. H. Benson.
Now between 1418 and 1484, when Erasmus, with his brother, left
Deventer, there is a great difference. In the early days Radewijns and
his successors, particularly Gerard Zerbolt, had to face persecution from
the mendicants, whom Erasmus, writing in 1510, actually links with the
Brethren ; and in those early days there was, as I suggested, little direct
education by the Brothers themselves, and certainly no forcing of pupils
towards monasticism. The brethren-house of St. Gregory at 's-Hertogenbosch had been founded in 1424 or 1425 by the Brethren at Zwolle.
Like Zwolle it supported separate dormitories for three classes of pupil,
poor, of moderate means, and wealthy—the three buildings of the Arme
Fraterhuis, the Mediocris Huis, and the Rijke Fraterhuis—and the boys
wore a uniform. 's-Hertogenbosch was, perhaps, the first real school
established by the Brothers, where at the end of the fifteenth century

---

[1] Quoted by Hyma, *The Youth of Erasmus*, p. 129.
[2] Quoted by Hyma, *op. cit.*, p. 131.

Latin and Greek were taught. It had a printing press, like Gouda : but before 1500 none of its leaders had made much of a reputation. As Hyma observes, it is very doubtful whether they had progressed as far on the road towards pure humanism as had Hegius at Deventer. And if we look at the inventory of the books, made when the survivors were finally sold in 1887, the forty-seven items appear to be more perfectly orthodox works of medieval philosophy. But perhaps the real secret of Erasmus' dislike can be seen in a more obvious contrast between the brothers of Zwolle and 's-Hertogenbosch. At Zwolle the tradition was to stand somewhat aloof and criticize the clergy : at 's-Hertogenbosch, just as at Gouda, the Brothers definitely co-operated with them ; they had a contract for masses at the Church of St. John. The atmosphere was clerical and orthodox.

How, then, did the *rapprochement* between the Brethren and the regulars begin ? If Deventer is any guide, the approach may have come from the religious orders themselves. In 1460 the great Netherland preacher, John Brugman, preached a sermon in the brother-house at Deventer, taking as his text, " Suffer the children to come to me and forbid them not, for of such is the kingdom of heaven." After alluding to Gerson's *De parvulis ad Christum trahendis*, he referred to Gerard Groote, who had tried to reform the immoral clergy in the Netherlands, and afterwards concentrated on training boys who might become reformers in turn.

> I like no order more than yours, except my own, namely the Franciscan order, and if there were no Franciscans, I would fall on my knees before you and beg for a place in your house. . . . I wish I had spent the time which I devoted to study in Paris at Deventer instead, for here knowledge and manners and virtues are taught which are more valuable than pure learning.

Then, addressing the pupils, he said :

> I expect you to listen attentively to your teachers in order that you may remember their precepts. But I also admonish you children always to keep God before your eyes in your studies, so that it may be your intention, when your studies have been completed, to serve God, according to the counsel of the brethren of the Heer Florens-Huis, who know which monasteries are good and which are bad.

Even if we take Erasmus with a grain of salt, these passages which I have quoted show that it is questionable whether the movement of the Brethren belongs directly to what has been termed, perhaps rather ambiguously, " the Christian Renaissance." Without wishing to be unduly narrow in defining terms, one is tempted to ask what can be meant by the expression, except the application of the standards and canons of Renaissance art and scholarship to Christian study and worship, e.g. the criticism and printing of the Greek New Testament.   Only in the work of a teacher like Hegius, first at Emmerich and later at the school attached to St. Lebwin's at Deventer, can we speak of the movement of the Brethren assimilating the new scholarship.   (While teaching at Emmerich, Hegius had learned Greek from Agricola ; but he never mastered it as well as some of his contemporaries.   He belongs to the earlier or Latin stage of the Renaissance, and, generally speaking, the movement was true in spirit and ideals to early, rather than to later, humanism.)   If, on the other hand, Renaissance means re-birth generally, and does not bear the exclusive connotation of scholarship, if it is religious revival that is intended, then we may fully admit that the Brethren definitely come within this category, and rank high among the reforming pietists of the fifteenth century.

Before ending, let us return to the more permanent and tangible legacies of the Brethren—their books.

To attempt to identify the work of the copyists would be a long and delicate task.   In the John Rylands Library there are interesting possibilities.   Latin MSS. No. 100, a volume of Augustinian nuns' offices which, Dr. James suggested,[1] may have come from the neighbourhood of Echternach in Luxemburg, is worth close examination in this connexion, as is the late fifteenth-century Horae, obviously of Flemish *provenance* (Latin MSS. No. 161).[2]   Another elaborate book of Hours which has the Prayers of St. Gregory (No. 163) [3] will obviously come into comparison, but of these two and of all manuscripts which can be called "illuminated," one thing must be said : the scriptor and the *pictor* or *illuminator* are usually quite different people, and their separate functions continue into the period of printing.   The early press very frequently omits the initial capitals, which are left to the limner to finish. To what extent the Brethren were artists and illustrators it is hard to say.

On the other hand, when we come to the Rylands incunabula, we are in no doubt.   The Library has five notable examples of the printing activity of the Brethren before 1500.   One of its best treasures is the Ghetidenboec issued by them at Gouda on 20 April 1496.[4]   This little book of Hours (*Getyde van onser liever Vrowen*) is specially remarkable for its illustrations and decorated borders.   The blocks for the illustrations were selected from a set of sixty-eight made by the " Second Gouda Woodcutter " for the printer, Gerard Leeu, and first used in Leeu's *Liden ons Heeren* in 1482.   Then they travelled round, and in 1483 at

---

[1] M. R. James, *Catalogue of the Latin MSS. in the John Rylands Library*, i. 181.
[2] James, pp. 274-276.   [3] *Ibid.*, pp. 279-281.
[4] M. F. A. G. Campbell, *Annales de la typographie Néerlandaise au xve siècle*, no. 840.

K

least thirty-two of the series were at Haarlem, for the printer Bellaert used them in the first book printed by him, *Dat Liden ons Heeren*.   They then returned to Leeu, who printed the whole in a *Devote Ghetiden*, published just after his arrival in Antwerp.   Next we find some being used at Deventer in 1493 ; and in 1495 fifty of them taken by Peter van Os for his *Ludolphus de Saxonia*,[1] published at Zwolle.   Thence they returned to Gouda in 1496 for the present Ghetidenboec.[2]

The other four now in the Rylands Library were printed by the Brethren at Brussels.   The rarest is probably the *Sporta* or *Sportula Fragmentorum*, by Aegidius Carlerius or Giles Carler,[3] dean of Cambrai. This consists mainly of essays and consultations on points of Canon Law. The date is either 1478 or 1479.   On 16 May 1480, the Brethren issued the *Breviarium Carmelitanum*, which the Library possesses, and perhaps— though not conclusively—the same year, the *Policraticus* of John of Salisbury, a particularly good piece of printing.   The Letters of Peter of Blois, undated like the *Policraticus*, but evidently printed about 1480–1481, make up its modest, but no less valuable, total.

[1] Campbell, no. 1184 ; Proctor, no. 9146.
[2] For their itinerary, cf. Sir W. M. Conway, *The Woodcutters of the Netherlands* (1884), pp. 40–53.
[3] Campbell, no. 398.

CHAPTER VIII

GERARD GROOTE AND THE BEGINNINGS OF THE "NEW DEVOTION" IN THE LOW COUNTRIES

UNTIL comparatively recently the origins of the movement known as the *Devotio moderna* attracted curiously little attention in this country. It was judged too medieval and too orthodox in character to have had much influence upon the course of reform, and the Anglican habit of relating all reforming movements to the Reformation did not allow it its rightful place in the history of the Christian spiritual life; from another angle, the sarcasms of Erasmus in his *Compendium Vitae* cast doubts upon the disinterestedness of its teaching, and raised among humanists suspicions that its aims and methods were ultimately obscurantist. Its reforming activities were mainly associated with the efforts of a single wing of, or group within, the movement that aimed at reforming the religious houses along the lines of the Augustinian convents of Agnetenburg and Windesheim, and small attention was paid to its appeal to the laity and its attempt to combat self-satisfied materialism among the prosperous middle classes in the towns. And the fact that it was, at any rate in its beginning, essentially a local movement, confined in the main to the western part of the ecclesiastical province of Cologne, still further confined its appeal.

In the present century the work of scholars like Albert Hyma,[1] Schoengen,[2] Maarten van Rhijn[3] and Post[4] has enlarged the social and intellectual content of the movement; and of late fresh studies of Thomas a Kempis have widened its historical connotation. Thomas, whom we now know indubitably to have composed *De imitatione Christi*,[5] wrote the life of the two men to whom the New Devotion owed most: Geert (whom we shall call Gerard) Groote and Florence Radewijns, and his absorption in their acts and writings, particularly in Chapter

---

[1] *The Christian Renaissance: History of the "Devotio Moderna"* (New York, 1925): "Drie en twintig Brieven van Geert Groote," *Archief voor de Geschiedenis van het Aartsbisdom Utrecht*, liii (1927), 1–54; liv (1929), 1–50; *The Youth of Erasmus* (Ann Arbor, 1930).

[2] *Die Schule von Zwolle von ihren Anfängen bis zur Einführung der Reformation*, Bd i (Freiburg, Switzerland, 1898); *Jacobus Traiecti de Voecht, Narratio de Incohatione Domus Clericorum in Zwollis* (ed. M.S., Amsterdam 1908).

[3] *Wessel Gansfort* (The Hague, 1917); and his *Studiën over Wessel Gansfort en zijn tijd*, (Utrecht, 1933).

[4] R. R. Post, *De moderne devotie, Geert Groote en zijn stichingen* (Amsterdam, 1940).

[5] L. M. J. Delaissé, *Le Manuscrit Autograph de Thomas a Kempis et l'Imitation de Jésus Christ* (Brussels, 1956), i. ch. iii, iv.

139

XVIII of the *Vita Gerardi Magni*, is reflected, as Fr. Debongnie has shown, in the first book (before 1424) of the *Imitatio* and other later passages in that work.[1] A large section of critical opinion tends to regard the *Imitatio* as a product of the Low Countries, in close relationship to the *Devotio moderna*, but until M. Delaissé edited the autograph many scholars were inclined to hold that so far from Thomas being the author of that work, he is not more than the second editor, the original being due to Groote himself. This theory, elaborated with great diligence by the late J. J. A. van Ginneken, is based on a study of vernacular " pre-Kempist " texts of the *Imitatio* and of Groote's Notebook,[2] and a minute examination of the manuscripts has led to revision and amplification of the original list published by M. J. Pohl. The argument is a highly specialist and technical one, and it would be impossible to give a full account of it here ; I can only say that the dating of these early texts raises problems which, in my judgment, have not been fully solved : but van Ginneken's work was certainly fruitful in calling attention to the literary form in which the precepts of the early pioneers of the *New Devotion* were embodied—the *rapiarium* or collection of ascetic or devotional exhortations, which grows, as it were, by accumulation, and may be re-cast by successive editors, and it does not detract from the honour of Thomas a Kempis if he gave permanent shape (and what a shape !) to the counsels of Groote and his disciples which the master himself and others may have committed to writing. Dogmatism in these matters must be avoided, but one fact stands clear : all the fifteenth-century accounts of the origin of the movement resulting in the institution known as the Brethren of the Common Life point to Groote and to the circle of Florence Radewijns at Deventer as the principal sources of inspiration.

If Gerard was, of set purpose, no academic theologian, and has not left works to equate him in production with his contemporaries Ruysbroeck, Wyclif, or even Hus, we possess a substantial group of *opuscula* by him that witness to his life and opinions,[3] and a number of

---

[1] " Les Thèmes de l'Imitation," *Revue d'histoire ecclésiastique*, xxxvi, Nos. 3–4 (1940), 309 f.

[2] J. J. A. van Ginneken, *De Navolging van Christus of het Dagbock van Geert Groote in den oorspronkelijken nederlandschen Texst hersteld*, s'Hertogenbosch 1929 ; *Trois textes pré-Kempistes du premier Livre de l'Imitation*, ed. et comm. par J. J. v. G. (Verhand. der K. Nederl. Akad. von Wetenschappen, Nieuwe Reeks, dl. 44, Amsterdam, 1940) ; *Trois textes pré-Kempistes du second Livre de l'Imitation* (Verh. der Nederl. Ak. v. Wet., afd. Letterk., Nieuwe Reeks, dl. 46, Amsterdam 1941). F. Kern adopts this point of view with somewhat indiscriminate enthusiasm in *Die Nachfolge Christi* (Olten, 1947), to which Mr. James Crompton kindly drew my attention.

[3] Dr. Paul Lehmann's reconstruction of the *Index Bibliothecarum Belgii* begun by the Ghent Dominican Vleeschouwer (d. 1525) and continued by J. van Bunderen

biographies[1] to illustrate his career and times. The oldest is the poem in Latin hexameters attributed to Windesheim and analysed by van Ginneken :[2] of the other seven, the best known are by Rudolf Dier de Muiden (1384–1459) who knew several of Gerard's more intimate friends ;[3] by Thomas a Kempis (1380–1471)[4] and by Peter Horn (1424–1479),[5] the latter account dating between 1440 and 1450. The two last were, of course, writing for edification or for reading aloud ; but neither can be called a hagiographer in the true sense of the word. These three accounts may be supplemented by the Windesheim chronicle of John Busch, who was born fifteen years after Gerard died ;[6] by the chronicle of Mount St. Agnes ;[7] and, as significant as any, by the story of the beginnings of the *Domus clericorum* in Zwolle written by James Voecht of Utrecht, a careful and faithful reporter of a very circumstantial oral tradition.[8]

In 1933 appeared the first complete critical edition, by the Jesuit father William Mulder, of Gerard's letters, which had hitherto been printed without full collation of the existing manuscripts. The edition owes much to the work of Dr. Acquoy, the pioneer of studies in Groote, whose section on the reformer in his book on Windesheim laid all students of the *Devotio* under obligation.[9] Mulder, who discovered 75 letters in all, collated The Hague and the Liège manuscripts of the

---

(d. 1557) in *Hist. Jahrbuch d. Görresgesellschaft*, bd. 40 (1920), 56–105, lists no less than 31 separate works.

[1] The best modern bibliography has been prefixed by K. C. L. M. De Beer, to his *Studie over de Spiritualiteit van Geert Groote* (Brussels and Nijmegen, 1938), in which the original writings of Groote are listed. See also n. 4.

[2] J. J. A. van Ginneken, *Geert Groote's levensbeeld naar de oudste gegevens bewerkt* (Verh. der Nederl. Ak. v. Wet., afd. Letterk., Nieuwe Reeks, dl. 47, Amsterdam, 1942).

[3] In G. Dumbar, *Analecta, seu vetera aliquot scripta inedita ab ipso publici iuris facta* (Deventer, 1719), 1–113.

[4] Ed. M. J. Pohl, *Thomas à Kempis Opera Omnia* (Freiburg-i-B., 1922), vii. 31–115.

[5] Ed. Kühler, in *Archief voor Kerkgeschiedenis* (Nieuwe Ser. 1909), vi, 332–370 : cited here as Horn.

[6] *Chronicon Windeshemense, Liber de Origine Devotionis Modernae*, ed. C. L. Grube in *Geschichtsquellen der Provinz Sachsen*, xix (Halle, 1886). Cited as Busch.

[7] *Chronicon Montis S. Agnetis* in *Thomas à Kempis Opera Omnia*, vii. 335–525.

[8] *Narratio de Incohatione Domus Clericorum in Zwollis*, ed. M. Schoengen (Werken uitgegeven door het Historisch Genootschap, Derde Ser., No. 13, Amsterdam, 1908). Cited as Voecht.

[9] *Het Klooster to Windesheim en zijn Invloed* (Uitgegeven door het Provincial Utrechtsch Genootschap van Kunsten en Wetenschappen, 1 dl., Utrecht, 1878, pp. 15–58). His (partial) edition of Groote's letters appeared at Amsterdam, 1857, as *Gerardi Magni Epistolae XIV e codice Regis Hagano nunc primum edito et perpetua annotatione . . . instructae*. For Windesheim, see *Acta Capituli Windeshemensis*, ed. Dr. S. Van Der Woude (Kerkhistorische Studien, Deel VI) (s'Gravenhage, 1953).

letters,[1] but departed from the order of the letters in these texts and arranged them chronologically, with admirable comment. His numbering and, to a large extent though not invariably, his dating are followed here. The new chronology[2] and the corrected and amplified text have thrown much fresh light on the circumstances of Gerard's life and circle, and carried readers far beyond the biographies of Bonet-Maury[3] and Grube.[4] It is clear that the medieval biographers of Gerard drew upon the more obviously didactic letters as *pièces justificatives*, but were not concerned with dating them, and recorded them either as manifestations of Gerard's opinions or as examples of effective writing. Gerard himself is equally unhelpful about dates. He often says where he is or where he has been or is going, but that is all : and often a vital addressee's name is missing. The fact that in The Hague manuscript Gerard's letters stand after a collection of the letters of Peter of Blois (whom Gerard much admired) indicates their value as literary patterns to the medieval student. It cannot however be said that they are easy, or that the student would have been wise in imitating their Latinity. Mulder is quite right in crediting Gerard with an obscure and contorted style, the reason for which is the intense Teutonic earnestness and passion with which he held his views, and his longing to engage the whole personality of his correspondent : not merely the mind, but the emotions. This can be seen in his characteristic outbursts and the wording of the final paragraphs, " Ach, ach, quando erimus ibi, ubi neque dolor neque labor ! " " Heu, heu, heu quando, quando, quando Domine ! Deus solus purus per se et plene ! " " Deficit pappirus, sed adhuc mens mea et amor vellent tibi loqui. Utinam scires ! "[5] Yet for all the explosive character of the language this is a notable collection, wholly redolent of its writer, burning with personal charity, with hatred of error, and with the dedication of a lofty spirit to the cause of reform.

The striking thing about Gerard is the shortness of his effective apostolate : only ten years, 1374-1384 : but they were the years that saw the outbreak of the Great Schism and the departure of most of the English masters from the University of Paris ; the publication of Wyclif's *De eucharistia* ; the revolts of 1378 in Florence and 1381 in England ; the quickening of the great controversy over Universals in the Carolinum

[1] *Gerardi Magni Epistolae*, quas ad fidem codicum recognovit, annotavit, edidit Willelmus Mulder S. J. (Antwerp, 1933), pp. xix-xxv. Cited as Ep.

[2] Previously as Acquoy observed, " De chronologische berekening van De Groote's leven is, zoover ik weet, nog nooit gemaakt." Van Ginneken (*Geert Groote's Levensbeeld*) has made a comparative table of the evidence, arranged chronologically, which utilizes the available sources.

[3] *Gerard de Groote, un Précurseur de la Réforme au quatorzième siècle* (Paris, 1878).

[4] C. L. Grube, *Gerhard Groot, und seine Stiftungen* (Görres-Gesellschaft, 1883).

[5] Ep. 64, p. 255 ; 18, p. 64 ; 25, p. 116.

at Prague ; the rapid growth of heretical movements both in the Netherlands and in England. The clergy of the diocese of Utrecht were talking about their own Lollards (Lollaert)[1] at the same time as the term became current over here. In this decade Gerard emerged as the Willibrord of the North, the evangelist to whom Voecht of Utrecht likened him.[2] In that decade he took his resolve, the result of a psychological crisis, to reject the world while living within it as a simple penitent ; formed his first community of renunciants, then under Ruysbroeck's influence sought temporary retirement in the Charterhouse of Monnikhuizen, to emerge (1378) in deacon's orders as an itinerant preacher under episcopal licence and as an incessant propagandist against the money-motive in the Church and relaxed morals among the beneficed clergy ; conducting a series of evangelizing tours throughout the diocese of Utrecht, into Brabant, Guelders and Holland, Zutphen and Groningen. *Discurrebat per patrias, scribebat epistolas, informavit pariter doctos et indoctos.*[3] The purpose of these visits was to recall the clergy from their increasing secularization and to draw into a spiritual community, a *civitas Dei*, whatever local form it was decided to adopt, both them and the laity, from the merchants and town councillors down to the humblest servant.[4] His campaigns he conducted not only by personal visits, but by didactic and pastoral letters, and occasionally by judicial action in the consistory court, in cases where the canons were obviously being broken and the *officiales* did nothing about it.[5] In 1381 he took the courageous step of denouncing, in the cathedral of Utrecht itself, the *focariste*, the clergy maintaining concubines,[6] and redoubled his activity against heretical sects, bogus medicals and divines, and preachers of hedonism on religious grounds.[7] His agitation and the actions he took to support

[1] "Domestici (heretici), dico Lullardos" : Ep. 9, p. 25 ; cf. Ep. 36, note a, where reference is made to the statement of William Heda (*Historia episcoporum Ultrajectensium*, 259) that Bishop Florence of Utrecht had the bones of a certain heretic, Matthew Lollaert, exhumed and burned in front of the door of his house. Cf. Horn, 346.

[2] Voecht, 5.　　　　[3] Horn, *loc. cit.*

[4] Ep. 19, to Henry de Schoenhove, gives various illustrations, showing that by 1381, the elements of a community life had become visible and that its members were sharing the modicum of property needed to sustain existence.

[5] Horn, p. 346 : " Egit eciam apud venerabilem pontificem Florencium ceterosque prelatos quatinus canonice contra eos procederetur " ; and Busch, pp. 260–261 (Bartholomew of Dordrecht) : " ad curiam Traiectensem eum citari procuravit."

[6] "Sermo contra Focaristas," ed. J. Clarisse in *Archief voor de Kerkelijke Geschiedenis inzonderheid van Nederland*, i (1829), ii (1830), 307–395; viii (1837), 5–107. That he was fiercely assailed for this is seen in the *Protestatio* published by Mulder in Ep. 57, pp. 214–215.

[7] E.g. Ep. 28, against John Heyden whom he found an ignorant impostor (" totum ignarum et nihil penitus scientem inveni," p. 123) ; Ep. 31 and 36, 37 against Bartholomew of Dordrecht who " penitenciam . . . et carnis afflictionem

it created a fierce wave of opposition in the diocese, that led to the bishop enjoining a suspension of preaching upon all clerks below the priesthood, and Gerard had never taken priest's orders, because he thought he was unworthy of them.   Being thus involved, the bitter disappointment, the frustration of his chosen task, may well have acted upon an already exhausted constitution to bring him to an early death at the age of 44 when plague visited Deventer.[1]   In the meantime he had given rudimentary form to the organization which was powerfully to survive his death : he had created groups of persons devoted to the Common Life.   The clerks and laity so converted and living, in Deventer, Kampen or Zwolle, lives of self-abnegation in common, Gerard called *Dei servitores* or *Deo servientes laici et clerici*, and during his lifetime the groups took definite, though varying, shapes.

In this brief paper three aspects of his life demand our attention.

1. His training. Gerard was *homo plene scientificus quasi in omni facultate*.[2] He was born (1340) of a well-to-do family in Deventer, one of the chief towns of Overyssel, a district within the principality of the bishop of Utrecht.   His father was an échevin and the family house was in the parish of St. Nicholas *in monte*.   Overyssel, which passed eventually into the domains of the Burgundian dukes, enjoyed under the Empire some measure of independence ; it was administered by a Council composed of representatives of the local nobility and the three cities of Deventer, Kampen and Zwolle.   Less wealthy than Brabant, less disturbed by feuds than the Liégeois, Overyssel was a trading and manufacturing centre with a tradition of learning and culture.   Its more promising boys were sent to join the Anglo-German nation in the University of Paris but some went to the Dominican school at Cologne, precursor of the University, or, after its foundation (1349) to the new *studium generale* founded by Charles V at Prague.   Significantly Gerard, a young clerk with means, is found at all these places.   At the University of Paris which he entered in 1355 he had taken the master's degree before 1360.   There he listened to the Ockhamist lectures of Buridan and to the theological teaching of Nicholas of Oresme, names distinguished in the development of fourteenth-century thought ; nor did he escape the new scientific current of speculation, derived from Oxford, that ran so powerfully in the French capital.   The constant mention of his studies in astronomy and of the books in magic which he possessed shows that

---

et similia verbo simul et opera dissuadebat, dicens Christum fuisse bonum socium " (Busch, 10-11).   He was supported by the Mendicants.

[1] By 1383 he had ceased to write : " nichil penitus scribo, sed obicientibus aliquibus respondeo " : he complained of weakness in the head : " infirmus sum cervice " : Ep. 61, p. 225.

[2] Voecht, 5.

he was deeply interested in experimental science. At Paris he became firm friends with one of the leading masters of the time, William de Salvarvilla, the Chanter, who after Gerard's suspension from preaching wrote to Urban VI commending his skill in the liberal, natural and moral sciences, and after his death praised him also for his knowledge of civil and canon law and theology.[1] The Chanter of Paris turned Urbanist in the Schism, when the court and the bulk of the University followed Clement VII, and had to leave Paris to take up the archdeaconry of Brabant in the diocese of Liège to which he had been provided. The provision brought to the north a notable reforming Frenchman, to whom Gerard could open his heart.

If by conversion he had abjured the world, he had not rejected theological studies, and the library he accumulated was, if highly selective, remarkably ample. Very soon after his conversion, he was found in penitent's garb in Paris spending a whole tankard-full of gold on theological texts ;[2] he was constantly borrowing from, and exchanging books with his friends ; frequently a text was loaned to him so that he could have it reproduced. He maintained, in his house, a special scribe Gherlac (the boy who later ran away) to copy manuscripts, and sometimes friends like John Cele, the master of the school of Zwolle, sent him money to pay the copyist for the work.[3] The copying tradition is one of the strongest legacies of Gerard to the brethren of the Common Life. Gerard was a keen book-hunter, and is found on one occasion securing for Cele a copy of the *Ethics* in Arnhem : he is deeply confused and ashamed of himself for retaining so long books that he had borrowed from Amsterdam : he *wants* to return them, but he is writing from Kampen and he will not send somebody else's books in the charge of a stranger. "God knows that when I send some one else's little book, I am more afraid for that little book than if I was to send all my own. Please send a messenger to Kampen and I will give the books to him."[4] On his preaching tours he took his books with him in a big crate or preaching case. Peter Horn relates that when about to embark for Holland, Gerard saw the devil sitting in a window and manifestly threatening him and saying : "If you take ship I will go with you." And when he was in the ship, there too were the powers

---

[1] Ep. 60, p. 223. Of Salvarvilla the best account is by Mulder in *Erf* (*Ons Geestelijk*), *Driemaandelijksch Tijdscrift voor de Studie der nederlandsche Vroomhied*, V (1931), 186–211.

[2] Rudolf Dier de Muiden in Dumbar, *Analecta*, p. 4.

[3] " Gherlaci scriptura utilissima est et labor continuus. Est iam in bono profectu, meo videre, et merito iuvandus est et diligendus " : Ep. 7, p. 16. Gherlac's escape is deplored in Ep. 25, p. 110 f. For payments by Cele, cf. Ep. 13, pp. 44–45.

[4] Ep. 13, pp. 45–46.

of the air, saying " let us give him some of the deep " (*demus sibi de gurgite*) : and they raised such a storm that the books which he had with him in the crate got wet, and he himself scarcely escaped.[1]

2. His ascetic ideals. Horn says that Gerard was converted by master John of Arnhem, canon of St. Peter's, Utrecht. Letter 43 written to John in 1382 ends with the words : " The Lord will not withhold his wrath (on evildoers) nor does he forget John and Gerard, that our estate may be renewed. *Miserere anime in eternum, Trinitas ineffabilis, maiestas interminata, felicitas et abissalis iucunditas. Et iterum dico, utinam saperemus et intelligeremus et novissima provideremus.*" [2]   These clausular outbursts are reserved for his most intimate counsellors and friends. But there is no other evidence for John of Arnhem's part. Rudolf Dier de Muiden has a different story. Gerard had fallen ill and was being brought the sacrament by his parish priest, who warned him to burn his book of magic ; for he had those books and taught the art, but did not practice it himself. Gerard declined and the priest went away : but after some thought, he had the man recalled, abjured his nigromancy and had the books (here it is plural) burned, whereupon he recovered and was changed into a new man.[3]   In other words his conversion is to be connected with a revulsion under some physical and mental stress against the Oresme tradition—and a determination not to concern himself with the astrological and mathematico-physical speculations of Paris.[4]   The simplest and perhaps the best explanation of the conversion is that of Thomas a Kempis who points out that he had been talked to by Henry Eger van Calcar, the Carthusian prior of Monnikhuizen, and that it was he who caught the great fish " on the hook of Christ." [5]   Gerard had been his friend at the University of Paris, and had been deeply influenced by his character and his ability.

For there is no sign that Gerard Groote had behaved as St. Augustine in his earlier years. He was virtuous as well as successful. Well dressed, hospitable, unselfish (when he entertained guests he was more intent on looking after their comfort than his own), he was a prosperous secular clerk, a pluralist with canonries and prebends in the cathedrals of Utrecht and Aachen, and, says Thomas a Kempis " other benefices," though it is not clear what these were. The first sign of ascetic reaction was that he divested himself of the possessions left him by his parents (which

---

[1] Horn, 341.   [2] Ep. 39, p. 157.   [3] Dumbar, *Analecta*, 2.
[4] Ep. 63, pp. 245–246, written to Rudolf de Enteren, dissuades him from reading the work of the famous astrologer Albumasar (Abu Maschar). " Praecipue accipiendum videtur de libris magicis et astrologicis, quos Parisiis legit et habuit, postea autem igni tradidit." Thomas a Kempis, *Vita Gerardi Magni*, Ch. 13 (*Opera*, ed. Pohl, vii. 69).
[5] *Vita Gerardi Magni*, Ch. 4.

shows that by 1374 they were dead) and assumed the dress and habit of a poor clerk. He gave his farm to the Carthusians of Arnhem ; five years later he turned his house into a hostel for pious women not under vows, and merely kept in it simple quarters for himself and one or two copyists : no servants, for he did all his own cooking. " He cooked his own food," Dier de Muiden says, " and that he might the more freely attend to sacred reading he was wont to prepare or cook peas, that do not require great care in the cooking, and when they were boiled sufficiently, he put in a herring which cooked along with the peas " : *et sic habuit potagium et piscem*[1]—a horrible concoction.

The early letters, a group of five written before he went to Monnikhuizen, are all concerned with securing the admission of a lady, Elizabeth de Gherner, whose father had been executed for felony, as a sister of the Clares at Cologne ; the problem of the woman who did not want to marry or who could not get married, perhaps because she had no charm or intelligence or money, was of some importance in the fifteenth century and Gerard was concerned about these persons. He wanted Elizabeth admitted " of si daer in commen mach sonder symonien " or, as he wrote to Arnold of Lochem, *sine symonia et sine pactu*—without a premium.[2]   This is the first note of Gerard's challenge to a common practice. She could, he says, writing to the abbess of the Clares, have produced letters of princes and other influential entreaties, but this business is " according to the flesh and one that walketh in darkness." [3]   But opposition developed to Elizabeth, who was suspected of being both dull-witted and indigent : and in despair Groote asked his correspondent for her admission to the Clares or to any similar house of women in a humbler capacity. " If she cannot be veiled because she is insufficiently taught and is ignorant of grammar, let her be put to the oar or to some lower place, if she is inadequate for better things. Truly, the lower places are safest in the ship of the church." [4]   Gerard had in the end, somewhat inconsistently, to tell his correspondent that she *had* temporal goods about which her friends could testify and that she *could*, if needed, produce testimonials. Throughout his remaining years Gerard was to fight both these fines upon entry, as much as the *proprietas* in which he saw—and correctly saw—the root of monastic corruption,[5] especially in those convents described by John Busch, to which only well-to-do ladies were admitted. All this, he thought, belonged to the *senium mundi et ecclesie*, the old, rotten order. Conversely he deplored the practice of well-to-do persons when entering a

[1] Dumbar, *Analecta*, 3.   [2] Ep. 1, p. 1 ; Ep. 3, p. 5.
[3] Ep. 2, p. 2.   [4] Ep. 4, p. 8.
[5] Ep. 41, pp. 162–163 ; 45, 177–183.

religious order of withholding their lands from the foundation and making them over to their relations, to the benefit of the family rather than of the Church.[1]

It was John Ruysbroeck who suggested to Gerard withdrawal to the Charterhouse at Monnikhuizen. Twice Gerard visited the prior of the Austin Hermits, at Groenendael, in 1374 and not long before his death in 1381, when Thomas a Kempis and Horn attribute to Gerard the revelation of the great mystic's approaching death which took place on 2 December. In Letter 24 written under the influence of his second visit, Gerard says that he would like to be the footstool under the feet of the prior and convent, to whom he was more attached by love and reverence than to any mortals.[2] He also translated two of Ruysbroeck's works from the German. At Groenendael he could find spiritual renewal which contrasted with his own mediocrity, and his admiration for Ruysbroeck reveals not a little. Historians have sometimes called Gerard a mystic, but the term does not fit him as it fitted the other man. The basis of Gerard's teaching was not Dionysian or " Platonic," but moral and practical. It was given orally or written with a Bernardine streak of poetic prose and sometimes with commanding intuition : he was indeed a contemplative, he discussed contemplation in one of his treatises, but he was not an original writer who could describe or analyse the search for the mystical experience of unity with God, as Ruysbroeck did. He had little use either for the allegories and the astronomical speculation that Ruysbroeck employed. If he had been more patient with himself and more tolerant of others, the regular life of solitude and prayer at the Charterhouse might have been the prelude to some greater finished treatise, and the world have been enriched by another Gerson or another Fénélon : but he was always unsatisfied, always wanting to gain souls, always aware of his own shortcomings : as he wrote to Ruysbroeck in 1381 : " there is nothing new to report about myself. I am always unprofitable (*inutilis*), always talking, always greedy, more than greedy for books : to which habit I am forced to set an end, partly for lack of cash, partly because I get tired of dealing with writers and all connected with that " (*ea, quae annexa sunt*).[3]

But in the reading and study and self examination of these years he had evolved the principles which Thomas a Kempis reports under the heading of " Resolutions and intentions set forth by Master Gerard in the name of the Lord, but not confirmed by vows " (m. 18). It is the

---

[1] Ep. 41, p. 167.
[2] Ep. 24, p. 107. The revelation is noted by Thomas a Kempis in *Vita*, Ch. 10 (*Opera*, vii. 54) and Horn, pp. 350-351.
[3] Ep. 24, p. 108.

Carthusian period in which his modern biographers, particularly van
Ginneken, lay particular stress, for it laid the foundation of his "following" or discipleship of Christ. He was to permit himself no temporal
preferment, no courting of the cardinals or great ecclesiastics ; no
petitions for benefices : as the appetite for more possessions must be
cut off, so any present possessions must be reduced by degrees to a
smaller compass. And, clear as it is now that recluses, just as hermits,
put their astrological knowledge and the powers of divination with
which they were credited at the service of secular patrons,[1] so Gerard
would have nothing to do with these professional consultations or with
observing seasons propitious for journeying or for blood-letting, "or
for any other thing save in the material sense of considering the density
of the atmosphere : I will never try to anticipate the future." The
knowledge that brings temporal wealth is to be shunned. "Do not
spend thy time in the study of geometrics, arithmetic, rhetoric, dialectic,
grammar, songs, poetry, legal matters or astrology : for all these things
are reproved by Seneca, and a good man should withdraw his mind's
eye therefrom and despise them." But "of all sciences of the heathen,
their moral philosophy is least to be avoided ; for this is often of great
use and profit both for one's own study and for teaching others." Gerard
resolved "never to take a degree in medicine or in Civil or canon Law :
for the purpose of a degree is either gain or preferment or vain glorifica-
tion and worldly honour." The *De imitatione* echoes the thought :
"Truly at the day of judgment we shall not be examined on what
we have read, but on what we have done. Tell me now, where are
all those doctors and masters with whom thou wast well acquainted
whilst they lived and flourished in learning ?"[2] Gerard enjoins again,
"Thou shalt not appear before a spiritual officer or judge, as a favour
to any friend or kinsman or other man, nor at all unless the most urgent
call of duty require it . . . Thou shalt not appear before the civil magistrates or the secular judge in Deventer save in the case of similar necessity,
for thy friends deal well enough with all such matters before magistrates."
The books which Gerard allowed himself to read were the Gospels ;
the Fathers and "Holy Books, such as the meditations of Bernard and
the Horologium of Anselm ; Bernard on the Conscience ; the Solilo-
quies of Augustine, and such like : the legends and devotions of the
Saints : the homilies of the Holy Fathers and of the four Doctors upon
the Gospels ; and all other works making for the better understanding
of the lectionaries and the Psalter ; and the historical books of the Old
Testament." But what of the Decrees, i.e. Canon law, "so as to know

[1] F. D. S. Darwin, *The English Medieval Recluse*, 39-41.
[2] De Beer, *op. cit.*, 126 f., lays much emphasis on this point.

what was determined of our forefathers and of the Church"?   One
must not strive to master them, answers Gerard, "but only to peruse
them; lest through ignorance of the law thou pervert piety into dis-
obedience."   It may be added that Gerard's citations from the Corpus
and the Glossators showed evidence of much more than perusal.[1]

3. The Common Life.   To remain in the world and not be of the
world—that was an even harder road than the entry into religion.[2]   It
seemed inadvisable to Gerard that a corporate body should be created.
There might be a common spirit, but as yet no legal person.

A new religious order was open to dangers as Groote said.   He
had carefully guarded himself when he composed a constitution for
the sisterhood living in his house : this was not to be a group of persons
under vows : any woman could leave when she so desired.   It was
just a hostel, looked after by two matrons who bought the supplies and
saw that the daily tasks were performed—dairying, sewing, weaving,
etc.; and its inmates, when not at these duties, devoted themselves to
prayer and pious works.   The finance was Gerard's : his lands he had
given to Monnikhuizen ; the remainder of his resources went to maintain the house at Deventer.   If there was to be a community for men,
Gerard felt it better that there should be an Augustinian convent built,
for a group living together under no vows would have appeared somewhat ridiculous.   And that took place, as John Busch tells us, at
Windesheim.

But the young copyists who wanted him to found a house for the
Common Life got their way in the end, after his death.   Rudolf Dier
de Muiden reports that the resources were amalgamated and individuals
no longer paid their own hostel expenses.   It was much the same at
Zwolle.   Here Henry Foppens of Gouda, sent by Gerard from Deventer,
collected the scholars who were coming in to work in the school under
John Cele (1350-1417), and had them in his house near the old Beguinage
convent, again as a sort of hostel.   The next stage was when three
laymen bought the area close by the Beguinage and adjoining Henry
of Gouda's house, and building a house there, began to live in common.
The laymen put up the money for the building, and when it was completed they handed it over to Gerard (1384).   Voecht, in his account

---

[1] Ep. 18, 21, 53 and 73 testify to careful study.   In 18 he debates, citing Innocent
IV, Hostiensis, Johannes Andreae and Vincentius Hispanus, whether a *scholasticus*
is able to receive money, and if he does, whether he is bound to restore it ; in 21
he discusses the relation between schism and heresy from the canonical point of
view, and cites Godfrey of Trano and Raymond of Peñaforte.   In 53 bastardy is
the point at issue, and in 73 the qualifications necessary for a clerk seeking a benefice
with cure of souls.   In every case he is *au fait* with the commentators, besides quoting the texts of the *Corpus Juris*.

[2] Ep. 61, p. 230.

of the house, observes that the three were on 4 July, " constituti in ea ipsa domo per eundem magistrum Gerardum, virum deo deditum, ad communiter in eadem vivendum sine cujusquam proprietate." Their first rector or procurator was John (Eskinni) van Ommen, " a blind man, but of illuminated mind," who brought with him his mother, the widow Regelande. The mother must have acted as a sort of house-keeper, and Gerard was looked upon as founder as well as trustee.

The alternative text of Voecht, called by his editor Schoengen " MS.B " (Royal Belgian Lib., Brussels MS. 8849) states (fo. 94 r.) that Groote bought the house and " again introduced into it the vendors to live there "; and that before he died " he entrusted that house for the same purpose to Florence (Radewijns) and John de Gronde, his disciples in Deventer," the reason being that John van Ommen with the two other original lay inhabitants had by this time gone off, under Gerard's leadership, to found Agnetenburg.[1]

During his life-time three types of association grew around Gerard, a natural creator of groups : there were the disciples, lay and clerical, who regarded him as their religious pattern and spiritual leader, persons not living in his house but constituting, as it were, his circle and later to be reckoned among the founders of the New Devotion through the active part they played in the creation of the " Brothers-houses "—men like John de Gronde, John Brinckerinck, John ten Water, and, above all, Florence Radewijns, whom Thomas a Kempis specially linked with Groote.[2] Living in his house there were the sisters, some of whose names are given by Dier de Muiden ; and there were the copyists, though most of this scholar-class were with Radewijns in his vicarage. Gerard, as his letters indicate, maintained several, for of one of them, called Gherlac, whom he employed upon patristic texts lent him by his friends, he had great hopes, at least in 1378 : " Gherlac's writing is very useful and he works continually. He is making good progress, I think, and is deservedly to be helped and loved ; and you "—that is his correspondent William Vroede—" are bound to help him and show

---

[1] Voecht, p. lxxxi. The original account is *ibid.*, 6–7.

[2] People who " niet in gemeenschap, doch als gewone burgers in de maatschappij leven " : De Beer, 25. On the relations of Groote, Florence and John de Gronde, cf. G. H. M. Delprat, *Verhandlungen over de Broederschap van G. Groote en over den invloed der Fraterhuizen* (2nd ed., Arnhem, 1856), 34. Acquoy, *Het Klooster te Windesheim en zijn Invloed*, p. 49, thought that Radewijns, more than Groote, was the founder of the movement : always, he wisely remarked, " met dien verstande dat, zonder De Groote Florens Radewijns er nooit zou zijn geweest." Busch, 255, speaks of Groote's associates drawing up " formam et modum in commune vivendi " *with the counsel of master Gerard* " together with his priests and clerks dwelling alike in the common life." This may be anticipating a little the formal beginnings of the organized common life.

affection to him and to strengthen him in the Lord, and to give him farther opportunities as you do for others of your scholars." But Gherlac did not remain faithful ; he left Deventer with some of Gerard's manuscripts (*exemplaria*) which he was evidently proposing to sell ; and in Letter 25 Gerard expresses his fear that the world had again claimed the ardent and inexperienced youth : " Your poverty would have sufficed you, if you had known how to count it wealth." He asks Gherlac to return : " fear not for the debts you owe me ; lo, when you enter Deventer, returned to the Lord and to me, I there remit you all the debt of those three florins (Gherlac had probably borrowed money to go away with)." But if he will not, Gerard tells him that whether he has gone to Cologne or to Strasbourg, he cannot escape. " Mark, I have friends in Cologne, and I could easily have you arrested when I wanted to." The letter however is one of affectionate and forceful appeal : " how delighted I was, how great were my hopes when I saw your eyes directed towards peace within, and when you knew and perceived the value that lay in your writings and when you considered and assessed this worth a kingdom. How true this was ! " [1]

We return to the first category. Besides the Sisters and the occasional copyists, clerks of Deventer and Zwolle were following Gerard's example and embracing poverty. Horn speaks of " his friends, that were priests, whom he begat to God, enlightened and nurtured," as gathered together one day with Gerard, and of Gerard's premonition that one of them would apostasize.[2] This is the John of Letter 19, and the precautions recommended by Gerard when the doubtful disciple wished to return to the stricter life are an interesting indication of what he required of anyone adopting the life of a poor clerk, though it must be remembered that John was suspect and the requirements are accordingly exacting. " First let it be inquired of him if he has freely resigned all his goods into the hands of the Bishop's commissary, so that the commissary may dispose of everything freely according to the dictates of divine and human law and the arbitrament of a good man (the commissary happened to be Gerard's correspondent) : secondly he must repent that he so misprises spiritual things and especially the mysteries and holy ministries of the Trinity . . . which lead to the life of grace and glory, to which all temporal things are ordained." He must above all be told mercenary practices and simoniacal profits are entirely to be avoided : that he must not take money for celebrating or preaching ; and if he does undertake the duties of a benefice, he must ask himself the motive for his acceptance of the responsibility. He must be told to restore to the Church what he has simoniacally gained, for it is his duty ; and if that

[1] Ep. 25, pp. 113-115.   [2] Horn, 361.

is too severe a requirement, the commissary should use the power of absolution and the commission given him to remit what needs be remitted, if John remains firm in his proposal. His books he should be allowed him for life, because of their importance to the Church as well as to him ; he is to sell his land or his lands as quickly as he can, and hand over the money to be disposed of by the commissary for some notable spiritual purpose ; he is to keep all the necessary furniture of his house—not the luxurious stuff—but what is sufficient for himself, one priest and one serving maid : everything beyond this should be sold and the money placed in the hands of the commissary ; if there are any curios, beautiful or precious or unusual objects which do not befit domestic sanctity and if cheaper substitutes will do, the *objets d'art* are to be sold and the simpler and useful goods bought ; and the same applies to ecclesiastical vestments. His home in Deventer he must no longer think his own, but the commissary should assign and adjudge it to the holy servants of the Church. He is to be allowed a lodging while he is at Deventer, in the house which is his property, now dwelt in by Walter the Échevin. John is to be assigned this lodging by the commissary, as a poor and indigent priest serving God.[1]

This remarkable document regulating the selling out of a rich priest for the benefit of the *Dei servitores*, those who have entered upon voluntary poverty, has evoked little comment from historians, saving only Acquoy. We do not know whether it took effect ; if it did, it would reveal a remarkably cooperative attitude on the part of the bishop of Utrecht, Florence Werbelijkhoven, who until the fierce reaction against Gerard began in Kampen and elsewhere during the course of 1382, had sympathized with his aims and had supported him against an active heretical opposition, as well as against the ordinary relaxed secular churchmen. The document attests a developing movement among the people of the diocese towards spiritual poverty, and it may be the threat of the social and tenurial changes involved, as much as his invectives against the focarists, that accounts for the bitterness with which Gerard was assailed by his opponents. We know from Peter Horn that at his death one of his enemies at Zutphen mounted the pulpit and announced Gerard's decease as a matter of public congratulation ;[2] he had been physically driven out of Kampen and there were areas where it was unsafe for him to go, for, as Horn says, such were the clergy of the diocese that with many it was thought a scandal that any of the clergy should not have a *focaria*. But the seed was sown and the moral foundations laid for the *Christi servitores* of the fifteenth century.

[1] Ep. 19, pp. 65–71.   [2] Horn, 366.

CHAPTER IX

CUSANUS THE THEOLOGIAN

I

W̶E are sometimes told that the fifteenth century saw the decline of scholasticism. Like all such generalizations, the statement contains a modicum of truth. It would certainly be more applicable to this country, where Wyclif had challenged the orthodox faith and had to be answered in terms which everyone could understand—Netter's *Doctrinale* points the way to simpler (though not less prolix) methods of exposition—than to the Continent, where, both at Paris and in the German universities, the philosophy of Ockham was strongly entrenched. But alike in England and abroad, there is undoubtedly a contraction of the field of influence once belonging to the scholastic method and the theologians trained along those lines.

That contraction came in numerous ways. In the Netherlands and in many districts of Northern Germany the teaching of religion on a simple and popular basis in the schools of the Brethren of the Common Life seemed a better preparation for the practical life of a parish clergyman than a discipline founded on the Sentences and ending, perhaps, with a degree that got one nowhere. In this country the former " artist " student was finding it very difficult to get a benefice in comparison with the less lettered protégé of the secular patron or the civil servant, and the general complaint was that the universities were losing in numbers. To speak more generally, as the century advanced, the growth of education and the increasingly vocational tendency of studies like law and medicine threatened to pass the professional philosophers and theologians by. And there was competition from another quarter. In Scandinavia, in England (especially East Anglia) and in parts of Germany, an emotional mysticism was claiming the attention of many who at an earlier date might have become orthodox academics or remained among the silent mortified devout. The solitary, living by rule, was coming into his or her own as the recipient of treatises or legacies ; [1] and the people were beginning to listen to other religious personalities who were by no means anchorites or recluses, as the career of Margery Kempe has made plain. Archbishop Arundel does not seem to have been angry with her, when she rebuked him for the laxity and extravagance of his household. Bishop Philip Repingdon treated her with

[1] Cf. *The Register of Henry Chichele, Archbishop of Canterbury, 1414–1443*, ii. 95, 380, 600, for testamentary bequests to recluses.

honour. She may have been a nuisance during divine service, and people grumbled ; but she was accepted, even if unwillingly, by her age. Art gives similar witness. The rich iconography of East Anglia in the fifteenth century points to something more than the stock work of a few firms of masons. There is a fine tangle of legend and fancy linked with the names of those popular saints of local devotion : St. Barbara, St. Dorothy, St. Edmund the king and martyr, St. Katherine, St. Margaret. It is the age of the women saints, when the Revelations of St. Bridget was almost the standard text-book of devotion.

Religious thought, therefore, was no longer content to dwell within the syllogism. In his earlier days, Nicholas of Cues had attributed an example of this method of proof to the working of the Holy Spirit.[1] In his later years he would scarcely have made such a suggestion. More than in the fourteenth century, dialogue was becoming a literary characteristic of the age ; and humanism, with its emphasis on formal beauty, on the perfection of a period and the cadence of words, was, as we all know, more than a little impatient with the *odiosa cantio* of the old disputations. On a different plane, popular devotion can be seen breaking out on all sides : in verse, in imagery (one recalls Descents from the Cross or the Man of Sorrows), in practical works of mercy and piety like the endowment of hospitals, or in campaigns against unorthodoxy that might lead equally to a crusade or the foundation of a college. It was the century of legacy and insurance for the soul ; and these religious currents, this world of exciting sensibility, must have alarmed quieter conservative spirits. The danger that the tides of sentiment might run uncontrolled should have been clear to any thoughtful observer about the time of the Council of Basel (1431). They had already shown what they could do in the Bohemian revolt. The problem was how to set the intellect free to serve the cause of religion without the academic contortions that served to alienate rather than attract. At the same time, as Gascoigne realized when he urged the need of preaching, religion, if it is to be vital, must be a force leading to action, to practical goodness before any intellectual enjoyment. It must move people to be better and more steadfast. This was the more necessary amid the bourgeois civilization of the fifteenth century. The opulent and comfortable life of the higher bourgeoisie needed some antidote to the pageants of its worship as well as of its secular ceremonies.

It can be seen, then, that the Church of the fifteenth century had to provide, apart from the elegant and fastidious prosodists, for two unlikely opposites, the visionary and the city magnate. The problem

---

[1] *De Concordantia Catholica*, II. xx. ; in *D. Nicolai de Cusa . . . Opera* (Petri, Basel, 1555), p. 748.

was not really new ; but now the necessity was upon her at a time when she herself stood deeply in need of internal strictness and missionary ardour, and was in danger of losing her power of instructing and illuminating her children.   Her weapon in this educational task had been the very discipline that had lost its freshness and compelling power.   This is not the time or place to venture any observations on the contribution made by the scholastic method to the cause of accurate thinking and the precise use of terms.   Every trained intellect of whatever rank in learned or administrative Christendom had been brought up in it, or had some contact with it, and its influence was everywhere.   Confronted with the new emotionalism, what was it to do ?   To those consciously or unconsciously in search of self-expression or seeking literary perfection, the laborious and often unremunerative toil of the schoolmen held out little attraction.   It was simpler to write homilies or pious meditations than a *quodlibet*, even if the scholastic terminology came almost as second nature.   This is no allusion to the work of pure and gracious minds like the author of the *Imitatio*, a classic in any age or generation : but to those writers, often in the vernacular, whose work is more enlightening to the philologist or to the student of behaviour than to the critic who inquires whither it is leading or what serious contribution it is making towards the philosophy of religion.

It fell to Nicholas of Cues to restore—or attempt to restore—the balance of reason and emotion by weighting once more the scale of reason, while at the same time demonstrating the limitations of the rational method.   To do this, he went back to Neo-Platonic sources ; but he is also a son of Master Eckhart, subtlest of German mystics, from whom he derived some of his terminology and a great part of his attitude towards ultimate reality.   So much has been written round his life that I need not sketch the career of the boatman's son who won fame at the Council of Basel, became papal legate in Germany, bishop of Brixen, and finally Cardinal of the Holy Roman Church.[1]   It is rather

[1] An admirable brief account is that of Dr. R. Klibansky, in *Enciclopedia Italiana*, s.v.   Among modern works, Paolo Rotta, *Il Cardinale Nicolò di Cusa* (Milan, 1928), is stimulating ; a useful book is that of Dr. Henry Bett, *Nicholas of Cusa* (London, 1932), but the best remains E. Vansteenberghe, *Le Cardinal Nicolas de Cues, 1401–1464* (1920).   The most notable recent works bearing upon his philosophy, of which Dr. Uebinger wrote, in 1888, the important book *Die Gotteslehre des Nicolaus Cusanus*, are Jos. Ranft, *Schöpfer und Geschöpf nach Nikolaus von Cusa* (Wurzburg, 1924) ; E. Cassirer, *Individuum und Kosmos in der Philosophie der Renaissance* (Berlin, 1927), which contains as an appendix the *Liber de Mente*, edited by Joachim Ritter ; and Joachim Ritter, *Docta Ignorantia, Die Theorie des Nichtwissens bei Nic. Cusanus* (Leipzig and Berlin, 1927).   Very useful also is Ernst Hoffman, *Das Universum des Nik. von Cues* (Heidelberger Abhandl., phil.-hist. Kl., 1929–1930).   For the Christology of Nicholas, the sermon " Dies Sanctificatus " (ed. Hoffmann and Klibansky, Heidelberg, 1929), is of considerable interest.

the sequence of his works and the environment in which he wrote them that should claim our attention here. Nicholas is an instance of a man whose most important work was his first serious essay in metaphysic. All the rest—and there is much of it—is a development of the ideas expressed in that treatise, until he had created his own system—the Cusan dialectic, we might call it—by building round its central conception, the notion of the one, changeless and transcendent deity, the structure of a finite universe subject to variation and mutability. In his early university years at Heidelberg he was in the town of the Ockhamist Marsilius of Inghen, the home of scholasticism; but at Padua, where he took his degree in canon law, the young lawyer was brought face to face with men and influences that left a permanent mark upon him. The mathematicians and the doctors, the latter Averroists, gathered there formed a brilliant and powerful teaching staff. Prosdocimo de' Beldomandi and Paolo del Pozzo Toscanelli must have introduced him to the Pythagorean doctrines so plainly reflected in his works. From them and from the Arabian traditions preserved by the medicals he may have learned the meaning of causation, and have become acquainted with the notion of law in nature, which, however paradoxical it may sound, underlay the astrology for which Northern Italy was famous. His great interest in Islam, that comes out in the *De pace fidei* and the *Cribrationis Alchoran*, and his respect for Avicenna [1] may well have been derived from his Paduan masters, not least perhaps from Ugo Benzi of Siena. "Ses vrais maîtres en philosophie, ce n'est pas a Padoue qu'il les faut chercher," M. Vansteenberghe has remarked.[2] This is perhaps a little hard on the Italian mathematicians, who worked deeply upon Nicholas's subtle and active intellect.

The pamphlet (1436) on the Reform of the Calendar may seem the only example of Nicholas's work that appears at all isolated from the rest. This impression will quickly disappear when the astronomical calculations are arrived at.[3] Though the first of his mathematical works was not issued till 1450, it is clear, even in the Concordantia Catholica (1433, the first major treatise, but, none the less, an *œuvre de circonstance*), that the Paduan leaven was early at work.[4] In the *De docta ignorantia* the mathematical influence is absolutely clear;[5] indeed, the notion of

---

[1] Cf. *Apologia doctae ignorantiae* (ed. Hoffmann and Klibansky, Leipzig, 1932), pp. 9–10. This is not to imply that he agreed in any way with Mohammedan theology. [2] *Le Cardinal Nicolas de Cues*, p. 13.

[3] *Opera*, p. 1157 f. The treatise contains a striking little historical survey of early chronological systems.

[4] Cf. especially the terms which he uses to describe the supreme agreement in God; *Opera*, p. 693.

[5] E.g. I. ii, x, xiii–xv, xxi, xxiii; II. i, v; ed. Hoffmann and Klibansky (Leipzig, 1932), pp. 7–8, 19–21, 25–30, 42–44, 46–47, 61–65, 76–78.

mathematical truth lies at the heart of the argument. Let us state his position in the words of the theological appendix to his *De Mathematicis Complementis*, which he dedicated to Nicholas V. The Pope, while pleased with the learned mathematical treatise, had expressed a little astonishment at the preoccupation of so leading an ecclesiastic with geometry and numbers, and Nicholas wrote to show him the logical implication of it all. True, the passage to be quoted was written thirty years after Nicholas's student days at Padua, but it reveals, as clearly as any other like quotation from his works, whither those early studies had led him :

> Everyone knows that in mathematics truth can be more surely reached than in the other liberal arts ; and therefore we see those who taste the discipline of geometry, remaining faithful to it in a remarkable love, as if a kind of food for the intellectual life is contained there more purely and simply [than elsewhere] ; for the geometrician does not care for lines or figures of bronze or gold or wood ; he cares for the lines and figures as they are in themselves, although they are not found outside the substances. He beholds, therefore, with the eye of sense figures of the sensible world, in order that with the eye of the mind he may be able to behold the figures of the mind. Nor does the mind see the mental figures any the less truly than does the eye the sensible figures ; but rather all the more truly, inasmuch as the mind beholds the figures in themselves, freed from material otherness (*alteritate*). But ordinary physical perception (*sensus exterior*) cannot reach them without that otherness ; for the figure acquires otherness from its union with the material substance, which varies and varies : on account of which there is one triangle on this pavement and another on the wall, and the figure is truer on the one than on the other ; and so under such conditions it always falls short of a higher degree of truth and precision. But mental perception in the abstract will see the figures free from all variable otherness ; since the mind discovers itself when the otherness of the senses is not there to impede it.[1]

A Platonist beginning, if we may take the first sentence to represent Nicholas's own experience. He remained faithful, indeed, to his geometry. Throughout his works there are passages contrasting the truth of mental perception with the conjectural " otherness " of sense-data. From a comparatively early period Nicholas must have been filled with the desire to pass beyond conjecture to the perception of eternal reality. Sensible things, he would argue, can never be precisely equal : there can only be approximate likeness. But the ideal quantities of the mathematician can be exactly alike, precisely because they are abstractions. In mathematical symbols precise and final truth can be attained. To put it in another way : truth, he observes in one passage,[2] is *adaequatio rei et intellectus*. The problem of knowledge is how to

---

[1] *Opera*, p. 1107.   [2] In the Compendium, *Opera*, p. 247.

bring about the assimilation. "Knowledge comes through likeness"; but in the finite world of sense-perceptions, real likeness is impossible. And how is the desired abstraction, reality, to be arrived at, when we are, so to speak, the prisoners of our own senses, the victims of *alteritas*? By what mental effort can mathematical certainty be brought into the service of philosophy? That is the question in its modern form.

There may be something fanciful in attributing so large a problem to the mind of Nicholas in the early days, when he was in Cardinal Orsini's household, hunting for classical manuscripts in Germany, or, later, winning his spurs over the Bohemians at the Council of Basel. The evidence for his mental growth before 1440 is slender; but the notions of equality and difference, of mutability and changelessness, and above all the concept of unity, to which he was always returning, did not come from the authors whom he cites in the mature treatises alone. Yet it was undoubtedly John the Scot that enabled Nicholas to ponder more deeply the philosophical implication of mathematical truth, and gave him the notion of the timeless, transcendent being, combining possibility and actuality, the being opposed to all alterity, eternally the same; and how deeply Nicholas had studied him both his early and his later commentators, especially Dr. Klibansky, have made plain. But Nicholas the theologian, as he stands to later ages, is compounded of something more besides. There is personal devotion, of the deepest and humblest kind, to the object of contemplation; and there is the mystic's language describing his approach to that ultimate reality, the use of analogy and symbol in which Eckhart was the instructor. If we are merely to attribute to Nicholas the negative theology of the Scot, we should miss an important positive element in his Christology: the doctrine of the Word as the mediator between the Creator and the human objects of his creation. One element of greatness in the Cusan is that he is able to bring together a being which he describes as absolutely greatest, and the concrete individual, without that individual losing his identity. He had to face the insistent problem of personality that besets the theologian of idealist leanings.[1] What does the Absolute care for the individuals whom it comprises? Does not the tremendous single-ness of God obliterate, in its unity, all those differences which to our finite minds are so precious? To the solution of these questions Nicholas brought a warmth of feeling that we are not always prone to expect in a writer who covers his pages with geometrical figures and diagrams.

[1] Nicholas viewed this problem chiefly in the light of the ascent of man towards God. How can finite man establish any contact with the divine Essence? For it is the human being that has to approach the God who beholds him, and has by intuition (which he describes in the *De visione Dei*) to arrive, through the darkness, at his essence.

But we are anticipating : for we left Nicholas at the critical point of transmuting mathematics into philosophy. This was the task of the busiest period of his life, from 1437 or thereabouts (the time, along with Cesarini, when he left the Conciliar party for the papal side), to 1453. Its landmarks are his leading work, the *De docta ignorantia*, and the *De conjecturis*, both of 1440 ; his vigorous support, in sermons and addresses, of the papal interest and his propaganda against German neutrality in the Council ; and his return, after that neutrality had been conquered by Aeneas Sylvius and Eugenius IV, to Italy, a cardinal for his pains : to Italy and—be it noted—to mathematics. To 1450 belong the *De transmutationibus geometricis* ; the *De arithmeticis complementis* ; and (his favourite theme), *De quadratura circuli*. The more mystical *De quaerendo Deum* was written while he was conducting the campaign against German neutrality (1445). 1451 and part of 1452 were occupied with his famous tour of his native land as papal legate. To 1452 belongs the *Conjectura de ultimis diebus*. It was 1453 that saw Cusanus, now bishop of Brixen, enter upon a quarrel with duke Sigismund of the Tyrol over the reform which he was attempting to impose upon the aristocratic nunnery of the Sonnenburg : a conflict which was to divide the local nobility, and ultimately to involve forces outside the immediate sphere of the disputants. Yet it was to 1453 that three works of serene imaginative power belong : the *De Visione Dei*, *De mathematicis complementis* and the *De pace fidei*. In the former he produced a work of devotion as well as of philosophical importance, wherein the novelty and paradox of the standpoint alone prevents it from ranking with the work of Thomas of Kempen. The astonishing fact about this period of legatine and diocesan work and activity in the life of Nicholas is the output of pure speculation amid all the disturbance that was going on about him.

After 1453 there is a gap. The conflict with duke Sigismund increased, and reached its climax in 1456–1457. None the less, in 1458 and 1460 came three works, *De Beryllo*, *De mathematica perfectione*, and, most characteristic of all, *De possest*. The latter and the *De non aliud* of 1462 are concerned most of all with the doctrine of God and his relation with the universe. They are his maturest theological works. I would quote here Dr. Bett's summary of his position :

> He began with a conception of God as the super-essential unity, which is opposed to no otherness, and in which all contraries coincide. He never really departed from that position. But he came more and more in later life to use phrases which stress the self-identity of the Godhead. God is *idem*, for unity, infinity, actuality, possibility, existence, nothingness, all that can be thought, all that surpasses thought, is the same in Him. He is *Non aliud*, for there is nothing to which He is other, since He is unrelated and unconditioned and absolute. He is the Possest, because in Him possi-

bility (*posse*) and actuality (*est*) are one. It can hardly be said that there is any real advance in thought here ; the notion of the changeless identity of the Deity is really involved in the conception, found in Nicholas's earliest books, of God as immutable Unity. But Nicholas came, in later life, to use new terms which stress the internal identity, so to speak, rather than the universal inclusiveness of the Absolute, and at the same time he came to emphasize the dynamic rather than the static aspect of the conception.[1]

In 1461, bitterly attacked by Gregory of Heimburg, with the Tyrolese dispute now assuming almost European proportions, Cusanus went to Rome. In the last two years of his life, no less than four treatises came from his pen.

In the final one, the *De apice theoriae*, he has given a little picture of himself which we may place alongside of the kneeling figure on Andrea Bregno's tomb in S. Pietro in Vincoli. The *De apice theoriae* is the report of a little conversation of the cardinal with Peter of Erkelenz, his secretary.[2] Peter observes that he has often seen his master so deeply sunk in meditation that he has not dared to disturb him. But now, finding him a little more relaxed and in less spiritual tension, he feels that he can make the venture, and ask the cardinal what he has been contemplating. The cardinal expresses satisfaction : he has often been surprised that Peter has never asked him what he was thinking about ; but now that his secretary has been ordained priest, it is right that he should ask to know. Peter replies that he has scrupled to ask because of his inexperience ; but, he adds ingenuously, " I thought that you had reached the end of speculation in your many various books." Cusanus replies that if the apostle Paul, wrapt up into the third heaven, did not comprehend the incomprehensible,[3] no one would ever be satiated by what surpasses all comprehension, but would ever try to comprehend the better. Then this exchange :

Peter. What are you seeking ?
Cardinal. You say rightly.
Peter. I ask you and you make fun of me. I ask you to say what you are seeking, and you answer " You say rightly." I was making no statement, only asking.
Cardinal. If you say " what are you seeking ? " you have spoken rightly : since I *am* seeking something. Who ever seeks, seeks somewhat. If he was not in search of anything, he certainly would not be seeking at all. Like all men given up to study, I am seeking something ; for I earnestly long to know what is the nature and essence of the thing so eagerly sought.
Peter. Do you think that it can be found ?

---

[1] *Nicholas of Cusa*, pp. 109–110.
[2] *Opera*, pp. 332–337.
[3] 2 Cor. xii. 2. St. Paul only says that he heard words which he may not repeat.

Cardinal. Certainly it can ; for the impulse (*motus*) which all scholars have
    is not in vain.
Peter. If so far no one has found it, why beyond all others do *you* try ?
Cardinal. I think that many people have seen it and have written about
    their vision. For the essence of it, which has always been sought, is
    being sought for now and will ever be ; if it was utterly unknown,
    how should it be sought ? When found, how should it remain unknown ?
    Therefore a philosopher said that it is seen by all, though from afar.

It recalls *La Saisiaz*, if only for the contrast in outlook :

I have questioned and am answered. Question, answer presuppose
Two points, that the thing itself which questions answers, is, it knows ;
As it also knows the thing perceived outside itself,—a force
Actual ere its own beginning, operative through its course,
Unaffected by its end,—that this thing likewise needs must be :
Call this—God, then, call that—Soul, and both—the only facts for me.

Browning's emphasis lay on the reality of the soul, the creature.
Nicholas's on the reality of the object sought, the being " beyond all
cognitive power and anterior to all variety and opposition " ; which
was not " now one, now another, but the *hypostasis* [the underlying
nature] of all." His works are one long act of contemplating this
being as it manifested itself in possibility and actuality, *posse* and *esse*,
at one and the same time.

II

First, the attitude of the seeker towards the object sought. Nicholas
speaks of truth or reality as *inattingibilis*, not to be attained. Is our
reason capable of attaining it ?

The answer that Nicholas would give is that we must realize our
own limitations. All research proceeds by comparison. The infinite,
because by definition it cannot be measured by anything, remains necessarily unknown. Knowledge or understanding of our native incapacity
compared with the knowledge that is God's he terms " learned ignorance," sometimes " holy ignorance.' This *ignorantia* has certain consequences : the man who has it will attach very little importance to the
affirmations which we commonly make about God ; for all the names
that we attribute to Him, all that we affirm of Him, are only " in respect
of His creatures " : they attach to Him some quality which His creatures
possess. Nicholas's first philosophical treatise, *De docta ignorantia*, lays
down, in the first book (ch. xxvi), the principles of the " negative
theology " which he derived from the Pseudo-Dionysius and from
Scotus Erigena. God, being absolutely greatest, is absolutely one.
There is no opposite to Him : His unity is not the unity which we
commonly oppose to plurality. In His oneness, which includes all things,

there is no distinction ; and so, strictly speaking, we cannot give Him any name or names. We can only say that He is not this, that, or the other. The theology of affirmation, Nicholas says, worships God by faith, attributing to Him names or values that we believe Him to possess ; but they are the names and values of our own making ; yet the theology of negation is equally necessary with that of affirmation, since without it God would not be worshipped as infinite, but rather as the creature, and such worship savours of idolatry.

> Holy ignorance teaches us that God is ineffable, and this because He is infinitely greater than all that can be named ; and because this is verily so, we speak more truly of Him by removal and negation, as great Dionysius did, who would not have Him as truth, nor as understanding, nor as light, nor as any of the terms usually ascribed ; whom Rabbi Solomon and all wise men follow. Whence He is neither Father, nor Son nor Holy Spirit, according to this negative theology, according to which He is infinite only.[1]

Now what is sometimes described as Nicholas's scepticism of the intellect is rooted in this idea of the absolute unity and infinity of God. *Docta ignorantia* is far removed from any despair or belittling of the human intelligence. No man with such respect for mathematical truth should be so accused. It implies a doctrine of the relation of the finite to the infinite which makes a severe demand upon the intellect, asking for an effort of abnegation, in order that through this act the creature seeking may come within the *visio* or glance of God, and through intuition perceive what the discursive reason cannot tell him. Let us explain this process still further.[2]

Finite and infinite, in the thought of Nicholas, do not stand in proportional relationship. In the universe, as we know it, things exist in grades of likeness, in relationships of space and time, and so forth. Our habit is to compare and relate one with another, and to try to comprehend their nature by means of likeness (*per similitudinem*). But, Nicholas maintains, no two things are so alike that they cannot be more alike *aeternaliter*. The finite understanding can never reach the essence of things (*quidditas rerum*) by means of the category of likeness ; for truth is an indivisible entity that can only be measured by itself. We can never, by our finite understanding, reach truth except in such a way that a more precise attainment is always possible. A mathematical analogy may help. If you multiply the sides of a polygon, you endlessly approach a circle ; but you never finally reach it. All that we know of the truth is that in its final, absolute form, it is unattainable to our reason.

---

[1] Ed. Hoffmann and Klibansky, pp. 54-55.
[2] In the analysis that follows I owe much to Dr. Bett's treatment of Nicholas's epistemology ; *op. cit.*, pp. 176-180.

Our human knowledge is *conjectura*. To be really wise is to understand this, and to realize that we must struggle ceaselessly towards a more perfect knowledge of the truth. Nothing could be more apposite than the passage from Pascal which Dr. Bett has adduced to summarize *docta ignorantia* :

> Les sciences ont deux extrémités qui se touchent. La première est la pure ignorance naturelle où se trouvent tous les hommes en naissant. L'autre extrémité est celle où arrivent les grandes âmes, qui, ayant parcouru tout ce que les hommes peuvent savoir, trouvent qu'ils ne savent rien et se rencontrent en cette même ignorance d'où ils étaient partis ; mais c'est *une ignorance savante* qui se connaît.[1]

How, then, can the eternal, undifferentiated Being have any contact with the world and its individuals ? How is the transition to be made from that unity to the changeable world of sense perceptions ? Nicholas does not adopt the Neo-Platonist plan of emanations or intermediate existences between God and the world. Just in the same way as he makes that absolute maximum and absolute minimum coincide in God —the foundation of his doctrine of the coincidence of opposites—so now he brings together under the single concept of reality God and the visible world, and speaks of reality as if it had two sides or aspects, one being God, the invisible and ultimate reality, the other the world, the visible and derived reality. *Quid est mundus nisi invisibilis Dei apparitio ? Quid Deus, nisi visibilium invisibilitas ?* The two are separate ; yet they are correlated. Using other terms, we might say that reality is both subject and object. As subject, it is God, originating, communicating ; as object, originated and communicated, it is the world.

If anything, it is the active and communicating aspect of reality which Nicholas emphasizes, and this receives illustration in his doctrine of the Trinity, perhaps the most difficult part of his work, but one of great importance, since to him, just as to Erigena, the Trinity was the plan of the universe. Readers of the *De concordantia catholica* will recollect the significance which he attaches to the threefold structure of the Church and the elaborate symmetry with which he works out the triad in her every past and activity.[2] The Scot and Eckhart had identified Father, Son and Holy Spirit with *essentia, virtus, operatio* : Nicholas adopts these terms on occasion, but his more general practice is to identify them with unity, equality and connexion, " Things in the world are many, but they are ever seeking unity ; they are different, but they are ever seeking equality ; they are divided, but they are ever seeking connexion."[3] True to his practice, Nicholas provides an *aenigma* or

---

[1] *Op. cit.*, p. 179.   [2] I. iv, v ; *Opera*, pp. 695–704.
[3] Bett, *op. cit.*, p. 149.

illustration of this, in his *Cribrationis Alchoran*. He depicts himself
as beholding a circular piece of water surrounded by meadows and
vegetation, and noting that though there was no apparent intake
or outlet, the water was quite fresh and greatly appreciated by the
natives of the country. This caused him surprise, till he saw that there
was a spring in the middle that fed a stream proceeding from it.
The water, therefore, was both spring, river and lake ; " and this
equally, since it was not more spring than river and lake ; and in the
lake was river and spring, nor was the spring river or lake, nor was the
river spring or lake ; nor was the lake spring or river. And I did not
see this, except when I considered with my intellect that the spring
of itself generated the river ; and therefore spring and river are
different, as generating and generated, like the Father and the Son.
Nor can the lake be river or spring, from which two it proceeds.
And I said : the spring is unity, the river equality and the lake is
connexion (*nexus utriusque*)." [1]

Dr. Bett has pointed out that these three attributes involve, in the finite
world, the existence of opposites—multiplicity, inequality and separa-
tion—and that such an antagonism is hardly consistent with Nicholas's
view, expressed elsewhere, that the world is the most perfect reflection
possible of the perfect nature of God. This is, I think, a just criticism of
a serious inconsistency. Yet there is in Nicholas's idea of the Trinity a
principle of some importance : it is the activity *within* the godhead
itself that distinguishes the deity of Cusanus from the abstract principle
of pure being conceived by the philosophers. In the God that he has
represented to us there is somehow or other expressed the vital pulse
and motion of existing nature. This is perhaps the significance of the
difficult chapter x of the second book of the *De docta ignorantia*, where
Nicholas discusses this *motus* or universal impulse in nature towards unity.
To him the Trinity is " the Trinity of the Universe." In God, the
absolute, is found the possibility that is limited in this world (he calls
this world the " contraction " of possibility and actuality) ; " in absolute
form, which is the Word of the Father, the Son of Holy Writ, are all
form and actuality ; in the absolute connexion of the divine spirit all
impulse to connexion, and the proportion and harmony that come
therefrom." [2] The Trinity is thus the indication of the perfect union
of possibility and actuality ; realizing what the material world is trying
to realize, but cannot, because its possibility and actuality are both limited.

Contemporaries must have found Nicholas's conception of God
very difficult. How was He to be made to enter the devotional life of
the ordinary believer ? At the Benedictine monastery of Tegernsee

[1] II. viii–ix ; *Opera*, p. 902.   [2] *Ed. cit.*, p. 99.

the prior, Bernard of Waging, was one of Nicholas's most fervent admirers,[1] and had introduced his doctrines to the convent. In 1453 Nicholas sent Bernard the treatise *De Visione Dei*, which was to explain to the brethren in simple language the meaning of learned ignorance and the notion of God which that involved. They had evidently asked to be initiated into the " mystical theology "—their phrase is interesting [2] —which he had made his own. The ascent or approach of the seeking believer is what they must have had in mind. But the *visio Dei* which Nicholas revealed to them is not what we mean when we speak of the " Vision of God." To Nicholas the vision is not man's view of God, but God's glance embracing man. Within that glance, " unlimited sight," as he calls it, man's small life is lived. " Thy look is my being. I am because Thou dost look at me. If Thou didst turn Thy face away, I should cease to be."

Nicholas proposed " by the simplest and most commonplace method to lead you by experience into that most sacred darkness." [3] The method is the metaphor of an *icon* or picture of a face with eyes that follow its beholders about wherever he stands or goes—" as though looking on all round it." He quotes a number of examples, particularly one " by the eminent painter, Roger [van der Weyden] in his priceless picture in the governor's house in Brussels." Put up the picture of God, says Nicholas, and stand a little way off : " and each of you shall find that, from whatever quarter he regardeth it, it looketh upon him as if it looked on none other." The astonishing thing is " the motion of its unmoveable gaze." The picture " keepeth in sight all as they go on their way, though it be in contrary directions ; and thus he [the beholder addressed] will prove that that countenance, though motionless, is turned to east in the same way that it is simultaneously turned to west, and in the same way to north and to south." God is called *theos* because He beholds all. It is not of the essence of sight to behold one object more than another,

> though it is inherent in sight, in its limited state [*contractus*, as above] to be unable to look on more than one thing at a time or upon all things absolutely. But God is true unlimited sight, and He is not inferior to sight in the abstract, as it can be conceived by the intellect, but is beyond all comparison more perfect. Wherefore the apparent vision of the icon cannot so closely approach the supreme excellence of Absolute Sight as can our abstract conception.

---

[1] See the account of him in E. Vansteenberghe, *Autour de la docte ignorance*, pp. 1–2, and his *opuscula* printed on pp. 163–188.

[2] How far had Cusanus intended his *De docta ignorantia* as a work of " mystical theology " for contemplatives ? It is very difficult to say. Even those brought up upon Eckhart would have found it extremely hard.

[3] I quote from the translation by Miss E. Gurney Salter.

And here is his view of the attributes assigned to God, the affirmations which we found the "negative theology" rejecting :

> The attributes assigned to God cannot differ in reality, by reason of the perfect simplicity of God. God, being the Absolute Ground of all formal natures, embraceth in Himself all natures. Whence, although we attribute to God sight, hearing, taste, smell, touch, sense, reason and intellect, and so forth, according to the divers significations of each word, yet in Him sight is not other than hearing or tasting or smelling or touching or feeling or understanding. And so all theology is said to be stablished in a circle, because any one of His attributes is affirmed of another, and to have with God is to be, and to move is to stand, and to run is to rest ; and so with the other attributes. Thus, although in one sense we attribute to Him movement and in another rest, yet because He is Himself the Absolute Ground in which all otherness (*alteritas*) is unity, and all diversity is identity, that diversity which is not identity proper, to wit diversity as we understand it, cannot exist in God.[1]

God's face is the archetypal face or, as we might put it, " face " ; and Nicholas's reflection upon its power leads him to a passage which explains the " sacred darkness " of the ignorance that he is expounding. The passage, which must be quoted in its entirety, here seems one of the most important for a full understanding of the Cusan dialectic (as I ventured to call it above). He imagines himself looking at a nut-tree, first with the visual eye, then with the mental, and lastly with the eye of holy ignorance :

> Thy face is that power and principle from which all faces are what they are ; and, this being so, I turn me to this nut-tree, a big tall tree—and seek to perceive its principle. I see it with the eye of sense to be big and spreading, coloured, laden with branches, leaves and nuts. Then I perceive with the eye of the mind that that tree existed in its seed, not as I now behold it, but potentially. I consider with care the marvellous might of that seed, wherein the entire tree, and all its nuts, and all the generative power of the nuts, and all trees, existed in the generative power of the nuts. And I perceive how that power can never be fully explicated in any time measured by the motion of the heavens ; yet how that same power, though beyond explication, is still limited, because it availeth only in this particular species of nuts. Wherefore, albeit in the seed I perceive only the tree, it is yet in a limited power only. Then, Lord, I consider how the generative power of all the divers species of trees is limited each to its own species, and in those same seeds I perceive the virtual trees.
>
> If, therefore, I am fain to behold the Absolute power of all such generative powers—which is the power, and likewise the principle, giving power to all seeds—I must needs pass beyond all generative power which can be known or imagined, and enter into that ignorance wherein no vestige remaineth of generative power or energy. Then in the darkness I find a Power (*virtutem*) most stupendous, not to be approached by any power imaginable, and this is the principle which giveth being to all generative and other power. This

---

[1] *The Vision of God*, p. 12.

Power being absolute and exalted above all, giveth to every generative power that power wherein it enfoldeth the virtual tree, together with all things necessary to an actual tree and that inhere in the being of a tree ; wherefore this principle and cause containeth in itself, as cause, alike enfolded and absolutely, whatsoever it giveth to its effect.

Like the Confessions of St. Augustine, the *Vision of God* is addressed to the deity. It is written with a warmth and emotion that glow particularly in the later chapters (xviii–xxv). The creature can only attain union with God because He is *amabilis et intelligibilis* ; He is to be loved as Deus genitus, the " absolute mediator," beloved of the Father, loving Him in turn. The son is *medium unionis omnium* : the means of uniting all. To Nicholas the mediator is the uniter. Human nature could not be united to the Father, save by the Son's mediation. " Who is not deeply ravished when he meditates carefully on this ? For Thou, my God, openest to me such a secret, that I see that man cannot understand Thee, the Father, save in Thy Son, who is intelligible and the mediator ; and that to understand Thee is to be united to Thee." The Son, medium of union, is human nature " profoundly united " to God. Jesus Himself is to be understood as the union (*copulatio*) of divine and human nature (ch. xx). Nicholas thinks of Him as " within the wall of Paradise," since His intellect is both Truth and the Image of Truth, and He both Creator and created ; not " without the wall," for that is not possible, since he combines the divine creating nature with human nature created. It is the humanity of Jesus that draws men to the Father. *Per te, Iesu, omnes attrahit Pater homines.* To Cusanus mediation meant the nexus of love.

In the sermon *Vere filius Dei erat iste*,[1] Jesus is represented as the Word of the Father sending the Father's message in brief over the earth.[2] The humanity of Christ, a living book, is the conclusion of all books, writings, forms, arts, technique. A conclusion is " a brief word, gathering up in its power all that could not be sufficiently explained in many books : for it is the conclusion for which everything is written ; for the things that are written are but its explication." Those who tend to think of Nicholas as the severe and abstract philosopher would do well to turn to the *De Visione Dei* and the Sermons. Here they will find passages of a serene and moving simplicity. His learning does not impede him here. Allusions to the canon law, his patristic learning and mathematical terminology are laid aside, and a poetic and humble spirit is revealed in the limpid prose of a great Latinist.

Cusanus is not a casuist ; he is no moral theologian. He is so wrapped

---

[1] *Excitationum Liber*, v ; *Opera*, p. 490.

[2] " Est verbum patris abbreuiatum super terram " : *loc. cit.* Cf. especially the " Dies Sanctificatus " (ed. Hoffmann and Klibanksy), pp. 34–36.

up in his vision that sin and error seem very far in the distance. There is scarcely any doctrine of the atonement; the sermons are mainly concerned with the nature of God and the person of Christ, but the sacrifice of the mediator is little dwelt upon. Nicholas had seen what corruption meant in high places. His reform of the German monasteries shows him to have been a shrewd and judicious churchman whose eyes were open to the abuses prevalent. Yet, save for the practical political chapters at the end of the *De concordantia catholica*, there is little in his work that is concerned with the problem of evil. His mind, which lights the whole fifteenth century, was the mind of a metaphysician, not of a moral philosopher. He saw the finite and infinite in terms of relationship, and looked for the union of created man with the creating Father through the mediation of the Son and the harmonizing of the Spirit.

CHAPTER X

"MIDDLE AGES" AND "RENAISSANCE"

IN one of his most entertaining letters, Mr. Justice Holmes observed that it was the end of man to form general propositions : but, he significantly added, most of them were "not worth a damn." His words, one fears, apply particularly to historians ; and perhaps there is no period of their study in which the truth of that great lawyer's remark is more evident than the fifteenth century.

"Middle Ages" and "Renaissance" are terms to which, as the result of nineteenth-century scholarship, very definite conceptions came to be attached. Profound differences appeared to exist between the two epochs, and the boundary was sharply drawn. Now it is clear that every historian, according to his own special interest, will draw that boundary-line differently ; and some will not draw it at all. This negative, we might even say evolutionary, point of view will not prevent us giving full credit to vitally creative personalities like Petrarch or Masaccio or Prince Henry the Navigator ; it implies that in the fourteenth and fifteenth centuries we must be prepared for the coexistence of the reactionary and the progressive, the obstinate remnants of the feudal world and the hopeful efficiencies of the new. It means, too, that the student of the Middle Ages will frequently recognize, even in the later examples of characteristically Renaissance work and institutions, much that is strangely familiar, however vigorously its authors protest their abhorrence of the "barbarous" ages before them. Often he will detect the old structure taken up and stylistically transformed. Each resumption will be with a difference, sometimes a serious difference, yet the medieval body will be there right enough, clearly recognizable through its modern trappings ; often through the medieval the new will be introduced.

All this sounds obvious : yet why have people been so slow to realize that it is not possible to jump out of one age into another ? It may be due to the depreciation by humanists like Poggio of the clerical past and all its works (he spoke of monastic libraries as the *ergastula* of barbarians) or to the laughter of the Aufklärung at the expense of everything "gothic" ; or to the general belief, fostered by all text-books (except by certain recent French and German examples), that at the Renaissance the individual "emerged" with a clear-cut and independent moral and aesthetic personality never acquired in his earlier institutional fetters. The Italian humanist has been the model. We

may best put the case in the words used by Walter Raleigh in writing
about Sir Thomas Hoby's translation of the *Cortigiano* : " the purpose
of the humanists was open and unashamed : man was to train himself
like a race-horse, to cultivate himself like a flower, that he might arrive
to such perfection as mortality might covet." It is rightly urged that
the purpose of the humanist was to invest his material, whether in
architecture, sculpture, painting or verse, with his own personality,
with the movement and the moods of a living man. Readers of Mr.
Berenson's criticism will recollect how often he uses the expression " the
tactile values " when appraising a piece of Renaissance sculpture : he
means that the artist is always appealing to our sense of touch, a veritable mark of the humanist. No one will gainsay the Renaissance artist's
freedom of conception, the naturalism based on close observation of
bodily motion, of the flight of birds, the massing of clouds, the purple
depth of landscapes, the contrasts of light and shade. No one will
deny that to the representatives or personifiers of the strongly self-
conscious " empires " which are the Renaissance States, contemporary
opinion attributed an indefeasible sanctity ; no one will dispute the
splendour of their courts or the art of their diplomacy. It is not the
place of the medievalist to contradict these things, although he may
legitimately urge that a monastic chronicler or a medieval university
student can be as self-revealing and as informing about his own or
other people's characters as any Renaissance diarist or ambassador, and
that his Latin is nearer to life than the Ciceronian correctness of the
Renaissance classicists. He will merely suggest that the majority of
human beings at the Renaissance were not humanists, nor courtiers,
but, whether of noble or of lowly birth, still the simple children of a
patria, like the good and lawful jurymen of a medieval assize roll, the
townsmen or the members of a tithing : men and women who grew
up in backgrounds of local custom and tradition, the sons and daughters
of their parish churches, which gathered up the social as well as the
religious life of their districts, and were the spiritual units of the country,
whatever that country might be. (Who can look at Burford, or St.
Thomas's, Salisbury, or the Sebalduskirche at Nuremberg, without
feeling this ?) He will venture to urge that the foundations of many
intellectual triumphs were laid in the scholastic past, and that humanism
is much too complex a phenomenon to admit of simple qualification
like " the emergence of the individual " ; that the arts of diplomacy
had long been practised in their subtlest forms by proctors at the Curia ;
that strong centralized administration, not unknown to the Normans,
had long been a source of complaint to feudal reactionaries both in
France and in England ; that the foreign exchange of which some

Renaissance writers complain so bitterly was a product of the Great Fairs. It may even appear to him that if there is any break in the continuity of European tradition, it is the break between the later Roman-early medieval epoch and the Middle Ages proper, as M. Ferdinand Lot has depicted it for us,[1] rather than between the Middle Ages and the Renaissance.

The great spell of Jakob Burckhardt in Germany and the influence of John Addington Symonds in this country—Pater, by including in his *Renaissance* essays both on early French romance and on Winckelmann, showed deeper insight—for long kept at bay intruders from an earlier period. Italy held the field, and under Burckhardt's influence a psychological method of writing history which concentrated attention upon representative types.[2] Literary and artistic figures that seemed to crystallize their periods or embody the atmospheres of their courts, cultured despots with the true gentleman's *sprezzatura* and clothes that showed to best advantage in the southern light, made a sure appeal against an age of respectability. English and German interest in the triumph of Italian nationalism, the romantic attraction for the Italian country and Italian monuments, which is the mainspring of Gregorovius and runs all through Browning : these, and the growing study of the Italian primitives popularized by men of versatile genius, kept attention away from transalpine developments just as much as from the study of Renaissance science and philosophy in Italy itself. The bulk of historians, reacting to these and other more formal influences, drew an Italian and aesthetic boundary-line between Middle Ages and Renaissance. For some it was the pontificate of Nicholas V, some put it more precisely in 1439 (the Council of Florence), but most were agreed that the first half of the fifteenth century was the place for it. In their several ways Petrarch (" the first modern man ") and Boccaccio were regarded as the " forerunners " of the fifteenth-century movement, though it was generally believed that in Italy the Renaissance arrived almost imperceptibly, long before it came to the rest of Europe, because there the classical tradition and classical architecture had never died out. It was barely remembered that Gothic in Italy, though originally an importation, became a very real thing in the fourteenth century, and that its minute naturalism in the smaller industrial arts had particularly interesting manifestations in Lombardy ; or that there were humanists in the time of Dante. Dr. Walter Goetz dealt decisively with the " Italian " point

---

[1] *The End of the Ancient World* (1931), especially p. 407.
[2] Richard Winners, *Weltanschauung und Geschichtsauffassung Jakob Burckhardts* (Beiträge zur kulturgesch. der M.A. und Renaissance, ed. W. Goetz, 1929), p. 34.

of view as early as 1907, and his judicious critique has never been discredited.[1]

In this country the change of view was long in appearing. For here the Wars of the Roses, which Stubbs taught us to regard as the struggles of a heartless pseudo-chivalric baronage, and the local corruption revealed in the Paston Letters, seems to epitomize the fifteenth century until Henry Tudor's coming, and the prevalent view of its culture was Denton's. There was also a natural reluctance to tackle the fifteenth century because of its genuine difficulties. Indeed, Professor Tout, in one of those moments of pessimism which sometimes affect the more buoyant natures, declared that the history of the fifteenth century could not be written : it was too hard. It was hard indeed because there seemed no clear line of advance in the various phases of the national life. In his Ford lectures, *Prejudice and Promise in 15th Century England*, Mr. Kingsford showed how brighter and more promising elements in intellectual life, how the desire for peace with our ancient rival, France, and for urban prosperity, co-existed with the old prejudices. It has fallen to the economic historians to draw a more complex picture that bears out the prejudice and promise of which Kingsford wrote. These scholars [2] have pointed out that it was a time of striking contradictions, alike of progress and retrogression : both in arable cultivation and in wool production, the period for England is one of decline " or at best stabilization," in contrast to the age of Edward I and II ; but at the same time, the development of capitalism, largely associated with the wool trade, not only produced individuals of great wealth, but also reached the middle ranks of the bourgeoisie, and led to a more modest and widely-distributed range of prosperity and influence. Socially, the rise of an intelligent middle class that demanded opportunities for education and better standards of comfort, laid the foundation of a firm middle element in the State, which was lacking in a country like Scotland. Yet the advance was in danger by a lack of public spirit and weakness at the centre : there were provincial growth and public apathy ; and constitutional studies have pointed to a similar phenomenon in legal and parliamentary institutions : this country in the fifteenth century, in its contrasts, its parochialism and its apparent isolation from the Continent,

[1] " Mittelalter und Renaissance," *Historische Zeitschrift*, 98, pp. 30–54.

[2] Notably M. Postan and E. Power, *English Trade in the Fifteenth Century, passim.* Dr. Eileen Power in *The Wool Trade in English Medieval History*, Lecture II, especially p. 35 f., summarizes the position outlined here ; cf. also her Lecture VI. For agrarian conditions, see M. Postan, " The Fifteenth Century " (Revisions in Economic History, ix.), *Economic History Review*, ix. 160–167, and John Saltmarsh, " Plague and Economic Decline in the Later Middle Ages," *Cambridge Historical Journal*, vol. vii. no. 1 (1941), 23–41. Professor Postan's article foreshadows his book on Manorial Profits.

provides, to modern research, problems of extraordinary fascination and difficulty,[1] all of them pointing to the basic amalgam of old and new from which anyone wishing to study the period must start.

These studies suggest that the purely intellectual and aesthetic approach to the problem of the relation between the Middle Ages and the Renaissance affords a very one-sided picture of the organic life of Europe, and this is equally true of an approach that is primarily religious. Yet historians of religion, just as much as students of economic history, have helped to transform our knowledge of that relationship.

In Germany the study of philosophy and later medieval religion, which we have come to associate with Prantl and Wilhelm Dilthey, led in the 'nineties to a closer analysis of European thought and spiritual experience. Pantheism, the new Platonism of the fifteenth century, the nominalism of Ockham and the revolt of Cusanus against the Aristotelian canons of ratiocination for the first time received the attention they deserved, and their bearing upon later developments in thought began to be seen. Perhaps the most influential factor of change was Reformation scholarship. The transformation of Luther's religious views between 1505 and 1515 was seen to require a deeper investigation than the old psychological explanation of that process permitted. Denifle in his *Luther* pointed to the medieval background of the Erfurt teaching, but his emphasis on Luther's " degeneracy " (which he set out to prove) kept him from doing justice to the Ockhamist theology which the future reformer imbibed. To Denifle Luther's theology was, in Dr. Boehmer's words,[2] " The degenerate product of degenerate scholasticism." It was left for more modern research to show what Luther rejected and what he retained out of the theological heritage that came to him, and how important his retentions were.[3] As Dr. Boehmer has pointed out, the value of Ockhamist criticism to Luther's development can hardly be overestimated, since it gave him " a whole arsenal of weapons to use in the struggle against Catholic dogma and the Catholic constitutional and legal system." Now Ockhamism it was which by its emphasis on the value of scientific experiment helped in the evolution not only of the early geographers and geographical discovery, but also of supreme Renaissance minds like Leonardo da Vinci. Like the philosophy of St. Augustine, it can bring to birth many new things, can be sceptical and destructive as well as (by its very method) creative. Its

---

[1] The difficulty arises mostly from the " sheer contradictoriness of our evidence, which is itself due in part to the seminal nature of the times " : S. B. Chrimes, *English Constitutional Ideas in the XVth Century*, p. 303.

[2] *Luther and the Reformation in the light of Modern Research*, pp. 23–24.

[3] *Op. cit.*, pp. 63–70. For the reaction against Ockham's doctrine of the will, see the *Times Literary Supplement*, 10 September 1931, p. 676.

creations are not "literary" ones, though it is not true to say, as Erasmus did, that Lutheranism spelled the death of letters.[1]   Literary performances do not exhaust the Renaissance, and the man who appeared a philistine to Erasmus was also the father of the German chorale.

Part of Luther's theological inheritance was the mystical piety that had its home in the Netherlands, a movement in great measure of the people and for the people, that *devotio moderna* which has been the subject of so much study in recent years. Ullmann's *Reformers before the Reformation* had long before pointed the way, but the emphasis laid there upon the "protestant" aspect of those North German devout spirits obscured their connexion with the Middle Ages and left them in a sort of unhistorical vacuum, while others described them erroneously as early humanists.   Only recently has it been understood that the pietist movement which started in the late fourteenth and was at work throughout the fifteenth century was compounded of many elements : that, as we suggested above, it cannot strictly be described, as Hyma describes it, as a "Christian Renaissance" unless by "Renaissance" is meant a movement for the revival of a Christianity based upon the gospel virtues of love and humility and unselfish co-operation.   It was really a lay experiment in the devotional life and the Christian education of young people, and, as such, it was one of that great complex of influences that had spread through the Europe into which Luther was born.   Other such influences, particularly in their bearing on the life of the people, Johannes Janssen, in reaction against the "political" history of Ranke, long ago portrayed in his *History of the German People since the End of the Middle Ages*.   The growth of capitalism in town and country, urban and rural communist reactions, were revealed by investigations of industrial organization and agrarian movements ; and now the study of the German universities, their curricula and the "school theology" taught there in the fifteenth century, has given us a remarkable picture of diversity in method, displaying upholders of the *via antiqua* (the older moderate realism) rubbing shoulders with, and often opposing, adherents of the *via moderna* (the nominalism of Ockham and d'Ailly),[2] and the coexistence of scholastic theologians and "rhetoricians" or humanistic exponents of classical style in the same homes of learning.[3]

This complex picture is not only true of Germany.   M. Champion's *Histoire poétique du quinzième siècle* presents literary France under an

[1] "Ubi regnat Lutheranismus, ibi litterarum intcritus."

[2] Gerhard Ritter, *Studien zur Spätscholastik*. II (Sitzungsb. d. Heidelb. Ak. d. Wiss., 1922).   Cf. especially pp. 124 *seqq.* for a discussion of the relations between humanism and *via antiqua*.

[3] Ritter, "Die Geschichtliche Bedeutung des deutschen Humanismus," *Historische Zeitschrift*, 127 (1923), p. 393.

equally variegated aspect, with that dualism in contemporary life which
Mr. Kingsford portrayed with such effect when he gave his Ford Lectures
on the fifteenth century in England. There are deep constitutional
complexities also. How shall we classify the monarchy of Louis XI or
of Edward IV ? Concentration of power and centralization are not
their only mark. There is the same consciousness in both monarchs
that government is an art, perhaps the highest game of skill. The use
by Commines of the terms *saige* and *sagesse*,[1] by Chastellain of *subtil*
and *subtilite* [2] in relation to Louis, take us out of the medieval world ;
and when Commines describes Edward as " Beau prince entre les beaux
du monde à l'heure qu'il fut de tous points au-dessus de ses affaires," [3]
do we not gain an impression never derived from the figures described
by Froissart, still less by English chroniclers ? [4]

And now, instead of looking for dualisms or the *concordantia opposi-
torum*, let us note, as briefly as possible, certain ways in which the Middle
Ages shared with the fifteenth and sixteenth centuries a common attitude
towards the classical past, and then turn to consider the persistence of
medievalism in what are normally considered full-blown Renaissance
activities.

First, the common aim to renew the Roman Empire. The effort
towards the restoration of imperial Rome (later we shall observe the
respect for *republican* Rome also) is one which is constantly occurring
both in the early and the later Middle Ages. We are all familiar with
Otto III's attempt to give his Empire a centralized Roman administration,[5]
to stabilize in the eternal city the power of the Emperor himself as against
the patriciate of the Crescentii. Dr. Percy Schramm, whose observations
on the occurrence of the Goddess Roma in early medieval art have
gained wide recognition,[6] has recently submitted the idea of *renovatio*
to an acute analysis, and shown what an important part it played in the
lives of the early Holy Roman Emperors and of the city itself. Under
Otto III it was the co-operation of Emperor and Pope which was to
bring about the restoration and guard against the dangerous plan of
making Rome dependent on the Basileus at Constantinople as of old.

---

[1] Cf. his famous picture of Louis XI (ed. B. de Mandrot, i. 73).
[2] E.g. *Chronique* (ed. Kervyn de Lettenhove), v. 456 : " Le roy cestes estoit
homme subtil et feint, savoit reculer pour saillir plus loin, savoit faire l'humble et
le doux a couverte fin, savoit . . . donner pour recevoir en double."
[3] Ed. B. de Mandrot, ii. 90.
[4] Except, perhaps, the translator of Livius.
[5] Cf. K. Hampe's " Kaiser Otto III und Rom," *Historische Zeitschrift*, 140 (1929),
513, and the earlier paper of L. Halphen, " La Cour d'Otton III à Rome," *Mélanges
d'Archéologie et d'histoire*, XXXV. 349–63.
[6] " Das Herrscherbild in der Kunst des frühen Mittelalters," *Vorträge der Bibliothek
Warburg* (1922–1923), i. 161 f., 214 f.

Schramm shows how the conception made successful headway against the influence of two documents which might normally seem opposed to it, the Donation of Constantine and Pippin's pact with the papacy, extended by Charles the Great, which guaranteed the boundaries of papal territory; [1] and by studying the lists of officials and the accounts of the ceremonies at the imperial court comprised in the various guide-books for the information of the medieval visitor, he proves that ever since the end of the ninth century the notion of an imperial hierarchy was kept alive at Rome, providing a kind of basis or justification for the attempts of the Emperors to turn their Italian supremacy into a reality within the city itself. [2] At the other end of the Middle Ages Dr. Konrad Burdach has given much attention to the meaning of the terms " renewal " and " re-birth." He finds them prominent in the letters of Rienzo, where they are used in connexion with the longed-for coming to Italy of an Emperor who is to be both Caesar and Messiah, and was to rule over an Italianized Empire; for Rienzo had the notion of the extension of Roman citizenship to all Italians, who were to concur, like the citizens of Rome, in the popular election of the new Emperor. [3] There can be no doubt that the word *renasci* was used of this projected imperial " re-birth," and that the conception was not unfamiliar to the early humanists from Dante's days onwards; but Burdach's method of pressing obscure artistic and literary symbolism into support of his theory gives the impression that the idea was shared by a much wider circle than in reality it was.

The continuity of the imperial idea in Italy through the Middle Ages into the early Renaissance, though it does not quite fall under our subject of Roman renewal, is an absorbing subject of study. It is worth observing the persistence of the concept in Italian public law. Signor F. Ercole, the author of an illuminating work on Dante as political thinker, has made some extremely suggestive observations upon its practical consequences; particularly upon its part in helping the modern state to birth. In early days the Communes might and did appeal to the Emperor against feudal authority; then came their struggle with the imperial power; their position now guaranteed by the Peace of Constance, with the growth of communal autonomy and the extension of communal territory, the imperial authority came to be only heeded

[1] *Kaiser, Rom und Renovatio* (1929), i. 21.

[2] *Ibid.*, i. 193 *seqq.* Schramm's study of the *Graphia aureae urbis Romae*, compiled in Rome about 1155, shows that the work incorporates the *Graphia Libellus* of Conrad II's time (1030) and the *Mirabilia Urbis Romae* (of *c.* 1140). The lists of officials in the *Libellus* show that " Antikes, Byzantinisches, Stadtrömisches und Ottonisches verschmolzen sind."

[3] *Vom Mittelalter zur Reformation*, II, i, 115–138. *Renaissance, Reformation Humanismus* (1926), especially pp. 77–84.

or invoked on occasion and for peculiar local reasons. Yet after the failure alike of the Hohenstaufen and of Henry of Luxemburg, even when the imperial vicariates were no longer, the idea of imperial sovereignty never died out. It was held that just as the Empire evolved from the Roman republic, so the imperial rule was the creation of the people, from which it derived its strength (the *Lex Regia* was prominently displayed in Rome during the fourteenth century). Republican Rome provided a powerful example for each city striving for constitutional liberty.

> Every commune felt itself, and was in fact, free to assume the constitution which suited it . . . and the people (*popolo*) of each separate commune seemed in itself to reproduce on a small scale the image of republican Rome ; took upon itself the rights and powers of the Roman people, had its own Senate, its own magistrates, its own consuls, and its own plebiscites ; experienced the struggles and fluctuations of parties . . . and like the people of Rome was able one day to renounce and lay in the hands of a single individual the power of all. The Signory, with an historical throw-back worthy of the closest attention, re-enacted on a diminished scale, in confronting the Commune, the very thing that had taken place on the grand scale when the Empire stood face to face with the republic ; and the *lex de imperio*, not without good cause, was the term used in a number of places for the act of electing the Supreme ruler.[1]

The ruler, as one exercising an authority delegated by the people, was not slow to concentrate all authority in his own hands, and to reduce the cities subject to him under separate pacts and agreements to a general condition of subordination, in which their differences in status disappeared, so that under the concept of the City State appeared that of the modern State. To these new units many of the juridical principles of absolutism and omnipotence found in Roman Law began to apply. A further step in the evolution of the modern State, Ercole argues, came through the recognition of the right of Pope and Emperor to legitimatize the forms of government adopted by the people. Pope or Emperor may come in at a comparatively late stage in the process when the legality of the permanent transfer of powers from the government to a despot is called in question, in which case the semi-feudal authority of one or other of these powers is invoked by the despot to stabilize his position.[2] Thus there is some use for one or other of the two great medieval luminaries even at the time of the Renaissance, and it is of no

---

[1] F. Ercole, " Impero e Papato nella tradizione giuridica Bolognese e nel diritto pubblico Romano," *Atti e memorie della R. Deputazione per Storia Patria per le Provincie di Romagna*, IV Ser., vol. 1 (Bologna, 1911), p. 128. Miss C. M. Ady kindly called my attention to this.

[2] This is the argument of G. B. Picotti, " Qualche osservazione sui caratteri delle signorie Italiane," *Rivista storica italiana*, vol. 43 (1926).

small interest to find what appears at first sight to be a thoroughly medieval authority helping in the evolution of "a modern" constitution.

Complementary to this notion of the political revival of Rome is that of an *aurea aetas*, an age of peaceful culture and civilization, imperially fostered and guaranteed. Something resembling this is, of course, given immortal expression in the *De Monarchia*. Giuseppe Toffanin in his highly stimulating, if a trifle over-imaginative, *Che cosa fu l'umanesimo?* [1] has pointed to the expectation of this age of tranquil *civiltà* entertained by contemporaries of Dante like Albertino Mussato. The language of such a future epoch was to be the speech of Cicero, who represented the championship of *pure* Latin as against the coarser idiom, the *devota rusticitas*, of the sects. The polemics of Petrarch against the Averroists of Padua and of Coluccio Salutati against Giovanni di San Miniato have more than a doctrinal significance : they stand for the assertion of a broad general *humana civilitas* against uncouth sectionalism. It is highly significant that Cicero is brought by Petrarch [2] into alliance with the Church. Toffanin thinks that it was Paduan Averroism that first brought about the project of such a literary union, and the heretical sects that generated in orthodox opponents the idea of a clerical-classical culture, which is the first definition that historically fits humanism.

This interesting view may be disputed, but it has at least one potent germ of truth. The tradition of Christian humanism does not die. It is the Schoolmen that do much to familiarize the West with classical culture. Years ago Lord Acton pointed out what a mistake it was to regard the Renaissance as, in origin, a pagan or un-Christian movement. What is essentially true of England is also true of the Continent. The Renaissance in its early stages is deeply connected with the clerical and scholastic past. To study the translations of Aristotle's Ethics made in the thirteenth century is to realize the spread of Greek ideas in the most "medieval" of all ages. The investigations of the Ethics in Latin form, begun a hundred years ago by Amable Jourdain and continued by Baur, Grabmann, Minges, Father Pelzer, have demonstrated the importance in this connexion of Robert Grosseteste, who, like Walter Burley and Henry Harclay in the next century, has lately received special attention. [3]

---

[1] Florence, 1929.

[2] In his *De ocio religiosorum*. Petrarch saw the danger lurking in Cicero's civic spirit, and did his best to emphasize the contrast "between his vain and restless political activities and the fruitful attitude of his old age" : Hans Baron, "Cicero and the Roman Civic Spirit in the Middle Ages and Early Renaissance," *Bull. John Rylands Lib.*, vol. 22, no. 1, April 1938.

[3] For a study of the Oriel College Oxford MS. of Grosseteste's translation, see F. M. Powicke, *Robert Grosseteste and the Nicomachean Ethics* (British Academy, 1930). Grosseteste's translations from the Greek are listed by S. Harrison Thomson, *The Writings of Robert Grosseteste, Bishop of Lincoln, 1235–1253* (Camb. 1940), pp. 42–71.

Naturally the Ethics is not always quoted for the moral inspiration or " inwardness " of Aristotle's counsel (for only in the matter of friendship did he ever pass beyond an " external " conception of the moral life), but for sensible and practical advice on the formation of good habits and the avoidance of bad ones. Yet even this quotation and his vogue mean something ; and it is hard to see why certain writers imply that a continuation of Aristotelian tradition should in some way detract from the " true " character of the Renaissance. Apart from the *Timaeus*, was it not Aristotle as much as Boethius who transmitted much of the substance of what Plato wrote to the West ? The fact that A is quoted in B's work does not necessarily mean that other people's knowledge of A will suffer from inaccuracy. Moreover, if we find " scholastic, Aristotelian, Averroistic material and astrological interpretation and discussion of the Platonic ideas in the second half of the Quattrocento," does this point to the fact that its Platonism was a " hollow pretence " ? [1] Surely it is the most natural thing in the world, when one considers the whole trend of contemporary philosophical training ; it helps to show that throughout most of the fifteenth century, even in Italy itself, the Renaissance was essentially a *Stilbegriff*, or, as we may say, a change in the way of putting things, rather than a change in essential ideas about those things. The Quattrocento brought about a revolution in style ; but can we honestly say that the search after new Greek models has gone so deep that the whole structure and method of scholastic argument is discarded ? The answer is emphatically in the negative.

The stylistic changes have long been coming. *Humana civilitas* demands an elegance of expression, after which the Middle Ages were increasingly in pursuit. Dr. Goetz's study of the sermons of King Robert of Naples shows that interesting monarch not only citing Latin classics of the golden and silver ages with the freedom of a John of Salisbury, but taking the themes of his discourses from Sallust and Seneca independently of the influence of Petrarch.[2] Those sermons, the discourses, be it noted, of a layman, are purely formal scholastic homilies of the most orthodox kind. This will not surprise any acquainted with the increasing classicism of the *Ars dictandi*. Moreover, the systematic

---

[1] So Lynn Thorndike, *Science and Thought in the Fifteenth Century*, pp. 177–178. Dr. Thorndike's conclusions on the slowness of the *quattrocento* to emancipate itself from medieval scientific conceptions are well worth pondering.

[2] König Robert von Neapel (1309–1343) : *seine Persönlichkeit und sein Verhältnis zum Humanismus* (Tübingen, 1910), especially p. 38. " König Robert ist mit seiner Vermischung von Scholastik und Antike ein Beweis dafür, und ebenso die Humanisten seiner Umgebung die nur eine mangelhafte Chronologie unter den Einfluss Petrarcas bringen könne." Cf. his very true remark (p. 42) : " Die Scholastik hat in erster Linie der Antike die Tore zur Renaissance geöffnet. Die scholastische Arbeit des 13 Jahrhunderts war reine Rezeption der Antike."

elaboration of style in Italy had its parallel north of the Alps. The Bologna masters of the Dictamen, about whom both Rockinger and Dr. Haskins wrote so attractively, had their spiritual progeny in England during the fourteenth and fifteenth centuries. As men groped towards Cicero, the high priest of all Latin stylists, a remarkable period of euphuism sets in, a sort of counterpart of the elaborate Gothic expression-ism found both in the Burgundian territories and in the sculpture of late medieval Germany. In his work on early English humanism [1] Dr. Walter Schirmer began the investigation of this new stylistic movement in England, and since then various studies, culminating in the recent work of Count R. Weiss, have traced the would-be humanism of those who, like Abbot John of Whethamstede, yearned towards Italian perfection, but were not able fully to attain it : patrons, learned abbots, diplomats, and administrators, none of whom had fully the time in which to acquire the concinnity of the new writing, but did their best either by the acquisition of classical works, or by the encouragement of Italian scholars, or in their own correspondence, to enter the grove of the Muses. With some, particularly Whethamstede, literary snobbery is carried to a high pitch. While staying at Venice on his way to Siena, the abbot fell ill and was given by an unknown Italian a recommendation to a certain doctor, who told the abbot that the unknown was a famous humanist : the abbot's reflections given in the St. Albans Annals [2] are worth quoting :

> O pain and mourning ! O tears, sighs and groans ! When I asked that great one repeatedly that at close of day he would tarry and sup with me, he made out that he must go further, and suddenly, before bread was broken, vanished from my gaze. After which, though at the time I had not been greatly disturbed nor cast down by the matter, yet, when I came into Galilee and heard from his disciples how that this man was another Cicero who, as Christ in Judaea by divine virtue made the deaf to hear and the dumb to speak, so by the art of his rhetoric made eloquent the tongues of the dumb and by the power of his speech taught the poor to preach the gospel and to work greater miracles than Amphion or Orpheus, I felt sadness in my inmost being, and in heaviness of spirit spoke : " Oh, if only, if only God had granted me to know so great a man, whilst he spoke with me in the way ! "

Dr. Schirmer's observations on Prior Selling of Canterbury give a not dissimilar picture.[3] Contemporary letter-writing shows us that the Dictamen has taken hold of England.[4] *Florida verborum venustas* is the

[1] *Der Englische Frühhumanismus* (Leipzig, 1931), pp. 88–91.
[2] Annales Mon. S. Albani (Rolls Series, 28, v.), i. 136 *seqq.*
[3] *Der Englische Frühhumanismus* (Leipzig, 1931), pp. 154–162.
[4] W. A. Pantin, " A Medieval Treatise on Letter-Writing," *Bull. John Rylands Library*, vol. XIII, no. 2, July 1929 ; N. Denholm-Young, " The *Cursus* in England," *Oxford Essays in Medieval History presented to H. E. Salter*, pp. 91–103 ; and H. G.

literary gift specially commended,[1] and it certainly complicated matters for the reader. Cicero is the main influence, not Greek yet, though we find the government after 1453 making payments to Greek humanists who had escaped from the siege of Constantinople, and in the middle of the century a new type of English professional humanist makes his appearance,[2] scholars like Robert Flemyng and John Free,[3] notable forerunners of Grocyn and Linacre. These flowers of style are not wholly medieval ; they remind one a little of classical Latin, trembling in the fifth century on the verge of the process many classical scholars call barbarization, though now it is the other way round. They herald a new and more artificial age, when Latin is no longer the flexible Esperanto of Europe, but the expert language of professionals.

Our picture then of early humanism is an extremely complex one. It advances through scholasticism and through the teachers of style : it coexists, as Dr. Ritter has shown, with the old forms of philosophy and theology, and will even, in Germany, support the adherents of the *via antiqua* against the so-called undermining influence of Ockham. It does not sweep away " medieval barbarism " with a fine gesture. But it advances. There could be no greater error than, in opposing the old view of Renaissance scholarship, to carry notions of the prolongation of the Middle Ages too far, either in literature or in art. After all, we know a Renaissance building when we see one. What is there of the Middle Ages in the Capella dei Pazzi in Santa Croce or in Santa Maria dei Miracoli in Venice ? The early humanists are the forerunners of the Renaissance : they do not represent the full product itself.

An important problem now before the historian of ideas concerns the dependence of the Renaissance in constitutional matters on medieval conceptions and medieval practice. We have already seen how the idea of the Empire could work itself into public law in Italy in a way which, incidentally, may reverse some of our views of the " utopian or unpractical " character of Dante's *De Monarchia*. But nearer still, at home, development of the notion of the State (as distinguished from the sphere and the capacity of the monarch) in the century before the Reformation, provides an absorbing example of the Middle Ages passing imperceptibly into the Renaissance. England in the fourteenth and fifteenth centuries illustrates the growth of a supreme public authority that had, as its core

Richardson, " An Oxford Teacher of the Fifteenth Century," *Bull. John Rylands Lib.*, vol. XXIII, no. 2, Oct. 1939.

[1] See Jacob, " *Florida verborum venustas*," *Bull. John Rylands Lib.*, vol. XVII, no. 2, July 1933 ; reprinted *infra*, ch. XI.

[2] Howard L. Gray, " Greek Visitors to England in 1455–1456," *Haskins Anniversary Essays*, pp. 81–116.

[3] R. Weiss, *Humanism in England during the Fifteenth Century*, pp. 97–112.

and centre, the mutually complementary [1] relationship of king and parliament.

Now parliament was not a simple phenomenon. It could be thought of, on the one hand, as an assembly of estates, acting for the generality ; on the other, as the king's high court, the highest in the land, a court that could not resist the king's will. Both these aspects of parliament were current in the fifteenth century and throughout the succeeding age ; though the second was predominant, the first never passes out of mind. And yet the aspect of parliament as the king's high court was the older and more primitive idea. The innovation, if such it was, lay in the strong emphasis laid upon that aspect during the Renaissance period. Then again, there is the concept of the king's conscience, which has a long history. In the fifteenth century it is being appealed to in matters which the Lords of the Council are not competent to decide. Through episcopal chancellors who set it in motion, it becomes, in chancery, the organ of *expertise*, to do what the more stereotyped common law cannot contrive or provide. With two exceptions (Thomas Beaufort, 1410–1412, and Richard Neville, earl of Salisbury, 1454–1455) the Chancellor is, in good medieval tradition, a churchman ; yet the chancery is the king's court. In his remarkable chapter on Wolsey as Lord Chancellor, Professor Pollard has written a passage which is well worth pondering :

> We cannot fathom that subtle and pervasive process, by which the *regnum* conveyed to itself so much of the jurisdiction, power and wealth of the *sacerdotium* in the sixteenth century, unless we take account of the conscience with which episcopal chancellors invested and endowed the king in chancery. If the state acquired a conscience, there was no knowing what might not happen to the church. Educated by the church and moved by its conscience, the state might even develop a religion of its own. [2]

Perhaps one who is engaged in examining certain phases of the relations between Church and State within this period may be allowed to point to other aspects of that " education," notably the close co-operation of king and ecclesiastics in the foundation of schools and colleges, the acquiescence of the Convocations in the royal determination

---

[1] " The king in parliament has the most incontestable right to the people's obedience. The king in parliament possesses the most solemn, strongest, and best-sanctioned rights of governance. But in the last resort conflict between king and parliament is unthinkable. No king, no parliament. The king's displeasure is enough to dissolve parliament's pretension, as his will is enough to dissolve its session. His demise is the demise of the parliament. His abdication invalidates writs for its summons. Parliament has no rights save by the grace of the king's majesty, who, so long as he remains a true king, maintaining the law, pursuing justice, defending his realm, is responsible to no human authority." S. B. Chrimes, *English Constitutional Ideas in the Fifteenth Century*, p. 349.

[2] *Wolsey*, p. 65.

to maintain parliamentary statutes affecting the Church, and the very close connexion of canon lawyers with the diplomatic missions and correspondence of their royal masters. It is possible that the reigns of Henry V and Henry VI will come to be regarded as the chief period of such an education, for the careers of lawyer-ecclesiastics, like Kemp, Bekynton and Stafford, have a significance not as yet fully recognized.

There is no need to point out that our tradition of central administration runs continuously from the Norman Conquest. The same is very largely true of those institutions which grew up under the House of Capet. But this centralization did not carry with it the doctrine that the State or its rulers and administrators are not under the law, whether it be the law and custom normally held and observed in their own countries or natural law. The idea, however, that for the State *necessitas legem non habet* is beginning to emerge in later medieval thought. Philip of Leyden, a clerk in the service of the Court of Holland, who wrote in the fourteenth century a treatise *de cura reipublicae et sorte principantis*, held the view that a landowner was justified in cancelling a privilege granted by him to a town or a private person if it offended *publica utilitas*. Gerson himself held that laws which adversely affected the maintenance of public peace should be interpreted differently or definitely set aside, and, not long after, it could be alleged by Jean Petit, on grounds of which many good moralists did not approve, that alliances or promises made by a prince could be repudiated by him, if they worked out to his own prejudice and to the prejudice of the public weal.[1] This doctrine, as we know, many repudiated as the " subversion de toute la chose publique." But the interesting thing is that it could be so confidently put forward. Reason of State has its roots deeper in time than we often imagine : the Renaissance deeper in the Middle Ages.

[1] Some instances quoted in F. Meinecke, *Die Idee der Staatsräson in der neueren Geschichte*, pp. 34–35.

CHAPTER XI

VERBORUM FLORIDA VENUSTAS

I

THE scribe who wrote in Archbishop Chichele's register the minutes of the Southern Convocation in October 1417, noted the appeal of Oxford University for the more effective promotion of its graduates in these terms : " [afterwards] mag. Robert Gilbert, Chancellor of the University of Oxford, commended in flowery beauty of words the state of the University and the promotion of its graduates." [1] The phrase occurs later (1426) when at the election of Alan Kirketon as abbot of Thorney, Dr. Stephen Wylton propounded the decree of election in this particular manner before the Archbishop's lawyers. [2] In close connexion with *florida verborum venustas* stand the terms *ornata verborum series*, to denote the rhythm and construction of the flowery sentences—perhaps the *cursus* in one of its forms. There are other instances where such expressions are used by the same registry : as, for example, when the Archbishop expounds the reasons for the summons of Convocation : *in maturo et deliberato verborum eloquio satis floride declaravit*. [3]

It may be no more than a busy clerk's method of abbreviating speeches which for official purposes did not demand special record. The medieval scribe followed the *grammaticus* of classical times in regarding carefully chosen words, like historical episodes, as flowers. We might easily translate the words of our title " in appropriate language " ; but by so doing we should miss the point. The garden of the early fifteenth century is a botanical garden, full of specimens, each bed carefully and curiously labelled. To be " natural," as we say, in speeches and correspondence is a modern requirement, a thing demanded by the plain man in a democratic age. In the early fifteenth century the plain man did not address Convocation, confirmed no elections, and wrote but little to the great. If ever he had to take up his pen to compose in Latin, he did so according to rules and examples that lay before him. In every age convention has dictated the tone and phrasing of letters and speeches, but in few epochs has it been so much king in learned, that is Latin, composition. It was the heyday of models. This is the more interesting because, as Professor R. W. Chambers once pointed out, much devotional

---

[1] *Reg. Chichele*, iii. 36 ; Wilkins, *Concilia*, iii. 381.   [2] *Reg. Chichele*, i. 100.
[3] *Ibid.*, iii. 54 ; Wilkins, *Concilia*, iii. 394. Cf. *Reg. Chichele*, iii. 36, " causas convocacionis eorum ad tunc elegantissime declaravit eisdem."

and mystical writing in English during the late fourteenth and early fifteenth centuries was the fine, straightforward outpouring of the heart, the " plain and open style " : and English, as an all-round vehicle of expression in prose, was rapidly gaining the ground it had lost at the Norman Conquest.[1]   Dr. Chambers rightly would not have it thought that all English had been or was now straightforward.   The Brewers, when in 1422 they proposed to use English in writing of their own affairs, after the manner of their sovereign Henry V, spoke of augmenting the English tongue,[2] and the increment only resulted in magniloquence. French models, which no one could forget, fostered the love of the ornate ; and indeed, when speaking of the separate identity of English in the early fifteenth century, we should never forget the close approximation of many of its individual words and expressions to Latin on the one hand and French on the other.   But the fact remains that until the desire " to embellish, ornate and make fair our English " prevailed and " Indenture English," which Ascham condemned in the chronicler Hall, became widespread, a pure and vigorous English prose did exist, the English of More, the child of what Dr. Chambers called " the ordinary medieval prose of pious instruction " ; [3] in vivid contrast with the ornamental Latin speech and tortuous processes of thought and sentence-construction which we are now to examine.   In proportion as this English develops, writing in Latin either becomes flowery and involved, or stiffens unmedievally with the imported classical forms of the early Ciceronian renaissance. In a paper of 1930 I suggested that one of the fascinating points of the fifteenth century lay in its contrasts and juxtapositions.[4]   These incompatibles were found in Latin style itself ; Thomas Elmham and Titus Livius, the two chief biographers of Henry V, have little in common ; and just as little the two writers whose periods overlapped in the house of St. Albans, the solid and prolific Walsingham and the temperamental but almost equally prolific abbot, under whose rule Walsingham's last days were spent.

[1] Speaking of Trevisa's observations when he was translating Higden in 1385, he remarks : " We might reasonably expect great changes when the children of 1385 had become the men of affairs of, say, 1410 or 1420.   Which is exactly what we do find.   It is interesting to compare the proportions of English to French in legal, civic and official documents by 1375 (when English is practically non-existent), by 1400 (when it is to be found, though it is not common), by 1425 (when it has become common) and by 1450 (when it is winning all along the line).   Then (except for its stronghold in Law French) French is driven out of England just as the English (save for Calais) are driven out of France : the two great consequences of the Norman Conquest vanish altogether."   *Nicholas Harpsfield's Life of More* (E.E.T.S.), p. cx.
[2] Chambers, *op. cit.*, pp. cxii–cxiii.
[3] Chambers, *op cit.*, p. cxvii.
[4] " The Fifteenth Century : Some Recent Interpretations," *Bull. John Rylands Lib.*, Vol. 14, No. 1.

In his study of early English humanism, Dr. Schirmer has devoted considerable attention to John the Sixth or John of Whethamstede, whom he ranks as a Maecenas, a patron of literature and art like Humphrey of Gloucester or Tiptoft.   Under him, Dr. Schirmer observes, " the attempt was made to garb the literary activity of the convent in the formal, aesthetic spirit of Italian humanism." [1] The time may not yet have arrived for a full estimate of this singular personality, for there is much work to be done upon the St. Albans manuscripts suspected to have been compiled by him or under his direction during his two periods of rule (1420–1440, 1452–1465), while the years which he spent at Gloucester College (where he constructed the library) demand investigation.   But one thing can be definitely stated : the problem of what Whethamstede wrote or did not write cannot be decided upon grounds of palaeography alone ; it will, needless to say, be necessary to make as complete a survey as possible of the various hands that occur in the contemporaneous St. Albans books and treatises connected with him, but the style and the peculiar and highly characteristic constructions he uses in his letters are the true starting-point, and if one works along these difficult and often baffling lines, certain conclusions that have a close bearing upon our subject appear not improbable.   The first is that in literary form the compilation known under the doubtful title of Amundesham's *Annales Monasterii Sancti Albani* and a considerable portion (covering at least the first printed volume) of the *Registrum* or " register " of Abbot John, both edited by Riley in the Rolls Series, are, whatever scribes were engaged in their actual production, due to the inspiration, if they are not the authentic work, of a single *dictator*. Otherwise, however good an imitator the so-called author Blakeney (or whoever is reported to have written the *Registrum*) may have been of the so-called writer Amundesham (or whoever is supposed to have written the *Annales*) [2] it was scarcely possible for him to have caught and sustained so consistently the mannerisms and the vocabulary of the

---

[1] *Der Englische Frühhumanismus*, p. 82.   Professor R. Weiss has devoted some attention to him in *Humanism in England* (1941), pp. 30–38.

[2] " John Amundesham, the presumed writer of the Annals of twenty years of John Whethamstede's first abbacy at St. Albans " : H. T. Riley, *Johannis Amundesham Annales Monasterii Sancti Albani* (Rolls Ser.), ii. ix.   " Scripsit acta Ioannis Whethamstede abbatis diui Albani " : Bale, *Index Britanniae Scriptorum*, ed. Poole and Bateson, p. 176.   " Mortuum [Whethamstede] usque adeo magnificat, ut accurata diligentia eius vitam perscriberet et obtrectatoribus imponeret frenum " : *Id.*, *Scriptorum Illustrium Maioris Brytanniae . . . Catalogus* (1559), p. 592.   Bale states that he saw certain works of Amundesham, two of which are apologies for the abbot, " in Ramesiensi monasterio."   It seems possible that these are the treatises embodied in the MS. Cotton Otho B. IV.   This badly charred volume contained, in addition to the items defending Whethamstede against the charges of his successor, " Gesta paucula abbatis Johannis sexti . . . de tempore illo quo prefuit primo in officio pastorali " (*Catalogus*, ed. T. Smith, 1696, p. 70), and thus may perhaps be the

narrative portions connecting the documents which he copies. The Arundel manuscript in the College of Arms (Whethamstede's " register " of his second abbacy) is not, in the strict sense of the term, a register at all, but is constructed on exactly similar lines as, though without many of the headings in, Cotton Claudius D. I (the account of Whethamstede's first abbacy by the so-called Amundesham). Both are written, to use the expression in the couplet beginning the " register," *more registrantis,* " in the manner of one who registers." Now the abbot's method of recording his own transactions may be gathered from a list of books given in the contemporary St. Albans volume, Cotton Otho B. IV. There was a large and there was a small volume for each period of his rule ; in the large his acts (*gesta magis notabilia*) were registered *plene et satis seriose* ; in the small, *parumper diminute* or *succincte.*[1] Whether the College of Arms or the Claudius texts are the full or the " succinct " versions it is not easy to say. I am inclined to believe that they are the full ;[2] that the short *chronicon rerum gestarum* in Harleian MS. 3775[3] and the burnt *Gesta* in Otho B. IV are abbreviations (though probably by different writers) in narrative form ; and that the register of the abbot was a peculiar and personal record, differing from the average register in certain distinctive characteristics. Both the College of Arms and the Claudius texts connect the abbot's *acta* by narratives or explanations that abound in elaborate scriptural allegory, allusions from poetry and mythology and reflections couched in execrable hexameters. These explanatory or connecting portions of narrative, which are the crux of the matter, differ, except for the later part of the *Registrum,* from the businesslike paragraphs of Walsingham in the *Gesta Abbatum,* or the short chronicle of the monastery in Harleian MS. 3775, to which we have alluded. In his biographies of the abbots Walsingham inserted documents in a very objective manner and connected them with straightforward and un-

---

authentic work of Amundesham. There is no positive evidence earlier than Bale's statement to connect Amundesham with the *Acta* or *Gesta* of Whethamstede ; and it is difficult to see what Bale really understood by the *Acta* at all. In one place (*Index*, pp. 263–264) he seems to refer to the " abbreviated register " in MS. Arundel 34 ; in another (*ibid.*, p. 462) he appears to refer to Cotton Claudius D. I. It is possible, however, that he is referring to Otho B. IV the whole time.

[1] Fo. 16 (foliation of the mounted and restored text). The four items, recording the full and the abbreviated versions, are numbered in the contemporary list 25–28. It is probable that Tanner (*Bibliotheca Britannico-Hibernica*, p. 40) consulted the list of books in Otho B. IV, as his footnote seems to indicate.

[2] Thus it must be the Claudius D. I text (or part of it) to which reference is made in the entry : " Item, in factura registri ejusdem, usque ad annum praelationis septimum, cum variis epistolis missivis xl s." : *Johannis Amundesham Annales Mon. Sancti Albani*, ii. 270.

[3] Fo. 102*a et seq.* printed by Riley before Amundesham's *Annals* (*op. cit.*, i. 3).

elaborate narratives, so that the record of an abbacy appears as much the
gesta monasterii as the *gesta abbatis*. This had frequently been the method
of monastic annals, like those of Burton, Waverley, Dunstable and
Barnwell, in the thirteenth century. But the two compilations before
us are strongly and unmistakably coloured by the personality of a single
commanding figure. In the twelfth century Abbot Simon had maintained " in his own chamber " two or three " very choice writers "
(*electissimos scriptores*), which resulted in a valuable store of excellent
books.[1] Is it too fanciful to see both in Amundesham's *Annals* and in
the abbot's *Registrum* evidence of a return to this practice ? The respectable sums paid for works *De propria compilatione* [2] may help somewhat
towards this point of view. At all events we are prepared for our second
conclusion : Whethamstede's speeches, letters and almost untranslatable
verses are not inserted and introduced by these lively and entertaining
passages purely for their evidential value, but in the main for their literary
merit. The records of his abbacy were to be literature as well as history,
for the abbot was the first exponent of composition in his day. On
3 July 1427, Archbishop Chichele requested him in the Council Chamber
at Westminster to write " certain letters of embassy " to Martin V " both
on behalf of the clergy of England and of the realm of England in
general." [3] Martin's attack upon Chichele for his suspected defence of
the Statute of Provisors was at its height, and in view of the difficulty
that Whethamstede found in complying with the Archbishop's request,
it is very likely that the letters formed part of the counter-propaganda
on Chichele's behalf which reached the Curia in August that year.[4]
That the abbot should have been chosen for this delicate task testifies, as
Riley well observed, to his reputation as a writer.

There was no more outstanding master of the flowery style and none
more thoroughly conscious of the fact than Whethamstede. The entertaining account of his visit, as representative of the English Bendictines,
to the General Council of Pavia (shortly afterwards removed to Siena)
in 1423 shows his conceits and mannerisms at their most typical.[5] He
had accepted deprecatingly, but with barely concealed pleasure, his
selection by the King's Council as one of the English delegation, and
like a good husbandman, he says, had first visited his vineyard, calling
upon his monks to reveal any matters that needed correction, with the
words : " a little while, brethren, and ye shall see me, and again a little
while and ye shall not see me, because I go to the Father " (Martin V,

---

[1] *Gesta Abbatum*, i. 192. See the remarks on him in Professor Claude Jenkins,
The Monastic Chronicler and the Early School of St. Albans, pp. 27–29.

[2] *Amundesham, Annales*, ii. 270.   [3] *Amundesham*, i. 17.

[4] Wilkins, *Concilia*, iii. 473–478.   [5] *Supra*, pp. 44–46.

his purpose being to gain privileges for the abbey).[1] Then followed an exchange of letters with the Archbishop, whose businesslike style contrasts markedly with the abbot's:

> Son in Christ and dear friend. We recollect, and assume that you do also, that in an earlier letter we told you of the King's wish that you should go to the General Council now imminent; it is our desire that you should inform us of your intentions in this matter, and in the event of your being disposed to start, that you meet us in London on Passion Sunday, to hear and understand, along with the other prelates who are crossing too, what conduct you shall pursue to the honour and profit of the English Church and its government in the business of this expedition. Fare you well in Christ, dear son and friend, now and, we trust, in the time to come.

Here is the abbot writing to Chichele (of whom he speaks elsewhere in bitter terms):

> In the humble service of our great President an offering of incense, worthy of God, for a sweet savour. Illustrious lord and father, through your merits honourable above others: after we had received with becoming reverence your lordship's letters and had read and fully understood their intent, we decided to inform you that, although our flesh beginneth to be sore amazed and very heavy, and even now to drink the cup of that journey beyond the seas, our spirit is none the less willing to take up the cross with Christ, and as resources of knowledge, ability or finance permit, to labour faithfully for the redemption of the Church now in bondage. If the Author of Salvation favour me, I shall come to London before or about Passion Sunday, ready then and, as my estate permits, disposed to climb new summits of Calvary, and to do all and sundry in this respect that the dread authority of your lordship shall enjoin upon me. Whom to the happy increase of his worship may the mercy of this world's Creator (*plasmatoris*) preserve for prosperous future days.[2]

All mention of pagan deities, mythology and ancient history has been appropriately excluded from this letter, which is in marked contrast to the one written by Whethamstede to the convent on landing at Calais after a tempestuous voyage:

> Dear friends: Concerning the great perils of the tempest at sea from which, now that the monster ocean has been appeased, we have by grace been preserved, we are erecting altars of incense to Neptune, who at the intercession of his Thetis calmed the watery storm into a breeze, and spake and the breath of the tempest was stayed and its waves were stilled. To begin, the nature of our business urging us on, we embarked on our mariners' vessels in the teeth of the wind and immediately upon going on board commanded that the main sail (*circumflexum velum*)[3] should be hoisted and bade our sailors set themselves to row, hoping that Aeolus, who favours sailing craft, would in the end be propitious; and that after a short while he would

---

[1] Given in *Amundesham*, i. 157–162.   [2] *Ibid.*, i. 118–119.
[3] So called probably from the shape of the rigging.

command Eurus who opposed us to go back to his cavern and that kindly Circius (the west wind) would blow in answer to our hope. But in no way did events follow our aspirations : since before the friend of Apollo had given us our full allowance (*plenam praebendam porrexerat*) and his steeds were tired, all at sea with us suffered the spirit of giddiness, and we, shame to say, were struck with terror and with all the others in every respect suffered watery sufferings (*aequoreas passi sumus passiones*).

Then follows a long passage, crammed with mythology, about the storm and its gradual decline : at which " we were glad, since the waves were silent ; and prostrating ourselves "—though doubtless prostrate already— " we offered incense to the marine deities, who had rescued us from the Scyllan gulf of the furious tempest. We therefore pray you also to offer with us similar sacrifice and to ask the sea gods this privilege and that after these perils of the waves that did so affright us, we may never be terrified henceforth . . . and on bended knees we beseech you to pray without ceasing for such an outcome." [1] The monks would doubtless know well how to interpret this playful polytheism, if indeed it ever got further than the abbot's notebook. His mythological manner meant that he was in good humour, and was less formidable than his biblical strain, which was specially reserved for monastic delinquents or his enemies at law. The poor brother who sought permission to migrate to Christ Church, Canterbury, on account of the musical facilities there, is castigated in the best homiletic style :

Out of the clay of the earth and out of the dust of poverty was this man created, and placed in a Paradise of contemplation, that there he might work according to rules, and to keep watch over it in monastic form ; it being granted to him freely to enjoy all claustral delights, and indifferently to eat of every tree of religion, provided only that he should keep one commandment, that is, faithfully abstain from the tree of knowledge, which tendeth to evil. Now a certain one, who was a crafty serpent, seeing this, who had theretofore himself departed from this cloistered heaven (*claustrali caelo*) and who was now enjoying a life at Christ Church more musical than monastic, envied the happy state of this man, and seeking the Paradise from which he had taken his departure, transformed himself into an angel of light, and offered this flexible brother a threefold apple (*pomum triplarium*) for him to taste. An apple, that is, of sweet refection, as touching [2] the stomach, an apple also of pecuniary profit, as touching the chamber, an apple too of free conversation, as touching recreation ; and further made promise to him of a knowledge of the art of music, which would make him equal with the gods therein, if he would but taste thereof.

That brother, acting the woman's part, seeing how honied was this apple to the taste, how golden to the sight, how honied, how golden, how silvery to the smell, gave heed unto the serpent's hissing, and, with the

---

[1] *Amundesham*, i. 126–127 ; Schirmer, *op. cit.*, pp. 88–89.
[2] The correct reading here is not *quam ad*, but *quantum ad*.

woman's impulse, seized the apple, bit a full mouthful of it and yielded unto the tempting snake his full consent to migrate. Consent therefore being given, and the sin of trespass in the matter of a habit being committed, it was devised and contrived on either side, with all possible clandestine craftiness, how that the fallen brother, throwing off the cowl of immortality, might by his departure put on the garment of mortality, and rejecting the clothing of original justice, might pass into the state of the fallen and relinquish his primeval rank of innocence.[1]

The written permit for the brother to change his monastery is described as *tunica migrationis pellicea*, " the skin coat of migration " ; it began with a greeting " in Him that put His hand to the plough and looked not back."

This is not the writing of a humanist, though humanists might be equally allegorical. The threefold apple (a preacher's fruit) would have put the genuine classic to flight. No humanist ill at Rome and turning his face to the wall would have seen in his sleep, as Abbot John did, St. Bernard promising him life, if henceforth he would read his books. It was the abbot's *Ciceronianus es*, his warning against too much literary paganism. Whethamstede could never have penned the gracious ending of one of Bishop Fox's letters to the President and Fellows of Corpus :

> Studete virtuti, et bonis literis omnibus viribus certatim operam inpendite, filii non minus quam si vos genuissem nobis carissimi.[2]

He was as great an exponent of courtly prose in his day as was Thomas Bekynton of the language of diplomacy ; but it was always the courtliness of the cloister and in the depths of his being he felt the fact. While unwell upon his Italian tour he was told by a courteous Venetian stranger of a doctor who could cure him, and later discovered that his informant was a leading humanist. His unbounded grief at not recognizing the great man " while he was with us in the way," and his preposterous letter to the *fons rhetoricae Venetiis scaturiens* (he kept a copy of it), exactly convey the futility of his efforts after the polished ease of the South.[3] But if he could not capture the spirit, he could at least teach others the mechanism ; and that is the point of his dictionaries and aids to elegant allusion, and the mass of notes and *obiter dicta* that are scattered over his various compilations. It was doubtless this erudition that won him the friendship of Duke Humphrey of Gloucester and Piero da Monte.[4]

---

[1] *Amundesham*, i. 89–90 ; Riley's translation (ii. xx–xxi) with some modifications. On the abbot's fondness for rounding off these homiletic passages with hexameters, see G. R. Owst, *Literature and Pulpit in Medieval England*, p. 579.

[2] *Letters of Richard Fox, 1486–1527*, ed. P. S. and H. M. Allen, p. 104.

[3] See Schirmer, *op. cit.*, p. 90 ; Jacob, " Changing Views of the Renaissance," *History*, XVI (Oct. 1931), 226–227. The remarks of Mr. L. F. Rushbrook Williams (*History of the Abbey of St. Alban*, p. 204) on Whethamstede's literary activity should be received with caution.

[4] For Piero da Monte's relations with Whethamstede, see Schirmer, pp. 85–87.

This body of joint classical and medieval learning has long been a puzzle to scholars. Whethamstede is known to have composed works entitled "Granarium," "Palearium," "Pabularium poetarum," and "Propinarium." The first and longest of these has been thought discoverable in three manuscripts, Cotton Nero C. VI, Tiberius D. V, and Additional MS. 26,674. Dr. Schirmer has rightly pointed out that Additional MS. 26,674 is not the "Granarium" at all, but the "Palearium" ; [1] but his views on the other two manuscripts, based on incomplete knowledge of the sources, appear open to correction in view of the very thorough survey of Whethamstede's writing in 1934 completed by Miss Esther Hodge,[2] who has proved, convincingly to my mind, that of the four volumes (not five, as Tanner thought) into which the large dictionary called the "Granarium" was divided, we possess two in the original version (Nero C. VI and Tiberius D. V, representing respectively entries under the letters A–L in Part I and the whole of Part II of the work), as well as excerpts, in other manuscripts, from the whole of Part I (A–Z), and a complete alternative transcript of Part II, while two articles from Part III also survive in the Bodleian Manuscript 585.[3] Of the two parts of the "Granarium" which have survived in the original version or in extracts, the first, labelled *de historiis et historiographis*, is a lengthy dictionary of historians and their works and of important institutions viewed historically (e.g. the entries *concilium, ciuitas, ecclesia*). The second part, headed *de viris illustribus illorumque illustriis, de doctrina philosophorum eorumque dictis et dogmatibus*, contains, as its title suggests, articles on the heroes of antiquity and is more concerned with moral adages than with institutions. The "Palearium," true to its name, holds the chaff rather than the grain ; [4] it is a dictionary of classical mythology and allusion, the fluttering gold of the ancient threshing-floor, valuable for anyone attempting the kind of panegyric that Lapo da Castiglionchio wrote for Duke Humphrey.[5] The fre-

[1] Schirmer, p. 93. This is of entirely different size, script and character from those of the Nero and Tiberius volumes.

[2] In her unpublished Manchester dissertation, *The Abbey of St. Albans under John of Whethamstede*. Schirmer appears to think (p. 92) that Tiberius D. V has been rendered illegible by fire ; and he neglects other manuscripts in which Miss Hodge has found excerpts from the original volumes.

[3] Miss Hodge has also identified the "Pabularium," but not the "Propinarium" which was apparently presented by Whethamstede to Oxford. (It is possible that the *Rupinarium*, referred to in the Cottonian Catalogue of 1696 (p. 70) as partly contained in Cotton Otho B. IV, is Smith's misreading of *Propinarium*.)

[4] Of one article in the "Granarium," he imagines his opponents saying " capitulum illud . . . non granum esse quod in sementem seritur, immo magis paleam, que vento leuissimo exsufflatur." MS. Cotton Nero C VI, fo. 56 v.

[5] The "Comparacio studiorum et rei militaris" : MS. Bodl., e Museo 119, fos. 116–143. On the use of classical mythology and ancient history by later

quent practice of early humanism was the comparison of the patron addressed to the heroes of ancient history or classical mythology, and the " Palearium " would here be a useful guide.   With these two works at hand, a writer would have at his disposal, alphabetically arranged, a *corpus* of Christian and pagan learning to tell him what authors to cite, what metaphors and allusions to employ, and how to moralize elegantly upon the vices and the virtues, fortune, conjugal fidelity and so forth. Whethamstede's dependence upon John of Salisbury and Vincent of Beauvais is very marked, and evidently he venerated their encyclopaedic learning.   It is much to be hoped that a study will be made of his authorities and the use he makes of them, as has been done for another and more weighty dictionary, the *Liber de veritatibus* of Thomas Gascoigne ;   for at the end of each article the abbot invariably cites both author and reference for his statements, and his sources can be traced in almost every instance.

In the " Granarium " the writing is sober and direct, and there is little exuberance.   It is essentially a work of reference.   Under each historian a brief analysis of his work is given :   the main classical writers and the apologists of the Christian Church are allotted summaries at lengths that vary according to their general currency at the time rather than their merit.   The greater figures of Western Christendom are discussed both in the light of ascertained fact as well as of legend and conjecture.   Where controversy exists, the arguments for and against are fairly stated, and the summing up is moderate and conservative. Under Brutus, " who according to the histories of the Britons (Geoffrey of Monmouth) gave his name to Britain," the abbot admits that according to other histories which some rank higher than the last-named, " the whole story of Brutus is *poeticus potius quam historicus*," and four reasons are stated why this is so.   One is that Britain is not so named from Brutus, but from brutality, because once upon a time " very brutal men lived in those territories."   According to these rationalists " it is a work of vanity and absurd to vindicate dignity of race without any basis for such vindication.   For only virtue renders a people noble, and it is only mind and reason that makes a man of gentle birth and ennobles him in his origin, since, as Seneca writes in his letters :   ' there is no one who is not originally descended from slaves, and no slave that is not descended from a King.' Let it be enough then for the Britons, in this question of noble origin, that they are powerful and strong in battle and everywhere defeat their adversaries, and suffer no yoke of slavery at all."   After this early " Rule

medieval writers, see J. Douglas Bush, *Mythology and the Renaissance Tradition in English Poetry*, ch. i, " Classical Themes in the Middle Ages," and ch. ii, § 2, " The Sources of Classical Mythology," pp. 30–35.

Britannia," he gives his authorities : " partly Isidore's Etymologies, the third chapter ; Ovid's Fasti, near the beginning, and the Transformations (Metamorphoses) [1] well towards the end ; partly Ranulph (Higden) in his Polychronicon, Book II, Chapter 27 ; and more summarily Geoffrey of Monmouth, *de gestis Britonum*, the first book, at the beginning." [2] *Ciuitas*, one of his longest articles, leads him into the etymology of town names ; and he gives a little urban geography of Europe, with the capitals and the names of their founders (" Cnossos, Crete, founded by the Curetes and Corybantes," etc.). His authorities here are interesting : the beginning of Livy ; Sallust's *Cataline Conspiracy* and the *Jugurthan War*; Solinus, *De mirabilibus mundi, passim* ; Justin's *Abbreviation of Trogus Pompeius* ; [3] Virgil's *Aeneid*, Book I ; Ovid's *Transformations*, Book III ; Josephus's *Antiquities*; Eusebius, *Historia Ecclesiastica* ; Jerome upon Genesis ; the eighteenth book of the *De Civitate Dei*, especially chapter ix ; Jordanes of Ravenna's *History of the Goths* ; Godfrey of Viterbo, William of Tyre, Orosius, and Boccaccio's *De genealogia deorum*. The last reference is worth noting. Only four works of the humanists are cited throughout : besides this, Petrarch's *De viris illustribus* and Leonardo Bruni's translations of Plutarch's Lives of Antony and of Cato. [4] One of the most illuminating articles is upon Constantine. Here he defends in a moderate way the legendary figure against the attacks of the rationalists. On three points, he says, my account of him has been challenged : the cure of his leprosy by Pope Sylvester, his endowment of the Church in the Donation, and his miraculous baptism. Take the first. If so remarkable an event had happened, surely Eusebius or some contemporary or later historian like Jerome, Eutropius or Orosius would have mentioned it. The writers of the Tripartite History altogether omit it ; and Godfrey of Viterbo declares it to be apocryphal. Against the Donation there are even stronger arguments forthcoming from historians to show that the Empire was both devised by Constantine and inherited by his descendants. Against his baptism, Sozomenus and the letters of Ambrose are cited by the modernists to prove that it was at the very end of the Emperor's life that he was baptized. To these arguments Whethamstede replies that the Bible story may provide an analogy and point a moral. The fact that certain events find no mention in the Evangelist does not preclude their likelihood. There is no mention in St. Matthew or St. Mark of the fall of the idols when our Lord came

---

[1] On the moralizing of Ovid in the later Middle Ages, cf. Bush, *op. cit.*, pp. 17–18.

[2] MS. Cotton Nero C. VI, fo. 33.

[3] This is one of his favourite works. On its popularity cf. Ruehl, *Die Verbreitung des Justinus im Mittelalter* (1871).

[4] MS. Cotton Nero C. VI, fos. 40–46. References to Leonardo's translations are also given on fos. 21 and 39, and to Petrarch on fo. 175.

into Egypt : " and yet it does not thereby follow that the statements of
Jerome upon Isaiah are mere tittle-tattle." Similarly from the omission
of the synoptic gospels to mention a fact or event it does not follow that
St. John is in error when he does so. On the question of the leprosy,
says the abbot, " in historical matters we ought to trust the more reliable
writers. Now the more trustworthy in their writings are James of
Genoa, Hugh of Fleury, Vincent of Beauvais, Gratian of Bologna, Isidore
of Seville, and Pope Gelasius the first, all of whom with one consent
approve this miracle." [1] This is a true medieval garner, and if one compares with it the titles of the books which he had made for the library
of the convent, there will be little doubt on which side of the dividing
line the learned abbot is to be found. Yet he wins our heart by his
devotion to that sanest and best of English medieval treatises, the *Policraticus*, and by his gathering of rarer flowers like Julius Firmicus Maternus,
Helinandus of Froidmont, Petrus de Palude, Alexander de Helpidio, and
Cardinal Adam Easton, the champion of St. Bridget.[2] The contrast
therefore between this grave work and the light-hearted " Palearium "
is very marked. Here beside the usual repertory of classical authorities,
Virgil and Livy, Ovid, Statius, Persius, Aulus Gellius, Valerius Maximus,
Servius on Virgil, Seneca's tragedies and letters, Pliny's *Natural History*,
and one mention, though without precise reference, of the *Odyssey*, the
dominating influence is Boccaccio's *Genealogy of the Gods*. Certain of
its articles come somewhat inappropriately from the abbatial pen.[3]

II

Not long ago, when a scholar secured admission to the Vatican Library
or Archives, he was very properly instructed, before setting to work, to
write a letter asking the Holy Father's permission to utilize the manuscripts
or records that bear upon the particular subject of his research. As he
cast about him in perplexity for the right words, the *ornata verborum
series*, a card was placed before him bearing the correct formula of
address and ending. In the Middle Ages not only was the outline provided, but in numerous cases the contents as well. Until the great
collections of English private letters (Paston, Cely, Stonor) make their

---

[1] MS. Cotton Nero C. VI, fos. 53 v.-56.

[2] The best of the semi-institutional articles are those on Ecclesia, fos. 71-73 ;
Eugenius (where, under Eugenius IV, he shows considerable knowledge of the
Council of Basel and quotes from its *Acta* : did he know the volume now MS.
Emanuel Coll. Cambridge, no. 142 ?) ; Johannes (especially John XXIII, and John
Hus ; in the former of these he quotes " auctor recollectionis actorum concilii
Constantiensis "), fos. 157-165.

[3] Add. MS. 26,764, especially those on Asellus (fo. 12), Lothis (fo. 83), Priapus
(fos. 104, 104 v.). The reference to the *Odyssey* is on fo. 12.

appearance in the fifteenth century, we owe the preservation of correspondence in the main either to administrative and official reasons, or to its aptitude in providing models for future use. It is this latter aspect that until recent times was much neglected in this country, in contrast to the systematic study of the *ars dictandi*, or art of composition in prose and verse, on the Continent and in America by generations of scholars from Ludwig Rockinger down to Professor C. H. Haskins. In one respect English scholars were not backward : in the editing and publication of our unique series of treatises upon administrative practice from the *Dialogus* as far as the sixteenth-century writers on the Justices of the Peace ; and in the sphere of justice, from the manor to the King's Court, we are reasonably well provided with printed tracts upon procedure. But English rhetoric has come off poorly, with serious consequences to other kindred subjects ; for, to quote Dr. Haskins, " while rhetoric was devoted chiefly to the art of letter-writing, it had at the same time significant relations with formal grammar, with the reading of Latin authors and with poetical composition." [1] In an earlier essay I ventured to give examples showing how considerably our appreciation of the influence of classical authors in medieval England might be improved by a less restricted selection of the materials for research.[2] But there are other fields of greater relevance where fresh initiative has already produced results. The analysis and publication of the letters of medieval students by Dr. Haskins [3] and Mr. Pantin [4] have suggested how much in regard to the technique of composition could be learned from this quarter ; and another branch that has long called urgently for attention is the style and method of the local chancery or registry, whether lay or ecclesiastical. By " local " here is meant non-royal and non-papal, e.g. the diocesan chancery.[5] It is from local sources for the most part that are derived, in the later Middle Ages, the letter-books and formularies which are the most important source of information for the *dictamen* in England. The chief English manuscripts illustrating and explaining the *cursus* have

---

[1] " An Italian Master Bernard," *Essays in History presented to R. Lane Poole*, p. 211.

[2] " Some aspects of classical influence in medieval England," *England und die Antike* (Vorträge der Bibliothek Warburg, ix, 1932), pp. 1–15.

[3] *Medieval Culture*, chs. i and ii.

[4] *A Medieval Treatise on Letter-writing, with Examples from Rylands MS. 394, Bull. John Rylands Library*, Vol. 13, No. 2, July 1929 : *Formularies which bear on the history of Oxford, c. 1204–1420*, ed. H. E. Salter, W. A. Pantin, H. G. Richardson, 1942.

[5] It is perhaps a better term than " private," regularly used by the Germans. Cf. H. Bresslau, *Urkundenlehre*, I (2⁰ Aufl.), 142 f. ; O. Redlich, *Urkundenlehre*, III Teil (Privaturkunden), 153–208, a chapter, with bibliography from German sources, on the development of the local chancery. Notable works in ecclesiastical diplomatic have been C. R. Cheney, *English Bishops' Chanceries* (Manchester, 1950), and Miss Kathleen Major's Introduction to her *Acta Stephani Langton* (Cant. and York. Soc., 1950).

now been classified ; [1] but there remains a mass of material with a very miscellaneous content, both official and non-official letters, some put together by monastic compilers,[2] others composed by and for administrators, civil or ecclesiastical. These letter-books may be purely utilitarian, got together for the needs of the office or the writer in his professional capacity (e.g. Harleian MS. 831, the book of a diocesan *officialis*, or Add. MS. 24,062, the collections of Hoccleve), or may combine both the utilitarian and the elegant, like the great *liber epistolaris* or "epistolary common-place book" of Richard de Bury,[3] amassed from such divers sources as Chancery files, official correspondence to and from Gascony, the letters received by the Vicar-General of the Patrimony of St. Peter in Tuscany, and from Oxford and Durham collections. The later thirteenth century is the time when epistolary elegance began to be systematically studied along the new rhythmical lines in the chanceries and registries. Somewhere about 1270 an English *dictator* at Paris, Johannes Anglicus, identified with Johannes "grammaticus" by Bale [4] and Tanner,[5] wrote in the course of his "poetria de arte prosaica, metrica et rithmica" an analysis of the various styles of the *cursus*, which is preserved along with an Orleans *dictamen*, now in Munich ; [6] and it was round about 1289 that Archbishop Pecham, no mean poet himself,[7] got the Italian notary, John of Bologna (whom he may have known at the Curia),[8] to send him a *summa artis notarie* for the use of the legal notabilities of the Court of Canterbury. It is worth quoting John's opening words :

> Since the holy Roman Church is mother and mistress of all, every one ought, in so far as God permits him, to imitate her in all her processes. Seeing then that your solemn court and the kingdom of England is almost entirely lacking in persons who have knowledge of the notaries' art according to the form of the Roman Curia or any suitable form, but that the

---

[1] By N. Denholm-Young, "the Cursus in England," *Oxford Studies in Medieval History presented to H. E. Salter* (1934), App. I, "The *Ars dictaminis* in England."

[2] See W. A. Pantin, "English Monastic Letter-Books," *Historical Essays in Honour of James Tait*, ed. Edwards, Galbraith and Jacob (1933), pp. 201–222.

[3] "Bury's is an unofficial formulary of letters copied with his own hand" : N. Denholm-Young (ed.), *The Liber Epistolaris of Richard de Bury* (Roxburghe Club, 1950), p. xxv.

[4] *Catalogus*, p. 325 ; *Index*, p. 176.   [5] *Bibliotheca*, p. 434.

[6] Printed by Rockinger in "Briefsteller und Formelbücher des eilften bis vierzehnten Jahrhunderts," *Quellen zur bayerischen und deutschen geschichte*, Bd. 9, i. 485 f. The Orleans *dictamen* is in *ibid.*, p. 97 f. See A. C. Clark, *The Cursus in Medieval and Vulgar Latin.*

[7] See the list of his poetical works by C. L. Kingsford and A. G. Little in their bibliography prefixed to *Fratris Johannis Pecham . . . Tractatus tres de paupertate* (Brit. Soc. Francisc. Studies, ii.), pp. 7–10. E. Blume, *Analecta Hymnica*, xxxi. 111–112.

[8] He was there *c.* 1277–1279. On him cf. D. Douie, *Archbishop Pecham* (1952), pp. 49–50.

proceedings in the cases, the processes before the judges, the verdicts in litigation and other matters pertaining to justice are written as they occur by men who, though probably well versed in other things, are entirely ignorant of the art of the notariate, one without which none can proceed in such matters unless he wishes to feel his way with a stick as if in the dark, (from which groping judges often suffer abuse and litigants inconvenience); led on therefore by my devotion to you and wishing to satisfy you and your court and the whole realm, as well as to further the profit of all, I have begun this little work. . . .[1]

It is seldom that one finds any allusion to this valuable and comprehensive formulary, perhaps the basis of much notarial work in the Primate's court, and a document which must have had an effect, indirectly, upon forms of procedure and methods of registration within the dioceses at large. The point to emphasize is that it was the later thirteenth century that transmitted to England some of the Continental enthusiasm for the *ars dictandi*, so that throughout it and the whole of the later medieval period, formularies, like collections of sermons, multiply. From foreign sources the compilations most frequently found in libraries seem to be those of Peter de Vineis, Thomas of Capua and the Roman notary Ricardus de Pophis. But from this new feeling for expression it must not be inferred that the *dictamen* is the art of writing involved and flowery epistles. To the writer of the Orleans *summa* the letter is but one form of prose composition (the others are *oracio* and *rhetorica*), and is defined as " oracio congrua, suis e partibus conuenienter composita, affectum mentis plene significans." [2] Apart from the information conveyed, its main interest, as a prose form, lies " in the conscious attempt to suit the style to the occasion, and thus to be in turns involved, artificial and fairly simple." [3] The letter-books of the fifteenth century could be all these, but the prevailing tendency in England during the early part of the period is towards the recondite and the precious, or towards an impressive rotundity. Not till the later part of the century was the Ciceronian *concinnitas* learned at all fully, and even then it was only very partially found. In the early sixteenth century Bishop Booth of Hereford gave his Cathedral registry a formulary, now Ashmole MS. No. 789, partly composed of letters passing between England and Rome during the pontificate of Martin V and the early years of Eugenius IV, and of diplomatic correspondence of the first half of the fifteenth century. In all these *exempla* there is practically nothing that owes its form and

---

[1] Rockinger, *op. cit.*, ii. 603–604. It would be interesting to know whether Pecham was acquainted with Johannes Anglicus at Paris. For his time there, cf. A. G. Little, " The Franciscan School at Oxford," *Arch. Francisc. Hist.*, 1926, p. 852 f.

[2] Rockinger, *op. cit.*, i. 103.

[3] C. Foligno, *Latin Thought in the Middle Ages*, p. 108.

vocabulary to the new classical scholarship. It is a purely medieval, a characteristically late medieval, letter-book.

It may be interesting to observe the equipment in this respect of Exeter during the rule of Bishop Edmund Lacy (1420–1458). One of Lacy's registrars, William Elyot, rector of Blackawton in the diocese of Exeter, and later archdeacon of Barnstaple, bought from the executors of his predecessor in the living, John Stevens, canon of Exeter, a large formulary, which is now All Souls College MS. 182.[1] Stevens had come in 1423 to Blackawton from the Battle living of Hawkhurst in the diocese of Canterbury by exchange with John Birkhede or Brekehede,[2] who was to be one of Archbishop Chichele's closest helpers in the foundation of All Souls College and ended his life as a canon of Chichester.[3] Elyot, when he died, left the volume to the College of which he had been a Fellow.[4] It is of some importance, for apart from the historical value of its contents it is deliberately a composition book, both in Latin and French. The first or Latin section of the book as far as fo. 189 contains a great number of Pecham's letters and injunctions, with additional material,[5] about which more presently. Then follows a long French

[1] The donation is given on fo. 190. The patrons of Blackawton were the prior and convent of Plympton.

[2] *Reg. Edmund Lacy*, ed. Hingeston-Randolph, p. 58.

[3] See C. T. Martin, *Catalogue of the Archives of All Souls College*, passim. In the All Souls Building Accounts Birkhede, who was steward of the Archbishop's household, figures as paying various sums to the clerk of the works, John Druell. Cf. my pamphlet (printed for the College), *The Archives of All Souls College*.

[4] It was appropriate that Elyot should purchase the book, for not only would the letters be of use, but also it had belonged to the friend of his own warden, Roger Keyes. In his will John Stevens left Warden Keyes (canon of Exeter 1436, archdeacon of Barnstaple in 1450 and precentor about 1460) two books, now in the Bodleian Library (MS. Bodl. 315) : Richard Rolle of Hampole on Job, and Grosseteste, *De oculo morali*, both bound up in a single volume with the *Policraticus* and the *Metalogicus* of John of Salisbury. (The will is given by Miss E. Lega-Weekes, *Topography of Exeter Cathedral Close*, p. 71.) The close connexion of Roger Keyes with Exeter is also probably to be seen, as Mrs. Rose-Troup once suggested to me, in the appearance of the local Devon saint, St. Sidwell, in a window of the antechapel in All Souls College, where Keyes, before he became warden, was supervisor of the works (25 Sept. 1441 to 31 Dec. 1443, All Souls Coll. Archives, Building Accounts, fo. 72 f.). The saint also occurs in a window in Eton College Chapel, where Keyes was master of the works from the Purification, 1448, to Michaelmas, 1450 (cf. Willis and Clark, *Arch. Hist. of the University of Cambridge*, i. 396). In 1437 an Act of Parliament had confirmed the dean and chapter of Exeter in their rights to the Fee of St. Sidwell, just outside the Eastgate of Exeter (Hooker, *History of Exeter*, ed. Harte, p. 174). Roger Keyes wrote an approbation of Bishop Lacy's office of St. Raphael in 1444.

[5] See the description in C. T. Martin, *Registrum Epistolarum Johannis Pecham* (Rolls Ser.), i. xliv–liii. The letters and petitions which it includes (but not, of course, the treatises) have been printed by M. D. Legge, *Anglo-Norman Letters and Petitions from All Souls College MS. 182* (1941). See the review by H. G. Richardson, *Eng. Hist. Rev.*, lviii (1943), 222–230.

series, which includes a group of parliamentary petitions and a long run
of diplomatic and semi-official correspondence, upon which Professor
Edmund Curtis drew extensively for his work on Richard II in Ireland ; [1]
and finally there are several treatises of instruction in French, the subject
of some notice by scholars abroad,[2] one by Walter of Biblesworth,
another a " Donat françois," by John Barton, scholar of Paris, " brought
up in all ways in the county of Chester." [3]   John Stevens, as Mr. H. G.
Richardson has pointed out, was an omnivorous collector and borrower.
" His associations with Lambeth will account for the presence in this
collection of letters ecclesiastical and secular, official and private, connected
with Roger Walden and Thomas Arundel " ;   and his inclusion of a
number of important letters in French from various high personages,
including Prince Henry of Monmouth while he was guarding the Welsh
marches from hostile incursion, and from Henry Despenser, bishop of
Norwich, is explained by the circumstances of his own career.[4]   For
our purpose, however, it is the Latin section which is of chief interest,
though it is difficult to say whether or not it was formed by the collector
of the French epistles.   The hand is of the early fifteenth century, and
it is consequently the more interesting to find the compiler going back
to Pecham for his models.   Among the Archbishop's letters he has
inserted a number of a less responsible kind, students' letters that form
a little commentary both on his own taste and on that of his contemporaries.   In one a student at Oxford recommends a younger friend to
study rhetoric, but to be careful in its use :

> These and similar words I write to you, my friend, that you may the
> more fervently delight in the art of rhetoric which, by happy communica-
> tion of itself, generalises the blessings of peace with remarkable sweetness,
> refreshing the spirit of its lover.   Its abuses, which surpass the sand of the
> seashore, affect the majority of men, as you know well ;   a few, however,
> lead even modern rhetoricians astray and deceive the professors of that art
> with their cloudiness (*nebulositate*).   Avoid obscure words which weaken
> the senses of the hearers, and use terms easily understood by the human

---

[1] " Unpublished letters from Richard II in Ireland, 1394–95," *Proc. Royal Irish
Academy*, vol. xxxvii, Section C, No. 14 (Dublin, 1927) ;   and *Richard II in Ireland
and the Submissions of the Irish Chiefs* (Oxford, 1927).

[2] E. Stengl, " Die ältesten Anleitungschriften zur Erlernung der Französischen
Sprache und Literatur," *Zeitschrift für Neufranzösische Sprache und Literatur*, i, i. (1879) ;
J. Morawski, *Les Diz et Proverbes des Sages* (Univ. Paris, Bibl. de la Faculté des Lettres,
2e série, 1924, which erroneously dates Walter of Biblesworth's treatise " end of the
fifteenth century ") ;   for the Walter of Biblesworth section, cf. P. Meyer in *Romania*,
t. xiii, 500 ;   he has printed the first eighty-six verses in *Receuil d'anciens textes*, Paris,
1877, p. 360.

[3] Is this John Barton, " medicus," the author of the *Confutatio Lollardorum* in All
Souls MS. 42 ?

[4] *Eng. Hist. Rev.*, lviii. 225.

intelligence ; for these hold the attention of readers by their attractiveness, and a friend can thus listen to your words and your solicitations are the more readily understood.   Take care, secondly, that your exhortations and those preliminaries which we call " never-ending " do not proceed eternally in a circle and lead to no conclusion.   Why give a picture of the heavens and complain that you are in an ill plight ?   Why begin with a description of the planets before lamenting your unhappy circumstances ?   And if you are asking a friend for money, what right have you to begin with the Incarnation of the Word ? [1]

This gentle castigation of modern rhetoric " written at Oxford " is not dated, but may well be of the late fourteenth century.   Of an earlier period is the elaborate fooling of a group of Oxford letters, in one of which " the glory in the highest revealed by divine inspiration" announces the election by the students in their drinking-place at an extraordinary hour, " as the custom is," of Robert Grosseteste, " knight in scholastic arms," as King of Christmas. [2]   In another, dated "in the luminous air above Bethlehem," Discretion addresses the king and informs him that while in the consistory of wisdom she was legislating for humanity, she decided to stop the strife between lascivious Happiness and Religion (*clerimonia*), a virgin attended by the seven liberal arts, who complained that Happiness was trying, *titillatoria voluptate*, to undermine the morals of the scholars.   Six of the " liberal sciences " were on the side of Clerimony, but music, the seventh, varied between one side and the other.   Discretion observes that she decided the strife by decreeing that, just as the face of the heavens changes with the passage of the months and stars give place to other stars, so at certain seasons, notably Candelmas, Happiness must give place to Clerimony ; " et ideo uolumus," she sums up very pompously, " ut iocunditatis et clerimonie talis fiat sacrosancta commixtio ut et clerimonia sit iocunda et iocunditas studiosa." [3]   A second address to the Christmas king from a deity described as " transetherius pater patrum et tocius ecclesiastice monarchie pontifex et minister " is dated " on the top of Mount Cancer," " pontificatus nostri anno non fluxibili set eterno." [4]   It is refreshing to find these tokens of the students' merry England amid the sober models of Pecham, and more pleasant still to think of Edmund Lacy's registrar reading and perhaps imitating them when he was off duty.   But the insertions are not all lighthearted : there is a letter of Sigismund to Henry V after the death of his father, Henry IV (1413), [5] and one from

[1] All Souls Coll. MS. 182, fo. 73.   The third piece of advice is worth quoting : " Cave tercio ne Scripture summas vel historias literales, quibus sentenciam decreueris perorare, ad materiam applices sub sensu mistico."

[2] All Souls Coll. MS. 182, fo. 94.   For the similar ceremony of electing a King of the Beans, or a Rex Collegii, at Merton, cf. *Registrum Annalium Collegii Mertonensis*, ed. Salter (Oxf. Hist. Soc.), pp. xviii–xix.

[3] All Souls Coll. MS. 182, fo. 92.   [4] *Ibid.*, fo. 92 v.   [5] *Ibid.*, fo. 113 v.

the Archbishop of Bordeaux to Henry VI during the early years of the minority.[1] The first of these is in the hand that copied the Pecham letters and is not an interpolation. I cannot help suspecting that this section of the manuscript was done by some one in close connexion with Archbishop Chichele, who had access both to the Archiepiscopal registers as well as to recent diplomatic correspondence ; by a man of conservative mind, who was prepared to lighten the collection with examples that made more appeal to modern taste. The contrast between the ecclesiastical character of the Latin section and the secular and governmental nature of the French is worth noting. One belongs to *clerus*, the other to *militia*.

The second Exeter book belonged to Edmund Lacy himself. His executors gave it to the Cathedral, " to be chained in the Great Library there." Whether it ever reached its destination seems uncertain ; it is now the first section of Bodleian MS. 859,[2] a composite volume containing the Distinctions of Bromyard[3] and some collections of sermons, with an attractive copy of Archbishop Pecham's Commentary on the Fourth Book of the Sentences at the end. The first forty-two leaves contain the collection of letters made by Gilbert Stone, canon of Wells, who was successively registrar to Robert Weyville, bishop of Salisbury (in his later days), Ralph Erghum, who followed him in that see and was translated to Bath and Wells, and then to Erghum's successor, the celebrated Richard Clifford, who was moved to Worcester and thence to London. Stone was faithful to each master, for Erghum took him from Salisbury to Wells, where he occupied one of the canon's houses,[4] and Clifford brought him from Wells to Worcester. He is described in 1398 as " clerk of the diocese of Lichfield, notary," [5] and to judge by his letters to the prior and convent of that place, Stone was certainly his home.[6] The metrical reflections of a scribe at the end[7] show that the letter-book in Bodley is a copy from the original which was sent, along with a dedicatory epistle, to Gilbert's friend and former fellow-student at Oxford, John Langrysh, prior of the Charterhouse of Witham,[8] whom

[1] *Ibid.*, fo. 160. [2] *Summary Cat.*, No. 2722.
[3] Fo. 60. Also " given " to the cathedral, though like Stone's letters, it is uncertain when it was ever chained in the library there. Between Stone and Bromyard a theological glossary has been inserted (fos. 44–58), perhaps bound up by the chapter with the two volumes of Lacy's bequest.
[4] *Cal. Papal Lett.*, v. 315 : " in the canon's house hard by the street known as ' Terre Lane.' " He held the prebend of Wedmore Secunda. In 1400 he acted as a commissary for Archbishop Arundel upon his visitation of Bath and Wells diocese *sede vacante* (p. 362).
[5] *Ibid.*, p. 157. [6] MS. Bodl. 859, fos. 1 v., 3. [7] *Ibid.*, fo. 42.
[8] See E. M. Thompson, *The Carthusian Order in England*, pp. 133–147 ; for the library, pp. 316–322.

he addresses in terms of admiration as a great exponent of composition. This connexion with Langrysh suggests that our Stone may be identical with the Carthusian who wrote the metrical account of Richard Fleming, printed by Mr. Salter in *Snappe's Formulary*.[1] The earlier letters can be dated shortly before 1381, and the latest not long before Robert Hallum's promotion to the episcopate,[2] probably in 1406, when he was at the Roman Curia.

The volume which he sends Langrysh contains mostly, but not entirely, his own letters. He inserts as a delicate compliment several examples by the Carthusian himself, one a very beautiful piece of writing addressed to a brother of the Charterhouse at Hull who had besought him for release from the duties of acting as proctor for the convent,[3] and another an exhortation to dovelike simplicity—" simplicitatis columbine redolens suauitas "—sent to the House in London.[4] There are quite a number by Richard II addressed to the Papacy (Boniface IX and Innocent VII), and one suspects that Stone may have had something to do with their redaction ;[5] for the heading makes it clear that they were written by him " nomine dictorum dominorum et aliorum amicorum suorum et eciam nomine suo proprio." There is one provincial constitution enjoining prayers for the souls of deceased bishops drawn up by the command of the Archbishop :[6] the last entry of all. Stone is very modest about the style of his writing. He reproaches himself for his leisureliness, his lack of systematic study while a young man and still more in advanced age, and asks Langrysh to correct, and absolve him from, any faults of poor composition (*sermo incompositus*). He confesses that he attaches no importance whatever to complaints made by clever young men of more voluble eloquence who presume, in the ingenuity of their literary skill (*curiositate dictaminum*), to say

Ecce quomodo sue innitens prudencie compilator merus iste, papirum denigrans frustra, in vanum laboraverat ydiota, dum vento glorie volatilis

---

[1] Pp. 138–144.

[2] Fo. 41 v. " Gaudet R. Clyfford Wygorn Episcopus de prosperitate magistri Roberti Hallum commorantis in Curia Romana, affectans continuacionem benevolencie sue, etc." The last dated letter is 12 Jan. 1406. *Ibid.*

[3] The reason being the desire to devote himself to contemplation. Langrysh replies : " Quanto enim fervencius diligimus, tanto perfectius contemplamur." True obedience is " the stable foundation and the lively origin and root of perfect contemplation." *Ibid.*, fo. 6.   [4] Fo. 5 v.

[5] E.g. three on behalf of Bishop John Waltham of Salisbury supporting his claim to visit the Chapter, fos. 15 v., 16, 16 v. and 17 ; to others at Rome about the same suit, fo. 17, 17 v. ; to Boniface IX against Cardinal Adam Easton, fos. 24 v., 25 ; a second complaint of similar nature, fo. 25 v. These letters are noted in M. E. Perroy's volume, *The Diplomatic Correspondence of Richard II* (Royal Hist. Soc.).

[6] Fo. 41 v.

intumescens talia nullius efficacie affatoria in unum memoriale pomposum satis inutiliter collegit, affectans preconiis varie laudis attolli, qui in iota minimo nequaquam meruit commendari.[1]

A diverting parody of the new pompous style. But it must be admitted that Stone can do as much himself on occasion. Let us take the beginning of the letter which he wrote for Ralph Erghum condemning the murderers of Archbishop Sudbury in 1381 : it illustrates particularly well his use of the double epithet and the climax of verbs :

> Vorax et horribilis impie rapacitatis auiditas inaudita, heu modernis temporibus sceleratius inualescens, dum oues pinguioris dominici gregis e[f]furit, ipsummet pastorem morsibus funestis dilacerat, deuorat et consumit.[2]

The unconscious humour of " the Lord's fatter flock " (an adaptation of a passage in Ezekiel) is worth noting. His best effort was written for Ralph Erghum, while at Salisbury, to the bishop of Lincoln urging him to take steps " against those committing idolatory at the new well near Bustlesham " (Bisham). Certain persons, " blinded by the phantasy of diabolical deceit," had been worshipping the well and paying profane and heathen devotion to a bird's nest hard by. The passage had best be left in its original form :

> Et pro eo quod, ut dicitur, in eodem fonte, iuxta quem in quodam arbore insuper nidificans quedam auis manibus hominum in nido suo tacta illorum, ut asseritur, non recessit, ymmo quia domestica et satis domita in nido reposita pacifice requievit, lippus quidam vir fantasticus, suos nuper lauans oculos defluentes estu feruido autumpnali adustos et potu superfluo plus solito humectantes, oculorum suorum lippitudines frigore aquatico naturaliter operante refrigescere senciebat, hoc nunc reputat pro miraculo multorum erronie credentium ceca leuitas scandalizans ; unde modernis temporibus ad fontem eundem tanquam ad locum sanctissimum multi confluunt, et ibidem offerunt et adorant. Quorum quidam in nidum dicte auis, vile gazofilacium suis et pullorum suorum stercoribus maculatum, es iactant, et nephanda manu prophanas oblaciones turpissima deuotione reponunt, in sancte matris ecclesie scandalum, fidei catholice preiudicium, perniciosum exemplum plurimorum, ac ipsorum sic ut premittitur ydolatrantium grave periculum animarum.[3]

The bishop had the well sealed up, but it was no good : the wretched people of Wycombe and Marlow opened it again, and in spite of Erghum's warnings and express prohibitions continued their worship ; he therefore requests his brother of Lincoln to have the penalties incurred by such conduct duly proclaimed in the churches. An interesting feature

---

[1] Fo. 1. [2] Fo. 2.
[3] Fo. 3. The *quia* in l. 3 is evidently a mistake of the copyist, and should be omitted. For similar practices at St. Edmund's Well in Oxford, 1291–1304, see A. B. Emden, *An Oxford Hall in Medieval Times*, pp. 86–87. I owe this reference to Mr W. A. Pantin.

of Stone's letters are the number addressed on behalf of his masters, especially the supple politician, Richard Clifford,[1] to the Holy See.[2] They point to the need for every bishop to have a registrar who could impetrate in the best curial style, and solicit whatever cardinal was his special protector.   There was a good practical reason behind these local works on the *dictamen*.   The favour of a friendly cardinal was half the battle, and it was advisable to approach him in the most ingratiating manner.   A suit in the Court of Rome was prepared and reinforced by an immense amount of extra-judicial solicitation.   Happy was the prelate who had a Gilbert Stone to do it for him.

Better examples of composition-books made in the fifteenth century could, no doubt, be found elsewhere.   The study of the letter-book is still in its early days, and the more work we can do upon it, the more light are we likely to gain from many different quarters upon the later Middle Ages in England.

[1] Clifford had started life in the king's chapel and had passed, via the Great Wardrobe, to the Keepership of the Privy Seal ; cf. T. F. Tout, *Chapters in Medieval Administrative History*, iv. 382, and the index, *s.v. Clifford, Richard* (vi. 205).

[2] E.g. fos. 24 v., 33 v., 41.

CHAPTER XII

ENGLISH UNIVERSITY CLERKS IN THE LATER MIDDLE AGES

1. THE PROBLEM OF MAINTENANCE

ONE who knew and learned from the late Dean Rashdall cannot discourse upon any aspect of the medieval University without some reference to that wise and inspiring teacher at New College. It was Rashdall who first made him interested in aspects of University history which received little more than cursory treatment in *The Universities of Europe in the Middle Ages*; for the book, despite its size and comprehensiveness, was in reality quite an early one in its author's career. A large residuum of learning and scholarship remained, never to be printed or even put on paper : Rashdall, first a busy tutor, then a busy dean, could not find the time. Much of that learning and scholarship bore upon those very phases and routine of University life which he seems to have somewhat neglected. As his big work stands it remains true, according to the judgment of his modern editors, that his concentration upon the heroic masters of dialectic or legal study around whom the Universities were, as he thought, constructed, led to a certain neglect of the internal organization and scholastic routine of the Universities he was discussing. Characteristically he always thought of the medieval English University in terms of colleges rather than of halls or inns : that is, of the privileged exceptions rather than of the less privileged many. It has been the task of Dr. Salter and Mr. Emden to restore the balance, as far as Oxford is concerned ; and nobody would have welcomed more keenly than Rashdall himself the new concentration upon the economic life of the University and the data forthcoming from a very important category of material in which the late Professor Haskins showed so much interest : the letters of students.[1]

Many of these have been revealed to us through the publication of the formularies and writing manuals of professional *dictatores* or teachers of composition, on the one hand, and of the early statutes, on the other. It is difficult material. Statutes may be printed by modern editors, but how in fact were they observed ? The writing masters may invent elegant and captivating forms for their pupils, but were the letters which they provided for all occasions actually sent ? Books of specimen letters

[1] *Medieval Culture*, pp. 1-35.

may easily have served to advertise the masters who composed them ; and in medieval times, as every student of constitutional history knows, statutes no less represented ideals rather than realities.   With the letters, however, it is the topics dealt with rather than the fact of dispatch that is significant ; and statutes at all events show the formulated purpose of authority, and are valuable for the evidence they give of the tensions and compromises of academic life.

As the financial resources of the University clerk is our main theme, one fact may be stated against the prevalent tendency to regard the University clerk in the later Middle Ages as invariably poor and living his life on a bare margin of subsistence : that indigence was by no means invariably the case.   To take three fifteenth-century bishops of Lincoln, it is difficult to imagine William Alnwick (well provided for by Stephen Scrope, archdeacon of Richmond), William Gray or Marmaduke Lumley as impecunious when in the schools.   Still less Richard or George Neville, the latter a target for Gascoigne's scorn.[1]   There was a fair sprinkling of *generosi*, young men of high birth, in the later medieval University.   This was especially so at Cambridge, where, in the rolls of petitions for benefices sent to the Roman Curia between 1372 and 1399, no less than fourteen young nobles are to be traced, including names like Grey, Despenser, FitzHugh, Bardolf, Zouche and de la Pole.[2] The personnel of King's Hall, the Cambridge home of the young man of position destined for ecclesiastical preferment,[3] would be worth study in this connexion.

What then of the great majority ?   Were they in the strict sense " poor " ?   And what does a " poor scholar " mean ?   Would the Middle Ages have regarded the present-day " State Scholar " as " poor " ?· Very probably : for poverty might mean lack of patrimony.   But there is a simple answer to the first question.   In the Middle Ages many students were poor because they were short of money ; and one obvious reason was that money itself was far from abundant.   There were, in the fourteenth and fifteenth centuries, periodical shortages of coin.   The years 1335–1343, when the output of coin was limited to bare halfpence and farthings, was such a period, which produced an economic crisis that came to a head in a petition to parliament.   The silver coinage of 1344–1351 helped to right matters for the time being, but the English coinage still remained under-valued in relation to foreign coins, the country was quickly drained of its supply, and there was not enough

---

[1] *Loci e libro veritatum*, p. 16.   [2] *Infra*, pp. 236–238.
[3] " These scholars and pensioners of King's Hall were many of them sons, relations or protégés of courtiers and civil servants lay and ecclesiastical . . . the scholars of King's Hall were ' the King's Childer,' after whom the lane that ran by their college was called."   G. M. Trevelyan, *Trinity College*, p. 5.

bullion. Import and export duties imposed, together with the prohibition on the export of coin and precious metals and gems, only served to
check trade. The output of the Mint dwindled, and from the end of
1403 the amount coined in gold and silver was almost negligible. In
1412 a new coinage with a noble of 108 grains of standard gold and
a penny of 15 grains standard silver was put into circulation. This was
immediately effective, and there was a large output of coin of both
metals for the next twenty years, after which bullion was again short,
except for spasmodic increases of silver. There was, therefore, no
constant and steady supply, a fact which, coupled with periodical dearth
(*caristia*), had serious economic consequences. Students will invariably
complain that they are short of ready money, but the constant theme of
their letters in the fourteenth century, particularly during the time of
the Stamford troubles, must be seen in relation to the general monetary
problem as much as to the circumstances of their parents.

In the young, the very young especially, to be out of pocket does
not always argue poverty : sometimes it points to " the detestable close-
fistedness of parents " ; not infrequently to extravagance. But Oxford
also suffered from the recurrence of *caristia*, dearth of provisions and
consequent high prices, nor was Cambridge an exception. Then there
was the parsimony shown by principals of halls, who may deliberately
have kept their young charges short, and only doled out a small proportion
of the sums which parents had entrusted to them. Needless to say, lack
of cash is one of the commonest themes of medieval students' letters.
The letters written by Thomas Sampson, the Oxford writing-master
(active 1350–1380), as models for his pupils in these emergencies, braced
the errant son to meet the reproaches of his father and suggested the
becoming answer, sometimes not wholly to the disadvantage of the
writing-master himself. A father is made to write angrily :

> In the manner you have described and in none other, greeting. The
> ways of life which you affect from day to day and which have been your
> undoing, ay and your apprehension by the authorities (as I have been given
> to understand by your companions on their visits here from time to time)
> have caused me great pain at heart and your mother too, so that at the sight
> of her grief I have been stricken with anguish, not least on account of your
> friends and ours who tell me what they have heard. Wherefore, to recover
> your honour and put slander under foot, you will now cease from such ribald
> behaviour, knowing that on no account will I give you any aid or financial
> help, if you require it, while you behave thus madly and outrageously, and
> that you will possess my curse as you had my blessing before. I cannot
> say any more now, but get your assistance elsewhere, if you want it.[1]

---

[1] *Formularies which bear on the history of Oxford, c. 1204–1420*, ed. H. E. Salter,
W. A. Pantin, H. G. Richardson (Oxf. Hist. Soc., New Series, IV, 1942), ii. 360–361.

Equal to any censure, the son replies :

> For his revered father his son humbly wishes all manner of honour, earnestly praying that our Lord in his power keep you night and day. As you have been given to understand that I have no desire to learn and that I am doing no work, pray believe me, sir, that my hope, on the contrary, is that you will understand matters aright, for, when I next come, I will tell you clearly how it is with me, and I will make you understand, and prove to you, that you have been told misleading tales. Wherefore I pray to God the Father on high that you will not have cause to forget my master, but will aid me to pay my expenses to him, as you can see in reading this letter. (Sampson's bill was probably enclosed.) I should like to say more, but at present am occupied in study with my dear master, so that there is no time to write or to say more. The Father, the Son, and Mary his Mother who are in undoubted bliss have you in his keeping night and day, so prays John your child.[1]

Affection for the master may indeed be genuine, as can be seen from a letter in which a scholar writes that he is bringing the master home for two or three days at Christmas.[2]

The youths who were sent by their parents or their patrons to the University are often described as considerably younger than the modern undergraduate. It is well to be careful here. Some confusion has been caused by the presence in the University towns of boys of 13-15 years, who were simply learning grammar as a preliminary to the Arts course, or were receiving elementary business training from resident teachers,[3] in whose houses they lived, while a considerable number were in the grammar halls. Some of these boys never took degrees at all ; others in time moved into the various halls or inns which after 1420 were the only permitted places of residence for the matriculated student, where they continued in the Faculty of Arts, and under properly accredited teachers, the grammatical studies prescribed by the medieval *trivium*. It is extremely difficult to discover the true age of these young men. Age has frequently been taken from matriculation entries : yet how misleading these entries are likely to be can be judged by a scrutiny of Foster's *Alumni Oxonienses*, a well-known book of reference largely used by family historians. Here the matriculation entry is always given where extant, this includes the age of the person in question. Sir Edmund Craster has kindly pointed out to me that in the entries of three members of his own family the age recorded in the matriculation register does not agree with the age derived from the actual date of birth. In two cases the age is decreased two years, and in the third case one year. Such discrepancies may be more frequent than is supposed. For example,

---

[1] *Oxford Formularies*, ii. 361.   [2] *Ibid.*, ii. 409.

[3] Cf. H. G. Richardson, " Business Training in Medieval Oxford," *American Historical Review*, XLVI (1941), 259 f. ; and *Oxford Formularies*, ii. 407.

Joseph Butler, afterwards bishop of Durham, is given as 17, whereas he was really 22 ; and Samuel Wesley, who matriculated in 1684 aged " 18," was also 22. These facts suggest that there may have been a " matriculation age " as opposed to the real age, so as to bring the person in question within the College Statutes. Such examples are, of course, from a post-medieval period : but they raise the whole question of proof of age, and suggest that much more evidence should be collected before we assume that the average University student began his career at 15, as has frequently been stated.

In medieval times students required more supervision than they are accorded to-day, and this was done in two ways : through the action of the Chancellor and proctors, whose duty it was to remove by banishment or quell by fining elements that might give trouble ; and through the discipline of the halls, which, though often privately owned, had principals licensed by, and responsible to, the University. At least once a year the principals and manciples of the halls at Oxford were convoked by the Chancellor, who inquired about disturbers of the peace and women of ill fame, the town and its suburbs being divided into six areas, to each of which a theologian, a jurist or decretist, and two masters of arts were appointed as a supervisory committee. The halls, which were fairly numerous, varied much in size and character. As Dr. Salter has remarked, a rich man might take a hall and use it as a residence and nothing more. The ordinary inmate (if the term is appropriate) paid the rent of his study, say sixpence a term, which served as a bed-sitting-room, paid for his commons weekly, and made a contribution towards the salary of the manciple and the cook. He had other expenses, e.g. for washing, for gaudies (special feasts) and the *commutacio*, a fee of twopence a term to the beadle of the faculty in which he was studying. There was also the terminal lecture fee, generally about 1s. 8d. paid to his hall ; and there would be personal expenses, e.g. a shirt, gloves, barbers' charges and so forth. A document published by Dr. Salter shows that the principal of a hall, accounting for one of his pupils during the Michaelmas term of 1424, gave the young man's expenses as 16s. 8d. : " and there remains in my hand," wrote the careful principal, " from the original sum 40d." The " original sum " reveals the system. " The tutor or principal is provided with a sum of money which he doles out to his pupil, as his needs require, and the undergraduate himself has nothing." [1]

We cannot, however, assume that this is necessarily the rule, and Dr. Salter himself draws a distinction between artists, who were mainly undergraduates, and legists, who were older men and tended to be of

[1] " An Oxford Hall in 1424," *Essays in History presented to Reginald Lane Poole,* p. 422.

higher social position.[1]   Older and more responsible students will pay
their own expenses, as can be seen from the letter of a legist, possibly
a bachelor of Civil Law, writing home to his father : it is in Rylands
Lat. MS. 394.

> Do not be surprised at me, even though I dare to molest the kindly ears
> of your compassion with the prayers I now pour forth. Since I cannot
> get through (*evadere*) without heavy cost, I have scarcely enough money
> for my expenses till the bearer of this letter returns ; for in commons I
> cannot manage (*evadere* again) with less than 8d. a week, but in other neces-
> saries also I have spent the money allowed me, and have to go on spending :
> to wit, in my journey to Oxford, for myself and my horse, 3s. 4d. ; in
> the purchase of two books at Oxford, namely the *Codex* and the *Digestum
> Vetus*, after I got here, 6s. 8d. ; item to the teacher from whom I hear my
> " ordinary " lectures, 2s. ; and when you reckon in the wages of our manciple
> and cook, the hire of my study and many other necessities with which I
> need not trouble you, because of their number, it will be obvious that my
> expenses are not unreasonable.[2]   Besides, I think I ought to tell you one
> thing : there has not been better study found in Civil Law than this year,
> since there are two doctors lecturing continuously here in the University,
> when before there was only one.   Each vies with the other in the elaborate-
> ness of his teaching, and in giving the most useful instruction.   In the hall
> where I reside the company is good and honourable, and we have sound
> discipline : whence, by God's grace and your assistance, I shall make a happy
> ending to the study I have begun.   Wherefore I think I must ask you in
> your kindness to send me what you can by the bearer of this letter, and send
> me too by the messenger a note of the amount you are letting me have,
> whenever you do so, and be sure this time to tell me the state of your health.
> . . .   These matters, as they stand, being fully and discreetly understood
> by yourself, I shall reckon that my entreaties have been handsomely answered,
> and will so labour in my academic task that I will never demean myself
> by the slumber of laziness, but will ever remain wakeful till I attain the
> knowledge I seek.   Farewell in Him whose mercies are unnumbered. . . .[3]

In this case the parents have not entrusted a sum to the principal of
his hall, but are sending their son his allowance direct.   The reference
to slumber is interesting (if not inapplicable to certain members of the
University throughout the ages) : for University life must have been
fairly strenuous in the Middle Ages.   Formal or " ordinary " lectures
began as early as 6 a.m. (hora prima), and lasted with certain breaks
till 11.   Disputations might go on till 7 p.m.   On certain days, of course,
there were no lectures or disputations (*dies non legibles* or *non disputabiles*).
Every student had to be on the roll of a regent master : he had to be

---

[1] *Op. cit.*, p. 433.
[2] Cf. the letter of the scholar to his Manciple, *Oxford Formularies*, ii. 401.
[3] *A Medieval Treatise on Letter-writing, with examples from Rylands MS. 394*, ed.
W. A. Pantin (reprint from *Bull. John Rylands Lib.*, Vol. 13, No. 2, July 1929),
pp. 54-55.

formally matriculated seven days after he joined his hall, when particulars of his name, age and place of birth were taken. The University was suspicious of the unattached scholar ; at Oxford an ordinance of 1420 compelled all scholars and their servants to take an oath to observe the Statutes and to place themselves under the guardianship of a principal, and not to live with townsmen. In college the problem was naturally simpler : most of all in Wykeham's College, where the life of the whole community was regulated to a degree scarcely known outside a monastic community.

So many of the letters to parents, preserved in the books of the *dictatores*, are in Latin that one is tempted to inquire whether the father or mother thus appealed to could read them. Latin is all right (one hopes) for a bishop or a learned clerk ; but comparatively few parents would keep chaplains who could translate such missives. It is worth noting, therefore, that in most of his letter-books, Sampson the *dictator* provided a French as well as a Latin version, not merely as an exercise for his pupil, but as an allowance to parental frailty. Here is an engaging request by a boy in an Oxford hall to his father, in both tongues :

> My revered Sire and lord, I commend me to you with all good wishes. I know not what to offer you, my sweet father, since I am your son and, after God, entirely your own creature, and so completely yours that I can give you nothing : for the law says " what is already mine cannot be to any greater degree mine than it now is." But if I can remember what the child's instinct prompts it to say, I might sing, as does the cuckoo unceasingly " Da, da, da, da " : which little song I am at this moment compelled to sing,[1] for the money which you so liberally gave me last time for my study is now completely disbursed, and I am in debt to the tune of five shillings and more. Therefore I beg you, my sweet father, with dutiful prayer, to let me have a sum of money to carry me on in the schools till Michaelmas : and may the All-Father preserve you safe in happiness for many years.[2]

The father thus solicited would probably have been unaware that he was receiving a model *epistola ex quinque (vel sex) clausulis pro subsidio obtinendo*, which followed a prescribed form in its *salutacio, narracio, peticio, conclusio and subsalutacio*. We can only hope that its pretty conceits appealed to him. It cannot, however, be maintained that, times of " dearness " apart, the necessities of life in Oxford were expensive. In 1450 it was possible for an undergraduate to be fed for 2½*d.* a week, if he had only one meal a day (a penny piece of beef would feed four persons) ; at the lowest, with food and clothing reckoned in, a careful student in a hall would not need to spend more than 50s. a year. But a B.A. would have to meet heavier expenses, both at his " determination "

---

[1] " La quelle chauntelette je sui constreint a chanter quant a ore."
[2] *Oxford Formularies*, ii. 390.

(taking his degree), and at the stationers from whom he purchased books. A scholar about to proceed to the degree of Bachelor of Canon Law writes :

> My dear friend : Since about All Saints day I am proposing with God's grace to take the bachelor's degree in Canon Law, to gain which degree with distinction (*laudabiliter*) I must have a complete copy of the *Corpus Juris Canonici* according to University custom, and that *Corpus* I can acquire for 20*l.* or 20 marks, but have no money at present to pay for it : I beg and beseech you, in whom I have special confidence above others, to provide me with that sum together with 10*l.* for the graduation breakfast, and to send the money with the bearer of this letter.[1]

These were large sums : but in the specimen reply ready assent is given, and the writer speaks of the joy which " all your spiritual sons " feel at the forthcoming promotion. The address is *reverendissime domine*, and the letter suggests that the friend who so obligingly undertook to send £30 may have passed the hat round among the spiritual sons, presumably the pupils and friends of the new bachelor.

How long, then, were parents and patrons prepared to maintain young clerks at the University ? Nobody could remain there without being " exhibited," that is, paid for in some fashion. Much would depend on the length of the degree courses ; but no satisfactory answer can be given to the question, since it raises a variety of complicated issues. Two indications may perhaps be noted : the growing anxiety shown by the Universities in the later Middle Ages that their numbers were falling because of the difficulties experienced by their graduates in securing promotion to benefices :[2] and the foundation of new colleges that enabled the clerk to continue his University studies beyond the goal of regency or the bachelor's degree in one or both laws. These suggest that possible maintenance by parents or patrons did not extend very far, and that, as a general rule, the clerk who wanted to stay beyond his fourth year had either to seek the help of a foundation, if he was not in one already, or to take Holy Orders and secure a benefice (and a dispensation to study) for his support.

It was the latter course which the majority had to adopt, for at both Universities colleges were the exception rather than the rule ; and medieval colleges were in the main comparatively small societies of privileged graduates. Writing of Oxford in 1360, Dr. Salter has estimated that the six existing colleges would contain about 10 undergraduates, 23 bachelors and 40 masters. The founding of New College

---

[1] *Oxford Formularies*, ii. 390.

[2] In December 1947, Chichele referred to the *gravis et frequens querela* of the Universities on this account and to the *desperacio promocionis : Reg. Chichele*, iii. 41–42. For earlier attempts to relieve this, cf. *ibid.*, i. clii–iii.

nearly doubled these figures, but if all the colleges had been dissolved in 1400, it would not have been a crushing blow to the University. The same is true of the eight colleges of medieval Cambridge that existed at the end of Edward III's reign, though there were fewer purely graduate foundations (Michaelhouse, Gonville Hall, Trinity Hall and the House of Corpus Christi). On the basis of the Oxford figures there would be, after the foundation of Wykeham's College, some 146–150 secular members of the University accommodated in colleges, out of a total of some 1,200 members of the University in all. Of these the mendicants might number 60–80 (perhaps an over-estimate), and the monastic colleges, Durham and Canterbury, about 50 at the most, while certain odd canons at Osney and St. Frideswide's might bring the number up to 150 regulars. If, then, there were 140 seculars and 150 regulars in collegiate foundations, that would leave 900 for the halls—a considerable majority. This was the figure which fell seriously in the period 1400–1438. It has been calculated that between 1300 and 1400 the total population of Oxford University dropped from about 1,500 to about 1,200 ; but that between 1400 and 1438 it sank still farther, to not more than 1,000. The Oxford authorities had no doubt about the reason : repeatedly they laid the blame upon the lack of provisions, the scarcity of benefices for graduates. Many clerks, they said, could not afford to stay beyond the first degree : seven years were proving difficult enough, and the fourteen normally required for inception in theology or for the doctorate in canon or civil law, almost prohibitive. The length of residence and the courses of study were prescribed for the Faculties by statutes made in more fortunate times ; statutes upheld and defended with impassioned obstinacy by seculars of the Faculty of Arts, especially the younger regents, who distrusted any concession to the religious, particularly to the mendicants. The "Faculty of Philosophy" they regarded as the foundation of Oxford learning,[1] and its curriculum must be maintained against any attempts at abbreviation : but that meant longer residence, and where was the money to be found ?

It may be estimated that a regent master had to pay about £5 a year in expenses of all kinds : perhaps an under-estimate, if purchase of books is taken into account. Supposing that he had no other resources, and was not in a foundation from which he drew commons and could borrow the books he needed, he would require a reasonably good benefice, even though he might make something by masses and other occasional offices. To stay away from his benefices he needed a licence as well as a substitute to serve his cure, and this might cost him as much as 8–10 marks annually.

---

[1] *Ibid.*, iii. 50 : " facultas philosophica que tam universitatis quam theologie est fundamentum."

He could scarcely sustain himself and preserve his status on what Mr. Moorman calculates to be the "average" living of 10*l*. annual income ; [1] and there is evidence from the province of Canterbury to show that the yield of benefices was declining in the first thirty years of the fifteenth century.[2] Tithe was not coming in as it should ; there was much devastation in southern coastal areas ; and the agricultural decline was having serious effects. Our information about the precarious position of the vicarage is on a footing with this conclusion.[3]

Hence the great advantage of the colleges and the competition to enter them, if it could be done. Within, allowances might be liberal. At Oriel every fellow was furnished with board and lodging, and 15*d*. a week, with 5*s*. at Christmas and Easter and 40*d*. at Whitsuntide. The original twenty scholars of Walter de Merton's community at Oxford had an allowance of 40*s*. a year ; generally speaking, table allowances were on a reasonable scale. At New College the fellows, chaplains and scholars received 12*d*. a week in times of plenty, and in times of scarcity 16*d*., increased to 18*d*. when corn was at more than 2*s*. a bushel. The contrast between conditions within and without help to explain the feelings of the baffled would-be entrant. Recent publication of University letters from a Durham register (end of the fourteenth century) shows the prior of Durham expostulating with the Warden and Fellows of Merton and then complaining to the bishop of Durham about the attitude of the college to clerks in his diocese. His argument is that since Merton has property in the diocese of Durham (Embledon) it is bound by its statutes and customs to elect a certain proportion of Fellows from the diocese ; but instead, the college has been favouring southerners ; for the last sixteen years there have been only two Fellows elected from the see of Durham, and those have been expelled.[4] It has been well observed by the editor of these documents that " strong local connections and fellowships confined to certain counties, which survived till quite recently, were not due to a freakish whim of founders, but were an intelligible part of the social system ; where a college draws revenues from a certain locality, the men of that locality, the compatriots, will look to the college to provide promotion for their relations and friends and tenants " ; [5] and, if this did not happen, the countryside would be up in arms. The prior of Durham, who took the lead on behalf of the *patria*, was not pushing the claims of his own monks, who could never be elected to a secular foundation : he was standing as a northern champion at the complaint of northerners both in the University and

---

[1] *English Church Life in the Thirteenth Century*, p. 136.
[2] Cf. *Reg. Chichele*, iii. 115–117.   [3] *Ibid*., i. ciii–iv, cl–i.
[4] *Oxford Formularies*, i. 227–231.   [5] *Ibid*., i. 222.

at home ; and he secured, for a time at any rate, the sequestration of Merton's northern revenues.

It appears from the prior's letter to the bishop that Durham scholars elected at Merton for a probationary period had not been admitted as Fellows when they had completed their year and a half ; " and now," observes the prior, " there are in Merton only three scholars from Northumbria (wider than the diocese), and these fear that, if your grace does not help, they will be expelled because of the complaints which they have sent you." These and other letters in the same register show that monks of Durham maintained their own secular scholars in the University, and sometimes used the monk-scholars of Durham College to convey messages to, and generally look after, the seculars of their maintenance. " Can the Principal of X College be induced to take my scholars on half commons ? " one will ask (*littera ut ponatur puer ad dimidias communas*). " I have tried," comes back the answer : " I did all I could with the said Principal who in truth replied that he would not grant this to his own uterine brother beyond the beginning of the year, since he does not know what and how many residents he will have in his hall then." " I know," the writer adds darkly, " that W. and all the scholars from our parts (*patrie*) who draw their commons there propose to evacuate that hall at the end of the year, so there is little hope in that quarter. But the said W. promised me faithfully that if he became principal of any hall next year (which he firmly hopes to do), he would see that your lad had first claim to half commons." [1] The keen—almost Scottish—interest of the *patria* in its own secular students at the University appears in an attractive letter of congratulation addressed to a northern graduate at Oxford. " Truly, if I am not mistaken, Rome was not happier when Megurca (? Jugurtha) was captured, or Paris when he abducted Helen, or Jason when he got the Golden Fleece, or Ulysses when he beheld Penelope, or the Holy Fathers at the advent of the Messiah than I was when I heard news of the prestige (*continencia*) which your reverence has achieved and of your other grateful successes." [2]

Provision was the cry of the secular clerk who stayed for any considerable length of time in the University. Many had to go down before taking a degree at all ; not a few had to leave before they achieved the higher status they were seeking. The letters preserved in the Formulary, MS. Bodley, Selden Supra 66, show the *Prior studentium* at Oxford asking a bishop to send back to the University two clerks who were bachelors in the higher faculties. [3] In several of the letter-books containing University material requests for the return of promising

[1] *Ibid.*, i. 237.   [2] *Ibid.*, i. 334.   [3] *Ibid.*, i. 212–213.

graduates occur.   Provision is the theme running through the letters in
Rylands Latin MS. No. 394, which belongs to the late fourteenth–early
fifteenth centuries, the compiler of which was most of all interested in
the struggling clerk.   One such announces with joy that he has escaped
from his " servile and weak condition " and become a rector : but for
this purpose, speedy ordination is required, and this must be arranged.
Another man, evidently a guardian or patron, writes to a confidential
friend asking him, since news has come that the church of C. is vacant,
to provide for his clerk : the friend answers that he is just two hours
too late (per duas horiculas), for the benefice has been snapped up by
a royal nominee.[1]   The problem of provision was not confined to the
two English Universities : it was one of the major issues faced by the
Council of Constance.   From the letters of Peter of Pulka, dean of the
Faculty of Theology in the University of Vienna,[2] we learn that representatives of Vienna discussed the matter with their opposite numbers
from the other German Universities, and that the problem was handed
to the original committee on reform.   If, as it had been suggested, papal
provisions were to be abolished, what would happen to the University
graduate who looked to the Papacy for his maintenance ?   Would
ordinary collators be able or willing to provide for him ?   The frequent
occurrence of this theme in Peter's letters is highly significant.   In another
context I have pointed to the great importance of the University roll
of petitions by graduates to the Curia and to the effect upon the
Universities of the attempt to restrict such practices.   It is impossible to
judge the economic position of the later medieval University graduate
aright, unless regard be had to the difficulties he experienced in securing
provision and the serious effects caused by the English statutory curtailment of the practice of petitioning Rome.

It must not be thought that such claims to promotion were made
only on behalf of, or by, the younger bachelors or junior regents who
aimed at incepting in a higher Faculty.   Very high dignitaries, who had
a good conceit of themselves, had no hesitation in advancing their claims ;
the University roll included the names of the most prominent senior
members.   In the notebook of William Swan, the English proctor at
the Roman Curia during the first thirty years of the fifteenth century,
there is a long memorandum, probably drawn up by Swan himself, in
support of the case for provision to a bishopric put forward by a distinguished client ; and that client was Master Richard Dereham, Chancellor of the University of Cambridge, 1404–1408.   The main facts of
his career are well known.   He came from the diocese of Norwich, had

---

[1] A Medieval Treatise on Letter-writing, pp. 44–45.
[2] Ed. Firnhaber, Archiv. für Kunde oesterreichischen Geschichtsquellen, t. XV.

been Chancellor of Cambridge in 1390–1391, was a Fellow of Gonville Hall, and, from 1399, Warden of the King's Hall. He was dean of St. Martin-le-Grand and held several prebends. He was a trusted diplomatic servant of Henry IV, to judge from the fact that in 1404 parliament demanded his exclusion from the royal household. In 1406 when Bishop Henry Despenser of Norwich died, the King (according to Dereham's own version) wanted to appoint the Cambridge Chancellor. On 3 September, the *congé d'élire* was issued to the chapter, but on 14 September the prior of Norwich, Alexander Totington, was elected, promptly to be imprisoned at Windsor for so manifest an act of defiance by the chapter. The death of Innocent VII in November 1406 improved Dereham's chances of gaining possession of the see. Gregory XII ordered an inquiry into the merits of the rival candidates, Antoine de Challant, Cardinal of St. Cecilia, being commissary for the investigation. The merits and admirable qualities of Dereham were accordingly set forth in a memorandum for which the Chancellor himself provided the facts. Each point claimed by him in his own favour was based on public notoriety.

Significantly, Master Richard Dereham's first claim was his work for the revocation of the Statute of Provisors in Richard II's reign (1390). In the time of Pope Boniface IX, the memorandum states, the excellent Doctor Bartholomew de Novaria, consistorial advocate, and the abbot of Nonantula were sent as ambassadors to England, so as to get the Statute against Provisors abolished and revoked, and then the said Master Richard, as the most excellent person available, was sent by the University of Cambridge to plead, along with the said ambassadors, for the revocation of the said Statute ; and for six consecutive years, in every parliament, he laboured strenuously, with all his might, on behalf of the University for the revocation of the same Statute. Three paragraphs are then devoted to his academic career. He had studied in the University for over twenty years, and obtained his doctorate, " with the rigour of examination." As the result of his learning and the gravity of his deportment, the venerable congregation of doctors and masters of the University elected him to be their chancellor, and while in that office he ruled the University well and by his strenuous efforts preserved its rights, privileges and honours. After emphasizing his close relationship with Henry IV, before whom he had said the canonical hours for six years and celebrated mass daily, having also been chosen to hear the King's confessions more frequently than any other, the memorandum points out the value to the Curia of Dereham in his dual capacity of defender of ecclesiastical liberty and trusted servant of the King. This is done by stressing the fact that, because he stood so high in the royal favour and at the same time saw that the Statute of Provisors prevented petitioners from accepting expectatives from Rome, he succeeded in obtaining from the King a charter, known as a royal letter patent, for all graduates and graduands in perpetuity, that they might be allowed to sue for expectative graces in spite of the Statute. On account of his request for this charter in favour of petitioners to Rome, Master Richard has suffered manifold insults and humiliations at the hands of many persons.[1]

Dereham's advocacy on behalf of the University graduate is an interesting point, though the facts he gives may have been somewhat stretched. In 1399 a licence, still in existence at Cambridge, was issued to the Chancellor and Scholars enabling them to petition Rome according to the form of the recent moderation of the Statute, and Cambridge accordingly sent a roll to the Pope. It is, however, difficult to infer from the working of the patent that Dereham's " charter " was in one sense a *perpetual* licence to send such petitions or that it conveyed any such hopes. Cardinal Challant was unconvinced by the eloquent testimonial. On 21 January 1407, Alexander Totington was papally provided to Norwich, and in the end Henry IV had to accept him.

To relieve the poverty of scholars at either University funds had been left from time to time by individual benefactors for the establishment of chests. These were mainly loan funds, each with its separate statutes prescribing the conditions of disbursement, and were an important means of alleviating temporary distress or embarrassment. Though most historians of the universities mention them, no authoritative study of the various chests has so far been written : they certainly deserve investigation. One of the earliest at Oxford must have been St. Frideswide's Chest, founded in 1284 by Robert Grosseteste out of the money paid by the burgesses of Oxford as amends for an attack on the scholars of the University. Statutes for subsequent chests followed the lines of Grosseteste's wording : the moneys therein could be " given under lawful pledge or caution to the indigent scholars of the University, unbeneficed or beneficed, up to an income of 10 marks," with the added proviso, when the loan was contracted, that if within a year from the time when the money was disbursed the loan was not redeemed, the keepers of the chest might realize the pledge, recoup themselves from the sale and pay any balance as the debtor should direct, or, if he died intestate, distribute the proceeds for his soul. The borrower was to draw up a written undertaking that on receipt of the money he would renounce all legal action of any sort against the Chancellor and obey his instructions in all things. In other words, he borrowed money under

[1] Bodleian Lib., MS. Arch. Seld. B. 23, fos. 113 v.–114.

conditions prescribed by the University. Most of the regulations for the chests at Oxford state the amount that can be borrowed by the varying grades of scholars, provide for the appointment of two recent masters as *custodes*, and give instructions about the pledge (*cautiones* or *pignora*) to be received and the account that is to be kept. Some interesting points emerge from the texts of these regulations.

As valuables of various kinds were deposited with the chest for security, it was necessary to have professional valuers in the University. Their services were in any case needed when a scholar died in the town, for the Chancellor had jurisdiction over his will and a " faithful inventory " was required. Most of all it was necessary to know the value of the pledge deposited, and as this was frequently a book, both at Cambridge and at Oxford, the *stationarii* or stationers, who were expert in this line, became the permanent clerks of the chests. They made the valuation, advised borrowers, and, as we hear, sometimes were not too scrupulous in selling pledges left unredeemed. Originally a stationer was a tradesman with a fixed booth or bookstall, like David in the market-place at Cambridge. He may have had copyists and even illuminators working for him, for it was his business to provide books for the scholars at a fixed tariff, get them bound and repaired, and frequently act as an intermediary between buyer and seller when the latter had a book to dispose of. The stationers, because of their position as valuers and as providers of essential texts and commentaries, were regular University officials and came within the Chancellor's jurisdiction. Both in the Cambridge Grace Book A and in the Statuta Antiqua of Oxford (before 1380) there is plenty of information about them. At Oxford the oath administered to them and the regulations they had to observe show to what temptations they might be exposed. When they sold a pledge they were bound to restore the money immediately to the chest, even if the keepers did not ask them to do so. Failure to do this may have been the reason why the Cambridge stationers Wake and Fydyon (1479–1482) owed the chests such large sums. After his death in 1480, Wake *multas pecunias debet diversis cistis*. When Fydyon died, Grace Book B minutes that the University authorities extracted from the common chest 12*l.* for the repair of several chests that were in low water (*in decasu existencium*) and repaid the money from the sale of Fydyon's effects. The stationers were not allowed to part with any pledge exposed for sale on approval for more than ten days. In the statute for the Chichele Chest at Oxford, a prospective buyer of the *pignus* could inspect it for eight days, but had to return it after that. One can easily imagine that a chest might become a sort of lending library. No stationer was allowed to sell any vendible goods in the chest without permission of the Chancellor or his commissary, the proctors and the keepers of the chest, and when he sold a pledge, he was bound to sell it fairly to a buyer in the University and particularly not abroad (*ad partes transmarinas maxime*). The valuation of the pledge must be made honestly, and the keepers must not sell without a proper valuation.

In spite of these undertakings, it is evident that the University was not always in a position to control its chests, or such would seem to be the conclusion to be drawn from the preamble to the regulations for the Audley fund (200 marks left by Bishop Edmund Audley of Salisbury) in which Archbishop Warham declared that he had reinforced the Chichele Chest, *nuper spoliata*, with Audley's bequest.[1]   In the regulations for the Fen Chest (1511) the keepers were ordered to have an indenture made when the sale of any pledge took place, one part to go to the stationers, the other to remain in the chest. It is unlikely that minor depredations accounted for the " spoliation " of the *cista de Chichele* : there was probably a larger raid. On 9 November 1457, the bailsmen of John Dyer, parish clerk of St. Mary's, Oxford, and George Davy, chaplain, undertook in the Chancellor's court to produce the two men, whenever called upon, to answer for abstracting (*ablatione*) 100*l.* from the Danvers Chest.[2]   This is a large sum : whether the defendants had done so, and what was their plea, we do not know ; but the Chichele Chest may have suffered a similar fate. It would, however, be hazardous in the absence of evidence to suspect misappropriation of funds. One chest, with much of its funds out on loan and various new demands to meet, may have borrowed from another and not have been able to repay.

No apology is needed for dwelling upon the economic difficulties of the University clerk, from undergraduates at one end to doctors at the other. We shall not appreciate the significance of much that is contained in the statutes of both Universities unless his needs are considered ; and in so doing we are brought face to face with one of the greatest problems confronting the medieval church : the problem of provision. It was appreciation of these needs that in the end converted the Universities from being assemblages of inns and *hospicia* into communities of colleges and greatly diminished the " non-collegiate " elements. A modern university with its halls and its large body of students unattached to any foundation comes much nearer to the medieval pattern.

<hr />

[1] *Statuta Antiqua Universitatis Oxoniensis*, ed. Gibson, p. 323.
[2] *Registrum Cancellarii Oxoniensis*, ed. Salter, i. 388.

2. Petitions for Benefices from English Universities during the Great Schism

Few topics in ecclesiastical history have demanded so much revision and revaluation as the papal collation of benefices. Earlier generations of historians, even if they treated with reserve the criticism of provisions voiced by Matthew Paris, nevertheless regarded the successive general reservations from 1265 to 1362 as a glaring invasion of the rights of ordinary collators : *juris ordinariorum locorum usurpacio*, as Dietrich of Niem called them in 1410.[1] Papal provisions of whatsoever category were represented as acts of administrative intervention which aroused national feeling, especially in this country, to statutory counter-measures ; as an abuse, not only because they introduced the non-resident alien into the English dioceses, but also because they diverted the normally resident incumbent from his cure in order to defend his title at the Court of Rome.[2]

In more recent years, with the growth of administrative studies, opinion has reacted sharply, perhaps even a little too emphatically, along lines which might be termed respectively diplomatic and canonist. The diplomatic method of approach to papal provisions in England is to view them, at all events until the second version of the Statute of Provisors (January 1390) and the outbreak of the struggle between England and Boniface IX, as a working, though somewhat precarious, system of give and take between a monarch determined to utilize every available means to assert his rights of patronage, primarily in the interests of his own servants ; and the Pope, whose eyes were chiefly turned towards the chapters of the English secular cathedrals, to provide for his brethren the cardinals and for the senior members of his own court. The second half of the fourteenth century, as M. Perroy's studies indicate, was a time of periodical (though increasing) friction and periodical (though increasingly unstable) settlement.[3] Upon this reckoning, provisions constitute one aspect, perhaps the predominant aspect, of the intercourse between two administrative organizations, royal and papal. This is an interesting, and in some ways an important conception ; but its emphasis on the professional element rather narrows the field and may hide the activity both of communities and of significant individuals that had no particular connexion with the Crown except for the fact that between 1351 and 1390 they had to buy a licence to seek the Curia.

The second, or canonist, method of approach is more fundamental,

[1] Dietrich von Niem, *Dialog über Union und Reform der Kirche*, ed. Heimpel, p. 19.
[2] For a modern expression of this view, cf. L. E. Binns, *The Decline of the Medieval Papacy* (1934), p. 118.
[3] E. Perroy, *L'Angleterre et le grand schisme d'occident* (1933), esp. chs. i, vii and viii.

and centres upon the act of provision. A papal letter of grace providing to a benefice is not to be interpreted as a final administrative mandate for A or B to be put in possession of this or that benefice ; but rather as a document initiating a *processus* which is to be carried to its legal termination by a group of *executores*, invariably the recipients of a mandate, concurrent with the provision, to inquire into the legal aspects of the grace and to discharge functions which are as much judicial as executive. In other words, the executors of a provision, even if it is their business to carry it to a conclusion, are inquisitors first and foremost. While, therefore, the disposal of benefices was an act of administration and in strict law could be carried out without any judicial action, in practice authoritarian action was avoided. To quote a recent opinion :

> As long as legitimate defence was not excluded, as long as the practice of provisions was governed by fixed juridical principles, as long as both sides had a recognised opportunity to maintain their own rights and to traverse the claims of their adversaries, there was no danger of the system of papal provision resulting more than any other method of distributing benefices, in injury to private rights, derogation of the public law of the Church, or impairment of the high standards of Church government.[1]

Petitions for provision, the favourable response (if given), and the letter conferring it should, if this view is correct, be regarded as the approach to promotion rather than as promotion itself. They are, in fact, a method of setting the machinery going. It was possible, though far from certain, that the petitioner would get something : by no means necessarily the actual benefice sought. For many clerks personally unknown to potential patrons it was a way of exploring the resources of patronage, of bringing their names forward for consideration.

The channels for the submission of such petitions were very important. It was advisable to find the best post-office to Rome. Well-sponsored collective petitions in the fourteenth century were more expeditious than individual requests that went into the *communis data* and had no priority in the office of the papal signature ; and there was a resulting economy in the expenses of transit. For the curial administrator, a tidy *rotulus* was better than a mass of individual schedules, whether the petitions were about the same subject or not. It seems likely that in the early days the grouping of the humbler sort of petitioners for benefices was done at the Curia, perhaps by some clerk of the *signatura* : the petition of 1343 containing the names of seventeen poor clerks from various English dioceses (along with those of others seeking the office of

---

[1] G. Barraclough, " The executors of Papal provisions in the Canonical theory of the thirteenth and fourteenth centuries," *Acta Congressus Iuridici Internationalis Romae 12–17 Novembris 1934* (Rome, 1936), p. 44.

public notary),[1] the groups supplicating in 1345,[2] the list of " poor priests and others" in 1348,[3] may well be of curial compilation ; and so too the roll of English *Romipetae*, graduates and priests, in 1363, which is followed in the Register by a lengthy collection of English clerks asking for benefices.[4] The persons included in these seem to have no English patrons to forward their claims, do not figure in the household lists of *beneficiendi* submitted by magnates or prominent ecclesiastics. Yet by the middle of the fourteenth century most petitioners appear to be finding sponsors and to be on somebody's roll. The " competition of rolls " (*concurrencium pressurae rotulorum*), of which the University of Cambridge a little later so bitterly complained,[5] was a reality ; and at least by the pontificate of Urban V, if not somewhat earlier, the headings of the *rotuli* indicate that they were compiled locally (e.g. a royal personage or an important magnate would have his own list),[6] while the proctor in the Curia employed by the petitioner-in-chief would, where necessary, make the required "reformation" or re-draft, so that the petitions might conform to the rules of the Chancery or take account of facts and conditions unknown to the sender.

The actual date at which English Universities began to collect and forward to Avignon the petitions of their scholars and graduates for benefices is uncertain. Rashdall thought that it might have been in the pontificate of John XXII or Clement VI ; he pointed out that the first actual benefice-roll sent by the University of Paris dates from the time of Clement VI.[7] The first uncontested example, in fact, dates from February 1335, when in letters to the King, the Queen, and the bishop of Lincoln, the University of Oxford asked support for the petitions on behalf of regent and non-regent masters, which were being sent to the newly-created Benedict XII.[8] The letter to the King refers to the

---

[1] *Cal. Papal Registers, Petitions*, i. 54–55.   [2] *Ibid.*, pp. 95–96.   [3] *Ibid.*, p. 136.

[4] *Ibid.*, pp. 426–435 ; cf. the " Roll of the English," pp. 447 f., 484–489, 501–502. For *rotuli* under John XXII, cf. *Regulae Cancellariae Apostolicae*, ed. E. von Ottenthal, p. 2.

[5] In the first petition of the " Colville " roll, described below.

[6] E.g. Roll of the Black Prince (1363), *Cal. Papal Reg., Petitions*, i. 454–456 ; of the earl of Warwick (1364), *ibid.*, 493–495.

[7] *The Universities of Europe in the Middle Ages*, ed. F. M. Powicke and A. B. Emden, i. 555 n. : "several Oxford rolls sent to Clement VI are among the Roman transcripts sent to the Public Record Office by Mr. Bliss." (Doubtless there is a reference here to the Oxford roll of 1343 printed by Bliss in *Cal. Papal Reg. Petitions*, i. 60.) Mr. D. E. R. Watt points out to me that one exists for Benedict XII : *Auctarium Chartularii Universitatis Parisiensis*, ed. H. Denile and E. Chatelain, i. 28.

[8] " Qil vullie de sa grace otreier les peticions queles lui seront purposees de par la Universite, en purvoiant au ditz maistres dauquns benefices de saint eglise " : *Formularies which bear on the history of Oxford, c. 1204–1420*, ed. H. E. Salter, W. A. Pantin, and H. G. Richardson (Oxf. Hist. Soc., New Ser., IV), i. 87. Mr. Pantin calls my attention to *ibid.*, i. 33 (1318).

practice of according graces *in summorum pontificum novis creacionibus*.[1]
Between March 1337 and July 1338 the University made a second appeal,
this time for regents alone,[2] and it is quite likely that a *rotulus* was prepared,
for when the University asked the chancellor, Robert de Stratford, to
use his influence with the King in support of their request, the chancellor
asked to see " the petitions." It is unlikely that he would be prepared
to wade through a file of supplications : it must have been a list for which
he asked, and, curiously enough, the list that he wanted to see was not
forthcoming, because Simon de Bredon, one of the proctors and so the
possessor of a key to the chest, disagreed with it and would not allow
the seal to be used. The University appears to have decided that the
outgoing proctors should have precedence in the list before the incoming,
and Simon was one of the new proctors.[3] That in 1337–1338 it was
the regent masters [4] who received consideration is suggested by the
return made to the earlier practice in 1344, when it was decided that
" at each new papal creation, when the University writes for regents
to secure grants, it should also write for non-regents who wish (to be
included), the lists (*cedule*) being collected together, sealed however with
the single seal of the University, the same date being kept in both lists
for composition, sealing, and presentation to the supreme pontiff " ; [5]
in other words, precautions were taken against any list or group of
names being inserted as an afterthought. This mention of the papal
creation makes more than doubtful, as far as Oxford in the fourteenth
century was concerned, Rashdall's statement that the *rotulus* was an
annual affair, whatever may have been the Continental practice. The
papal Registers of Supplications certainly do not support his view as
regards England ; and the examples from both Universities which I shall
briefly review are mainly creation or jubilee rolls.

By 1362 the competition of non-university interests was becoming
felt ; for in that year Archbishops Islip and Thoresby and the bishops
of Exeter, Rochester, Ely and Ossory sought and were accorded permission to confer a limited number of benefices upon masters of theology
and doctors of canon and civil law owing to the pressure of non-university
provisors with expectatives. The archbishops could confer six each,
the bishops three.[6] At the end of the year, however, as the result of

[1] *Oxford Formularies*, i. 86.
[2] *Ibid.*, pp. 90–91.   [3] *Ibid.*, p. 92.
[4] For a comparison of the rights of regents and non-regents at Oxford, cf.
S. Gibson, *Statuta antiqua Universitatis Oxoniensis*, pp. xxii f.
[5] Gibson, *Statuta*, p. 143 : " diversis cedulis colligatis, unico tamen sigillo
universitatis consignatis, eadem data concepcionis, consignacionis ac summo pontifici
presentacionis utriusque cedule conservatis." " Conservata " would be the form
expected, but this is a sense construction.
[6] *Cal. Papal Reg., Petitions*, i. 387.

Urban V's creation, both Universities submitted *rotuli*,[1] while at the end of January 1363 another *rotulus* was forthcoming from English jurists and artists with academic degrees being then present in the Roman Curia. The long roll of non-graduate *Romipetae*, to which I have alluded, was also submitted in 1363, so that the pressure of other interests is evident. The Oxford list, both for regents and non-regents, was followed by an additional petition for persons not contained in the former roll ; [2] furthermore, the Cambridge roll [3] received two supplements,[4] one of which is termed in the Register of Supplications a *reformatio* or modification, revising or re-wording some of the petitions (e.g. since by inadvertence it was omitted to state whether the benefices asked for were with or without cure, the Pope is prayed to extend the grant so as to include both). No mention of any Cambridge *nuncius* occurs, but shortly afterwards the undated reply to a petition shows that the chancellor himself, Dr. Michael Causton the elder, had seen fit to go to the Curia, perhaps to "labour" there on behalf of his graduates.[5] We also know the names of three Cambridge men who were there too : William de Gotham, described as "of the dioceses of Lincoln and Evreux" ; [6] Robert de Wistow, *rectius* Robert Weston, who complained that he had been left out of the roll ; [7] and Michael Causton the younger, then only a B.A. and 23, but included in the roll, who was praying for a dispensation on account of age.[8] Whether Gotham, Weston and the younger Causton presented the roll or followed it in order to secure a *reformatio* to meet their cases, there seems no way of knowing. The mention of numerous errors and omissions in the composition of the roll shows, as we have suggested, that making it up was a ticklish business. The order of the petitioners had to be correct, both as regards status and degree ; the wording of the supplications had to comply with the requirements of the Chancery : any error or omission called for an *emendatio*, so that a long roll demanded quite a list of *addenda* and *corrigenda*.

Much of the technique of composition can be illustrated from the

[1] *Ibid.*, pp. 390–392.   [2] *Ibid.*, pp. 404–408.   [3] *Ibid.*, pp. 404–408.
[4] *Ibid.*, pp. 435–438 ; 441–442.   [5] *Ibid.*, p. 408.
[6] "Whereas he is of that of York" : *Cal. Papal Reg., Petitions*, i. 411, 415.
[7] *Ibid.*, p. 415.
[8] *Ibid.*, pp. 415–416. *Alumni Cantabrigienses* does not distinguish between the two Caustons, both named Michael, both of the same diocese (Norwich). The elder was Chancellor of Cambridge University in 1361, 1362, 1363, rector of East Dereham in 1371 and until his death in 1396 (Reg. Fordham, fo. 53) ; the younger was B.A. in 1363 (when the elder was S.T.P.). In 1370, when he petitioned for a canonry and prebend in Chichester, Michael Causton junior is described as clerk of the diocese of Norwich, M.A., scholar of laws, and rector of Hamerton (Hunt, a living in the gift of the abbot and convent of St. John of Colchester). He was fellow of Pembroke, whereas the elder Causton was master of Michaelhouse.

drafts of three *rotuli* from the second half of the fourteenth century in the possession of the University Registry, Cambridge.[1] Extensive notes on these rolls, with lists of petitioners, were made by the late Dr. A. H. Lloyd, the historian of Christ's College, and by his daughter, the late Miss M. E. H. Lloyd.[2] Through the generosity of Mrs. Lloyd, who sent me all the relevant papers of her husband and her daughter, I have been able to study their notes, many from the Vatican Archives, while through the courtesy of the University Registry I was allowed to inspect a draft of the longest of the rolls.[3]

More than 200 years previously the Cambridge antiquary, Thomas Baker, had made brief extracts from these rolls of petitions, which he found at the Registry in the cylinder (*capsula*) marked P, when he was planning an *Athenae Cantabrigienses*. His nomenclature for the first of the three was *Rotulus vetustior*, which we may adopt. This is the earliest, and contains 75 names. It is not in order of degrees, as the other two are, and the fact suggests that it is an early draft, perhaps an incomplete draft, of the final roll. In the two later Cambridge rolls, masters (i.e. professors) of theology and doctors of decrees and doctors of laws stand first : then the rolls differ. The earlier of the two puts the bachelors of laws, decrees and the scholars in canon law, theology and laws, in front of the masters of arts ; the later places masters of arts just after doctors of laws, and the bachelors of laws and decrees at the end.[4] The dating of *Vetustior* can be gauged with some degree of accuracy. The *regesta Avinionensia* (Vatican Archives) contain the majority of provisions solicited in *Vetustior*, most of them granted in February, 1 Gregory XI (February 1371). Now on Roll 173 of that series, under similar dates, is to be found a parallel group of provisions accorded to graduates of Oxford, when the name of the Oxford *nuntius* who presented the roll, John Mandour, LL.B., is given. These University rolls, *Vetustior* and the Oxford list, must have been prepared in 1370, and sent to Avignon late that year for the creation of Gregory XI.

[1] Cambridge University Registry, " Livings," no. 1.
[2] Their interest in the rolls was partly biographical. It was clear to them that the 360 petitions there contained added a considerable number of new names (*c.* 258) to *Alumni Cantabrigienses* ; and they made a number of valuable biographical notes on these newly revealed members of the University published as " Notes on Cambridge Clerks petitioning for Benefices, 1370–1399," by Mrs. Jessie Lloyd, *Bull. Inst. Hist. Research*, XX, no. 61 (1945), 75–96 and 192–211.
[3] My thanks are due to Mr. William Baker, of the University Registry, for these facilities. Owing to circumstances arising from the war, I was unable to see the originals of the first and third of the rolls, and have to rely on Dr. Lloyd's full and careful calendar of the petitions they contain.
[4] The Paris *rotuli* put doctors and masters under their respective faculties : Theology, Decrees, Medicine and Arts, in that order, and Arts, as might be expected, is subdivided into nations, French, Picard, Norman and English.

The second Cambridge *rotulus*, of the time of the chancellor William Colville (which we may accordingly term *Colville*), survives in one complete copy, one slightly less complete draft, and several small and incomplete rough drafts. This little series shows how much time and care the composition of a *rotulus* must have involved. The scribe may have begun copying either before the full complement of petitions had come in or before the order of the petitioners had been fully settled. In the longest version, Colville contains no less than 265 petitioners, including nine members under age and three married bedels. At the end of the roll is a petition, tendered on behalf of all those supplicating, for general permission to continue in the University for a period of five years, and while absent, either to enjoy the fruits of their benefices, or to lease them (*arrendare*) to others. The roll begins with a flowery exordium requesting that men whose light has been hidden under a bushel may now be erected upon the candlestick of promotion, and that those who have to face the competition of rolls backed by powerful persons shall not have to stand outside the door while others " enter to enjoy the delights of the marriage." Biblical allusion apart, the dates of Colville's chancellorship, 1388–1391, and the mention, in the roll, of John Wace and Richard Baston as proctors (*rectores*—they held office in 1388–1389) point to the marriage of Boniface IX to the Church. *Colville* is both a creation roll and a jubilee roll, for the new Pope, to whom it was sent, held his first jubilee in 1390. 1389 or early January 1390 must be its date, for after 29 January 1390 licences out of the Statute of Provisors were, in accordance with the terms of the reissue, heavily penalized, and no such licence for Cambridge occurs or indeed was likely to occur among the letters patent of 1390, as it was to do in 1399, when Richard II had been given power to modify the statute.

The third roll was sent during the chancellorship of Eudo la Zouche, and may accordingly be termed *Zouche*. This is merely a draft. There are 109 petitions in all, but as many as 16 have no names attached, and 6 appear very doubtful, as the usual particulars of the petitioners are missing. The date is a more difficult matter than with *Vetustior* and *Colville*. The two proctors mentioned in *Zouche*, William Alyn and John Hollebrooke, held office in 1397–1398.[1] Now Richard II had been granted power in 1392 and again in 1397 to modify the Statute of Provisors according to his discretion, and it seems unlikely that a body like the University could have availed itself of the King's moderating power to get permission to petition Rome without the consequent licence appearing on the Patent Roll. On 27 April 1399 the University

[1] For Alyn, cf. *Alumni Cantabrigienses*, I, i. 20 ; for Hollebroke (later Master of Peterhouse and Chancellor), *ibid.*, I, ii. 388.

secured such a licence, " according to the form of the moderation," to petition for benefices,[1] and the patent, tested by the King, and with part of the great seal in white wax attached, is still preserved in the University Registry. It seems likely, therefore, that the first efforts to compose the roll were made in the second half of 1398, and that the roll was sent in 1399 after formal permission from the Crown had been received. 1399 is probable, too, because in 1400 Boniface IX was to hold his second jubilee. It is interesting to note that the patent to Cambridge was granted " on the information of John Rome." Rome was rector of Fenstanton and an important official in the Privy Seal office, who later, under Henry IV, became clerk of the parliament.[2] *Zouche* gives the name of the *nuncius* who bore the roll to the Curia, *presentis rotuli portatori pro ipsius expedicione deputato* : it was Dr. John Ixworth, the distinguished proctor in the Curia, the senior colleague of William Swan and Visitor of Clare College.[3]

While there are minor divergences, the essential form of these rolls is the same. The *rotulus* is an ordered and edited assemblage of individual petitions, headed by the petition of the chancellor himself. It is therefore, just as at Paris, a document from which no scholar of any standing in the University would wish to see himself omitted. The formidable list of seniors, *olim cancellarii*, who figure in *Colville* was not likely to encourage the hopes of a young petitioner. Each supplicant in the roll gives his diocese, his degree, the category of benefice at which he aims, and in a final *non-obstante* clause the benefice or benefices which he at present occupies, if any, or any other fact that might require dispensation : e.g. that he has lost half the little finger of his right hand. These *non-obstante* clauses would be required for the concurrent tenure of a rectory with the canonry and prebend or office sought. Where serious incompatibility is involved, a petitioner makes, as he is bound to do, the offer to resign one of the benefices, and in the papal reply such resignation is liable to be imposed.[4] There are five types of petition for canonry and prebend. In the highest, confined to the senior doctors, the chancellor and former chancellors, the petitioner supplicates for a canonry " under " (i.e. with) expectation of a prebend " as well as (*necnon*) of a dignity, ' parsonage,' administration or office with cure or without, even if the

---

[1] *Cal. Pat. R.*, 1396–99, 547.

[2] See the account of him in A. F. Pollard, " Fifteenth-century clerks of parliament," *Bull. Inst. Hist. Research*, xv (1937–38), 141–142.

[3] For his preferments, cf. *Cal. Papal Lett.*, v (1396–1404). 596–597, and Jacob, " To and from the Court of Rome in the fifteenth century," *Studies . . . presented to Mildred K. Pope*, p. 163.

[4] Among the seniors pluralists are fairly numerous. They deserve the analysis given by Professor Hamilton Thompson to the Lincoln pluralists of 1366 in *Associated Architectural Societies' Reports and Papers*, vols. 34, 35, 36 (1919–1922).

dignity itself is elective and the highest (*maior*) after the episcopal, and one which a man reaches normally by election." The other variants, for graduates lower down the scale, omit some or all of these latter offices and qualifications. The second and more numerous type of petition asks for a benefice of so many pounds value with cure or without —the proportion is normally £40 with cure, £20 without—in the gift of the bishop, or of the bishop, dean and chapter of this or that cathedral church, or for a benefice in the presentation of a monastic house. The wording of the petitions is made to conform to the style of the Curia.

Petitions for benefices in the gift of the religious are, on the whole, in the majority. It is natural therefore to ask upon what principle petitioners name the bishop, cathedral or monastery whose patronage they desired to secure, for the *rotuli* leave no doubt that local ties were by no means the prevailing reason. It is not surprising that in 1370 a canon of Chichester, Thomas Wyrmonde, should be found asking for a dignity, "parsonage" or office in the cathedral, nor that the rector of Eversham, York, should the same year seek a canonry and prebend in the mother church. For Cambridge men, too, the liberties of St. Edmunds and St. Albans were conveniently local dispensers of patronage : but why should the rector of Barnack near Stamford ask for a canonry and prebend in Chichester, or the vicar of St. Edward's, Cambridge, seek a benefice in the gift of Glastonbury ? Why in *Colville* should so many petitioners look to the Prior of Lewes, when in *Vetustior* and *Zouche* they do not ? The only possible answer is that roughly within their own ecclesiastical province petitioners glanced in the direction of the largest and most likely ecclesiastical sources of supply, wherever they were to be found. They asked for anything that might be going. It would be convenient to suppose that the University authorities had some inside intelligence about those sources of supply, some means of estimating the possibilities : did Cambridge, for instance, draw upon sees and monasteries untouched by Oxford ? A comparison of the 1363 rolls does not encourage any such hypothesis. All that the Cambridge University authorities ask in their nation-wide search is that the Pope shall pay regard to seniority and experience. In one of the drafts of the Colville roll, Boniface IX was asked that in cases where several graduates petitioned for the same collation, or for a provision in the same church, preference should be given, among the seniors, to the holders of the more important degree (*pociores in gradu*), and that when the degrees of the candidates were equal, the older candidate should be preferred.

The main problem raised by these rolls is : how many of these 360 petitioners got what they asked ? The question is complicated by serious archival gaps. For 1389 and 1399 no register of supplications has survived, and it is to that particular record that we should normally look to find brief notes of the papal replies. For 1 Gregory XI, the Avignonese series of papal registers supplies the collations made ; but for 1389 and 1399, years of the Schism, there is no corresponding source.[1] Nor are the Cameral records of any avail ; the class of benefices with which we are dealing were not conferred in Consistory, and therefore do not show in the *Obligationes et solutiones*, while the *Libri annatarum*, so valuable for provisions in the fifteenth century, do not begin until 1421. All we can safely rely upon is the bishop's registers for the institution of the provisors, where it took place. The latter qualification is worth underlining, because as we saw, papal provision, under whatever formula granted, does not necessarily imply that the clerk secured his title. Each provision was accompanied, as requested in the petition itself, by a mandate to the executors, but the executors, who were as much investigators as administrators, had to observe law and custom, had to ascertain whether the provision was judicially practicable. At an earlier date Bishop Simon Montacute's Ely register records the appearance of an executor charged with putting a provisor into possession of Cottenham, a Ramsey living. The executor's commission instructed him to inquire into the life and conversation of the poor clerk so provided, and to hold a discussion with representatives of the abbey, who are invited to come and state their case (*ea que proponere voluerunt*), before action is taken.[2] In 1375 the record of the Ely Consistory shows Master Edward Beylam, LL.B., of Cambridge (who had petitioned in 1370), presenting his letters of provision together with the *processus* (the statement of legal action that followed), and being instituted by the bishop to a benefice which it had taken four years to secure.[3] This is not a long period, as things went, for provisions which necessitated the examination of the candidate, let alone expectatives, which might take much longer to mature.

All save fifteen of the petitioners in *Vetustior* received provision, most of them on 28 January, a few not until Michaelmas 1371 : by no means everyone to the benefice desired. Michael Causton the younger, the nephew (it is to be surmised) of the Chancellor, supplicated for a canonry and prebend in Chichester—he was under age and had to be dispensed— but was provided to the prebend of Howden in York.[4] He does not appear ever to have secured possession. Thomas de Ely, M.A., who

---

[1] The " Lateran " registers of Boniface IX contain only *Littere de Curia* or *Littere Secrete*, and are therefore useless for the present purpose.

[2] Reg. Montacute, fo. 27b.

[3] Ely Consistory Court, Reg. D. (1378–1381), fo. 33. His provision is in Regesta Avinionensia, vol. 178, fo. 499.

[4] Reg. Avin., vol. 178, fo. 471 v. References to this source are Miss Lloyd's.

sought a benefice of £40 with cure in the gift of Lewes Priory, was provided to one of £30 with cure, or £20 without, in the gift of Castle Acre.[1] Robert de Tunstede, M.A., S.T.B., rural dean of Hingham, Norwich diocese, who asked a £40 or £30 benefice in the gift of the Prior of Christchurch, Canterbury, was rewarded with a prebend at Llandefi-Brefi, near Lampeter.[2] Take again the three clerks of the name of Eltesley, Thomas the elder, master of King's Hall, Thomas the younger, LL.B., rector of Croxton, and Robert, LL.B., all petitioners in *Vetustior*.[3] The elder Thomas, who had asked for a canonry and prebend in Lichfield, received provision of one in St. Paul's ; [4] the younger, who had sought a prebend in York, one in Beverley.[5] Neither, as far as can be discovered, ever got possession. The position of the younger is revealed in a papal mandate of 19 November 1373, by which the Official of Ely was directed to assign to him, if found fit after examination, the canonry and prebend of the free chapel of Wolverhampton.[6] He had, the mandate states,[7] already been provided to a canonry in Beverley, upon getting possession of which he was bound to resign Croxton. So far he had not got possession, but in the meantime had exchanged Croxton for Teversham in the same diocese, and subsequently Teversham for the Wolverhampton canonry ; the present provision, which he had solicited and received, permitted him, notwithstanding the resignation clause in the letters of provisions, to hold Wolverhampton along with the Beverley canonry. The mandate cautiously adds, "*when he gets them.*" We know that by November 1373 he had secured neither, so that the Teversham-Wolverhampton exchange cannot have materialized, and his position cannot have been very promising. It is worth observing that the Official of Ely was one Thomas de Eltesley. Was this his elder namesake ?

Ten of the petitioners in *Vetustior* had been in the Cambridge University roll of 1363. Of these, in spite of mostly favourable replies, only Robert de Sutton the younger (to be distinguished from Robert de Sutton, LL.D., rector of Glatton in Lincolnshire, who appears in Sudbury's return of pluralists in 1366 [8]) seems actually to have got

---

[1] "Castillacie" : Reg. Avin., vol. 178, fo. 471 v.

[2] Reg. *Ibid.*, vol. 177, fo. 87 v.

[3] The relationship between the two Thomases is a little difficult to trace ; on 18 April 1349 the elder Thomas, as rector of Lambeth, presented the younger Thomas to the rectory of Eltisley (Reg. de Insula, fo. 18b, 36), and towards the end of the elder's life they exchanged (29 March 1375) their respective churches of Landbeach and Granchester (Reg. Arundel (Ely), fo. 6). In 1371 Robert was rector of Histon (Reg. Avin, vol. 181, fo. 81 v.) ; in 1382 he exchanged Hecham for the rectory of Fletchergate, Lincoln (Reg. Arundel, fo. 41 v.). See Lloyd, *op. cit.*, pp. 88–89.

[4] Reg. Avin., vol. 179, fo. 583 v.   [5] *Ibid.*

[6] Provision in *ibid.*, vol. 188, fo. 529.   [7] *Cal. Papal Lett.*, iv. 193.

[8] *Reg. Sudbury* (C. and Y.S.), ii. 181.

possession of the benefice he was seeking, one " value 30*l*. in the gift of the abbot and convent of St. Mary's, York." [1] Thomas de Eltesley, junior, who asked for a canonry in Witton (Ely), obtained one in Lincoln; and Robert de Tunstede, M.A. and S.T.B., rural dean of Hingham, did not get the benefice he was hoping for from Christchurch, Canterbury, but the rectory of Eversholt in Bedfordshire. Thomas de Bingham, M.A. and S.T.B., asked for a canonry and prebend (name erased) and was provided to a benefice in the gift of the prior and convent of Spalding. The latter he failed to obtain : but in *Vetustior* he is described as rector of Westmill (Hunts). The impression gained from the prebendal odysseys of these University graduates is that while a canonry was undoubtedly a prize, the process of acquiring it was an uncertain affair : a rectory was a sounder investment : it formed the permanent foundation of the University graduate's career. None the less, the desirable course for the higher academics was, through dispensations, to combine rectory with canonry and prebend.

In *Colville*, there are eighteen petitions for canonries and prebends in Salisbury alone. Only one succeeded, Walter Eston's petition for a priest's instead of a subdeacon's prebend. For canonries in Lincoln, there are likewise eighteen, none successful. Papal provisors to canonries in St. Paul's met with the same fate. Even Bartholomew Sidey, archdeacon of Middlesex, Simon Sudbury's former domestic clerk, who held the prebend of Neasdon from 1370 and at one time held Twyford,[2] did not succeed in gaining a more lucrative stall. The petitioners who sought these higher promotions must have known that the chances were against their obtaining possession, even if the papal signature was favourable ; the young regents have been only too conscious that the roll contained a substantial number of senior non-regents and of graduates holding respectable positions outside the University, using the Cambridge *rotulus* as a convenient way of bringing their names forward. At the same time, generalization on this head is dangerous, until we know much more about the permanent personnel of the University in the later years of the fourteenth century. One indication of limited value we do possess : the lists at our disposal are separated by periods of seven, nineteen and ten years. A comparison of the names and status of a supplicant whose name occurs twice, that is, in successive rolls, should give some indication of what success he has met with in the interim.[3]

---

[1] *Cal. Papal Reg., Petitions*, i. 406. He got St. Mary's, Binbrook (Lincs).

[2] *Reg. Sudbury*, i. 271, 274. Cf. also Lloyd, *op. cit.*, p. 205.

[3] It is not always possible from this conjunction to argue for that individual's continuous residence, because some clerks leave the University, then return for a period sufficient for the academic grace they will be seeking, then leave again. This particularly applies to the civilians and the canonists (in the majority in the three

We may begin with Thomas Baketon or Bacton, a distinguished ecclesiastical lawyer, who in *Vetustior* is called clerk of the diocese of Norwich, doctor of laws, and petitioner for a canonry in Hereford. He received provision to one in Lincoln,[1] but he does not appear to have obtained possession. By an earlier petition in the roll of 1363 he had secured the rectory of St. Gregory, Sudbury, and this he was ordered in 1370 to resign.[2] Bacton was a lawyer of considerable experience : the Close Rolls (1375) show him engaged in transactions over Cambridge landed property,[3] and during the middle of Richard II's reign he is named upon various commissions as doctor of laws.[4] In 1381 Archbishop Courtenay made him Dean of the Arches and he later appears as Commissary General in the Court of Canterbury as well as Commissary of the Prerogative, with a house in the parish of St. Nicholas, Cole Abbey.[5] Here then is a jurist to whom at any rate the first of the Cambridge *rotuli* proved fruitful. Next comes John de Burgo, reputed author of the popular manual of ecclesiastical duties and administration, the *Pupilla oculi*, who is said in *Alumni Cantabrigienses*, on the authority of the *Dictionary of National Biography* (which apparently took the statement from Pits), to have died *c.* 1386.[6] But he was alive in 1389, when he asked for a canonry and prebend in Lincoln. In *Vetustior* he appears as master of arts and as proctor, supplicating for a £40 benefice with cure in the gift of the abbot of Selby. In reply, he was given one of £30 or £20 in the patronage of Peterborough Abbey.[7] This was South Collingham, Yorkshire, which he was holding when he made his second petition in 1399. Between 1370 and 1389 he had been chancellor, and had proceeded to the mastership—that is, the doctorate—in theology. He was, I think, a veritable resident who secured a benefice at the first asking, but probably did not live to follow up any grant made to him by Boniface IX. One stalwart, John Pulham, appears in all three rolls. In *Vetustior* Pulham described himself as priest of Ely diocese, master of arts and scholar of theology. He had just been proctor (1369–1370).

---

rolls), many of whom took service under a bishop or archbishop, thereafter obtained licences to study for three or five years, and, having got their degrees, passed on to their former, or more profitable, employments. This can be illustrated in the next century by the careers of some of Archbishop Chichele's lawyers who were mostly Oxford graduates. There is reason to think that Chichele himself left his practice in London to return to Oxford for a period of further study so as to take his doctorate in civil law. Experience in the ecclesiastical courts (*practica*) might count in the requirements for a lawyer's degree : cf. *Reg. Chichele*, i. xxi.

[1] Reg. Avin., vol. 174, fo. 210 v.   [2] *Ibid.*   [3] *Cal. Close R.*, 1374–77, 203.
[4] E.g. *Cal. Pat. R.*, 1381–85, 356, 425, 498, 587, 596 ; *ibid.*, 1385–89, 85, 169, 173 ; *Cal. Close R.*, 1381–85, 460, 561 ; *ibid.*, 1385–89, 104.
[5] I. J. Churchill, *Canterbury Administration*, i. 396–397, 398, 445. He died in 1396 : Lloyd, *op. cit.*, p. 78.   [6] i. i. 257.   [7] Reg. Avin., vol. 178, fo. 401.

He asked for a benefice of £40 with cure in the gift of St. Mary's, York. He was provided to one of £30 or £20 in the gift of the bishop of Worcester.[1] In his petition of 1389, when he sought a benefice of £40 or £30 in Ely diocese, he described himself as licentiate in theology, and as engaged in litigation for St. Mary's in the Strand, without being in possession. The patron of this church was the bishop of Worcester, so it seems that the executors of Gregory XI's provision had met with legal opposition. In 1399 Pulham was still of the same degree, still asking for a similar benefice and still litigating, he states, for St. Mary's in the Strand.

Both in *Colville* and *Zouche*, Eudo la Zouche, LL.D., brother of Lord Zouche of Harringworth, petitioned for a canonry and prebend in Salisbury. On neither occasion was he successful. In *Colville* he described himself as *olim cancellarius*, as canon of Lincoln [2] and rector of Hogsthorpe. In 1399 he was chancellor again, prebendary of Langford in Lincoln Cathedral, and archdeacon of Huntingdon. More successful than the chancellor was another doctor of laws, Brian Fairfax, clerk of the diocese of York. He was LL.B. in 1389 when he petitioned for a canonry and prebend in York. In 1399, now a doctor, he described himself as rector of East Gilling, near Richmond, and asked for a valuable benefice in the gift of the bishop of Durham. It seems that for some period within those ten years he had been residing, for by the will of John Fairfax, rector of Prescot, dated 7 June 1393, a bequest of books in canon and civil law and the sum of £40 came to Brian " for his sustentation while attending the schools." [3] He was instituted to the rectory of Long Marston (Glos) on 17 May 1394, exchanged it for Foxhall (Suffolk) on 18 April 1398, and Foxhall for East Gilling on 28 April that year. In 1399 he secured leave of absence " causa standi in scholis." It seems likely that he spent two or three years away from Cambridge, and returned, probably to take his doctorate. In the end he got his desire. In 1410 he was collated to the precentorship of York and, in 1420, to the prebend of Langtoft, and died at a good age in 1436.[4] In the absence of any recorded papal reply, it is doubtful whether his cathedral appointments can be connected with his petitions ; but in any case the chapter of York might very well have been aware that Fairfax had turned his youthful eyes in their direction and have not forgotten him.

The younger applicants in *Colville* are worth some analysis, since some of them appear again in *Zouche*. In the former roll, the Bachelors of Arts stand just after the Licentiates in Arts. In *Colville* there are as many as 45 : 28 are in priest's orders, the remainder are described as

[1] Reg. Avin., vol. 181, fo. 317 v.   [2] Provision in *ibid.*, vol. 179, fo. 183.
[3] *Testamenta Eboracensia*, i. 187.   [4] Lloyd, *op. cit.*, p. 90.

clerks. Eight are also scholars in canon law, mostly in their second or third year, and 2 are also scholars *in utroque*, while 1 from York diocese is also a Master of Grammar. In most cases which I have been able to trace, it was the second petition, not the first, that brought them some measure of success. But early difficulties should not be over-exaggerated, since in *Colville* there is a group of 10 clerks, described as scholars, most of them under 23 years of age, who petition for dispensations to hold expectatives, mostly of benefices in the gift of the religious. If it was worth while for such young men to supplicate, it could not have been entirely unfruitful for the bachelors of arts, who were of full age. Probably much depended on who you were. In the Colville roll William Airmyn, clerk of the diocese of York, B.A., petitioned for a canonry and prebend in Southwell. Airmyn bore a well-known name. He was possibly great-nephew of William Airmyn, the administrator of Edward III's early years, the " pushing clerk," as Professor Tout called him, who became bishop of Norwich 1344–1353 ; [1] and a kinsman of William Airmyn or Ermyn, treasurer of Calais under Richard II and a baron of the exchequer under Henry IV. Airmyn had already (1388) been presented by the Crown to the prebend of North Newbald in York : [2] he did not get Southwell : but in 1392 he was collated to a prebend in Exeter, which in 1394 he exchanged for a canonry in the collegiate church of Abergwilly.[3] Prebends came with some ease to the well-connected. A not dissimilar case, though he is a much older man, is that of Robert Foljamb, LL.B., of the diocese of Lichfield. Foljamb was the son of Sir Godfrey Foljamb of Nottinghamshire, a prominent shire knight and tenant-in-chief (d. 1389). As early as 1362 we find Robert holding a prebend in Lichfield. In 1366, when he was a scholar of canon law, he was on the *rotulus* of the duke of Lancaster, asking for a prebend in Beverley, which he did not get.[4] But he must have had good helpers, for when he petitioned in 1389 he was holding the prebend of Morehall in the collegiate church of Noseley. He was never provided to Lichfield, but, strangely enough, to a prebend in the King's free chapel of All Saints, Derby, for in 1391 he was ordered, with others, to come before the King's Council for infringing the King's privileges in that chapel by accepting a benefice in virtue of a provision by the Pope.[5] Boniface IX could not have done a more maladroit thing in answer to Foljamb's petition in the Colville roll.

[1] *Chapters in Medieval Administrative History*, ii. 366–369, Tout calls the Airmyns " quite an official family."

[2] *Cal. Pat. R.*, *1385–89*, 478 ; described as " late Treasurer of Calais," *ibid.*, p. 99, which does not distinguish between the two Williams.

[3] *Reg. Brantingham*, part I, p. 134.

[4] *Cal. Papal Reg., Petitions*, i. 529.   [5] *Cal. Pat. R., 1388–92*, 523.

But there were more exalted petitioners than Airmyn and Foljamb. In the Colville roll, there is a little group of *generosi* beginning with Thomas Grey, licentiate of laws, rector of Wethersfield, *de nobili genere procreatus*. Dr. Lloyd thought that he was a different person from Grey, bachelor of laws, *de generoso sanguine procreatus*, the son of Sir Thomas Grey, who is found petitioning in *Vetustior*, but I see no reason to distinguish them. Thomas Grey may have been son of Sir Thomas Grey of *Wark* (not Sir T. Grey of Heton, the author of the Scala-chronicon). His first petition was in 1364 for a canonry and prebend in Salisbury, and it was granted with the qualification " if he is eighteen years of age." [1] In *Vetustior* he states that he had been granted a prebend in Salisbury by Urban V, but had not obtained it ; and so he asked for it again. Whatever Gregory XI's reply may have been, there is no evidence that he secured it at the second attempt. By the time of the Colville roll he had been presented by Alice Lady Neville to Wethersfield, London diocese.[2] He died in 1396, and is therefore missing from *Zouche*. More successful than Thomas de Grey was Roger de Grey, son of Lord Grey of Ruthin, described in *Colville* as clerk of the diocese of Bangor, and scholar of canon law in his third year, who asked for a canonry and prebend in Abergwilly. He declared that he was holding the prebend of Netheravon in Salisbury cathedral, and his estate in Netheravon had been confirmed to him by the King in 1388.[3] He did not get possession of Abergwilly, but on 26 May 1394 his father gave him a good living in Norfolk. Other Cambridge *nobiles* on the Colville roll are Roger Cromwell, son of Ralph, Lord Cromwell of Tattershall ; William Bardolf, brother of Lord Bardolf ; Roger le Despenser, son of Sir Philip le Despenser (grandson of Sir Edward le Despenser) ; and Edmund Clifton, *de nobili genere procreatus*, who was probably son of Sir Nicholas Clifton, deputy admiral in the west. None of them was above the status of B.A., and Bardolf, Despenser, and Clifton had as yet no degree. It is therefore reassuring to find that they, like humbler and perhaps abler young clerks, did not succeed at the first attempt. In *Zouche* there is, besides the chancellor and Grey, only one *nobilis*, John de la Pole, son of Richard's friend, the chancellor Michael, earl of Suffolk. He is bachelor of both laws and in his petition asks for a benefice value £200 vacant or to be vacant, in the gift of the Archbishop of Canterbury, as well as for a canonry and prebend in Lincoln. He declared that he held the canonry and prebend of Wistow, York, and the canonry and prebend of the altar of St. Andrew in Beverley. The latter declaration is interesting, because this prebend had been the subject of a famous prolonged suit in

---

[1] *Cal. Papal Reg., Petitions*, i. 490.   [2] *Newcourt, Repertorium*, ii. 654.
[3] Cf. *Cal. Pat. R., 1385-89*, 478 ; Lloyd, *op. cit.*, p. 93 for further details.

the Curia between Pole and Thomas de Wallington, Papal chaplain, who claimed that he had been collated to it as a reserved benefice by Urban VI, and pleaded that, after holding it some time, he had been ejected from it by Pole. By Rome it was adjudged first to Wallington, then to Pole, then to Wallington again.[1] But in the end Boniface IX, *motu proprio*, four months after his judgment ordering the executors to turn Pole out, annulled the previous sentence, and awarded the prebend to Pole.[2] The last mandate shows that this is a case where the same benefice was granted twice, a phenomenon much less common than critics of papal provisions imagine. Did Pole ever get the Lincoln canonry ? Probably not, for it seems unlikely that he is to be identified with the Thomas Pole, M.A., who received Corringham prebend in July 1426 ; Professor Hamilton Thompson was undoubtedly right in asserting that this Pole was a son of the second earl of Suffolk.[3]

This little assembly of facts is far from being an adequate basis for generalization about the effectiveness of the University *rotulus*. All that can be shown is that some petitioners were successful through the action of executors, or after litigation, some not. The proportion is hard to determine. Yet had the University roll been a mere waste of labour, would it have been prepared and sent ? And would the Oxford Convocation in 1417 have defended the " approved custom of writing for benefices "[4] which Archbishop Chichele's projected constitution seemed likely to supersede ? If the roll was more or less a lucky dip, it was at least a method of enabling the University clerk to compete with others more advantageously placed through being under the protection of the influential, or known to local patrons.[5]

[1] *Cal. Papal Lett.*, iv (1362–1404), 369–370.   [2] *Ibid.*, pp. 409–410.
[3] *Lincoln Visitations*, i. 194.   [4] *Reg. Chichele*, iii. 50.
[5] My best thanks are due to Professor J. A. Twemlow for a number of suggestions and corrections embodied in this chapter.

NOTES AND COMMENTS ON CHAPTERS I TO X

CHAPTER I

P. 3: "Modern Conciliar Study." For recent work, see my article "The Conciliar Movement in Recent Study," *Bull. John Rylands Lib.*, Vol. 41, No. 1 (September 1958).

P. 7: "inevitably such questions had been asked before." As H.-X. Arquillière showed in two papers published in 1911 ("L'origine des théories conciliaires," *Séances et travaux de l Académie des sciences morales et politiques*, N.S., LXXV. 573-586, and "L'appel au Concile sous Philippe le Bel et la genèse des théories conciliaires," *Revue des Questions Historiques*, XLV. 23-55), Conciliar thought was not a body of doctrine suddenly devised to meet the emergency of 1378, but had much earlier origins. Recent studies, however, indicate that these origins are to be found not so much in any single crisis in the relations of Church and State (e.g. 1297, to which Arquillière pointed), or in the works of individual political publicists, as in the thought and doctrines of the canon lawyers themselves. Along such lines, Conciliar thought can hardly be represented as a reaction against what Dr. Figgis called "the canonist theory of sovereignty": it is, more truly speaking, the logical culmination of certain ideas advanced in the course of earlier canonistic discussion. It is not imposed from without the Church, it arises from solutions given by the masters to questions canvassed within, particularly during the formative period of the Canon Law.

The most comprehensive and effective synthesis of these ideas was made by Cardinal Zabarella in his so-called *Tractatus de Schismate*, an extensive gloss on I.6.6. in his *Commentary on the Decretals*, the importance of which, for Conciliar studies, Dr. Walter Ullmann was the first to indicate (*The Origins of the Great Schism*, 1948, p. 176, Appendix, "Cardinal Zabarella and his position in the Conciliar Movement"). Professor Brian Tierney in his *Foundations of the Conciliar Theory* (Cambridge, 1955) has traced the ideas back from Zabarella to their source in the Decretists and Decretalists, particularly in Huguccio (d. 1210) and in Hostiensis (Henricus de Segusio, d. 1271); has noted the transference of some of these ideas to the sphere of political controversy in the *De Potestate regia et papali* of John of Paris (during the controversy between Philip IV and Boniface VIII); and has pointed to their survival even in the glosses of some of the strongest upholders, among the fourteenth-century canonists, of the papal *plenitudo potestatis*. Canonist sources, some of which Dr. Tierney has analysed in certain Cambridge manuscripts, indicate two developments of special significance for Conciliar thought: on the one hand, there is Huguccio's insistence that any acceptable theory of Church Government must be founded on a clear distinction between the authority inherent in the whole *congregatio fidelium* and the powers that could be exercised by the institutional *Romana ecclesia* which he identified with the Pope and Cardinals (cf. Dietrich of Niem's use of the distinction, p. 40 *supra*) ; on the other, there is the construction, by Hostiensis, of a coherent theory of the distribution of authority within an ecclesiastical corporation. Just as the bishop is part of the corporation of his cathedral church, sharing with the canons the responsibility for guiding its affairs and possessing proctorial powers to act on its behalf, so the Pope is part of the College of Cardinals, and in turn Pope and Cardinals stand in a similar relationship to the *universitas fidelium* in which ultimate sovereignty resides. Before this wider view of the Church as a whole could be accepted, it was necessary to establish that the *corpus mysticum* was indeed a corporation, i.e. that the *universitas fidelium* was a *universitas* in the most technical and legally precise sense of the term ; and this has been done by Huguccio when he maintained that the Church as a whole was subject to the same rules of corporation structure as any lesser chapter or college. It must not be thought that these liberal constitutional theories were those of the majority of canonists ; but they survived the criticisms of contemporaries and of the strongly pro-papal lawyers of the Avignonese epoch, and were welded into a whole by the genius of Zabarella. Thus on p. 3, l. 4 *supra*, the word " juristic " should be added after " theological," and the canonistic contribution given its due weight.

Later medieval canonists like Petrus Anchoranus, Antonius de Butrio and Panormitanus (Nicholas de Tudeschis) invoked extra-legal methods of combating the *plenitudo potestatis* by maintaining that the Pope is bound by the faith that he owes to the Catholic religion and to the Church as its organ to uphold the example of Christ. If he falls away from this and his action scandalizes the Church, measures can be taken against him by the whole body of the Church represented by the Council. The views of these and other canonists are discussed by Ludwig Buisson, *Potestas und Caritas* (Stuttgart, 1958).

P. 14, ll. 19–20 : J. B. Morrall, *Gerson and the Great Schism* (Manchester, 1960) traces the progress of Gerson's views on the Council.

CHAPTER II

P. 24 : " Hoccleeve, secondary in the privy seal office." Dr. A. L. Brown kindly pointed out to me that Hoccleeve, though almost forty years in the Privy Seal office, was never secondary. Professor Tout thought that there was a regular series of appointments to this position in the fifteenth century, but it appears to have been filled very irregularly. There was no successor to John Prophet until 6 October 1406, when Prophet's nephew, Thomas Felde, was appointed (" significantly two days after his uncle was appointed Keeper "). After Felde's transfer to Canterbury the position was vacant again until about 1420 when Robert Frye was appointed.

P. 40 : " A passionate nature and realistic mind." Dietrich's invective against papal fiscality and the legislation which gave it effect was the result of his own experience during the Schism ; but that experience may also help to resolve the difficulty noted on pp. 21–23 above. The financial disturbance of that period was critical and prolonged. The *Avisamenta* or recommendations of the reforming Commissions at the Council of Constance, the legislation of the 43rd Session and the *Concordata* made by the several nations with the Papacy, all advocate or enjoin the abolition of papal grants, licences and dispensations made *since the outbreak of the Schism*. For the reformers 1378 is the fatal date after which papal expedients for replenishing Apostolic *camera* multiplied in the courts of Avignon and Rome. Recent research has shown that it was, during those forty years, the intensification of such grants, the lack of local inquiry from, and consultation with, the diocesans (e.g. over unions and appropriations) and the unscrupulous pushing of annates, especially by Benedict XIII and Boniface IX (cf. the account in F. Baix, *La Chambre apostolique et les " Libri Annatarum " de Martin V (1417-1431),* 1942, p. cdiv f.), that underlined already existing grievances, and made reform of the head seem a paramount necessity. It is difficult to estimate the financial effect of the Schism upon the Papal Court. At a first glance there is every indication of growing stringency, and the position suggested by recent studies might thus be described. During the Avignonese period both the cash on deposit in the papal palace (part of the " treasure ") and the yearly surplus of income over expenditure had been diminishing ever since the pontificate of Clement VI. Clement started with a balance of 1,428,115 fl. (the cameral florin = 28s. Avignon) : he left, at his death, only 35,000 fl. (H. Hoberg, *Die Inventare des päpstlischen Schatzes in Avignon, 1314-1376,* 1944, p. xviii) ; in 1369 the treasure had fallen to 15,000 fl., and it was even lower under Gregory XI (Hoberg, p. xxii f.). Hoberg rightly remarks (p. xxv) that nobody can fairly maintain that the Avignonese Popes amassed any substantial sum in money or precious objects. K. H. Schäfer, in computing the total annual expenditure of the Curia (*Die Ausgaben der apostolischen Kammer unter Benedikt XII, Klement VI und Innocent VI,* 1944, and *Die Ausgaben . . . unter den Papsten Urban V und Gregor XI (1362-1378),* 1937), has pointed to its notable rise under the last two Popes : in certain years it exceeded income, e.g. in 1372 by 2,527 fl. ; in others, e.g. 1375, it fell only a little behind (401 fl., *ibid.,* p. 567) ; the largest credit balance of Gregory XI was only 4,861 fl. (*ibid.,* p. 500). By 1376 the Papacy was spending rather more than 338,000 fl. annually, and the expense of defending the papal state in Italy was monopolizing large sums. Thus in 1376 Gregory XI spent on war, in May, 58,201 fl., and in August, 87,024 fl. (*ibid.,* p. 627). This recalls John XXII who is estimated to have disbursed as much as 67·3 per cent. of his whole revenue in warlike expenditure in Italy (E. Göller, *Die Einnahmen der apostolischen Kammer unter Benedikt XII,* 1920, p. 10*).

By 1378 therefore the Papacy was only just paying its way, and could barely stand the financial shock of a Schism. Though many of the Cameral records have disappeared, along with the secret correspondence of the time, it is plain that the Popes were forced to borrow more heavily than before from merchants as well as from princes and from the College of Cardinals, and to do so upon a diminishing credit. Tribute and census now reached their lowest levels ; the States of the Church could scarcely pay for their own administration, while the direct taxation of spiritualities was now mainly in the hands of the monarchs of Europe. Gregory XII and John XXIII had to fall back upon the sale of offices and property, and the imposition of larger Chancery fees. During the Schism the taxes on sealing and registration constituted one of the main sources of income (P. M. Baumgarten, *Aus Kanzlei und Kammer*, 1927, p. 251 ; W. von Hoffmann, *Forschungen zur Geschichte der Kurialen Behörden von Schisma bis zur Reformation*, 1914, i. 244 f. ; ii. 128–130). Benedict XIII, by his close-fisted policy after the French restoration of obedience, had worked the *servitia* and annates so hard that in 1413 John XXIII was forced, out of compassion for the economic plight of the French benefices, to concede that for the next five years he would only take half the annates and the services (P. M. Baumgarten, *Untersuchungen und Urkunden über die* Camera Collegii Cardinalium *für die Zeit von 1257–1437*, 1898, p. 80). Until the middle and southern territories passed out of the hands of Ladislas of Naples, John XXIII was in an acutely difficult financial position, and one can sympathize with his desire to restore papal authority in those lands after the death of Ladislas (1414) instead of going to the Council of Constance.

On the other hand, the Papacy, from the Avignonese period onwards, had subsidiary funds which never found their way into the main accounting system of the Apostolic Chamber. Of these historical scholarship has in consequence taken little account. Chief among them was what is described as the secret fund or account, the *pecunia secreta*. Although under Clement V its existence probably did not imply a division of actual treasuries, under John XXII the moneys and material it contained are mentioned as being left in separate coffers in the papal *studium*. If the continuous *physical* existence of a secret treasury is not easy to demonstrate, the fund itself is undoubted. Dr. P. D. Partner, who has made a special study of the secret accounting, kindly points out to me that while the earliest records of them that survive are from the mid-fifteenth century, the curial inquiries of 1318–1321 and of 1336 into Clement V's donations and legacies reveal the evidence of a secret treasure of substantial proportions (cf. F. Ehrle, " Der Nachlass Clemens V und der in Betreff dersselben von Johann XXII (1318–1321) geführte Process," *Archiv für Literatur und Kirchengeschichte des Mittelalters*, V, 1889, and in particular the evidence given in 1320 by Johannes de Lescapone ; whose " liber tam de secretis receptis quam expensis," discovered, after his death, in the Apostolic Chamber, contained under sixteen heads the secret income and expenditure of Clement V). Under Innocent VI the ordinary ledgers of the Camera mention very large sums being transferred from the chamber to the secret account, " assigned to the lord pope " (K. H. Schäfer, *Die Ausgaben . . . unter Benedikt VI and Innocent VI*, pp. 510, 813–814, etc.). Similar transfers are recorded for Urban V (Schäfer, *Die Ausgaben . . . unter den Päpsten Urban V and Gregor XI*, 1937, pp. 7, 381). The sources of the income of the secret fund increased in number, until by the end of the fourteenth century it seems to have been usual to appropriate almost any kind of papal income for the purpose. At the beginning of the fifteenth, other special accounts for moneys specially reserved to the Pope came into existence, like that kept under Boniface IX, by Stefano Geri da Prato, Bishop of Volterra, papal *cubicularius* and registrar of apostolic letters (part published by C. Guasti, " Gli Avanzi dell' Archivio di un pratese Vescovo di Volterra," *Archivio Storico Italiano*, 4 Ser., XIII (1884)). See P. D. Partner, " Camera Papae: problems of Papal finance in the later Middle Ages," *Journal of Ecclesiastical History*, IV (1953), 55 f.

P. 43 : " the historic duty of the Emperor." Dr. G. J. Jordan, *The Inner History of the Great Schism in the West* (1930), p. 132, points out that, before Dietrich, Zabarella had already made the suggestion that the Emperor should summon the General Council. Dietrich's interest in imperial history can be seen in the *Privilegia* (printed by Schard, *De iurisdictione, autoritate et praeeminentia imperiali* . . . Basel, 1566, pp. 785–859) and his *Viridarium imperatorum et regum Romanorum* (ed. A. Lhotsky, " Das Viridarium imperatorum et Regum Romanorum," *Sitzungsber. der Österreichischen Akad. der Wissenschaften*, Phil.-Hist. Klasse, 226 (1949), 93 f.). The sources for the Saxon and Hohenstaufen periods which he uses in the latter are analysed by K. Pivec, " Quellenanalysen zu Dietrich von Niem I : Die Ottonenzeit im Viridarium imperatorum und die Gesta Saxonum," *Mitteilungen des Instituts für Österreichische Geschichtsforschung*, 58 (1950), 386–440. Pivec stresses his out-of-date imperialism : " without any understanding of the growing financial problem of the Papacy or the new forces of organization in state and church, in his political tracts he advocated for the contemporary age the ideal of an order long buried in the past, which could no longer apply to the times in which he lived." Dietrich's other historical writings, particularly those in which he extols the Emperor Henry VII and criticizes Clement V, are discussed by Professor Hermann Heimpel in K. Pivec and H. Heimpel, *Neue Forschungen zu Dietrich von Niem* (Nachrichten der Akad. der Wiss. in Göttingen, 1, Phil.-Hist. Klasse, No. 4, 1951).

CHAPTER III

P. 55 : " The English . . . had already sent a small number of prelates over to Basel." The first English delegation did not, in fact, arrive till the latter part of February, 1433 (22 February is the date given by A. Zellfelder, *England und das Basler Konzil*, p. 63). The bull of dissolution had been dated 18 December 1431. The resolution to allow an English delegation, in defiance of the papal bull, to go to Basel was taken by the King's Council at the instigation of Humphrey, duke of Gloucester, who had been won over by the pleading of Gerald Landriani, Bishop of Lodi. The Convocation of Canterbury admitted (September 1432) that the bull was valid, but decided that the delegates should go, and at the same time that from giving them " certain notable persons should be sent on an embassy to Eugenius IV " (*The Register of Henry Chichele*, ed. Jacob, iii, 232–233), presumably to assure the Pope of the loyalty of the English Church and to tell him that the delegation was going to Basel primarily to confute the Hussites. Chichele remained loyal to Eugenius throughout, and especially in 1436–1437, when England refused to support the action of the Council of Basel in abolishing annates.

P. 56 : " It was in this year that the great chance of solid peace was permanently lost." It was probably lost in 1433 when, after Easter, the meeting of Henry VI's English and French Councillors in Calais failed to put forward any effective plan for securing peace with France through the mediation of the Council of Basel. Basel was by this time deeply under suspicion in the English Council for imposing an Oath of Incorporation and for refusing to adopt the Constance plan of organization by nations. See A. N. E. D. Schofield, " The First English Delegation to the Council of Basel," *Journal of Ecclesiastical History*, XII. 2 (October 1961), pp. 186–9.

" an insularity . . . on the part of Archbishop Chichele." The difficulties of Chichele's position should be realized. Since 1424 an archbishop was technically a salaried member of the King's Council, now during the minority of Henry VI the governing authority in the kingdom and the controller of foreign policy. The objection which Chichele took through his proctors in April 1433 (see his protest read by Peter Partrich in Zellfelder, *op. cit.* pp. 250-252) to the use of the deputation rather than of the nation system in the Council of Basel must have been based on the fact that the Council, disregarding Lancastrian France, had already incorporated representatives of the French Church from the provinces recognizing Charles VII, and of Charles VII himself, in defiance of the Treaty of Troyes (1420). This action of the assembly at Basel, prejudicial to the future course of relations with France and with Burgundy, could scarcely be tolerated by anyone as faithful as Chichele to the policy of Henry V. It is not difficult, therefore, to understand the return from Basel, by the end of June 1433 (*The Correspondence of Thomas Bekynton*, Rolls Ser., ii. 144), of the greater part of the first English delegation, whose members had been reluctant to sit in the large mixed international committees alongside of political antagonists, who, in English eyes, had no right to be there. I have discussed Chichele's attitude in *Henry Chichele and the Ecclesiastical Politics of his Age* (Creighton Lecture, 1951).

CHAPTER IV

P. 64 : Richard also consulted Cambridge, and received from the University a reply, printed by W. Ullmann, " The University of Cambridge and the Great Schism," *Journal of Theological Studies*, IX. i (April 1958), 53 f. Cambridge advised no recession from Boniface IX, but suggested a General Council, if the measures advocated fell through.

P. 73 : " Since 1389, Prophet, as clerk of the Council." Dr. A. L. Brown has kindly pointed out that while Prophet was writing for the Council about 1389, he was not described as " clerk of the Council " until 1392. He became " secundarius " only in 1394. He appears to have left the office in 1395 and returned as Keeper on 4 October 1406. Richard Clifford had been exonerated from the Keepership on 2 November 1401, and two Keepers, Thomas Langley and Nicholas Bubwith, were in office before Prophet's appointment.

CHAPTER V

P. 85 : " He seems to have spent his early university years at Oxford only, where he joined the Franciscans." . . . " The first certain date in his life is 1324, when he was summoned to the Court of Avignon." It seems that Ockham was ordained subdeacon on 26 February 1306 (*Registrum Roberti Winchelsey*, ed. R. Graham (Cant. and York Soc.), *pars nona*, p. 981). He lectured on the *Sentences* at Oxford *c.* 1307 to *c.* 1319. The latest bibliography of his works is in A. B. Emden, *A Biographical Register of the University of Oxford*, ii. 1384–1387 (Oxford, 1958). Emden maintains that he was " seemingly not identifiable with fr. Wm. Ocham (Okam), O.F.M., Reading Convent, licensed to hear confessions between 1318 and 1320."

P. 88 : " Ockham is essentially a scholastic." This chapter does not discuss the question of the relation between Ockham's non-polemical works and his political writings. To R. Scholz, who emphasizes Ockham's " critical radicalism and practical conservatism . . . a typical English trait," they appear to be in separate compartments (*Wilhelm von Ockham als politischer Denker und sein " Breviloqium de principatu tyrannico,"* Schriften des Reichsinstituts für alt. deutsche Geschichtsk., Leipzig, 1944, p. 18) ; to M. Lagarde, on the other hand, in his notable *La Naissance de l'esprit laique*, esp. vols. V and VI, there is the closest connexion ; Ockham helps to destroy the medieval synthesis because his philosophy provides the justification for the independent and individual existence of the innumerable particulars which have replaced the universal Christendom : it has provided the theoretical bases for the groups or estates which are " the true political reality in the fourteenth century" (*La Naissance*, iii. 6). M. Lagarde's work is not yet finished, but some of the problems to which it gives rise have been briefly noticed in my lecture, *Some Recent Contributions to the Study of the Later Middle Ages* (Oxford, 1951). A very different approach to the question is that of M. Léon Baudry, " Le philosophe et le politique dans Guillaume d'Ockham," *Archives d'histoire doctrinale et littéraire du Moyen Âge*, Ser. 1937–1938, 209 f. Ockham's philosophical views, M. Baudry thinks, led him to be highly suspicious of anything resembling " group personality " or any theory that regarded *universitates* as either real or fictitious persons, and that this suspicion emerges in his treatment of the Franciscan Order : " Fratres sunt ordo et ordo est fratres. Ex quo sequitur quod ordo non est persona imaginaria et repraesentata, sed ordo est vere personae reales." The factor that maintains the Church as a Church is not the Pope, not a group of persons like the College of Cardinals, but the unity of belief, the one hope, the supernatural life.

Even if, in the end, there is found to be only very indirect connexion between Oxford and Munich, and we can echo the view of Dr. J. B. Morrall that it is " only in writers influenced by the Neo-Thomist interpretation that we meet with the idea that Ockham's polemical position was a necessary result of his philosophy " (" Some Notes on a Recent Interpretation of William of Ockham's Political Philosophy," *Franciscan Studies*, vol. 9, no. 4, New York, 1949, 338), the method adopted in both places is, with the exceptions noted in chapter v and immediately below, very much the same. The same meticulous and balancing care with which Ockham developed his theory of universals, hesitating between the "fictum" and "intellectio" explanations and rejecting other possibilities (cf. Ph. Boehner, "The Realistic Conceptualism of William of Ockham," *Traditio*, iv (1946), 315–319), is witnessed in the larger political dissertations from the *Opus Nonaginta Dierum* to the *Dialogus*. The word "obscurity" used on p. 88 is out of place in these discussions : Ockham may be difficult, but he is never obscure ; and "inconclusiveness" (*ibid.*, almost as questionable an epithet) will only daunt those who fail to realize that the political writer is also the author of the *Perihermenias* and the *Quaestiones super libros Physicorum*.

P. 88, n. 2 : For "the remainder of which will constitute vol. II." *read* "the remainder of which, edited by Professor H. S. Offler, is in vol. II."

P. 98, n. 3, add : On Ockham's Conciliar views, see B. Tierney, "Ockham, the Conciliar Theory and the Canonists," *Journal of the History of Ideas*, XV (1954), 40–70.

P. 100 : " clearer and more unequivocal statement." The clearest is the unfinished *Breviloquium de potestate Papae*, composed during the pontificate of Benedict XII, perhaps in 1341 (Léon Baudry, *Guillaume d'Occam, sa vie, ses idées sociales et politiques, 1949*, p. 219). Here Ockham departs from the method of the *Dialogus*, where opinions contrary to his own are discussed with balance and objectivity, and his own views are made perfectly clear, as he proceeds " in aliqua asserendo constanter, aliqua absque assercione temeraria opinando." The first two books are a powerful attack upon the extreme papalist theory of the *plenitudo potestatis* from a purely theological point of view, for it is the business of theologians to know what power the Pope possesses *jure divino* (*Breviloquium*, ed. L. Baudry, 1947, i. 7, p. 10). The doctrine that the Pope has complete power both in temporal and in spiritual matters to do all things not repugnant to divine law and the law of nature is branded as an assertion not only false and dangerous to the whole community of the faithful, but actually heretical, " because it is manifestly repugnant to holy scripture " (ii. 2–3, pp. 18–20). *Horrendissima servitus* is his description of such a theory when put into practice, for it violates the evangelical law of liberty. The second part of Book II is devoted to the " absurdities " which follow from taking the words *Quodcunque ligaveris* literally and without allowing for exceptions (ii. 15–16, p. 48). In Book III he argues against the position, taken by thinkers like Giles of Rome, that outside and apart from the Church no true power exists, and that *imperium est a papa, ita ut nullus possit esse verus imperator nisi qui a papa fuerit confirmatus vel electus* (iii. 2, p. 71). Historically, as the Old Testament shows, infidels possessed true *dominium* and temporal jurisdiction. If the Church alone could legalize temporal power and ownership, there would result the position that children, before they were baptized, would have no right to succeed to their parents' property, an *absurditas vix oppinabilis* (iii. 5, p. 83). It is " a heretical opinion to maintain

that there has been and is no true *dominium* or jurisdiction outside the Church "
(iii. 16, p. 100). The fourth book is on the theme that the Roman Empire
non est a papa.

CHAPTER VI

P. 106 : " Most scholars now accept Dr. Lapsley's contention that Henry was
anxious to avoid a parliamentary deposition." Professor B. Wilkinson has
pointed out that the idea of a parliamentary deposition involves a conception
of Crown and parliament as two distinct entities which was " contrary to all
that we know of their constitutional relations in the fourteenth century or for
long after " (" The Deposition of Richard II and the Accession of Henry IV,"
Eng. Hist. Rev., LIV, 1939, 220) ; and that " even the idea of a deliberate rejec-
tion by Henry of the authority of parliament, in the procedure he ultimately
adopted, can have little to commend it " (p. 230). What actually happened,
Professor Wilkinson argues, was, *mutatis mutandis*, a reversion to the precedent
of Edward II's deposition, when the assembly of lords acted with the *collaudatio*
and approval of the *populus*. Richard II was deposed, as the " record and
process " of the deposition has it, in an assembly consisting of *status et populus* ;
and the " estates," he maintains, were the magnates, the lords spiritual and
temporal, the noble as opposed to the non-noble element (p. 233). The non-
nobles, the *populus*, approved, while judgment on Richard was that of the *status*
alone. The difficulty about this hypothesis is, as the author admits, the joint
expression, the words *status et populus* themselves, which give the impression
that the commons were the judges of Richard as much as the nobles: an impression against which the commons later protested.

Is there, in fact, any solid reason why *status* should not mean the three estates,
the lords spiritual, the lords temporal and the commons, the most important
part of which were still the quasi-aristocratic element of the shire knights (cf.
J. S. Roskell, " The Social Composition of the Commons in a Fifteenth-Century
Parliament," *Bull. Inst. Hist. Research*, XXIV (1951) 154) ? *Status et populus*
is a method of expressing two aspects of the situation on 30 September 1399 :

1. The writs had already gone out for a meeting of the estates on the 30th,
   and there was a strong reason for not cancelling it. It might do what
   Henry wanted, and in view of opposition in the North, there was no
   time to lose.

2. Henry Bolingbroke was going to have his case against Richard II decided
   somehow. The decision was to be followed (or accompanied) by an
   electio in regem in which " the people," in past instances the Londoners,
   traditionally took part by approving. Those advisers of Henry who
   made themselves responsible for investigating precedent—and there is
   evidence that precedent was studied with the greatest care—must have
   been well aware of the Londoner's role.

What met on the 30th therefore, was an assembly convened to record the
fact that Richard II, by his conduct, had divested himself of the " character "

of King. It was this assembly that set up the committee of deposition, accepted their report and gave approval to Henry's *calumpnia*, his judicial challenge of the Crown, but it was neither a parliament, nor intended to be a parliament. See the treatment of these events in A. Steel, *Richard II*, ch. ix and in E. F. Jacob, *The Fifteenth Century* (Oxford, 1961), ch. 1.

CHAPTER VII

P. 125, n. 2, add : Much important detail will be found in *Consuetudines fratrum Vitae Communis*, ed. W. J. Alberts (Groningen, 1959).

CHAPTER VIII

P. 145 : Several of Groote's letters, Nos. 9, 20 and 51, were written to the Chanter. In the first of these Gerard replies to Salvarvilla's expressed intention of preaching to schismatics and heathens in the East, and urges him to stay in Paris, where he is much more needed than among the Scythians, Greeks or Balts who will not understand his Latin and whose learning is of the devil ; or among the Mathametici (Mohammedans) who will be as inveterate in their errors as any western heretic. Physically and morally France is his home : he will hook more fish in France and Italy than in the East (Ep. 9, p. 25). Paris needs converting ; and Gerard has much to say about scholastic sermons and their makers who love to be called Rabbi and have the first seats in the synagogues ; for by their methods of sermonizing practically the whole of Europe is infected. To Paris, the frontal and original member of Western Europe, the medicine should be applied, before it is spread to the Roman Curia and to all apostates (Gerard was, on balance, an adherent of Urban VI). Paris, which Gerard interestingly likens to Jerusalem, is the home of " Pharisees, jurists and religio us (mendicants)," teaching the tradition of the elders and the commands of men, and how to transgress God's commandments (Ep. 9, p. 27). The letter is characteristically filled with citations from St. Augustine and St. Jerome, recalling the emphasis laid by Thomas a Kempis on Gerard's remarkable knowledge of Augustine, especially the letters. Apart from the scriptures and Aristotle's *Ethics* (frequently cited), and classics like Seneca and Valerius Maximus, St. Augustine and St. Bernard are Gerard's models. Bernard he had studied deeply (See Mulder's list of citations, p. 338.) It is to be seen in letter 8 how quickly he can detect a treatise which purports to be by St. Bernard, but is not: the work *De amore*, which his friend William Vroede had thought genuine, is not only repugnant to Bernard's intention (*thesi*) but has neither the style, nor the beauty of language (*flores Bernardini*), nor the gravity ; and the incipit is wrong (*liber iste diversimode incipit*, Ep. 8, p. 7). The latter point is characteristic, for Gerard was a tireless reader and student of texts. His books were part of his life.

P. 150 : While some of Gerard's best letters were written to those entering religion or about to assume the office of prior or prioress and while he honoured all

R

strict religious, he was not an indiscriminate propagandist for the religious orders. He was keenly aware of the dangers of *proprietas*, and some of his strongest letters were directed to the Cistercian house of Camp on the lower Rhine and to the nunnery of Honepe, against the *detestabile malum* ; he recognized how extremely hard was the practice of obedience and loyalty to superiors, and the duty of refraining from passing judgment upon superiors, and how insidious was the reaction that made the monk feel "*minus utilis, minus fervidus vel minus bonus quam . . . in seculo.*" Letter 69, printed for the first time by Mulder, is addressed to a Carthusian who had been a secular priest and had felt that he would have greater scope for his administrative talents in some more relaxed order, where he might become abbot or prior : the feeling of wasted talent, says Gerard, is dangerous and is a sign of self-reliance rather than of humility (Ep. 69, pp. 270–272) : and to a new monk he writes to combat the sense of frustration which is insidious (Letter 16): " And know that often a man is more deserving when he is in a less fervour than when he is in a greater, and then is the time of deserving, when God leaves a man and withdraws his hand." This is wholly in the spirit of II.x and III.xx of the *De imitatione Christi* ; it is taken up, again, in Letter 62 on patience and perseverence : *caveamus ne tristicia absorbeamur.* But while the entry into religion with the will to persevere and change one's life is " as a second baptism, according to St. Bernard in his *De Praecepto et dispensacione,*" he will not advise it for all his friends. To William Oude Scute, a priest and a secular whom he called *habitator senior cordis mei,* shocked at the prohibition of Gerard's preaching into thinking that he might do better in a religious order, he wrote : " As I see it, I would not dare to counsel you to enter religion, though I have no confidence nor should you trust me in this, since I do not know God's way. The desire I have in my heart—it may be foolish—is that you should remain in the world, and not be of the world, since the world will hate you, and many so-called religious, because they are of the world and seek their own, will hate you too." (Ep. 62, p. 235). Instead, he advises William to hold communication with Ruysbroeck's monks and with those of Rougecloitre (near Brussels) : they will understand him.

CHAPTER IX

P. 156, n. 1 : Dr. Joseph Koch published a collection of the letters of Nicholas of Cues in *Sitzungsberichte der Heidelberger Akademie der Wissenschaften,* Phil.-Hist. Klasse 1942–1943, 2 Abhandlung. In 1948 appeared his comments on the letters in the same Heidelberg series, Jahrgang 1944–1948, under the title, *Nikolaus von Cues und seine Umwelt.* This contains the itinerary of Nicholas' legation in Germany, 1451–1452, and a bibliography which ignores works published in English. The most useful modern monographs are those of Peter Menniken, *Nikolaus von Kues,* 2e Aufl. 1950, and (in relation to his political thought) G. Heinz-Mohr ; Unitas Christiana : *Studien zur Gesellschaftsidee des Nikolaus von Kues,* 1958. R. Haubst, *Die Christologie des Nikolaus von Kues* (Freiburg, 1956) is valuable. Of the letters of Nicholas published in *Cusanus-Texte,* Briefwechsel, Erste Sammlung (*Sitzungsberichte der Heidelb. Ak. d. Wiss., Phil.-Hist. Klasse, XXXIII*), no. 4 is crucial for the passage of Nicholas to the papal side. In it Nicholas replies to a Carthusian who asks him a number of searching questions on the relations between the Council and the Church, e.g. " Are not the Councils the Church at least from the point of view of representations ? " and "if dissension arises in a Council duly and properly summoned to what side should one adhere ? "

The texts of Nicholas's philosophical writings have begun to be published at Stuttgart (Kohlhammer, from a collation of the Paris 1514 and Basel 1565 editions). The first volume has an introduction by the editor, Dr. Alfred Petzelt. The critical text, Latin and German, is now appearing under the editorship of E. Hoffman and R. Klibansky, in *Heidelb. Ak. d. Wiss., Phil.-Hist. Kl.*, 192/98-1960.

CHAPTER X

P. 172 : " The great spell of Jakob Burckhardt in Germany." And, it should be added, in England as well as in America. A good account of his influence on historiography will be found in Wallace .K. Ferguson, *The Renaissance in Historical Thought* (Cambridge, Mass., 1948), pp. 178-252. See also the notable article on Burckhardt by Dr. Hans Baron in *Renaissance News*, Vol. 13, autumn 1960. During the last fifty years certain medievalists have tended to contest the very existence of the Renaissance. In danger of being carried too far, this reaction has received a valuable corrective from Ernst Cassirer who, after analysing Renaissance philosophy from a mathematical and physical point of view (*Individuum und Kosmos in der Philosophie der Renaissance*, 1927), came at the end of his life to see in the Renaissance a shifting in the balance between particular forces in civilization—" society, state, religion, church, and science "—and therefore a new equilibrium (*Journal of the History of Ideas*, IV. 55). The Renaissance, as Erwin Panofsky recently puts it in other terms, was " a period of de-compartmentalization, of mixture and interpenetration "(*Renaissance News*, V, no. 1, p. 7). Re-statements of the position are to be found in D. Hay, *The Italian Renaissance in its Historical Background* (Cambridge, 1961), and (with special reference to periodization) by Delio Cantimori in *Relazioni del X Congresso Internazionale di Scienze Storiche*, IV. 307-344 (Florence, 1955).

In their prolongation of the Middle Ages, the medievalists to whom we referred have received assistance from the students of medieval science. The continuity of scientific thought, in particular of Aristotelian studies, in the Italian Universities of the fifteenth and sixteenth centuries, has been treated in a number of places (especially " The Development of Scientific Method in the School of Padua," *ibid.*, i. 177) by John Herman Randall, Jnr. As Randall pertinently remarks: " At Padua, Bologna and Pavia, to a less extent at Siena and Pisa and the brilliant university of Ferrara, Aristotelianism was still a living and growing body of ideas. What Paris had been in the thirteenth century, Oxford and Paris in the fourteenth, Padua became in the fifteenth " (p. 188). One of the most judicious re-statements of Renaissance humanism is, however, to be found in E. Cassirer, Paul Oscar Kristeller and J. H. Randall, Jnr., *The Renaissance Philosophy of Man* (1948), where classical and medieval influences are shown both as blended and as distinguishable.

On the side of pure scholarship, the work that has gone into the Italian national edition of Petrarch is having the effect of demonstrating the great importance of Petrarch and his circle on the constitution of classical texts. The study of the manuscripts of Livy owned and annotated by Petrarch has led the editor, Dr. G. Billanovich (in his important article " Petrarch and the Textual Tradition of Livy," *Journal of the Warburg and Courtauld Institutes*, vol. XIV, 1951), to show how important were the private libraries of fourteenth-century humanists for the identification as well as the copying of classical manuscripts. The importance of fourteenth-century classical studies in Northern Italy is also emphasized by R. Weiss, *Il primo secolo dell' umanesimo* (1949), in which he demonstrates the literary relations of leading Paduan humanists with their fellow-enthusiasts in Venice, Verona, Vicenza and Bologna. One of the more interesting is Jeremias of Montagnone, the Paduan judge, who was particularly occupied with Catullus (cf. R. Ellis, *Catullus in the Fourteenth Century*). It is the fourteenth century on which some of the liveliest minds are now concentrated.

To them the continuity of the classical tradition, in poetry, history and iconography, is the all-important topic of study. The concern of scholars like Jean Seznec (*La survivance des dieux antiques*, 1940) and B. L. Ullmann with the transformations of classical myth and legend (cf. the latter's edition of Coluccio Salutati, *De laboribus Herculis*), or of Hans Baron with the interpretation of Cicero's literary and philosophical treatises from the twelfth to the fifteenth century, points to the later Middle Ages as the essential and transforming link between the classical past and the newer age. To art historians, on the other hand, something more decisive may be said to have occurred between 1250 and 1550, and they suspect that that decisive thing happened in Italy during the fifteenth century. Was it, perhaps, the perfection of anatomical study, the science of perspective or, more generally, the union of science and art, as contemporaries understood these expressions, whereby representation became portraiture, space lengthened into distance and technology served the cause of beauty as well as of utility ?

The modern interpretation of the Renaissance is essentially dynamic : it is not bound to chronology. The Renaissance is not valued so much for the new content it created—though this is infinitely rich—as for the new energies it awakened and for the intensity with which these things acted. It represents a change of emphasis, rather than a repudiation of the whole medieval past.

INDEX OF PERSONS AND PLACES

Aachen, 146
Abergwilly, canonry of, 237, 238
Acquoy, J. G. R., 141
Acton, Lord, 179
Adam of Usk, 24
Aeneas Sylvius, *see* Pius II
Agnetenberg, 122, 130, 131, 139, 141, 151
Agricola, Rudolf, 137
Ailly, Peter d', 3, 6, 14, 15 and n. 1, 38, 40, 49, 50, 61 n. 2, 93, 130, 175
Airmyn, Ermyn, William, bishop of Norwich, 237
— —, treasurer of Calais, 237
Alan of Lille, 130
Albergen (Eastern Over-Yssel), 125
Albert of Saxony, 130
Albumasar (Abu Maschar), 146 n.
Aleman, Louis, Cardinal of St. Cecilia, 7
Alexander V, 28, 73, 74, 75
— — (Peter Philargi), Cardinal of Bologna, 39
Alnwick, William, bishop of Lincoln, 208
Alyn, William, 229
Ambrose, St., 195
Amersfoort, 124
Amsterdam, 145
Amundesham, John, 187 and n. 2, 188 and n. 2, 189
Anagni, 3, 29
Anchoranus, Petrus, 241
Andres of Escobar, 37
Anselm, St., 149
Antioch, Patriarch of (Jean Mauroux), 6
Antwerp, 125, 138, 149
Aquinas, St. Thomas, 88, 110, 111, 112, 115, 116, 119
Aragon, 2, 46
—, King of, 65 n. 3
Aristotle, 81, 88, 110, 114, 116, 131, 179, 180
Arnhem, 145
—, Charterhouse of, 147
—, Master John of, 146
Arquillière, H.-X., 240
Arundel, Thomas, Archbishop of Canterbury, 57, 71, 76, 82 n. 3, 107, 154, 201, 203 n. 4
Ascham, Roger, 186
Athanasius, 87

Athens, 131
Audley, Edmund, bishop of Salisbury, 222
Augustine, St., 16, 17 n. 2, 18, 112, 146, 168, 174, 195
— —, of Canterbury, 81
Aulus Gellius, 196
Avicenna, 157
Avignon, 5, 7, 21, 26, 51, 85, 86, 101, 103, 225

Bacon, Francis, 110
Bacton, Baketon, Thomas, Dean of the Arches, Commissary General and Commissary of the Prerogative, 235
Baden, 6
Baix, F., 21
Baker, Thomas, 228
Bale, John, 187 n. 2, 198
Barbara, St., 155
Barbarossa, Frederick, 24
Barcelona, 49
Bardolf, William, 238
Barnack, nr. Stamford, rector of, 231
Barnet, 46
—, John, bishop of Ely, 226
Baron, Hans, 251, 252
Barraclough, G., 20, 21, 22, 23, 224 n.
Barrow, William, bishop of Carlisle, 73
Barton, John, 201 and n. 3
Bartoš, F. M., 38
Basel, Bâle, Council of, 6, 7, 15, 17, 27, 47, 52, 53, 54, 55, 56, 69, 155, 156, 159, 196 n. 2, 244, 245
—, bishop of, *see* Coudenberghe, William de
Baston, Richard, 229
Bath and Wells, bishops of, *see* Clifford, Erghum, Weyville
Battle, monastery of, 200
— —, Hawkhurst, in patronage of, 200
Baudry, L., 246
Baur, L., 179
Beaufort, Thomas, 183
Bedford, John, duke of, 53, 54, 55
Beer, K. C. L. M. de, 249
Beer, prebend of Salisbury, 82 n. 1
Bekynton, Thomas, 184, 192
Beldomandi, Prosdocimo de', 157
Belleart (printer of Haarlem), 138

Benedict, St., 127 n. 1

Benedict XII, 19, 93, 225 and n. 7, 246

— XIII (Peter de Luna), 2, 7, 27, 38, 69, 71, 72, 74, 242

Benson, R. H., 135

Benzi, Ugo, of Siena, 157

Bereford, William de, 109

Berenson, B., 171

Berlière, Dom U., 21

Bernard, St., 45, 123, 192

—, of Waging, prior of Tegernsee, 166

Berry, John, duke of, 5

Bessarion, 130

Bett, H., 160, 161, 164, 165

Beverley, canonry of, 233

—, prebend of, 233, 237

— —, of the altar of St. Andrew, 238

Beylam, Edward, 232

Billanovich, G., 252

Binbrook (Lincs.), St. Mary's, 234 n. 1

Bingham, Thomas de, rector of West-mill (Hants), 234

Birkhede, Brikehede, John, canon of Chichester, 200 and n. 3

Bisham (Bustlesham), 205

Bisticci, Vespasiano da, 69 n. 2

Blackawton (Devon), rector of, see Elyot

Blanche, daughter of Henry IV, wife of Rupert of the Palatinate, 70

Blois, Peter of, 142

Boccaccio, 172, 195, 196

Boehmer, H., 174

Boethius, 180

Bohemia, 47

Bologna, 45, 181, 251, 252

—, Cardinal of, see Alexander V

Bonagratia of Bergamo, 86

Bonaventura, St., 131, 139

Bonet-Maury, 142

Boniface VIII, 7, 19, 24, 36, 240

— IX, 27, 28, 34, 35 and n. 2, 36, 39, 42, 50, 51, 57, 60, 62, 63, 64, 65, 66, 67, 68, 71, 72, 204 and n. 5, 219, 223, 229, 230, 231, 235, 237, 239, 242, 243

Booth, Charles, bishop of Hereford, 199

Bordeaux, Archbishop of, see Monte-ferrando, David de

Borsano, Simon de, Cardinal of Milan, 3, 32

Boüard, M. de, 4

Bozen, 45

Bozo, Cardinal, 24

Brabant, 45, 143

—, archdeaconry of, 145

Bracton, Henry of, 93, 110

Brakel (Westphalia), 26

Brancacci, Carlo, papal nuncio, 57

Bredon, Simon de, 226

Bregno, Andrea, 161

Bremen, Archbishop of, see Otto

Brewers, company of, 186

Bridget, St., 81, 155, 196

Brinckerinck, John, 151

Brixen, bishop of, see Cues, Nicholas of

Bromyard, John, 203

Brown, A. L., 241, 245

Brown, Robert, canon of Salisbury, 79

Browning, Robert, 162, 172

Bruges, 13

Brugman, John, 136

Bruni, Leonardo, of Arezzo, 25, 195

Brunswick, see Engelhus

—, duke of, 27, 33

Brussels, 125, 138

Brynkley, Master Richard, dean of the Arches, 58

Bubwith, Nicholas, archdeacon of Dorset, canon of Salisbury, 79, 245

Burckhardt, J., 172, 251

Burdach, K., 177

Burgo, John de, 235

Burgundy, duke of, Philip (d. 1404), 5

— —, John the Fearless (d. 1419), 5, 56

— —, Philip the Good (d. 1467), 84 n. 3

Buridan, 144

Burley, Walter, 179

Bury, Richard de, 198 and n. 3

Busch, John, 141, 147, 150

Butillo, Francesco, 30, 32

Butler, Joseph, bishop of Durham, 211

Butrio, Antonius de, 241

Calais, 8, 45, 190

—, treasurer of, see Airmyn

Cambrai, 125

—, dean of, see Carler

Cambridge, 221

—, St. Edward's, vicar of, 231

—, stationers of, see Fydyon, Wake

—, University of, 208, 209, 215, 219, 220, 221, 225, 228, 229, 230, 231

— —, Chancellors of, see Causton, Colville, Dereham, Zouche

— —, Christ's College, 228

— —, Clare College, Visitor of, see Ixworth

— —, Corpus Christi, House of, 215

— —, Gonville Hall, 215

Cambridge, University of, King's Hall, 208 and n. 3
— — — —, Master of, see Eltesley
— —, Michaelhouse, 215
— — — —, Master of, see Causton
— —, Pembroke College, 227 n. 8
— —, Trinity Hall, 215
Canterbury, 8, 25
—, Archbishops of, see Arundel, Chichele, Courtenay, Islip, Pecham, Sudbury, Warham, Winchelsey
—, Christ Church priory, 191
— — —, prior of, see Chillenden
Capri, 29
Carler, Giles (Aegidius Carlerius), dean of Cambrai, 138
Carlisle, bishop of, see Barrow, Strickland
Carlyle, Dr. A. J., 13
Castellamare, 29
Castiglionchio, Lapo da, 193
Catullus, 252
Causton, Michael, the elder, Chancellor of Cambridge, Master of Peterhouse, 227
—, Michael, the younger, rector of Hamerton (Hunts), 227 and n. 8, 232
Cele, John, 123, 124, 129, 145, 150
Celestine, 14
Cesarini, Cardinal Guiliano, 16, 17, 55, 160
Challant, Antoine de, Cardinal of St. Cecilia, 219, 220
Chambers, R. W., 185, 186
Champion, P., 175
Charlemagne, 99, 177
Charles IV, Emperor, 101, 102
— VI, King of France, 5, 71 n. 1, 73 n. 1
— VII, King of France, 54, 56, 245
—, of Durazzo, 33, 35
Chastellain, Georges, 176
Chaundler, John, dean of Salisbury, 78, 79, 82 n. 1
Cheyne, Sir John, ambassador to Rome, 70, 71 and n. 1
Cheyney, William, knight of Queen Joan, 78 n. 5
Chichele, Henry, Archbishop of Canterbury, 45, 53, 55, 56, 58 and n. 5, 59 n. 2, 75, 76 and n. 1, 81, 82 n. 3, 185, 189, 190, 203, 214 n. 2, 234 n. 3, 239, 244, 245
— —, ambassador of Henry IV, 70

Chichele, Henry, bishop of St. David's, 73, 79
— —, Chancellor and canon of Salisbury, 79
Chichester, bishop of, see Sydenham
—, canonry and prebend of, 227 n. 8, 231, 232
—, canons of, see Birkhede, Wyrmonde
Chillenden, Thomas, prior of Christ Church, Canterbury, 53
Chrimes, S. B., 107
Cicero, 179, 181, 182, 252
Clement IV, 19
— V, 19, 243, 244
— VI, 101, 102, 225 and n. 7, 242
— VII, 145
Clifford, Richard, bishop of Bath and Wells, later of Worcester, afterwards of London, keeper of the privy seal, 58, 71, 72, 73, 203, 206 and n. 1, 245
Clifton, Edmund, 238
Cnossos (Creet), 195
Coke, Lord, 110
Cole Abbey, 235
Cologne, 28, 45, 46, 125, 130, 143, 147, 152
—, Archbishop of, see Frederick
—, Dominican School of, 144
Colville, William, Chancellor of Cambridge University, 229
Commines, Philippe de, 176
Conrad of Gelnhausen (Provost of Worms), 5, 9, 10 and n. 2, 11
Conrad of Mengenburg, 87, 102, 103
— — Soltau, bishop of Verden, 27
Constance, 14, 38, 44, 48, 49, 50, 76, 80
—, Council of, 4, 5, 6, 19, 22, 25, 37, 38, 39, 44, 47, 48, 49, 50, 51, 52, 53, 54, 58, 75, 76, 77, 82, 83, 93, 147, 218, 243
Constantinople, 76, 182
—, Patriarch of, see Rochetaille, Jean de la
Corinth, 131
Corsini, Peter, Cardinal of Florence, 3
Cossa, Baldassare, see John XXIII
Coudenberghe, William de, bishop of Tournai and of Bâle, 8 n. 5
Courtenay, William, Archbishop of Canterbury, 235
Craster, Sir Edmund, 210
Creighton, Bp. Mandell, 25, 48
Cremona, 45
Cromwell, Roger, 238
Croxton, rector of, see Eltesley

Crukadan, Geoffrey, canon of Salisbury, vice-general of Robert Hallam, 79

Cues, Cardinal Nicholas of, papal legate in Germany, bishop of Brixen, 6, 15, 16, 17 and n. 3, 18, 89, 125, 133 n. 1, 154–169 passim, 174, 250, 251

Curtis, E., 201

Cyprian, St., 7, 16, 17

Damasus, 87

Damiani, Peter, 105

Dante, 36, 76, 89, 93, 99, 105, 177, 179, 182

Davy, George, 222

Debongnie, Fr. P., 140, 248

Delaissé, L. M. J., 140

Delft, 124, 125

Denifle, H., 174, 225 n. 7

Denton, W., 173

Derby, King's free chapel of All Saints, prebend in, 237

Dereham, Elias de, 78

—, Richard, Chancellor of Cambridge, dean of St. Martin-le-Grand, 73, 218, 219

Despenser, Henry, bishop of Norwich, 7, 201, 219

—, Roger le, 238

Destrez, J. A., 123

Deventer, 122, 123, 124, 125, 135, 136, 137, 138, 140, 143, 149, 151, 152, 153, 250

Deverose, John, 66 n. 1

Dier, Rudolf, de Muiden, 124, 141, 145 n., 146, 151

Dietrich of Niem, 3, 19, 20, 23, 24–43 passim, 50, 96, 223, 240, 241, 244

Dilthey, W., 174

Doesburg, 125

Dordrecht, Bartholomew of, 143 n.

Dorothy, St., 155

Druell, John, 200 n. 3

Du Boulay (Bulaeus), C. E., 60

Durandus, 59

Durham, bishop of, see Butler

Dyer, John, 222

East Gelling (Yorks), rector of, see Fairfax

Easton, Adam, Cardinal of St. Cecilia, 196, 204 n. 5

Echternach (Luxemburg), 137

Eckhart, Master, 156, 159, 164

Edmund, St., king and martyr, 155

Edward I, 173

— II, 173, 247

— III, 73, 100, 101, 120

— IV, 176

Eger, Henry, of Calcar, 146

Ellesmere, Lord, 110

Elmham, Thomas, 186

Eltesley, Robert, 233

—, Thomas, the elder, master of King's Hall and rector of Lambeth, 233 and n. 3

—, Thomas, the younger, rector of Croxton, 233, 234

Ely, bishops of, see Barnet, Montacute

—, Thomas de, 232

Elyot, William, rector of Blackawton, 200

Embledon, co. Durham, 216

Emden, A. B., 207, 245

Emmerich, 137

Engelhus, Dietrich, of Brunswick, 27

Enteren, Rudolf de, 146

Erasmus, 21, 134, 135, 136, 175 and n. 1

Ercole, F., 177, 178

Erfurt, University of, 27, 174

Erghum, Ralph, bishop of Bath and Wells, 203, 205

Eskinni, John, of Ommen, 151

Eston, Walter, 234

Eton College, Chapel of, 200 n. 4

Eugenius IV, 7, 17, 55, 56, 160, 199, 244

Eutropius, 195

Eversham (York), rector of, 231

Eversholt (Beds), rectory of, 234

Exeter, bishops of, see Grandisson, Lacy, Stafford

—, canon of, see Stevens

—, prebend of, 237

Fairfax, Brian, rector of East Gilling (Yorks), 236

—, John, rector of Prescot, 236

Farnier, William, 86

Felde, Thomas, 241

Fénélon, 148

Fenstanton, rector of, see Rome

Ferguson, W. K., 251

Ferrara, University of, 251

Ficino, 131

Figgis, J. N., 1, 2, 6, 7, 17, 46, 240

Fillastre, William, Cardinal of St. Mark, 6 and n. 1, 38, 54

Finke, H., 28, 37, 38, 46, 47, 49, 50, 82

FitzNeal, Richard, 24, 32

FitzRalph (Armachanus), 66

Flandrin, Peter, Cardinal of St. Eustace, 3 and n. 2

Fleming, Richard, bishop of Lincoln, 45, 54, 204

—, Robert, 182

Florence, 25, 45, 131, 142

—, Capella dei Pazzi in, 182

—, Cardinal of, see Corsini, Peter

—, Council of, 172

Foljamb, Sir Godfrey, 237

—, Robert, 237

Fondi, 32

Foppens, Henry, of Gouda, 124, 150

Fortescue, Sir John, C. J., 106–120 passim

Fox, Richard, bishop of Winchester, 192

Foxhall (Suffolk), rectory of, 236

Frankfurt, Reichstag, 64

Fraunceys, John, 35 n. 2

Frederick, Archbishop of Cologne, 28

—, of Austria, 100

—, bishop of Regensburg, 102

Free, John, 182

Froissart, 176

Frye, Robert, 241

Fydon, stationer of Cambridge, 221

Gansfort, Wessel, 125, 129, 130, 131, 132, 133, 134

Gascoigne, Thomas, 155, 194, 208

Gelasius, Pope, 196

Genoa, 5, 69

Geoffrey of Monmouth, 194, 195

Geri, Stefano, da Prato, bishop of Volterra, 243

Gerson, 5, 9, 10 and n. 1, 11, 12, 13 and ns. 3 and 5, 14, 15, 28, 37, 38, 40, 50, 60, 68, 84 and n. 3, 96, 110, 113 n. 3, 130, 136, 184

Gervase of Tilbury, 34 and n. 3

Ghent, 125

Gherlac, scribe, 145 and n., 151

Gherner, Elizabeth de, 147

Gilbert, John, bishop of Hereford, 37 n. 3

—, Robert, Chancellor of Oxford University, 185

Giles of Rome, 8, 112, 247

Gilson, J. P., 60

Ginneken, J. J. A. van, 140, 149, 248, 249

Glendower, Owen, 71

Gobelin Person, 25, 30, 32

Godfrey of Viterbo, 24, 195

Goetz, W., 172, 173, 180

Goldast, M., 88, 93

Gotham, William de, 227

Gouda, 125, 136, 137, 138; see Foppens, Henry

Grabmann, M., 179

Granchester (Cambs), benefice of, 233

Grandisson, John, bishop of Exeter, 226

Gratian, of Bologna, 94, 196

Gray, William, bishop of Lincoln, 208

Gregorovius, F., 172

Gregory the Great, 63, 81

Gregory VII, 36

— IX, 42

— XI, 26, 30, 228, 232, 236, 238, 242

— XII, 4, 27, 28, 36, 39, 57, 71 and n.1, 72 n. 3, 73, 74, 219, 243

Gregory of Heimburg, 161

Grey, Lord, of Ruthin, 238

—, Roger de, 238

—, Sir Thomas, of Wark, 238

— —, of Heton, 238

—, Thomas, rector of Wethersfield, 238

—, William de, 69 n. 2, 81

Grocyn, William, 182

Groenendael, 148

Gronde, John de, 151

Groningen, 125, 130, 131, 143

Groote, Gerard, 122, 123, 124, 136, 139–153 passim, 249, 250

Grosseteste, Robert, bishop of Lincoln, 82, 179, 200 n. 4, 202, 220

Grube, C. L., 142

Grunnius, 134, 135

Guelders, 143

Guppy, H., 126

Gwynn, A., 8

Haarlem, 138

Hadle, John, 140

Hague, the, 141

Hall, Edward, 186

Haller, J., 19, 20, 22, 40, 41, 53, 75, 88

Hallum, Robert, bishop of Salisbury, 53, 58, 59 and n. 2, 68, 70, 75–84 passim, 204

Hameln, 26

Hamerton (Hunts), rector of, see Causton

Harborough, Henry, precentor of Salisbury, 79 n. 2

Harclay, Henry, 179

Hardt, H. von der, 37, 47, 48

Harlegh, John, canon of Salisbury, 79 n. 2

Haskins, C. H., 181, 197, 207

Hattem, 125

Hegius, 129, 130, 136, 137

Heidelberg, 157

Heimpel, H., 37, 38, 244
Helinandus of Froidmont, 196
Helpidio, Alexander de, 196
Hengham, Ralph de, 109
Henry II, Emperor, 43
— —, King of England, 24
— III, Emperor, 43
— —, King of England, 106
— IV, King of England, 4, 57, 58, 70, 71, 72 n. 3, 73 and n. 1, 74, 75, and n. 1, 106, 107, 108, 202, 219, 220, 230, 248
— V, King of England, 49, 54, 55, 59 and n. 2, 73, 77 n. 1, 78 (Prince of Wales), 80, 184, 186; see Henry of Monmouth
— VI, King of England, 203
— VI, Council of, 54, 56, 107, 108, 184, 244
— —, Emperor, 24
— VII, Emperor, 24, 102, 244
— —, King of England, 173
— of Hesse, see Henry of Langenstein
— of Langenstein, 1, 5, 8 and ns. 1 and 2, 9, 39 n. 1, 60
— of Luxemburg, 178
— of Monmouth, 201
— Prince, the Navigator, 170
Hereford, bishop of, see Spofforth
—, canonry of, 235
—, Nicholas, 37 n. 3
Heyden, John, 143 n.
Higden, Ranulph, 186 n. 1, 195
Hilary, St., of Poitiers, 84 n. 2
Hingham, rural dean of, see Tunstede
Hirsche, C., 148
Histon (Cambs), rectory of, 233
Hobbes, Thomas, 18
Hoby, Sir Thomas, 171
Hoccleve, Thomas, 24, 74 n. 1, 75, 198, 241
Hodge, Esther, 193
Hofer, J., 84 n.
Hoffman, E., 251
Hofmann, W. von, 36
Hogsthorpe (Lincs), rector of, see Zouche
Holland, 143
Hollebrooke, John, 229
Holmes, Mr. Justice, 170
Horn, Peter, 141, 145, 148, 152, 153
Hostiensis (Henricus de Segusio), 240
Houchyns, Simon, 81
Hübler, B., 48
Hugh of Fleury, 196
Huguccio, 240, 241

Hull, Charterhouse of, 204
Hulsbergen, 125
Humphrey, duke of Gloucester, 78, 187, 192, 193, 244
Hungary, 39
Huntingdon, archdeacon of, see Zouche
Hus, John, 50, 52, 76, 140, 196 n. 2
Hyma, A., 122, 124, 136, 139, 175

Indersdorf, monastery of, Upper Bavaria, 150
Inge, W. R., 152
Innocent III, 118
— VI, 243
— VII, 27, 31, 35, 36, 70, 74, 204, 219
Isaiah, 196
Isidore of Seville, 195, 196
Islip, Simon, Archbishop of Canterbury, 226
Ixworth, John, Visitor of Clare College, Cambridge, 230

James of Genoa, 196
— of Viterbo, 7
Jarrow, 148
Jeremias of Montagnone, 252
Jerome, St., 87, 195, 196
Jerusalem, 41
Joan, Queen of Henry IV, 78
Johanna of Naples, 33
Johannes Anglicus, 198, 199 n. 1
John, St., 196
John XII, 37, 97
— XXII, 19, 31, 86, 90, 91, 92, 93, 97, 102, 225, 242, 243
— XXIII, 4 (Baldassare Cossa), 5, 6, 11, 25, 28, 37, 38, 39, 49, 50, 196 n. 2, 243
— of Bologna, 198
— of Gaunt, 65
— Henry of Luxemburg, 90
— of Jandun, 86, 102
— of Ketel, 250
— of Paris, 240
— of Salisbury, 24, 130, 138, 180, 194
— the Scot (Scotus Erigena), 159, 162, 164
— of Segovia, 47
Joinville, 24
Jordan, G. J., 244
Jordanes of Ravenna, 195
Josephus, 112, 195
Jourdain, Amable, 179
Julius Firmicus Maternus, 196
Junghanns, H., 70, 71
Justin, 195

Kampen, 144, 145, 153
Katherine, St., 155
Kemp, John, 184
Kempe, Margery, 154, 155
Kempen, 152
Kempis, Thomas a (Hemerken, Thomas, of Agnetenberg, Thomas of Kempen), 122, 123, 130, 139, 141, 146, 148 and n., 160, 249, 250
Kempten, 45
Keyes, Roger, 200 n. 4
Kingsford, C. L., 173, 176
Kington St. Michael's nunnery (Salisbury diocese), 82 n. 2
Kirketon, Alan, abbot of Thorney, 185
Koch, J., 250
Kristeller, P. O., 252

Lacy, Edmund, bishop of Exeter, 200 and n. 4, 203
Ladislas of Naples, 5, 36, 243
Lagarde, M., 246
Lagharun, Richard, Fellow of Magdalen College, 61 n. 2
Lambeth, 201
—, rector of, see Eltesley
Landbeach, benefice of, 233 n. 3
Lando, Franciscus, Cardinal of Venice, 26, 33
Landriani, Gerald, bishop of Lodi, 244
Langley, Thomas, 245
Langrysh, John, prior of Witham, 203, 204
Lapsley, G. T., 106, 247
Launce, John, 28 n. 1
Leeu, Gerard, 137, 138
Lenz, M., 38, 49
Leroy, Pierre, 41
Lescapone, Johannes de, 243
Lewis of Bavaria, 86, 89, 90, 91, 93, 99, 100, 101, 102
Lichfield Cathedral, canonry of, 233
— —, prebend of, 237
Liége, 125, 141, 142, 144
Linacre, Thomas, 182
Lincoln, bishops of, see Alnwick, Fleming, Gray, Grosseteste, Lumley
— Cathedral, canonry of, 234, 235, 236
— —, — and prebend of, 235, 238
— —, prebend of Corringham in, 239
— —, — of Langford in, 234, 236
—, Fletchergate, rectory of, 233
Lionel, duke of Clarence, 111
Livius, Titus, 186
Livy, 195, 196, 252

Llandefi-Brefi, prebend of (St. David's), 233
Lloyd, A. H., 228, 238
—, Miss M. E. H., 228
—, Mrs. Jessie, 228 n. 2
Lochem, Arnold de, 147
Lodovico of Volterra, papal collector, 57
Lollaert, Matthew, 143
Lollards, 143
London, 45, 49, 190
—, bishop of, see Clifford
—, St. Martin-le-Grand, dean of, see Dereham
—, St. Mary in the Strand, benefice of, 236
—, St. Paul's Cathedral, canonry of, 234
— — — —, prebend of Neasdon in, 234
— — —, — of Twyford in, 234
Long Marston (Glos), rectory of, 236
Lorenzo de' Medici, 131
Lot, F., 172
Louis XI, 176
Louvain, 125, 130
—, St. Martin's Priory at, 149
Lowthorp, Louthorp, George, canon of Salisbury, 79 n. 2
Lucca, 27, 28
Lumley, Marmaduke, bishop of Lincoln, 208
Lüneberg, 27
Lupold of Bebenberg, 99
Luther, Martin, 131, 132, 174, 175
Lutterell, Hugh, knight of Queen Joan, 78 n. 5
Lyndwood, William, 54

Maastricht, St. Salvatius at, 28
McIlwain, C. H., 87, 103, 105, 113
Mainz, 45
—, Archbishop of, 100
Maitland, F. W., 106
Malden, A. R., 78, 80
Mandour, John, 228
Maramaldi, Cardinal Landulf, 28
Marcellinus, 97
Margaret, St., 155
Mark, St., 195
Marlow, 205
Marsilius of Inghen, 130, 157
— of Padua, 41, 42, 85, 86, 87, 88, 89, 93, 102, 105
Martin V, 15, 28, 45, 46, 49, 52, 53, 54, 55, 189, 199
— of Troppau, 89
Masaccio, 170

Matthew, St., 195
— of Cracow, 35
Maultasch, Margaret, of the Tyrol, 90
Meibomius, 25
Melancthon, 130
Meran, 45
Michael of Cesena, general of the Franciscan Order, 86, 90 and n. 3, 91, 93
Middlesex, archdeacon of, see Sidey
Milan, Cardinal of, see Borsano, Simon
Miller, Dr., 132
Minges, P., 179
Monnikhuizen, Carthusian monastery of, 123, 143, 147, 148, 150
Mont St. Michel, abbot of, 60
Montacute, Simon, bishop of Ely, 232
Monte, Piero da, 192 and n. 4
Monteferrando, David de, Archbishop of Bordeaux, 203
Moody, E. A., 88, 89
Moorman, J. H. R., 216
More, Thomas, 186
Morena, Acerbus, Podesta of Lodi, 24
Morrall, J. B., 241, 246
Mortimer, Anne, 111
—, Philippa, 111
Mottrum, Adam, precentor of Salisbury, 58, 79
Mount St. Agnes, see Agnetenberg
Mulder, W., 141, 249
Munich, 86, 198
Münster (Westfalen), 125
Mussato, Albertino, 179

Naples, 30, 32, 33
—, Archbishop of (Jordan Orsini), 33
—, see Johanna, Ladislas, Robert of
Neville, Alice Lady, 238
—, George, Archbishop of York, 208
—, Richard, 208
—, —, earl of Salisbury, 183
Nicholas V, 158, 172
—, of Butrinto, 24
—, of Fakenham, 59, 60 and n. 1
Nieheim, Niem, Nyem, 26; see Dietrich
Nocera, 29, 30, 33
Nonantula, abbot of, 219
Norwich, bishops of, see Airmyn, Despenser
—, prior of, see Totington
Noseley, prebend of Morehall in collegiate church of, 237
Novaria, Bartholomew de, 219

Nuremberg, 91, 102

Ockham, William of, 41 and n. 2, 85–105 passim, 154, 174, 175, 182, 245, 246, 247
Oresme, Nicholas of, 144, 146
Orleans, Louis, duke of, 5
Orosius, 195
Orsini, James, Cardinal of St. George in Velabro, 3
—, Jordan, Cardinal of Albano, later of Sabina, 159
Osmund, St., 78, 79, 80, 81, 82
Ossory, bishop of, see Tatenhall
Otto I, 37
— III, 49, 176
—, Archbishop of Bremen, formerly bishop of Verden, 27
— of Freising, 24
Ovid, 195, 196
Owst, G. R., 7
Oxford, Oseney Abbey, 215
—, St. Edmund's Well at, 205 n. 3
—, St. Frideswide's, 215
— University, 1, 7, 60, 62, 64, 69, 76, 79, 185, 193 n. 3, 144, 201, 203, 207, 209, 211, 212, 213, 214, 215, 216, 217, 220, 221, 225, 226 and n. 4, 228, 231, 234 n. 3, 246, 251
— —, All Souls College, 200 and ns. 3, 4
— —, Canterbury College, 215
— —, Chancellors of, see Gilbert, Stratford
— —, Convocation of, 239
— —, Durham College, 215, 217
— —, Gloucester College, 187
— —, Merton College, 202 n. 2, 216, 217
— —, New College, 213, 214, 216
— —, Oriel College, 216

Paderborn, diocese of, 25
Padua, University of, 157, 158, 179, 251
Palude, Petrus de, 196
Panofsky, E., 251
Pantin, W. A., 197
Paris, 145, 198
—, University of, 1, 5, 11, 14 (College of Navarre), 37, 49, 53, 55, 59–65 passim, 84, 85, 122, 123, 130, 136, 142, 144, 146, 154, 228 n. 4, 251
Paris, Matthew, 223
Parma, 45
Partner, P. D., 243, 244
Pascal, Blaise, 164

Pater, W., 172
Paul, St., 11, 63, 95, 116, 131, 161 n. 3
Pauli, Michael, de Pelagallo, bishop of Siena, 41
Pavia, 44, 45
—, Council of, 189
—, University of, 251
Payne, Peter, 52, 56
Pecham, John, Archbishop of Canterbury, 198, 199 n. 1, 200, 201, 202, 203
Pelzer, A., 179
Perche, Master John, registrar of the Court of Canterbury, 58
Perroy, E., 4, 51, 223
Persius, 196
Perugia, 34
Peter of Blois, 138
— of Erkelenz, 161
— of Pulka, dean of theology in Vienna University, 218
Peterborough, abbey of, 235
Petit, John, 184
Petrarch, 170, 172, 179, 180, 195, 252
Petrus de Ebulo, 24
Petzelt, A., 251
Philip IV, King of France, 7, 240
— of Leyden, 184
Piacenza, 45
Picardy, 45
Pippin, King of the Franks, 177
Pisa, 251
—, Council of, 3, 4, 6, 25, 28, 39, 44, 47, 48, 51, 53, 54, 58, 71, 74, 76, 79, 82, 84
Pius II (Aeneas Sylvius), 118, 160
Pivec, K., 244
Plaoul, Pierre, 41
Plato, 114, 180
Plummer, A., 109
Poggio, 170
Pohl, M. J., 140
Pole, John de la, 238, 239
—, Thomas, 239
Pollard, A. F., 183
Polton, Thomas, successively bishop of Hereford, Chichester, Worcester, 79 and n. 1
Poole, R. L., 24, 85
Post, R. R., 139
Pountney, chapter clerk of Salisbury Cathedral, 78, 79 n. 2, 80
Pozzuoli, baths at, 34
Prague, University of, 123, 143, 144
Prantl, C. von, 174
Prescot, rector of, see Fairfax

Prignano, Bartholomew, see Urban VI
Prophet, John, dean of York, 73, 74 and n. 1, 241, 245
Pseudo-Dionysius, 162, 163
Ptolemy of Lucca, 112
Pulham, John, 235
Pupper, John, of Goch, 132

Radcliff, Nicholas, prior of Wymondham, archdeacon of St. Albans, 65–68
Radewijns, Florence, 122, 123, 124, 135, 139, 140, 151 and n., 250
—, vicarage of, 250
Raleigh, Prof. Sir Walter, 171
Ramsey, abbey of, 232
—, Cottenham (Cambs), in patronage of, 232
Randall, J. H., Junior, 251
Ranke, L. von, 175
Raphael, St., 200 n. 4
Rashdall, Hastings, 88, 207, 225, 226
Reading, Franciscan convent of, 245
Repingdon, Philip, 37 n. 3
— —, bishop of Lincoln, 154
Reuchlin, John, 130
Rhijn, Maarten van, 139
Richard II, 51, 60 n. 1, 64, 65, 106, 107, 201, 204, 219, 229, 248, 249
—, duke of York, 107, 108, 109
—, earl of Warwick, 107
— of Meneville, 88
Richardson, H. G., 201
Richenthal, Ulrich von, 50, 76
Richmond (Yorks), archdeacon of, see Scrope
Rieder, K., 21
Rienzo, 177
Riezler, S., 88
Ritter, G., 182
Robert of Geneva, see Clement VII
—, King of Naples, 180
Rochester, bishops of, see Whittlesey, Young (Ingh)
Rockinger, L., 181, 197
Rolle, Richard, 200 n. 4
Rome, 5, 16, 25, 26, 27, 28, 29, 31, 40, 70 and n. 1, 72, 89, 130, 131, 176, 177, 178, 179, 220, 224, 229, 230
—, English hospice of St. Thomas the Martyr and Holy Trinity, 29
—, German hospice of Santa Maria dell' Anima, 29
—, St. Peter's, 53
—, S. Pietro in Vincoli, 161
—, John, rector of Fenstanton, 230

Rose-Troup, Mrs. F., 200 n. 4
Rothenburg, 27
Rovere, Francesco della, see Sixtus IV
Rupert of the Palatinate, King of Germany, 27, 70
Ruysbroek, John, 123, 140, 143, 148

St. Albans, 44, 45, 46, 57, 65
—, abbot of, see Whethamstede
—, archdeacon of, see Radcliff
—, manuscripts written at, 187–189, 193–196
St. David's, 71
—, bishop of, see Chichele
St. Eustace, Cardinal of, see Flandin, Peter
St. Germain, Christopher, 110
St. Mark, Cardinal of, see Fillastre, William
St. Victor, Hugh of, 123, 130
— —, Richard of, 123
Salerno, 33
Salisbury, Cathedral of, 78–82
— —, bishops of, see Audley, Hallum, Mortival, Waltham
— —, canonries and prebends of, 234, 236, 238
— —, canons of, see Brown, Bubwith, Harlegh, Mottrum, Polton, Sydenham, Ullerston
— —, dean of, see Chaundler
— —, prebend of Netheravon, in, 238
—, John of, see John
Sallust, 180, 195
Salter, Rev. H. E., 204, 207, 211, 214
Salutati, Coluccio, 179, 252
Salvarvilla, William de, chanter of Paris, 145 and n.
Sampson, Thomas, 209, 213
San Miniato, Giovanni de, 179
Sangro, Cardinal Leonardo de, 30
Sarvavilla, William de, 122
Savoy, 47
Schaffhausen, 6, 11, 147
Schirmer, W. F., 181, 187, 193
Schism, the Great, 142, 145
Schoenhove, Henry de, 143
Schoengen, M., 125, 139
Scholz, R., 41, 87, 246
Schramm, P. E., 176, 177
Schwab, J. B., 37
Scotland, 8
Scotus, Duns, 88
Scrope, Richard, Archbishop of York, 107

Scrope, Stephen, archdeacon of Richmond, 208
Selling, William, prior of Canterbury, 181
Seneca, 180, 194, 196
Serravalle, Giovanni da, 76
Seznec, Jean, 252
Shaftesbury, St. Edward's shrine at, 76
s' Hertogenbosch, 125, 134, 135, 136
Sidey, Bartholomew, archdeacon of Middlesex, 234
Sidwell (Sativola), St., 200 n. 4
Siena, 27, 181
—, bishop of, see Pauli
—, Council of, 15, 44, 45, 53, 54, 55, 189
Sigismund, the Emperor, 5, 6, 9, 39, 49, 54, 56, 59, 80, 202
—, duke of the Tyrol, 160
Sikes, J. G., 99
Simon, abbot of St. Albans, 189
Sixtus IV (Francesco della Rovere), 130, 131
Socrates, 114
Solinus, 195
Solomon, Rabbi, 163
Sonnenburg, nunnery of, 160
South Collingham (Yorks), benefice of, 235
Southwark, Church of St. Mary, 85
Southwell, canonry and prebend of, 237
Sozomenus, 195
Speyer, 45
Spofforth, Thomas, abbot of St. Mary's, York, later bishop of Hereford, 53
Stafford, Edmund, bishop of Exeter, 70
—, John, 184
Stalberg, Johannes, 27
Stalbridge (Salisbury diocese), 82 n. 2
Statius, 196
Stefaneschi, Cardinal James, 24
Stephen, bishop of Tournai, 42
Stevens, John, canon of Exeter, 200, 201
Stone, Gilbert, canon of Wells, 203, 204, 205, 206
Strasbourg, 123, 152
Stratford, Robert de, chancellor of Oxford, 226
Strickland, William, bishop of Carlisle, 73
Stroziis, Marcellus de, 82 n. 4
Stubbs, W., 84, 173
Sudbury, St. Gregory's rectory, 235
—, Simon, Archbishop of Canterbury, 205, 233, 234
Sullivan, J., 87

Sutton, Robert de, rector of Glatton (Lincs), 233
—, Robert de, the younger, 233
Swan, William, 28 n. 1, 29, 218, 230
—, Joan, wife of William, 29, 31
Swete, A. B., 11
Sydenham, Simon, dean of Salisbury, later bishop of Chichester, 79, 80
Sylvester, Pope, 195
Symmachus, 37, 96
Symonds, J. A., 172

Tanner, Thomas, 198
Tatenhall, John de, bishop of Ossory, 226
Tegernsee, Benedictine monastery of, 165
Teversham (Cambs), benefice of, 233
Theobald, Archbishop of Canterbury, 24
Theodoric, 37
Thérouanne, bishopric of, 8
Thessaly, 131
Thomas, duke of Clarence, 202
—, of Capua, 199
Thompson, A. Hamilton, 239
Thoresby, John, Archbishop of York, 226
Thorney, abbot of, see Kirketon
Tierney, B., 240
Tihon, A., 21
Tiptoft, John, Lord, 107, 187
Toffanin, G., 179
Toscanelli, Paolo del Pozzo, 157
Totington, Alexander, prior of Norwich, 219, 220
Tournai, bishop of, see Stephen, William de Coudenberghe
Tout, T. F., 173, 237, 241
Trento, 45
Trevisa, John of, 186 n. 1
Tudeschis, Nicholas de (Panormitanus), 241
Tunstede, Robert de, rural dean of Hingham, 233, 234
Twemlow, J. A., 239 n. 5

Uguccione, Cardinal (Archbishop of Bordeaux), 4, 73 and n. 2
Ullerston, Richard, Chancellor of Oxford University, canon of Salisbury, 8, 61 n. 2, 70, 79 and n. 2, 80, 81, 82
Ullmann, C., 175
—, W., 240, 252
Ulm, 45

Upton, Nicholas de, 81
Urban V, 225, 227, 238, 242, 243
— VI (Bartholomew Prignano), 3, 8, 26, 27, 29, 30, 31, 32, 33, 35, 65 n. 3, 68, 72, 122, 239
Uthred of Boldon, 65
Utrecht, 143
—, bishop of (Florence de Wervelijkhoven), 122, 143 n., 153
—, cathedral of, 143, 146
—, eccl. principality of, 144

Valerius, Maximus, 196
Valois, Noel, 4, 46, 54, 60, 70
Van der Weyden, Roger, 166
Van Os, Peter, 138
Van Rhijn, M., 130
Venice, 181, 252
—, Cardinal of, see Lando, Franciscus
—, Santa Maria dei Miracoli, 182
Verden, city and bishopric, 27; see Otto, Dietrich of Niem
Verona, 252
Vicenza, University of, 252
Vienna, University of, see Peter of Pulka
Vincent of Beauvais, 194, 196
Vinci, Leonardo da, 174
Vineis, Peter de, 199
Vinogradoff, Paul, 110, 119
Vintschgau, 45
Virgil, 195, 196
Viringe, chapter clerk of Salisbury Cathedral, 78, 79 n. 1
Visconti, family of, 5
Viterbo, 27
Voecht, James, of Utrecht, 141, 143, 150, 151
Volterra, bishop of, see Geri
Vos, John of Heusden, 122
Vroede, William, 151

Wace, John, 229
Wake, stationer of Cambridge, 221
Walden, Roger, 201
Walincourt, monastery of, 150
Wallington, Thomas de, 239
Walsingham, Thomas, 186, 188
Walter, échevin, 153
—, of Biblesworth, 201 and n. 2
Waltham, John, bishop of Salisbury, 204 n. 4
Ware, Master Henry, 57
Warham, William, Archbishop of Canterbury, 222
Water, John ten, 151
Weiss, R., 181, 252

Wells Cathedral, canon of, *see* Stone
—, prebend of Wedmore Secunda in, 203
Wesley, Samuel, 211
Westminster, abbot of (William Colchester), 73
—, Palace of, 4, 60, 89
Weston (Wiston), Robert, 227
Wethersfield, rector of, *see* Grey
Weyville, Robert, bishop of Bath and Wells, later bishop of Salisbury, 203
Whethamstede, John, abbot of St. Albans, 44, 45, 46, 54, 55, 181, 186, 187 and n. 2, 188, 189, 191, 192 and ns. 3 and 4, 193 and n. 3, 194
Whittlesey, William, bishop of Rochester, 226
Wilkins, David, 80
Wilkinson, B., 247
William of Tyre, 195
William of Wykeham, 35 n. 2
Willibrord, 143
Winchelsey, Robert de, Archbishop of Canterbury, 85
Winchester, bishop of, *see* Fox
Winckelmann, J. J., 172
Windesheim, Congregation of, 122, 123, 124, 130, 139, 141, 150
Windsor, 219
Winterbourne Came (Salisbury diocese), 82 n. 1
Witham, prior of, *see* Langrysh
Witton (Ely), canonry of, 234
Wolsey, Thomas, 183
Wolverhampton, prebend of, 233
Workman, W., 79 n. 2
Worms, 45
—, Provost of, *see* Conrad of Gelnhausen
Wyclif, John, 8, 37, 47, 140, 154
Wycombe, 205

Wylie, J. H., 70, 74
Wylton, Stephen, 185
Wymondham, priory of, 65; *see* Radcliff
Wyntershulle, William, 65 and n. 5
Wyrmonde, Thomas, canon of Chichester, 231

Yelverton, J., 119
York, Archbishops of, *see* Neville, Scrope, Thoresby
—, prebend of Howden in, 232
— —, Langtoft in, 236
— —, North Newbald in, 237
— —, Wistow in, 238
—, precentorship of, 236
—, St. Mary's Abbey, 234
—, — —, abbot of, *see* Spofforth
— Minster, dean of, *see* Prophet
Young (Ingh), Richard, bishop of Bangor, then Rochester, 71, 72
— —, auditor of the Sacred Palace, 72, 73 and n. 1
Yssel R., Valley of, 124

Zabarella, Francesco, Cardinal of St. Cosmas and St. Damian, 240, 241, 243
Zerbolt, Gerald, 135
Zouche, Eudo la, Chancellor of Cambridge University, canon and prebendary of Lincoln, archdeacon of Huntingdon, rector of Hogsthorpe, 229, 230, 236
—, lord, of Harringworth, 236
Zutphen, 143, 153
Zwolle, 123, 124, 125, 130, 131, 135, 136, 138, 141
—, Mount of St. Agnes near, *see* Agnetenberg

Printed in Great Britain by Butler & Tanner Ltd, Frome and London